The Dark Side of T Leadership

MW00775253

Most research into leadership presents leaders as heroic, charismatic and transformational 'visionaries'. The leader, whether in business, politics or any other field is the most important factor in determining whether an organization succeeds or fails. Despite the fundamental mistakes which have directly led to global economic recession, it is often still taken for granted that transformational leadership is a good thing, and that leaders should have much more power than followers in deciding what needs to be done.

The Dark Side of Transformational Leadership confronts this orthodoxy by illustrating how such approaches can encourage narcissism, megalomania and poor decision making on the part of leaders, at great expense to those organizations they serve. Written in a lively and engaging style, the book uses a number of case studies to illustrate the perils of transformational leadership, from the Jonestown tragedy in 1978, when over 900 people were either murdered or committed suicide at the urging of one man, to an analysis of how banking executives tried to explain away their role in the 2008 financial crisis.

This provocative but hugely important book offers a rare critical perspective in the field of leadership studies. Concluding with a new approach that offers an alternative to the dominant transformational model, *The Dark Side of Transformational Leadership* will be an invaluable text for researchers interested in leadership, students on leadership courses requiring a more critical perspective, and anyone concerned with how the practice of leadership can be improved.

Dennis Tourish is a Professor of Leadership and Organization Studies at Royal Holloway, University of London, UK. He has published seven previous books on leadership and organizational communication and serves on the editorial boards of several journals, including *Human Relations* and *Management Communication Quarterly*, where he was previously an associate editor. He is a Fellow of the Leadership Trust Foundation and a co-editor of the journal *Leadership*.

The Dark Side of Transformational Leadership

A critical perspective

Dennis Tourish

Routledge
Taylor & Francis Group

LONDON AND NEW YORK

First published 2013
by Routledge
27 Church Road, Hove, East Sussex, BN3 2FA

Simultaneously published in the USA and Canada
by Routledge
711 Third Avenue, New York, NY 10017

*Routledge is an imprint of the Taylor & Francis Group,
an informa business*

British Library Cataloguing in Publication Data
A catalogue record for this book is available from the British Library

Library of Congress Cataloging in Publication Data
A catalog record for this book has been requested

ISBN: 978-0-415-56427-4 (hbk)
ISBN: 978-0-415-56428-1 (pbk)
ISBN: 978-0-203-55811-9 (ebk)

Typeset in Times New Roman
by Cenveo Publisher Services

This book is dedicated to my wife, Naheed Tourish, in grateful thanks for all her support, love and collaboration over many years. This book and much else would never have been accomplished without her by my side.

Contents

List of boxes and tables   ix

Acknowledgements   x

PART I

Leadership agency unravelled   1

1   Why the dark side? Why now?   3

2   Transformational leadership: the dynamics of excessive
    leader agency   20

3   Coercive persuasion, power and corporate culturism   40

4   Spirituality and leadership: using ideology to enhance
    leaders' power   59

5   The dark side of leadership and silence in the workplace   77

6   The folly and the dangers of leadership education in
    business schools   96

PART II

Case studies   115

7   The dark side of leadership in corporate America: Enron revisited   117

8   The Militant Tendency's long march to oblivion: conformity and
    authoritarian leadership on the left   136

9   Leadership, group suicide and mass murder: Jonestown
    and Heaven's Gate through the looking glass   157

10 Accounting for failure: bankers in the spotlight   178

PART III
Conclusion   197

11 Reimagining leadership and followership: a processual,
    communication perspective   199

    References   216
    Index   244

Boxes and tables

Boxes

5.1   The impact and benefits of upward feedback   79
5.2   Improving critical upward communication:
      the ten commandments   88
6.1   Transformational leadership promises made by
      business schools   103
6.2   Pedagogic approaches to leadership   107

Tables

2.1   Key ingredients of transformational leadership and cults   30
3.1   Key techniques of coercive persuasion   43

Acknowledgements

I am grateful to all those with whom I have collaborated on leadership research over the years. These include Joel Amernic, Jim Barker, David Collinson, Russell Craig, David Dickson, Colin Hargie, Owen Hargie, Ashly Pinnington, Paul Robson, Karyn Stapleton, Naheed Tourish and Tim Wohlforth. Several of the chapters that follow draw from earlier work published with their collaboration. All of these have been significantly amended and updated in this book. None of the above necessarily share any or all of my conclusions, and responsibility for any errors of fact or misinterpretation in this book is mine alone.

Part I
Leadership agency unravelled

1   Why the dark side? Why now?

Introduction

Elmer Gantry is a 1960s film about a dedicated female evangelist, Sharon Falconer, played by Jean Simmons, and the title character, played by Burt Lancaster, who is a fast-talking travelling salesman.[1] Attending one of Falconer's events, he is attracted to her and even more to the realisation that money can be made from what he sees as little more than a racket. A riveting performer, Gantry buries his shady past to become the star of the show, wowing audiences throughout America, until exposure, disaster and – perhaps – some kind of moral reawakening takes place. Whatever his genuine beliefs, the fame and success that he enjoys in his role of travelling preacher man takes precedence over his purported message and the good of whatever followers his proselytising manages to attract. Never has charisma been so seductive – or so tawdry.

If there is any redemption for Gantry, it is only partial. For at least one follower, Sharon Falconer, it is too late. Devoted to the beliefs that she at least articulated with complete sincerity, she perishes in a fire, unable to face the truth of Gantry's betrayal. Nothing is as it seems. In this film, sincerity may be real but it is attached to dubious beliefs; inspiring rhetoric camouflages malign intent; love is a tool of manipulation; high ideals are a ploy to win people's hearts, all the better to purloin their wallets. The more charismatic and impressive a speaker may be, the wider is the chasm between him or her and the authentic interests of their followers.

The contrast with the way in which would-be leaders are depicted elsewhere could not be more striking. In more recent Hollywood movies, US presidents are played by such stalwarts as Danny Glover, in the movie *2012*, courageously deciding to perish with his people rather than escape disaster in a specially prepared ship, or Harrison Ford in *Air Force One*, single-handedly taking on – and whipping – terrorists who have seized the presidential jet. This twin-step approach by Hollywood says much about how most people these days approach the subject of leadership. In one version, leaders are duplicitous and not to be trusted. In another, we are encouraged to believe that leadership is necessary and to invest many hopes in those who hold leadership positions. The corollary is that our own ability to act is diminished. As Banks (2008: 11) puts it: 'Conventionally, leaders show the way, are positioned in the vanguard, guide and direct, innovate, and have a vision for change and make it come to actuality. Followers on the other hand conventionally track the leader from behind, obey and report, implement innovations and accept leaders' vision for change'. Most leadership scholarship thus tends to assume that visionary leadership is powerful, exciting and necessary, with leaders acting as a force for good whose efforts almost invariably produce positive outcomes (Collinson 2012). Followers, meanwhile, have walk-on parts in the drama of their own lives.

In an organizational context, much of this attributional process is vested in the persona of the chief executive officer (CEO). Their charisma, reputation and symbolic power are assumed to impact positively on corporate reputation (Cravens *et al.* 2003) and firm performance (Rajagopalan and Datta 1996; Pollach and Kerbler 2011). Within the public sector also, there has been a growth of rhetoric around what has been described as 'leaderism' (O'Reilly and Reed 2011), in which it is assumed that some form of leadership – drawing heavily on private sector models – is vital for improved effectiveness (Martin and Learmonth 2012).

In line with this, influential practitioner journals such as the *Harvard Business Review* regularly devote space to the need for 'better' leadership. They provide forums in which influential CEOs proclaim their business 'secrets' and methods of doing management as models that should be more universally applied (see article by CEO of Heinz [Johnson 2011] for a typical example). Macho imagery is rife. One edition of the *Harvard Business Review* in January 2007 devoted to 'the tests of the leader' adorned its cover with an image of a male business executive performing push-ups on a boardroom table. The job of such leaders is then to cajole, convince or bully followers into embracing the leader's vision. If the global economic crisis is any indication, the results of this approach have not been inspiring. In a slightly less crude form, this is more or less what transformational leadership theories seek to legitimate. I argue in Chapter 2 that such a stress on how leaders transform others inevitably changes the relationship between leaders and followers from a two-way exchange into a one-way process of domination that has an inherently autocratic potential.

More studies are appearing, however, that explore 'toxic' leader behaviour (Pelletier 2010), 'bad' leadership (Kellerman 2004), 'narcissistic' leadership (Kets de Vries 2006), the prevalence of 'destructive leadership behaviour' (Aasland *et al.* 2010) and 'leadership derailment' (Furnham 2010). 'Negative' leadership has been variously conceived as behaviour that is insincere, despotic, exploitative, restrictive, failed, laissez-faire and involving the active and passive avoidance of leadership responsibilities (Schilling 2009). But within the field of leadership studies, every study pointing to the dark side is met by a chorus of voices that present leaders as saints, commanders, architects (redesigning society), pedagogues (teaching appropriate behaviours) and physicians (healing stricken organizations). Such metaphors are widely employed by leaders themselves, determined to present themselves as indispensable for human prosperity (Amernic *et al.* 2007).

A fascination with leadership?

In good times or bad, it appears that most of us remain fascinated by leadership and enthralled by leaders. Indeed, as many have suggested (see, for example, Lipman-Bluemen 2008), it may even be that difficulty and uncertainty heighten our tendency to hope for the appearance of a Messiah figure and in the process render us more susceptible to the persuasive charms of snake-oil salesmen, whatever the toxicity of the brew they are peddling. By definition, such hopes are combined with contempt for actual leaders practising leadership in the world that we see before us. From this perspective, the first decades of the 21st century have been a boom time for peddlers of illusions, vain hopes and bombastic promises, seeking to capitalise on the uncertainty, economic chaos and disillusionment that has engulfed society. There are plentiful business 'gurus' who claim to have identified a few simple steps capable of producing lasting success, possibly with nothing more complex than the adoption of seven habits deemed to be 'highly effective' (Jackson 2001). Sun Myung Moon, who died in 2012, claimed to have found the one true path to God and mobilised unknown thousands to that end within the Unification Church, better known as the Moonies. They have many rivals offering similar promises, potions and prescriptions. For those of a more secular disposition, there are numerous psychotherapies that promise to free the human psyche from distress. Some seek to accomplish this by regressing people to traumatic memories of past lives or fast forwarding them to ones they have not yet experienced (Singer and Lalich 1996). All that one needs to do is to suspend one's own critical judgement and defer to the wisdom of someone else.

Ultimately, this book challenges our enduring preoccupation with leader agency, while the rest of us are expected do little more than admire or critique their efforts. It is a warning against trusting too much in the judgement of others and not enough in our own. If power corrupts, then the same might be said of powerlessness. It corrodes our ability to act purposively, take responsibility for our actions and manage our own destiny but it enhances our tendency to ridicule the imperfect efforts of others, to little positive effect. Passivity also provides the unscrupulous with opportunities to manipulate others against their own real best interests. This book explores these dysfunctional processes in detail, in the hope that more balanced attitudes towards leadership can be developed and that we can find better ways to practise leadership than are mostly in evidence at present. Given the economic calamities that have befallen the world since 2008, the need for better leadership has rarely been so clear.

Leadership and 'the great recession'

A contemporary focus on the dark side of leadership is indebted to bankers – a rare sensation, it must be said, for a taxpayer. They have come to symbolise much that is wrong with leadership and the paradoxes of our attitudes to it. Two cartoons in the UK newspaper, *The Daily Telegraph*, during July 2012 sum this up. In one, a secretary is reading out a list of messages to a worried-looking banker.

She concludes: 'And your mother called to say she thinks you should be in jail'. In another, a woman is saying to her banker date: 'I told my mother you were a Scientologist, but I didn't dare tell her you were also a banker'. Bankers themselves have been slow to recognise their fall from grace. They have been reluctant to apologise and have developed accounts of the 2008 crisis which persistently fail to draw meaningful lessons about what needs to change in their behaviour (see Chapter 10).

Evidence seems to emerge on an almost daily basis that demonstrates lax ethics and a culture of self-enrichment at odds with any model of leadership that purports to serve the common good. Barclays is one of the world's biggest banks. Its leaders spent much of the summer of 2012 dealing with accusations that they had manipulated interest rates – particularly the London Interbank Rate (LIBOR) and the Eurobank Offered Rate (EURIBOR) in ways that may yet attract criminal charges. The Financial Services Authority (2012) issued a damning report and it was ultimately fined £290 million by US and UK regulatory authorities. Its chairman, chief operating officer and CEO had to resign, the latter facing a lengthy grilling from Members of Parliament (MPs). By then, such shenanigans and attendant grim publicity had become almost routine.

But what began as a banking crisis in 2008 has also sent economic shockwaves around the globe, threatened the Eurozone and the wider European project, brought whole populations in countries such as Greece to levels of destitution unheard of since the 1930s and stimulated a mass 'Occupy' movement throughout the world. Many now question the validity of capitalism as the best system for generating long-term prosperity. Thus, bankers may be the most pilloried exemplars of business leadership gone awry but they do not stand in the dock alone. The UK, in 2012, witnessed the previously unthinkable, as the once mighty Rupert Murdoch, owner of News International, faced a wave of scandals, particularly concerning illegal phone hacking by his newspapers' journalists. He had to close one of his most profitable and long established papers, *The News of the World*, and endure intense questioning from a select committee of MPs. His son and heir apparent was forced to resign from a senior role in the company, while several other top executives now face criminal charges.

Critical attention has also been directed at pay levels for those who hold top leadership positions. *The New York Times* reported in April 2012 that the median pay for CEOs in the USA had reached US$14.4 million, compared with an average salary for employees of US$45,230 (Singer 2012). The newspaper bluntly asked whether they were worth it. A report by Incomes Data Services (2011) on directors' pay, prepared for the UK's High Pay Commission, noted that in the previous ten years the average annual bonus for FTSE 300 directors had increased by 187 per cent but the average year-end share price had gone down by 71 per cent over the same period. As their report noted: 'Pay for performance has added to the staggering complexity of executive packages and yet there is no clear evidence that it works' (p.5). Challenges to the legitimacy of business leadership thus reach way beyond the banking sector. Kellerman (2012) cites a 2011 Gallup survey in the USA, where, by a ratio of six to one, respondents said that corporate leaders had done more to hurt than help the economy. The same survey found that only 13 per cent of Republicans wanted major corporations to have more influence in the future than they have had in the past. These findings are now typical. Established institutions, political parties and business leaders are held in lower regard than any time in living memory.

It is obvious that the practice of leadership has gone badly wrong. As a result, the heroic myths of leadership that were so dominant for many years are under scrutiny and by people far beyond 'the usual suspects' on the left. The *Harvard Business Review* has published a number of critical articles (at least, by its normal somewhat sycophantic standards), including a piece by the global managing director of McKinseys, entitled 'Capitalism for the long term'. This fundamentally challenges the shareholder value-first priorities of the previous booming decades and urges leaders to change their basic models of business or face the possibility of more stringent outside regulation being foisted on them (Barton 2011). Gary Hamel is a well-known business analyst and commentator, visiting professor at the London Business School, author of several bestselling management books and a frequent contributor to the *Harvard Business Review*. His latest book (Hamel 2012: 10) argues that 'The worst economic downturn since the 1930s wasn't a banking crisis, a credit crisis, or a mortgage crisis – it was a moral crisis, wilful negligence in extremis'. He goes on to specify these failings in terms that include deceit, hubris, myopia, greed and denial. It is a devastating charge sheet.

Questioning leadership theory

While present economic strains may ease at some point, wider questions about the nature of leadership have been inescapably posed. There are calls for more regulation, a greater focus on ethics, a change in culture, a rebalancing of capitalism, a change of leadership personnel in banks and, in many cases, suggestions that politicians should also be dispatched to the scrapheap. But something, it seems to me, is missing. Leadership theory also needs to change. It has done much to encourage an overemphasis on leadership and, in some cases, has legitimised the actions of megalomaniac leaders, who have become convinced that powerful, visionary leadership is helpful, healthy and wise – and, of course, that this means more power should be ceded to leaders. I challenge this view, and what I see as the complacency that goes with it. Different models of leadership are required. The concentration of power in the hands of a few has not been a successful experiment in decision making. We should not be so surprised by this. It has long been noted that out of control leaders in charge of countries invariably lead them to ruin, as in Iraq, Zimbabwe or Libya, and that centralised command economies of the kind currently found in North Korea do not work. It is difficult to see why it should be otherwise within individual organizations. Theories that seek to entrench leader power without considering the downsides of doing so need to be challenged. Business schools, therefore, also need to revisit how they approach the teaching of leadership – a point I develop further in Chapter 6.

Leadership theorists have too often presented an idealised image of leadership – a magic mirror that is economical with the truth. It is time to catch up with reality.

The dark side and the psychology of power

A core argument throughout this book is that leaders wield enormous power, not always wisely. Power is generally defined in terms of our ability to influence other people and derives in part from our ability to control such things as resources, rewards and punishments. As See and colleagues (2011: 27) note, 'A growing body of research has shown that power has strong effects on those who possess it'. These effects range from the benign to the malign. Regardless of this, many accounts of power take it as natural that it should be concentrated in the hands of leaders and regard it as a neutral resource to be used as they see fit. Pfeffer (2010) is one example. An organizational theorist of great renown and a persuasive advocate of humanistic workplace relations, his book on power nevertheless functions as a guidebook on how business leaders can acquire more power, avoid losing whatever power they have and so direct more effectively the efforts of others. In his view, the world is as it is, not as we would like it to be. Some people have power and others do not. Pfeffer admonishes his readers:

> Don't worry about how your efforts to build your path to power are affecting your employer, because your employer is probably not worrying about you. Neither are your coworkers or "partners", if you happen to have any – they are undoubtedly thinking about your usefulness to them, and you will be gone, if they can manage it, when you are no longer of use. You need to take care of yourself and use whatever means you have to do so.
>
> (Pfeffer 2010: 217–18)

In this dog-eat-dog world, if people want power then Pfeffer's book provides the techniques that will lead them to their heart's desire. It is someone else's job to worry about the consequences.

It is obvious that I take a more critical approach in this book. The Great Recession serves as an excellent illustration of what happens when power is concentrated in the hands of a few people, who then use it to advance a self-serving agenda with minimal regard for its wider consequences. It has long been clear that models of leadership which assume that powerful leaders can be relied upon to behave wisely, ethically and for the public good are mistaken. Power adversely affects our ethics, perceptions of others, levels of testosterone and our inclination to engage in risky behaviours. Some examples illustrate the point.

Lammers *et al.* (2010) designed an ingenious set of experiments with 61 subjects designed to manipulate how powerful people felt. They were asked to recall a time when they felt either powerful or powerless. Levels of hypocrisy instantly increased. Those who felt more powerful were more inclined to condemn cheating – but only in others. When given the chance to decide how many lottery tickets they would receive by privately rolling dice, they were more inclined to lie about their scores to obtain extra tickets. Subjects were also more likely to condemn tax dodging, speeding or holding on to stolen goods but thought it less heinous if they did it themselves. Power, it seems, breeds a sense of entitlement and an inclination to hold others to standards of behaviour that we cannot live up to ourselves. Even when we do not have formal power 'over' others, we still have power 'to' them, since we can behave towards them in ways that may be enabling or indifferent, unethical and judgemental (Courpasson 2011). Social influence and power relationships are always present.

The effects of power on people who see themselves as lacking it are also marked. Galinsky and colleagues (2003) ran an experiment in which people were, once more, primed to feel powerless or powerful. They then entered a room to look through some papers. But fans were strategically positioned to blow air into their faces in an irritating manner. Subjects who felt powerful were inclined to move the fan. Those who felt powerless were more likely to tolerate it. If being powerful encourages self-centred behaviour, a sense of powerlessness seems to work equally well – but in the opposite direction.

Nor does it require much to induce either feeling in us. In another experiment, people were given maths problems to solve as individuals (Langer and Benevento 1978). They were then given similar tasks in pairs. Some subjects were supplied with stopwatches and given the job of timing how long this took. In some groups, they received neutral labels, such as 'timer'. In other two-person groups, however, the person with a stopwatch was called 'the boss', while some subjects were given the label 'assistant'. Lastly, everyone once more solved problems on an individual basis. I find the results astonishing. Those who had been given the label 'boss' showed a marked improvement in their performance. 'Timers' or 'solvers' showed no change in performance. But those who had been 'assistants' showed a decrease in performance.

There are, I believe, important implications for leadership. It seems that we are by nature highly sensitive to either the presence or absence of power and fine tune our behaviours accordingly. When people have a label applied to them such as 'boss' they seem to feel more responsible for the task at hand and intensify their efforts accordingly. But when given a label such as 'assistant' their competence goes down, possibly because they conclude that they are less responsible for the task. After all, there is a 'boss' to assume ultimate responsibility. Regardless, most organizations seem to stress status differentials and many managers long for large offices and imposing titles to describe their role. Organizations typically have 'directors' of every function under the sun, while vice-presidents swarm through every corridor, crowding out everyone else. They may be unwittingly adding to the burden of expectation that they carry, while ensuring that their ability to do their jobs goes down. Meanwhile, others grow less and less willing to assume responsibility.

In a further twist, it seems that how considerate we are in our use of power is bound up with our sense of competence. Fast and Chen (2009) illustrated this effect by manipulating the sense of power and self-worth in 90 subjects. The subjects then 'punished' people who made mistakes. They did so by sending horn sounds at lower or higher decibels. Those who felt more incompetent but who also felt that they had more power were willing to administer the harshest punishments. Evidently, there is a risk of power going to our heads. But the more incompetent we feel, paradoxically, the more likely this is to happen – and the less caring we then are to those around us.

This lack of care is not limited to punishing behaviour. It includes a willingness to take a greater share of even small rewards and engage in disinhibited social behaviour. Keltner *et al.* (2003) illustrate this very well. They had three-person student teams engage in a joint writing exercise together. More precisely, two people engaged in the task while one had the job of evaluation – in essence, they were allocated the role of a boss. When at a certain point a plate of cookies was provided, the evaluators were more inclined to take a second one, while also chewing with their mouths open and spraying crumbs in all directions. Sutton sums up the leadership implications as follows:

> When people (regardless of personality) wield power, their ability to lord it over others causes them to (1) become more focused on their own needs and wants; (2) become less focused on others' needs, wants and actions; and (3) act as if written and unwritten rules others are expected to follow don't apply to them.
>
> (Sutton 2010: 28)

These hazards may be particularly pronounced in male dominated environments – such as banking. Coates and Herbert (2008) spent eight days shadowing 17 male traders on a typical trading floor in the city of London. Using saliva samples, they measured their levels of testosterone. As a typical finding, one trader had a winning streak that saw his profit levels exceed his historic average by over 100 per cent. His testosterone levels also soared – by 76 per cent. Success, at least in this environment, produces more testosterone but the higher its levels, the more risky our behaviour is likely to be. Nevertheless, we regularly put people in social situations where they have considerable power, often experience the buzz and rewards of success and are tempted to engage in risky behaviours, since the pay-off is so great. The problem is that the consequences of failure for others can be catastrophic. Most leadership theories pay far too little attention to the need for counterbalancing mechanisms, in which, for example, leaders receive much more critical 'upward' communication on their behaviour (see Chapter 5) and where clear limits are placed on their power. I now turn to one crucial reason why this may be the case.

The over-attribution of agency

A part of the reason why we give leaders too much power has been an all-too-common tendency to commit what Rosenzweig (2007) has termed 'the halo error' – that is, to over-attribute either success or failure in business, politics, sport and elsewhere, to the role of those who hold a handful of top positions. Arnulf *et al.* (2012) conducted a study of this phenomenon from the world of football, focusing on the hiring and firing of managers in the Norwegian Premier League over a 12-year period. Their analysis demonstrates that, had the managers not been fired, their teams' performances might have improved just as well or even quicker. They suggest that decision makers are often fooled by randomness, have overly heroic expectations and are reluctant to permit the time required for deep learning and the development of sustainable leadership capacity at all levels. Team performance in sport, over the long haul, turns out to be a complex phenomenon that cannot be reduced to the behaviour of a single leader, whether it is good or bad. But such simplistic attributions continue to be widely made.

In business, this error is particularly pronounced in the influential work of Jim Collins, best-selling co-author of *Built to Last* (Collins and Porras 1994), of *Good to Great* (Collins 2001), *How The Mighty Fall* (Collins 2009), and now *Great by Choice: Uncertainty, Chaos and Luck – Why Some Thrive Despite Them All* (Collins and Hansen 2011), which attributes total agency to the intentions and actions of top CEOs. Despite occasional disclaimers, Collins' work draws heavily on the retrospective accounts of organizational actors (usually in a senior role) and business commentators without considering whether their accounts have been tarnished by precisely a tendency towards over-attribution. The managerial voice dominates, functioning like an omniscient narrator who talks over the opening titles, main action and closing credits of a movie. Moreover, Collins explicitly invokes the notion of cults, arguing that leaders of organizations should seek to infuse them with a 'cult like' enthusiasm for greatness. It seems clear to me that social systems are far too complex, emotionally charged and contested to be reducible to simple models that not only assume too much agency but also concentrate that agency in too few hands. The sense-making models that both leaders and followers employ to co-construct each other is a vital aspect of the leadership process and one which traditional trait, situationist, contingency or transformational models have been slow to recognise.

Consistent with this, the assumption of absolute leader agency is also a given in much of the literature on organizational failure. For example, Amar and colleagues (2012: 69) assert that 'The reason organizations fail to respond to market conditions is the inability of their senior leaders to manage their organizations to the complexity and dynamism of their business environment'. In then arguing for more distributed forms of leadership to deal with this problem, they suggest that:

> The right approach for responding to these changes requires vesting the authority to lead where it is needed for quick reading and responding. A management style consistent with this principle will allow employees at every level to assume leadership roles, make decisions and manage their part of the business like the top managers of the organization manage corporate strategy, compliance and other corporate tasks.
>
> (Amar *et al.* 2012: 69)

Agency is here viewed as totally in the hands of leaders in terms of responsibility for problems.

Paradoxically, in seeking to critique such leadership practice, the exaggerated view of agency that accompanies it may have the effect of reinforcing the very problem that is at issue – our tendency to see agency in organizations as primarily a matter of leadership, with followers cast in the role of compliant but relatively powerless disciples. Thus, simultaneously, in Amar *et al.*'s (2012) concept, leader agency remains intact in terms of deciding what authority (if any) should be relinquished. It is also assumed that formal leaders retain exclusive oversight of the key directional issues that confront organizations. Those forms of 'empowerment' that are considered relate exclusively to how those in 'follower' roles can make the vision and strategies of their leaders more effective. In such literature, the co-construction of goals and strategies and associated stakeholder models of organizational participation, as advocated for example by Deetz (1995), is typically not considered. Rather, the assumption remains largely intact that organizational leaders need 'to do the same things they always have done – demand compliance from those in less powerful positions' (Stohl and Cheney 2001: 387). In consequence, the door to destructive, tyrannical and disempowering leadership remains open.

Rather than allow ourselves to be seduced in this way by the rhetoric of visionary leaders, the challenge is to assume responsibility for our destiny ourselves. We can question, dissent and resist – and many of us do (Zoller and Fairhurst 2007). But it is generally easier to condone the status quo, particularly under conditions of autocracy. While dissent and resistance clearly exist and may be growing, it is not unusual for people to merely to transfer their allegiance from one false god to another. The attitude often is: if one messianic leader has failed, let us canonise another.

Despite this, the need to question and challenge will not go away. This book encourages its readers to resist the status quo, question authority and always approach the practice of leadership and its claims with a healthy feeling of scepticism.

A personal perspective

My own interest in the dark side of leadership is born from the intersection of many factors – personal and professional. The professional is rooted in a disciplinary background of communication studies, heavily shaped by linguistics, sociology and social psychology. How one person influences another is an intrinsically fascinating question. Moreover, all of us both influence other people and are influenced by them. In studying such issues, we are really learning how to understand ourselves better.

The personal emerges from my experience of being subject to and an observer of leadership practice in both functional and dysfunctional contexts. I grew up in Northern Ireland at the height of what has been termed 'the Troubles'. Over 3,700 people were killed and 47,500 injured. On a pro rata basis, the death toll would have been equal to 115,000 people had it occurred in Britain or 600,000 in the USA (Hargie and Dickson 2003). Seemingly charismatic and indubitably influential individuals advocated political ends, in the pursuit of which the lives of their followers, not to mention those of their enemies, were of little significance. Leaders came and went – some summarily dispatched by followers who had grown weary of attempts at compromise or a perceived failure to achieve much-ballyhooed goals. Yet some also endured through all the strife, unaffected by fashion, failure or the lethal disdain of their opponents. What distinguished those who achieved lasting influence from those who held exalted positions one day only to be discarded the next? How come so many people were willing to follow some leaders to the precipice and even beyond?

Thus began a preoccupation with leaders who hold followers in thrall by dint of their rabble-rousing oratorical gifts; who offer an appealing simplicity of purpose in the face of life's complexities; who compel a transformation in follower attitudes, thereby converting apparently 'normal' people into devotees of rigid ideologies, totalistic beliefs and violent means; who exploit the devotion and commitment of their followers to further an agenda frequently at odds with its proclaimed emancipatory intent; and leaders who promise to right all wrongs, only to add fresh layers of hurt to an already besmirched human condition. Leadership for me has always been about studying the limits on the power of leaders to do good and the propensity of some to champion an agenda that may exercise a destructive impact but which nevertheless exerts a powerful emotional appeal. Echoing Winston Churchill, many leaders promise blood, sweat, toil and tears but few do so for equally worthwhile ends. So the study of leadership inevitably becomes an exploration of leader and message effects and of how leaders and followers exercise a reciprocal influence on the mindsets and practices of each other. This book seeks to challenge those approaches which take leadership influence for granted and which pay too little attention to the negative consequences that follow. How can such crude approaches have been so influential? And why have we been so blind to its potentially negative effects?

Part of the answer is our forgetfulness, a forgetfulness I seek to dispel in this book. In medieval days, it was commonly believed that monarchs held their position by virtue of 'the divine right of kings'. They were the anointed representatives of God on Earth and to challenge the legitimacy of their rule was to flout the will of the divine. It sometimes seems as if mainstream leadership work, lacking a sense of historical continuity, offers a similar view: 'the divine right of leaders'. To offer one example, the growing interest in 'evidence-based management', championed by most contributors to a key text edited by Rousseau (2012), adopts a purely functionalist view of the leadership role. The argument is that management – and leadership – practice should be based on the evidence about 'what works' and that management research must therefore be more relevant to the needs of 'practitioners'. Practitioners are defined purely in terms of a managerial elite, whose legitimacy is taken for granted rather than interrogated. It is assumed that decision-making power rests with managers, who are free to make decisions on all key issues without their subjects being required to offer a voice. Employees, cast in the role of infantilised dependants, must grant power of attorney over many of the most important aspects of their lives to powerful others.

This promotion of unbridled leader agency does not square with my life experience of leadership or what I have found in my research. Nor is it possible to reconcile it with perspectives that stress ambiguity, indeterminacy of meaning and the subtlety and range of human-inspired messages – in short, with the world as most people really experience it. To study leadership must be to study voice, power, words, discourse – and not just those of the élite. Leaders have no divine right to exercise absolute authority over followers. Rather, the challenge is to delineate the limits of their power; to explore the sense-making processes whereby this power is enacted in the minds and lives of leaders and followers alike; to ascertain what it is that holds people in thrall to flawed visions and dysfunctional leaders; and to continually question and challenge the legitimacy of a leader centric view of the social world we inhabit.

What this book is, and is not

Many readers will be aware of the burgeoning literature within the tradition of what is known as critical management studies (CMS) and will instinctively appreciate its useful emphasis on issues of power and agency. More recently, Collinson (2011) has suggested that we can now speak of 'critical leadership studies' (CLS), since more leadership scholars are exploring such issues as power, identity and resistance, with a view to developing post-heroic perspectives on leadership. Yet, for all its value, it seems to me that many critically oriented researchers imagine that their work stops with critique, rather than starts. I recall a colleague discussing a seminar presented by a leading CMS scholar. When asked 'yes, but what is your alternative', the speaker paused for a moment and then replied: 'Well, there is no alternative'. In short, oppressive power relations are inscribed on all human interaction, meaning that leader–follower relations remain inescapably tortured, conflicted, alienated and incapable of resolution.

In common with many others (for example, Thompson 2005), I find this an underwhelming response to the challenges that we face as the dominant species on the planet. The world is on fire and it will take more than a spirit of sorrowful torpor to extinguish the flames. I do not want scholars engaged in CLS to become so preoccupied by leadership abuses that they neglect to develop alternatives. It is certainly vital that we deconstruct leadership, that we ask critical questions of its practice and that we open up our research to different voices and interests. But it is also important, I think, that we attempt to offer solutions. If the world cannot be made perfect, then perhaps it can at least be made better. And this is a challenge which, in fairness, at least some CMS scholars (for example, Cunliffe 2008) are beginning to address, particularly in terms of critical management education. Symptomatic of this trend, the *British Journal of Management* published a special issue in 2010 which explored the role of business schools from a critical perspective. There have also been calls for a 'critical performativity' approach to leadership (Alvesson and Spicer 2012: 368), which recognises the 'potentially positive value of functional exercises of authority' and which questions the usefulness of abandoning all notions of leadership.

I do not therefore reject the need for leadership. While my focus is on its dark side, leadership is often necessary, justly exercised and has a positive impact on followers, organizations and societies. Consider well-known exemplars of such leadership – Dr Martin Luther King's advocacy of civil rights in 1960s America, Nelson Mandela's struggle against apartheid and then for reconciliation in South Africa and Aung San Suu Kyi's struggle against military rule in Burma, which included spending 15 years under house arrest. These are inspiring examples. But what makes them stand out and are they really so rare?

When we think of how functional authority can be exercised in a positive manner, clear patterns emerge. Positive leadership exists, I argue, when we attempt to influence others, ideally for a common purpose. It is not about imposing one's will on recalcitrant others, as Hitler and Stalin did on a devastating scale and as many still try to do on a smaller canvas. It is about debate, persuasion and a willingness on the leader's part to change their own actions, minds or plans when it is the logical thing to do. An openness to reciprocal influence is critical – a theme I develop in greater detail in Chapter 5. However, it is also about exercising authority. There are times, particularly under crisis, when either an individual or a small group must make a final decision on behalf of the collective. This is not an endorsement of totalitarianism but it is a recognition that participatory rather than representative democracy is not possible under all conditions. Balance is critical. This sometimes means taking an unpopular stand and running great risks, in the hope that vindication will come but knowing that it may not.

Such leadership is not necessarily bound up with formal hierarchy. Sometimes people show it when they have no formal power at all. Bob Geldof emerged in the 1980s as a major campaigner against famine in Africa, organizing events that inspired the world and saved millions of lives. He represented no organization but he had sufficient authority as a musician to galvanise his peer group into participating in a successful event. A forceful personality also helped. This willingness to act for a noble purpose when others hesitate seems to me to be part of positive leadership. It also requires people to be in a position when they recognise themselves as having a leadership role and are acknowledged by others to have that role as well. Credibility is a key ingredient of authority. An example of this credibility in positive action is the Bill and Melinda Gates Foundation, run with the participation of Warren Buffet, which focuses on alleviating extreme poverty and poor health in developing countries, alongside addressing the failures of America's education system.

In exploring the dark side throughout this book, I consider what we can do to bring the positive much more to the fore. This means trying to answer some rather awkward questions. These include:

- What do leaders really need from their followers? Is it blind obedience, input, critique or something we have not yet figured out?
- What do followers really want from their leaders? Is it mainly financial reward? Or is it forms of recognition, empowerment and autonomy that are to some extent inherently in conflict with modern business organizations?

If so, what can we do about it? What is that remains constant in leader–follower relations and what is there about such relations that are subject to change? These issues are a recurrent theme in the chapters that follow.

- We hear much in the literature these days about 'authentic leadership'. What about 'authentic followership'? Can followers genuinely bring their real selves into the workplace or are existing power structures too pervasive and destructive to permit this? In Chapter 4, for example, I consider the tensions inherent to the notion of spiritual leadership that purports to fulfil this enabling role. For that matter, where does pathological leadership (of which there is much) fit into the schema of authenticity, which seems to assume that an authentic inner self is invariably positive in nature (Fairhurst 2007)?

- The sociological theorist, Robert Michels, famously summed up his view of organization over a century ago as follows: 'Who says organization, says oligarchy' (Michels [1911] 1962: 365). Interestingly, in view of my arguments about authoritarianism within certain kinds of leftist facing organizations in Chapter 8, many of Michels' ideas on this derived from his own disillusioning experience as a member of the then left-wing German Social Democratic Party. He noted that, as organizations grow in size, opportunities for direct participation diminish, with more authority ceded to smaller groups of members to act on behalf of the collective. This raises such issues as the limits on freedom and agency within social systems. Moreover, is hierarchy innately oppressive or is it indispensable for organizational life? How, if at all, can its downsides be curtailed or eliminated? If oligarchy is inevitable, must it be absolute or, as Tolbert and Hiatt (2009) suggest, can it be considered as a matter of degree?

- To what extent are followers often complicit in their own subordination? People can be reluctant to challenge power, even when there is no obvious sanction at the disposal of the powerful. We are easily overawed by authority, celebrity and wealth. Passivity in the face of power is more common than resistance. I show, for example, in Chapter 7, how little resistance there was within Enron to the corrupt business models of that organization's leaders. We need to consider why this is so often the case, how leaders can become more tolerant of dissent and how followers can acquire courage.

I don't entertain any illusions that these issues are capable of ultimate resolution. Human beings have shown a remarkable capacity for reinforcing destructive hierarchy, even as we pronounce our intention of abolishing it, including when that effort has taken the form of revolutionary action. But that is not the point. I do not believe that merely uncovering dysfunctional dynamics is sufficient. People are trying to make sense of their social world but most also want to improve it. To remain only at the level of critique is to evade our most fundamental responsibility of all, as citizens of the planet. We need to use the intellectual tools at our disposal to do better. And this must mean seeking to answer the question: what is the alternative? Where does our journey seek to take us?

The voyage ahead

This is a book about charismatic visionaries whose charisma is an illusion planted in the minds of their followers and whose vision is feeble, illusory or inappropriate, despite its appeal to many. It is a book about the limits on the ability of leaders to do good and the tendency of many to put their own self-interest above the collective good of their followers. It is about how so many invest so much hope in so few, almost always embarking on a journey towards disappointment. It is about the techniques that some leaders use to manipulate people into endorsing their fantasies and how followers subordinate their own genuine needs to those decreed by the leader. As we shall see in the case study chapters that constitute Part 2 of this book, it is about how some leaders project the impression of greater insight than what they actually possess in order to take advantage of our desire to anoint a saviour in religious or secular form.

In exploring these issues, I do not intend to imply that leaders can ever achieve total control over followers. Fairhurst and Zoller (2008: 141) rightly note, following Foucault, that 'attempts at control inevitably breed corresponding attempts at resistance. It is the reason that company grapevines flourish the most in organizations with the tightest control of information'. This also applies where tyrannical power is at its most extreme. For example, Langbein (1995) – himself a holocaust survivor and a leader of resistance efforts at Auschwitz – has documented open revolts in Nazi concentration camps, including Auschwitz, Treblinka, Birkenau and Sobibor. Power is never omnipotent, even when wielded through the barrel of a gun.

The 'Arab Spring' is a good contemporary example. Beginning in December 2010, uprisings forced regime change in Tunisia, Egypt, Libya and Yemen. Major protests broke out elsewhere, including Syria, Algeria and Jordan. I recall running a leadership development programme in early 2010 in the Middle East. Several of the participants took me aside individually, to patiently explain that any suggestion of valuing dissent or encouraging critical upward communication would not work in the region, given its tradition of respect for authority and the nature of the regimes that had long been in place. One said: 'This is the Middle East, and things are different here'. It occurs to me that, in offering such feedback, they were themselves demonstrating the very behaviours that they were attempting to suggest were impossible. Those who have most power are (relatively) powerless in some domains of action, while those who appear to be without power retain agency in some deep recess of their being. What has been characterised as 'dualistic understandings' between force and consent, the individual and society, and power and powerlessness needs to be challenged (Knights and Vurdubakis 1994).

But all things have limits. While I cite examples of resistance in the chapters that follow, my main focus is on those leadership practices that seek to atomise and individualise people's experiences of dysfunctional power, thereby turning them 'inwards' and away from the possibility of an effective collective response (McCabe 2007) or which attempt to reframe their perceptions of overweening power by internalising ideologies that legitimise it.

Such atomisation is at its most acute under totalitarian state regimes, such as in Stalin's Russia or Saddam Hussein's Iraq. But the ingredients of totalitarian power are replicated in micro form within many smaller social systems – as my discussion of Jonestown in Chapter 9 suggests. Under these conditions, resistance is a particular challenge for those in senior positions, even when their own self-interest suggests that it would be wise. Stalin's entourage offers a good example. They were the most vulnerable to his repeated rounds of purges. Almost 117,000 members of the Communist Party were imprisoned or executed between 1937 and 1938; 139 people were elected to the Central Committee of the Party in 1934; 102 of them were shot, while five more killed themselves to avoid this fate. More than half of the top officers within the Red Army were executed (Figes 2007). No one felt safe and the more senior their role the less safe they were. Why did they not remove him?

Opportunities to do so did exist. In June 1941, when the Nazis invaded Russia, there appears to have been a few days when Stalin's morale collapsed. After some initial meetings, he disappeared to his *dacha*, physically exhausted and depressed by the disintegration of his strategy of accommodation with Hitler. When his top aides eventually caught up with him, some sources indicate that Stalin imagined they had arrived to arrest him. But no. They had come to insist that he resume his hold on power (Sebag-Montefiore 2007). By then, the habit of servitude was deeply ingrained. Only Stalin, it seems, did not realise by how much. The atomisation of the individual will through strict surveillance had eliminated, for now, the possibility of collective resistance. I suggest that the possibility of arrest in previous years, and the scrutiny that went with it, created the belief that to discuss resistance with others meant certain death. The alternative was ever more sycophantic displays of loyalty. Within Stalin's own circle, officials felt obliged to defer to his every passing whim, indulge his passion for all night dinners and drinking sessions, laugh uproariously at his infrequent jokes, re-enact the last moments of selected execution victims (such as the former Chairman of the Communist International, Grigory Zinoviev) and affirm that they regarded him as a genius (see Sebag-Montefiore 2007 for many excruciating examples). While the terror was random and such demonstrations were of limited value, they at least offered some hope. Hope, however fleeting, is always preferable to despair. Thus, an authoritarian leader may not be able to keep a total check on many millions. But he or she can keep a close eye on those in their immediate circle. The courage of followers, subordinates, hirelings and sycophants only grows when the leader's power visibly wanes, through old age, the decay of systems of surveillance and revolt in the wider society.

This is therefore a voyage around the dark side of human nature. But I hope that it is a voyage that informs our thinking and actions beyond these pages. In analysing what I think goes wrong with leadership practice, I repeatedly point to suggestions for alternatives in the chapters ahead. There is no one ready-made approach that can guarantee to always avert shipwreck. But in the struggle to contain the dark side, to reclaim power and to gain wisdom, the first step is awareness.

In that spirit, the voyage begins.

Points for discussion

1. How would you differentiate between 'positive' and 'negative' forms of leadership influence?
2. Consider powerful individuals you have known. What behaviours did they typically show towards others? To what extent can the psychological experiments discussed in this chapter explain their conduct, good or bad?
3. Identify a recent media story about the success or failure of a business organization. How much does the coverage stress the role and decisions of individual leaders? Is such an emphasis justified?
4. If the theory and practice of leadership needs to be improved, what are your initial thoughts about how this should be accomplished?

Note

1 The film is based on a 1926 novel of the same name by Sinclair Lewis. The movie version departs significantly from its source material.

2 Transformational leadership

The dynamics of excessive leader agency[1]

Introduction

Our voyage begins with a study of transformational leadership. A recent review described this as 'the single most studied and debated idea within the field of leadership studies' during the previous 30 years (Díaz-Sáenz 2011: 299). As an indicator of its popularity, I entered the term 'transformational leadership' into Google Scholar in mid-2012. It reported over 82,000 hits. A search of *Amazon. co.uk* at the same time found over 4,600 books with 'transformational leadership' somewhere in their title. A random selection from Amazon's listings is instructive. They include: *Inspirational Presence: The Art of Transformational Leadership* (Evans 2009); *Transformational Leadership: Shared Dreams to Succeed* (Godard *et al.* 2000); *Improving Organizational Effectiveness Through Transformational Leadership* (Bass and Avolio 1993) and *Transformational Leadership in Nursing: From Expert Clinician to Influential Leader* (Marshall 2010). These reveal much about the intent and promise of transformational leadership. It is about transforming others rather than oneself, projecting charisma, building shared dreams and ensuring that organizational performance – as defined by powerful elites – is improved. As the title aimed at nurses suggests, it seems that there is no limit to the professions or sectors which can benefit from such an approach. Even clinicians stepping into frontline leadership roles are encouraged to adopt a 'transformational' mind-set.

In this chapter, however, I explore the largely unintended consequences of this approach. In stressing the need for leaders to 'transform' others – a project which increasingly seeks to reshape their most private values, attitudes and aspirations – transformational leadership has been complicit in attempts to extend the power of formal organizational leaders in ever more intrusive directions. Influence is conceived largely in unidirectional terms. It flows from powerful leaders to more or less powerless others. The job of followers is, in the main, to accept the wise counsel they receive from elsewhere. While the power of some is enhanced, that of others is diminished.

It is instructive to compare the key ideas of transformational leadership to what we know of dysfunctional leadership practice in organizations widely regarded as cults, as I do in this chapter. Such an approach reveals what few leadership scholars appear to have noticed. Fundamentally, the techniques of influence advocated by those who promote transformational leadership are uncannily similar to those used by the leaders of cults such as Scientology (famous for having such luminaries as Tom Cruise, John Travolta and Kirstie Alley among its members), the Moonies and a myriad of others. Transformational leadership has had an influential trajectory. How much of this has been positive is a different matter. I argue here that it serves mainly as a warning of the dangers that arise when leader power is taken for granted and challenge the tendency of many scholars simply to reproduce and reinforce the power of leaders without sufficiently considering the potential for the abuse of power that invariably arises.

Transformational leadership defined

Most interest in transformational leadership dates from the late 1970s. At that point, Burns (1978) proposed that leadership could be conceptualised in two factor terms, as being either transactional or transformational. His work is considered seminal in the field. Within transactional models of the leadership process, the independence of the goals of both leaders and followers is a given (Flauto 1999). Goods, services and other rewards are exchanged so that the various parties achieve their independent goals. The emphasis is on exchange relationships between followers and leaders, in line with the traditional nostrums of social exchange theory (Anand *et al.* 2011). Burns (1978: 425) critically observed that the object of this transactional approach 'is not a joint effort for persons with common aims acting for the collective interests of followers but a bargain to aid the individual interests of persons or groups going their separate ways'. The culture that results from a transactional approach to leadership is likely to be one characterised by dissent, which may be more or less tolerated, and reduced cohesion – outcomes which most managers instinctively reject.

Transformational leadership is presented in a different light. Here, the leader is encouraged to change the goals of followers, subordinates or (in the case of cults) devoted members. Put in its most positive form, the new goals are assumed to be of a higher level in that, once transformed, they represent the 'collective good or pooled interests of leaders and followers' (Burns 1978: 426). Clearly, such a positive assumption requires a large leap of faith. There is no a priori reason to presume that the goals proposed by a transformational leader represent a deeper mutual interest among organizational partners and, hence, express the best interests of all concerned. If a leader secures sufficient power to adjust the psyche of his or her followers, in the form of transforming their independently determined goals in a communal direction, such power could just as likely be used for the sectional good of the designated leader. This dilemma has been dubbed 'the Hitler problem' (Ciulla 1995): in essence, can Hitler be viewed as a transformational leader? Is he in the same category as Martin Luther King or other more moral leaders? If not, who sets the standards for what constitutes morality, using what criteria and validated by whom? As Grint critically observes:

> There is … little evidence that admiring followers of Mao, Stalin, Hitler or Osama bin Laden followed their leaders because they were psychopaths

(though that would be a good reason to avoid contradicting them if you were not a loyal follower) and much more evidence that these followers assumed their leaders were ethical; it's just that their ethics do not match ours and their scapegoats often include us: we were and are their 'other'.

Grint (2010: 97)

The model proposed by Burns (1978) is a highly idealised version of an inherently problematic process. This is evident in the following depiction of the process:

In contrast to the transactional leader who practices contingent reinforcement of followers, the transformational leader inspires, intellectually stimulates, and is individually considerate of them … The transformational leader emphasizes what you can do for your country; the transactional leader, on what your country can do for you.

(Bass 1999: 9)

Despite the invocation of Kennedy, the type of appeal described was also one made by the regimes of Hitler, Stalin and other totalitarian leaders.

By definition, transformational leaders need more power rather than constraints (or 'regulation'), presumably to restrain the power of their potential dissidents. Their eccentricities, like those of a kindly uncle, must be tolerated. Bass (1990: 26) argues: 'Organizational policy needs to support an understanding and appreciation of the maverick who is willing to take unpopular decisions, who knows when to reject the conventional wisdom, and who takes reasonable risks'. The conception, however, is clearly one in which the leader is liberated to act as a maverick, while limiting the ability of followers to behave in an equally unpredictable fashion.

The perils of excessive conformity

The dangers are considerable. Research has long shown that new group members, or those with low status, tend to acquire influence within a group by overconforming to its emergent norms (Jetten and Hornsley 2011). Otherwise, they are penalised, usually through the withdrawal of valued social rewards. Leaders, on the other hand, have greater status, authority and power. They have more freedom than followers to violate long-established norms. The risk is of followers prematurely complying with destructive forms of action to ingratiate themselves with leaders (Jones 1990). The leader, meanwhile, takes the absence of overt dissent as assent and, moreover, views it as supplementary evidence that the given course of action is correct – what has been termed consensual validation (Tourish and Robson 2003). Transformational leadership is liable to exacerbate these problematic processes yet further, with negative consequences for the quality of a leader's decision making.

Undaunted, transformational leadership theorists typically argue that leaders should seek to influence the identity of their followers to indirectly increase their commitment (Chemers 2003). It is argued that leaders need to satisfy followers' needs, values and goals and confirm their identities as part of a process of shaping attitudes to make them conform to a common, unitary interest. In the process, personal and organizational goals are aligned, heightening employee commitment (Bass 1985). Thus, an organization's 'vision' becomes one that is described as 'shared' by employees and leaders (Conger *et al.* 2000). Empirical studies also suggest that transformational leadership fosters much closer identification with both the leader and the designated work unit – an outcome generally viewed by its advocates as desirable (Kark *et al.* 2003). A powerful expression of such thinking is provided by two of the foremost advocates of transformational leadership:

> Transformational leaders … are those who stimulate and inspire followers to both achieve extraordinary outcomes and, in the process, develop their own leadership capacity. Transformational leaders help followers grow and develop into leaders by responding to individual followers' needs by empowering them and by aligning the objectives and goals of the individual followers, the leader, the group, and the larger organization … transformational leadership can move followers to exceed expected performance, as well as lead to high levels of follower satisfaction and commitment to the group and the organization.
>
> (Bass and Riggio 2006: 3)

This comes close to what I would describe as a 'Superman' or 'Superwoman' view of leadership. As Alvesson and Sveningsson (2012: 203) critically observe, in overviewing the field of leadership, 'there are no limits to what leadership is supposed to accomplish in terms of improving the feelings, thinking, values, ethics, change-mindedness, satisfaction, and performance of followers'. Unfortunately, in the world that most people inhabit, such limits on leader effectiveness can be observed every day – as they are in the behaviour of every human being. Most of us stumble and fall on a regular basis. Leaders are no different.

In addition, the view of organizations implied by authors such as Bass and Riggio is unitarist. They argue that 'Transformational leadership involves inspiring followers to commit to a shared vision and goals for an organization or unit' (Bass and Riggio 2006: 4). This approach assumes that 'all organizational members share the goals of the organization and are thus motivated to act in ways that will ensure the realisation of such goals' (Hay and Hodgkinson 2006: 148). And yet, simultaneously (and without any acknowledgement of contradiction), it proposes a leadership model in which leaders tightly control the behaviour of their followers: leaders have the power to reward, punish or fire followers, depending on how enthusiastically they embrace the goals set for them by leaders. It is a model which can too easily see a kindly uncle morph into an angry god.

Charisma, vision and individual consideration

Bass (1990) extended Burns' ideas from the political sphere and into small-group and organizational settings. This trend has been maintained in the research of others, including Tichy and Ulrich (1984), Tichy and Devanna (1990) and Aryee *et al.* (2012). Three transformational attributes have been consistently identified in this literature: charismatic leadership, individual consideration and intellectual stimulation (Díaz-Sáenz 2011). The transformational leader is assumed to possess and energetically communicate 'a vision' for the organization. A vision has been defined as a mental image that a leader evokes to portray an idealised future (Conger 1989). As Awamleh and Gardner (1999: 346) point out, 'an idealized vision is generally considered to be a prerequisite for a leader to become transformational or charismatic'. Charismatic leaders have been defined as people who 'by the force of their personal abilities are capable of having profound and extraordinary effects on followers' (House and Baetz 1979: 339). Thus, charisma is something that has variously been described as residing in the person (House and Howell 1992), a behavioural phenomenon (Conger and Kanungo 1994), concerned with some aspects of social exchange (Bryman 1992) or ultimately an attributional phenomenon (Lord and Maher 1993).

The vision (again, in the most optimistic rendition of the process) performs an integrative role, combining the members into a collective whole with a shared set of aspirations capable of guiding (or moulding) their everyday behaviour. The act of communicating such a vision is highly dynamic, requires intense charisma and transforms relational dynamics throughout the workplace. In particular, Shamir and colleagues summarise the literature on this by saying that transformational leaders:

> cause followers to become highly committed to the leader's mission, to make significant personal sacrifices in the interests of the mission, and to perform above and beyond the call of duty … Theories of charismatic leadership highlight such effects as emotional attachment to the leader on the part of the followers; emotional and motivational arousal of the followers; enhancement of follower valences with respect to the mission articulated by the leader; follower self-esteem, trust, and confidence in the leader; follower values; and follower intrinsic motivation.
>
> Shamir *et al.* (1993: 577)

This is clearly a radical agenda, proposing a collective rebirth into new organizational configurations, self-perceptions and transformed relationships whereby one dominant culture is likely to emerge. For the most part, Weber's (1968) interest in charisma as a form of domination rooted in the relationship between a leader and the leader's followers has been supplanted by a narrowly functionalist perspective, with most research focusing on its 'effectiveness' and how this effectiveness can be measured (Conger and Kanungo 1998). As Ladkin (2010) has observed, this puts much less attention on the role of followers and context in the development of charismatic leadership. Rather, it is taken for granted that charisma is a useful thing to have, since some people have more of it than others, and that the main task of leadership scholars is to explore how it can be exercised more 'effectively'.

Hansen *et al.* (2010) provide a typical example of where a functionalist perspective of this kind leads us. They surveyed 2,000 CEOs worldwide to identify in their article's title 'The best-performing CEOs in the world'. The key question this seeks to address is 'Who led firms that, on the basis of stock returns, outperformed other firms in the same country and industry?'. The point here is not whether – or to what extent – leadership makes a difference to organizational performance, however narrowly such performance is defined. Rather, it is that in this example – routine in the positivist and functionalist research on leadership – total agency is invested in the leader. Critical perspectives, which draw attention to the exercise of untrammelled authority as a form of 'symbolic violence' (Robinson and Kerr 2009), examine how it can put undue emphasis on the need for individual rather than system-wide change (McCabe 2011) and stress its potential for dysfunctional domination are still relatively rare.

What of the people required to be charismatic, transformational leaders and, hence, spearheads of this new revolution? Most managers do not exude charisma in the manner assumed to be necessary. Indeed, quite a few have a well-deserved reputation for being boring. It is possible that a significant number of those exceptionally endowed with charisma possess uncommon personality traits, good and bad. In particular, Maccoby (2000) suggests that many charismatic leaders are narcissists – that is, people with an inordinately well-developed self-image, in which they take great pride and on which they reflect frequently. They are also likely to have a strong need for power, high self-confidence and strong convictions (De Vries *et al.* 1999). Rather than flexibly responding to feedback, the narcissistic but charismatic visionary leader is inclined to perceive reality through the distorting prism of his or her vision.

The problem is compounded by the fact that leaders within corporations, in particular, possess more power than ever before (Guthey 2005). Corporate chieftains, such as General Electric's former CEO, Jack Welch, have been lionised in the business press and wider media, often credited with sole responsibility for their organizations' success during their tenure and upheld as role models for other emergent business leaders across the globe (Amernic *et al.* 2007). For such leaders, the management of meaning through the framing of an alternate vision of reality is crucial to the consolidation of their power. Frequently, this also compels a harsh attitude towards dissent. As Stein (2008: 75) has noted: 'Corporate executives … use language in an effort to manage (which most commonly means to control) dissent. Their tactics include denying, constraining, subverting, transforming, quashing and discrediting challenges that oppose orthodox ideologies and policies'.

In this scenario, the leader may be able and willing to impose his or her vision on recalcitrant followers, however erroneous it is. The edge of a cliff might seem the starting point of an adventurous new journey. Sceptics are pushed and pulled to the precipice. Unable to resist the argument that an overwhelming external threat ('the competition') leaves no room for doubt and dissent, they leap – to death or glory. Fear of an external threat, however imaginary, is also a powerful means of promoting in group cohesion – as my discussion of Jonestown and

Heaven's Gate in Chapter 9 demonstrates. In addition, whatever their virtues, narcissists can be overconfident in their abilities, unwilling to compromise, have an excessive need for power, lack empathy, be a poor listener, have an intense need for the admiration of others, be arrogant and also be overly self-absorbed (DuBrin 2012). Precisely such behaviours and traits have been found to be characteristic of cult leaders, in all manner of cultic organizations (Tourish 2011).

The handling of dissent is one of the most problematic aspects of transformational leadership theory and one where comparisons with cultic organizations are most pertinent. Even managers introducing change who are not explicitly guided by the precepts of transformational leadership theory frequently view resistance as something to be overcome, rather than useful feedback (Lewis 1992; Spicer and Levay 2012). Researchers into transformational leadership are especially prone to this conceptualisation (Yukl 1999). This is despite the well-documented fact that many charismatic leaders have an exaggerated impression of precisely how effective or useful their vision is (Conger 2011). An alternative perspective, based on the institutionalisation of feedback into organizational decision making, is rarely considered. The problem is inherent to myths of heroic leadership and the behaviours that are associated with it. As Yukl (1999: 40) has argued: 'expressing strong convictions, acting confident, and taking decisive action can create an impression of exceptional expertise, but it can also discourage relevant feedback from followers'. Given its emphasis on the agency of leaders rather than followers, transformational leadership is inherently disposed to produce this unfortunate side effect.

Illusions in leadership

A number of psychological processes facilitate undue faith in transformational models of leadership, despite their weaknesses. Firstly, an abundance of research evidence suggests that people have a tendency to exaggerate the contribution that designated leaders make to organizational success (Meindl 1995). This may be particularly so in extreme situations, irrespective of the validity of the notion itself (Meindl *et al.* 1985). The perception that we have unmet needs, particularly if we are already anxious, increases our receptiveness to supposedly charismatic or transformational leaders, whether or not they can actually meet the needs in question (Hansbrough 2012). Under pressure, our need for causal explanations (with both an explanatory and predictive power) increases, since it enables us to reduce uncertainty. As Gemmill and Oakley (1992: 115) have pointed out, 'As social despair and helplessness deepen, the search and wish for a Messiah (leader) or magical rescue (leadership) also begin to accelerate'. There is a widespread desire to believe in the possibility of an omnipotent leader, capable of resolving all our problems (Schilling 2009).

This desire lends itself also to support for leaders with extreme views. Such views 'are clear cut and unambiguous; by glossing over nuances and intricacies they afford sweeping generalizations that permit certainty and assurance' (Kruglanski and Orehek 2012: 13). This assurance is enormously consoling.

Leaders are often inclined to use self-deception and various impression-management techniques to convince followers of their ability to deliver on such a challenging agenda (Gray and Densten 2007). It is evident that the explanations generated by all these endeavours need not be accurate to feel compelling. Sense making in organizations is often driven by plausibility rather than accuracy (Weick 1995). In particular, experimental evidence suggests that positive leadership attributions are increased when the saliency of leadership behaviours is exaggerated (Pfeffer and Cialdini 1998). The transformational model lends itself to such processes, stressing as it does the central contribution that transformational leadership is assumed to make to business success.

Within cults, the saliency of leadership behaviours is also routinely exaggerated. For example, most of a cult's key documents (usually billed as articulating seminal developments in the ideology of the group) are written by the leader, who also makes the keynote speeches at cult gatherings and is in every way deferred to by a largely passive and uncritical followership (Tourish 2011). Such followers are heavily penalised if they dissent. Sceptics and dissenters, the weak and the wavering, are forced to leave if they maintain a questioning attitude. The absence of overt dissent encourages the wide adoption of the fallacious view that everyone agrees with the general line and imbues it with a spurious legitimacy it lacks in reality. Typically, CEOs come under pressure to replicate these dynamics. They can derive theoretical sustenance for this effort from the writings of transformational leadership theorists.

Once committed, it is hard to detour from the road already well travelled. An extensive literature shows that people tend to regard themselves as more intelligent, skilled, ethical, honest, persistent, original, friendly, reliable and even more attractive than others (Myers 1996). This can be defined as a self-efficacy bias (Gist 1987). Thus, once we have embarked on a course of action, our assumptions about our own abilities cause us to exaggerate its virtues, minimise its problems and exaggerate its gains. This research also suggests that leaders are liable to rate their own leadership behaviours as more effective than those of other people – perhaps more so, if they have explicitly developed a self-image consisting of charismatic attributes. From this, it is a small step to assuming that an organization's successes are the result of the leader's efforts, while its problems derive either from uncontrollable external factors or insufficiently committed behaviour by followers. It follows that more rather than less charismatic leadership is required. For example, investigations of annual reports show that bad performance is attributed to general economic or industry conditions. Good performance, on the other hand, is attributed to management and internal organizational factors (Salancik and Meindl 1984).

Such a flawed conception is not limited to leaders. De Vries *et al.* (1999) surveyed 958 people and found that subordinates with charismatic leaders had a higher need for leadership than those with noncharismatic leaders. The evident encouragement of such dependency attitudes is scarcely consistent with the empowerment imperative. However, it is wholly consistent with flawed group dynamics that place too much power in some hands and too little in others.

The downsides of faith in transformational leaders

It is apparent from this that transformational leadership theories may well become unfalsifiable. Whatever happens, or whatever could possibly happen, is evidence of the theory's correctness and leads to its wider implementation. Success is due to the correct application of the transformational leadership model. Failures are due to external factors beyond its control. In either case, the solution is more transformational leadership. Thus, the theory of transformational leadership becomes impervious to refutation.

Conger, in the main an enthusiast for transformational leadership, acknowledges that:

> though we tend to think of the positive outcomes associated with leaders, certain risks or liabilities are also entailed. The very behaviours that distinguish leaders from managers also have the potential to produce problematic or even disastrous outcomes for their organizations. For example, when a leader's behaviour become exaggerated, lose touch with reality, or become vehicles for purely personal gain, they may harm the leader and the organization.
>
> (Conger 1990: 44)

The problem is that the model tends to preclude the possibility of corrective feedback from followers to leaders. In some cases, this might have little adverse impact. There are organizations that are led by inspiring people, capable of fashioning competitive strategies that help their organizations to survive. However, the ubiquity of transformational leadership ideas can persuade even the most uncharismatic that they too must develop, articulate and inculcate a compelling vision. In many cases, it is as though the tone deaf have become convinced that they are the bearers of songs which must be sung. Thus, organizations are sometimes led by CEOs who are esteemed by the stock market (at least initially), but who turn out to be wrong, mad, bad or daft.

In such circumstances, corporate paranoia, frenetic activity and group norms that penalise open discussion may rapidly take root. Organizational problems are inevitable when leaders develop a monomaniacal conviction that there is the one right way of doing things and believe that they possess an almost divine insight into reality. The potential for this development is inherent to transformational leadership theories of leadership. Thus, Conger acknowledges the following possible liabilities in the leader's communication and impression management skills, of particular importance in this case:

Exaggerated self-descriptions.
Exaggerated claims for the vision.
A technique of fulfilling stereotypes and images of uniqueness to manipulate audiences.
A habit of gaining commitment by restricting negative information and maximizing positive information.

Use of anecdotes to distract attention away from negative statistical information.
Creation of an illusion of control through affirming information and attributing negative outcomes to external causes.

(Conger 1990: 50)

The consequences of such defects are clear. They include the elimination of dissent; the accumulation of power at the centre; a failure to sufficiently consider alternative courses of action, when they appear to conflict with a centrally ordained and divinely inspired vision; and a growing belief on the part of the leader that, other evidence notwithstanding, he or she is more essential than ever to the organization's success. One result is an implacable conviction on the part of leaders that they have a duty to fashion a vision and – come what may – push it down the ranks of their organizations.

Transformational leadership and cults: the parallels explored

In Table 2.1, I summarise the defining traits of transformational leadership and, alongside these, indicate how their most destructive manifestations are replicated within cults. These similarities are systematically explored in the rest of this chapter.

Cults have been defined as organizations which remould individuality to conform to the codes and needs of the cult, institute taboos which preclude doubt and criticism and generate an elitist mentality whereby members see themselves as lone evangelists struggling to bring enlightenment to the hostile forces surrounding them (Hochman 1984). A standard definition proposed by one of the premier research and educational organizations on this issue defines cults as:

A group or movement exhibiting great or excessive devotion to some person, idea or thing, and employing unethical manipulative or coercive techniques of persuasion and control ... designed to advance the goals of the group's leaders, to the actual or possible detriment of members, their families or the community.

(American Family Foundation 1986: 119–20)

Other definitions highlight the centrality of particular forms of leadership to the cultic phenomenon. For example, Lalich describes a cult as:

A sharply bounded social group or a diffusely bounded social movement held together through shared commitments to a charismatic leader. It upholds a transcendent ideology (often but not always religious in nature) and requires a high level of personal commitment from its members in words and deeds.

(Lalich 2004: 5)

Table 2.1 Key ingredients of transformational leadership and cults

Traits of transformational leadership	Traits of cults
Charismatic leadership	Charismatic leadership: • Leader viewed in semi-divine light by followers • Leader sole source of key ideas • Power increasingly concentrated in leader's hands, who has absolute authority • Leader has privileges far in excess of other group members
A compelling vision	A compelling vision: • Vision 'totalistic' in its implications • Agreement with vision precondition of group membership • Vision communicated unidirectionally from top to bottom • Dissent from vision penalised, by withdrawal of valued social rewards and/or expulsion
Intellectual stimulation	Intellectual stimulation: • The vision presented as an intellectual key, unlocking secrets that others cannot comprehend • Vision monopolises the time, thoughts, emotions and physical energies of members. Stakhonivite work norms prevail
Individual consideration	Individual consideration: • Followers rewarded for compliance, and penalised for dissent • Indoctrination rituals that alternate between stressful and exhilarating • Leaders maintain the vision is perfectly tailored to the deepest needs of followers • Continuous indoctrination, to reinforce initial sense of affiliation • Followers encouraged to believe that the leader has a vested personal interest in their welfare
Promotion of a common culture	Promotion of a common culture: • Members begin to copy each other's speech mannerisms, dress codes and non-verbal gestures. Total conformity prized • Unidirectional communication – downwards • Negative information suppressed and positive information maximised • Common culture seen as precondition for group's ultimate success

Members typically display high commitment, replace their pre-existing beliefs and values with those of the group, work extremely hard, relinquish control over their time, lose confidence in their own perceptions in favour of those of the group (especially of its leaders) and experience social punishments such as shunning by other group members if they deviate from carefully prescribed norms (Langone 1988; Singer 1987). Cultic organizations achieve their effects by controlling people's social environment, particularly their time; placing them in a position of powerlessness relative to an apparently all-knowing leader; eliminating opportunities for members to provide corrective feedback to their leaders or to receive much in the way of feedback themselves from the outside world; and manipulating complex systems of reward for conformity, while administering punishment for dissent.

The extent to which these practices obtain varies widely from group to group. Accordingly, it has been suggested that the typology of cult behaviour represents a continuum along which individuals, groups and whole communities can move from time to time (Tourish and Irving 1995). It can thus be argued that cults are socially harmful. I discuss two particularly strong examples of such groups in Chapter 9. Such harm will be all the greater depending on the degree of control exercised by a cult's central leadership, the more power its leaders have to fashion the belief systems of their followers, the more followers become uncritical acolytes for the ideas of others, the heavier the workload demanded of enthusiastic converts and the more unethical the persuasive processes (for example, the withholding of crucial information) that are employed to maintain feverish support for the group's ideology. I do not suggest that the practice of transformational leadership will automatically transform host organizations into cults, no more than I would claim that one episode of drunkenness turns someone into an alcoholic. However, I do argue that the core defining traits of transformational leadership have the potential to move organizations further along the cult continuum than is desirable. Such a possibility can be clarified if we consider how the dominant traits of transformational leadership theory (as summarised in Table 2.1) overlap with the dysfunctional world of cultism.

Charismatic leadership

Charismatic leadership is an indispensable ingredient of cultic organization (Tourish 2011). It has been observed in doomsday cults in the 1950s (Festinger 1957), the Jonestown cult of the 1970s (see Chapter 9), the suicidal Heaven's Gate cult in California (see also Chapter 9) and more recently in the homicidal Aum cult in Japan (Lifton 1999).

Frequently, the charisma that followers attribute so fervently to the leader turns out to be no more substantial than the magical powers possessed by the Wizard of Oz. Cult leaders have been variously exposed as alcoholics, drug addicts or semi-literates, whose major pronouncements are often written for them by others (Langone 1993) – the equivalent, in a sense, of over-reliance on a corporate public relations department. However, such is their position of prominence and the desperate need of their followers to believe, that manifold glowing qualities are attributed to them. In turn, such attributions activate powerful expectancy effects (Blanck 1993). Followers often believe that their leaders are people of genius, insight, outstanding organizational ability and uncommon compassion. They then perceive only munificent qualities in the leader's behaviour, irrespective of what they actually do: expectations have become self-deluding prophecies. Likewise, I suspect that the charismatic reputation of many corporate gurus, dutifully chronicled in the literature, is much exaggerated by the social attributional processes sketched here.

A compelling vision/intellectual stimulation

Typically, cults are organized around what has been defined as a 'totalistic' vision of a new world order. The group's leaders suggest that their vision is capable of fundamentally transforming an impure reality. The resulting mood of absolute conviction has been defined as 'ideological totalism' (Lifton 1961). Ideas are embedded so deeply in people's heads that they grow inoculated against doubt. Provisional theories about the world become sacred convictions, dependent on the word of hallowed authorities for their validation rather than evidence. In religious cults, the worship of God is transformed into the worship of his messenger on earth – the leader of the group (Tourish and Wohlforth 2000). In the corporate world, a messianic leader may seek ever more enthusiastic expressions of agreement from the organization's employees. The vision maintains an attitude of certainty towards issues that are objectively uncertain. An absence of critical feedback then reinforces belief in the compelling vision of the leader.

In its sharpest form, Lifton defines ideological totalism as follows:

> The totalistic milieu maintains an aura of sacredness around its basic dogma, holding it out as an ultimate moral vision for the ordering of human existence. This sacredness is evident in the prohibition (whether or not explicit) against the questioning of basic assumptions, and in the reverence which is demanded for the originators of the Word, the present bearers of the Word, and the Word itself... the milieu... makes an exaggerated claim of airtight logic, of absolute 'scientific' precision.
>
> (Lifton 1961: 427–8)

Thus, a compelling vision, passionately argued for, has a head start over a sober presentation, in which doubt, uncertainty and an acknowledgement of the possibility of error hold sway. The more uncertain the external environment, the more likely it is that a compelling vision will encourage followers to over-identify with a group, its goals and its leaders. Knowing this:

> some leaders may manufacture events and circumstances and more generally cultivate very high levels of uncertainty for malevolent purposes – that is, as a means of social control and domination over the group and to bring an

extremist vision into fruition … These leaders may deliberately employ tactics that capitalise on preexisting uncertainty, provoke chronic uncertainty, and then reduce uncertainty by encouraging a staunch and singular identification with their extremist groups.

(Seyranian 2012: 229)

They do so largely by offering a compelling vision which will resolve an anxiety that the leader him or herself has created. Likewise, a corporate vision whose truth is held to be self-evident, whose tenets cannot be questioned and whose acceptance is assumed to be indispensable for the organization's salvation has the potential to provide considerable intellectual stimulation and unleash passionate forms of ideological totalism, which are reliant upon irrational viewpoints.

Individual consideration

Cults make great ceremony of showing individual consideration for their members. One of the most commonly cited cult recruitment techniques is generally known as 'love bombing' (Hassan 1988). Prospective recruits are showered with attention, which expands to affection and then often grows into a plausible simulation of love. This is the courtship phase of the recruitment ritual. The leader wishes to seduce the new recruit into the organization's embrace, slowly habituating them to its strange rituals and complex belief systems. At this early stage, resistance will be at its highest. Individual consideration is a perfect means to overcome it, by blurring the distinctions between personal relationships, theoretical constructs and bizarre behaviours.

Thus, cult leaders and other members go out of their way to praise the potential recruit's contributions in group meetings. Points of similarity with the group (such as dress codes, positive statements about aspects of the sacred belief system, a concern for the welfare of the underprivileged, attendance at meetings or participation in demonstrations) are celebrated and encouraged. This could be defined as 'individual consideration'. It certainly represents an enormous amount of individual attention. However, it may be more appropriate to define it as *manipulation*.

A more technical term for the practice of love bombing, derived from the literature on interpersonal perception, is *ingratiation*. As one of the pioneer researchers in this area summarised it:

There is little secret or surprise in the contention that we like people who agree with us, who say nice things about us, who seem to possess such positive attributes as warmth, understanding, and compassion, and who would 'go out of their way' to do things for us.

(Jones 1990: 178)

People generally cling to those who encourage the further expression of their opinions, display approving non-verbals such as smiles and eye contact, express agreement with our beliefs and shower us with flattery or compliments.

Meanwhile, the *law of attraction* (Byrne 1971; Oren *et al.* 2012) holds that the more similar attitudes people have in common then the more they will like each other. Cults encourage the fallacious notion that all members are more alike than they really are, and are more dissimilar from non-members than is actually the case. The clear objective is to create an overwhelming sense of group identity, infused with a spirit of cohesion, loyalty and commitment to the group's goals – all outcomes generally valued in the corporate world and esteemed in most writing on transformational leadership. When this is combined with ingratiation, the consequences are that the people ingratiating themselves become perceived as familiar and similar to us (Jones 1990). They become a liked 'insider' rather than a stereotyped 'outsider' (Goldhammer 1996). Joining with them to form a group seems a natural and risk-free next step.

Furthermore, relationships are often characterised by an imbalance of power. This is especially true of cults and is certainly true within most corporations. For my purposes here, the key point to note is that a person of lesser status attaches more importance to being liked by those of higher status than the other way round (Rosenfeld *et al.* 1995). This encourages them to agree with such a person's opinions, ape their mannerisms and adapt to their belief systems, thereby achieving significant influence with them. Thus, those solicited by the cult find themselves inherently motivated to offer the organization's leaders the most positive feedback possible – agreement with their opinions and compliance with their demands. Meanwhile, potential recruits are showered with attention from precisely these figures. Cognitive dissonance theory (Aronson 1997) suggests that most of us would be inclined to rationalise a growing belief in a leader's ideas as an independently made choice – thereby ensuring that it takes even deeper root in our psyche.

Conversion

When someone responds to intense individual consideration from higher status leaders and is desperate to affiliate with them, the outcome of their shift in attitudes can be regarded as conversion. It occurs when a person experiences fundamental changes of knowledge and beliefs, values and standards, emotional attachments and needs, and of everyday conduct, so that previously existing values and beliefs are abandoned in favour of new ones articulated by the leader. New dress codes, behaviours, beliefs and modes of being are embraced. Each reinforces the other. A new dress code is likely to encourage the adoption of behaviours normally associated with the dress code; novel behaviours strengthen the attitudes that underpin them; the overall effect is, frequently, what outside observers come to see as a fundamental personality transformation, or new mode of being, on the part of the person concerned (Jenkinson 2008). The process has been described as one of identity stripping, identification and symbolic death/rebirth (Zablocki 2001).

Unsurprisingly, transformation is a dominant theme in the practice of cultic organizations and their leaders – the more, the merrier (Tourish 2011). The prospect of permanent revolution suggests that people must be inspired by a compelling vision that is powerful enough to sweep aside all reservations. The following quotation conveys the mental state that it is frequently implied should be aroused by the energetic communication of such a vision. It is worth reflecting on:

> To say that one had 'seen the light' is a poor description of the mental rapture which only the convert knows (regardless of what faith he has been converted to). The new light seems to pour from all directions across the skull; the whole universe falls into pattern, like the stray pieces of a jigsaw puzzle assembled by magic at one stroke. There is now an answer to every question, doubts and conflicts are a matter of the tortured past – a past already remote, when one had lived in dismal ignorance in the tasteless, colorless world of those who *don't know*. Nothing henceforth can disturb the convert's inner peace and serenity – except the occasional fear of losing faith again, losing thereby what alone makes life worth living, and falling back into the outer darkness, where there is wailing and gnashing of teeth.
>
> (Koestler 1949: 23)

The quotation is from the writer Arthur Koestler, describing his mood of exaltation while a member of the Communist Party in the 1930s. It is included in a volume of reflections on the period aptly entitled *The God That Failed*, which documents a mindset that can only be called cult-like. It is in this direction that would-be visionary, charismatic leaders often seek to transport their followers and, in the process, make use of cult-like tactics.

Clearly, I am not suggesting that leaders should avoid showing consideration to others, individual or otherwise. I am suggesting that when an imbalance of power is institutionalised into the relationship and dissent is equated with subversion, such consideration becomes a form of manipulation. It may not represent an expression of the follower's real best interests. In particular, individual consideration is often predicated on the false assumptions that:

- the leader knows best;
- all change must come from the top;
- the leader must have a compelling vision and communicate it energetically;
- we need one unifying culture around here.

Under these conditions, individual consideration can become a form of 'love bombing' likely to blur the recipient's ability to freely determine where their own mind ends and that of the organization begins. The negative consequences implicit to this characterisation become even more apparent if we look critically at the issue of corporate culture.

Promoting a common culture

I have, earlier, pointed out that notions of corporate culture, particularly as articulated in the literature on transformational leadership, under-theorises the role of dissent. Monoculturism is the implied ideal state, in which difference is banished to the margins of the group's tightly policed norms. The search for a unifying corporate culture and the transformational leaders who promised to deliver it was hugely inspired by the work of Peters and Waterman (1982), who argued that it would create turned on workforces wholly committed to corporate objectives. Western (2008) argues that it led to a search for 'designer employees' who were responsive to management's quest for better competition in the global marketplace. While this sounds ominous enough, the major problem arises in overtly coercive environments with totalistic environments. These ensure that:

> tremendous overt and covert pressure is brought to bear on everyone to con-form publicly, to participate actively, and to work hard, while a facade is maintained that such conformity and dedication is entirely voluntary or the product of successful ideological persuasion.
>
> (Schein *et al.* 1961: 80)

Total conformity along these lines leads to the disabling and well-documented phenomenon of groupthink, an infection which thrives particularly well in the overheated atmosphere of cults (Wexler and Fraser 1995).

Various techniques are employed to achieve a monocultural environment within cults, some of which seem tailormade to realise the conformist vision implied in much of the transformational leadership literature. In particular, cults express an insistent demand for purity, in which 'the experiential world is sharply divided into the pure and the impure, into the absolutely good and the absolutely evil' (Lifton 1961: 423). Dissent is demonised, rendering it all the more unap-pealing, since people quickly grasp that to associate with dissenters is to volun-teer for a Salem-style witch hunt. They are consoled with the view that the group's vision offers a superior insight to any other perspective on offer. Dress codes, language and styles of interaction are all highly regulated (Tobias and Lalich 1994), reinforcing the monochrome environment that has come to define the members' social world. Reluctant converts eventually become True Believers. Typically, the culture is one of impassioned belief, incessant action to achieve the group's goals, veneration of the leader's vision and a constraining series of group norms designed to quell dissent.

The general literature on influence would suggest that when people freely embrace such norms (or, more accurately, can be convinced that their conversion is a voluntary and enriching process) then the dominant belief system will be inter-nalised still further (Cialdini 2009). When people adopt irrational behaviours they generally feel compelled to develop rationalisations that justify such actions. Their self-image requires a convincing motive. The most readily available explanation is the conviction that their actions made sense and were freely chosen. Much of the literature on excellence and cultural change is likely to activate this process of self-deception. It seeks to limit people's scope for manoeuvre, while simultane-ously convincing them that they are empowered and autonomous individuals. We thus have 'the twinning of freedom and control' (Hope and Hendry 1995: 61).

It has been suggested that this is part of 'a broader drift of Anglo-American business away from enforceable employee rights towards a discretionary, enlightened despotism' (Ackers and Preston 1997: 679). There can be few better illustrations of Orwellian 'doublethink' (Willmott 1993).

More fundamentally, the twinning of freedom and control rests on a mutually contradictory set of assumptions. Most models of leadership and power generally work a crucial missing variable – tyranny (Bies and Tripp 1998). Power itself is a frequently unacknowledged variable in organization theory. However, people are habitually assured that they are empowered and free and, indeed, are often encouraged to roam in any direction that they wish. The problem is that they roam at the end of a leash, constrained to move within an orbit sharply defined by the governing cultural assumptions of the organization. Culture thus becomes another form of social control. That such control is less overt than that found with traditional bureaucratic models simply makes the process more insidious.

Within cults, the dominant culture is likely to be totalistic, punitive, self-aggrandising and all-embracing in its messianic scope. The leaders of modern corporations may feel compelled to move in similar directions. As du Gay summarises it:

> Excellence in management theory is an attempt to redefine and reconstruct the economic and cultural terrain, and to win social subjects to a new conception of themselves – to 'turn them into winners', 'champions', and 'everyday heroes'. As much as anything, Culture Excellence is a struggle for identities, an attempt to enable all sorts of people, from highest executive to lowliest shop-floor employee, to see themselves reflected in the emerging conception of the enterprising organization and thus to come increasingly to identify with it.
>
> du Gay (1991: 53–4)

In this environment, those who insist that a widget is just a widget, bereft of transcendent qualities, may get short shrift. Thus, autonomy is simultaneously affirmed and negated. Through imposing a uniform definition of meaning, we have also an attempt at thought control. Transformational leadership theorists, who generally approach the leadership phenomenon with the minimum of scepticism, have liberally dispensed licences endorsing such mind-altering practices. In contradistinction to this, and in common with others, I view scepticism as the indispensable basis of rationality.

Conclusion

The theory and practice of transformational leadership has the potential to encourage authoritarian forms of organization. The popularity of transformational leadership, despite its weaknesses, can be viewed as a form of nympholepsy (that is, a state of ecstasy or frenzy caused by a desire for the unattainable). On the one hand, it aspires to produce a turned on, highly motivated and even largely self-governed workforce. On the other hand, it seeks to position the CEO as the fount of all wisdom and certainly as the final arbiter of anything resembling an important decision. This 'vision' has a ready appeal for CEOs, frequently motivated by a noble desire to produce results for shareholders, employees and customers but also convinced by the literature that they are charismatic visionaries rather than people in suits. The contradictions to which these conceptions gives rise inspires ever more frenzied activity, rather than a re-evaluation of the original concept. As often seems to be the case, the more elusive the goal, the more intense the effort devoted to its attainment.

The consequences for leaders may also be less than pleasant. Socrates, in *The Republic*, long ago pointed out that authoritarian leaders are compelled to be suspicious of dissenters:

> He has to keep a sharp eye out, then, for anyone with courage, self-confidence, intelligence or wealth. He has no choice in the matter: he's bound to treat them as enemies and to intrigue against them, until he's purged the community of them. That's the nature of his happy state… They never have any friends, then, throughout their lives: they can only be masters or slaves. Dictatorial people can never experience freedom and true friendship.
>
> (Socrates 1993: 565–76)

But it is possible to visualise alternatives. At a minimum, these would:

- *Re-emphasise the key elements found in transactional leadership*: these include recognising the independent goals of leaders and followers; the exchange of rewards in systems of reciprocal influence; and people's right to retain a sense of identity, place and purpose beyond their employer's orbit.
- *Acknowledge the ubiquity of power differentials in the workplace and the damaging effect such differentials can have on perceptions, attitudes, relationships and organizational effectiveness*: I have, for example, alluded to the fundamental difficulty of people with superior status obtaining accurate feedback about their performance from people with lower status – an issue explored further in Chapter 5. This impairs decision making and may encourage those at the top of organizational charts to exaggerate their contribution to obtaining corporate goals, while diminishing that of others. Alternative leadership models would legitimise the existence of multiple visions and facilitate their resolution through processes of negotiation, conflict resolution, debate and free speech.
- *Look again at democratic and stakeholder perspectives for organizational restructuring*: transformational leadership models presume the right of those at the top to a disproportionate role in the decision-making process. I suggest that we need a new ethic of managerial leadership, in which both sides recognise the need to frequently cross the line between leadership and followership.

It is not my intention to question the need for leadership *per se*. But it is my intention to argue that the dominant models within the rubric of transformational leadership are fundamentally flawed. In particular, they promote, unintentionally or otherwise, group dynamics often found in cults rather than in 'normal' business organizations. More inclusive and participatory models of the leadership process are required. It is a conclusion to which I return repeatedly in this book.

Points for discussion

1. How different is the idea of transformational leadership from other leadership theories of which you are aware?
2. To what extent can 'bad' leaders, such as Hitler or Stalin, be considered transformational?
3. What factors can cause people to put too much power in the hands of leaders?
4. What safeguards would you suggest to ensure that leaders do not acquire absolute power within organizations or society?
5. Are any safeguards that you can imagine compatible or incompatible with organizational efficiency and effectiveness?

Note

1 Some of the ideas in this chapter were originally published in Tourish, D. and Pinnington, A. (2002) Transformational leadership, corporate cultism and the spirituality paradigm: an unholy trinity in the workplace? *Human Relations*, 55: 147–72.

3   Coercive persuasion, power and corporate culturism[1]

Introduction

I argued in Chapter 1 that today's organizations are marked by the steady accumulation of power by corporations and senior executives. This power is often exercised through coercive control mechanisms designed to ensure conformity (Tracy *et al.* 2006). Here, I argue that these forms of control can be better understood if we see them as examples of what has been termed 'coercive persuasion'. Coercive persuasion refers to the ways in which leaders socially construct discursive systems of constraint that are difficult for followers to challenge and resist. Examples of this dynamic in practice include the tragically flawed decision making by Morton-Thiokol executives leading up to the Challenger disaster (Starbuck and Milliken 1988; Tompkins 1993; Vaughan 1996) and the disciplinary processes within Enron which demonstrated how excessive levels of conformity and compliance could have dysfunctional and even dangerous consequences for organizations (see Chapter 7). While there has been some critical questioning of this growing coercive force of corporate power in our lives, scholars have yet to fully explore the processes whereby unchallenged coercive persuasion becomes manifest in the daily lives of subordinates, followers and employees.

This chapter explores the key dynamics of coercive persuasion and contextualises these dynamics within modern corporate culturalism, one of its strongest manifestations. I begin by developing coercive persuasion as a concept and situate its roots in contemporary theories of power, conformity and leadership. I draw extensively on Schein's (1961) foundational work on coercive persuasion to develop a framework for describing and assessing the techniques that often shape conformity in organizational practice.

Leadership, power, and conformity

The issue of conformity and its relationship to leadership is relatively under-examined in the literature. On these grounds, I have critiqued theories of transformational leadership in Chapter 2. Such approaches tend to assume that leader action is inherently rational. Moreover, 'The interests of the organization and those of management are seen to be largely coterminous' (Gordon *et al.* 2009: 16).

Similarly, Lord and Brown (2001, 2004) have defined leadership as a social process through which leaders change the way that followers envision themselves. They recommend that leaders should link motivation and reward to followers' identities, 'activating' the appropriate self rather than directly stressing specific goals. Few studies in this tradition explicitly recognise that unquestioning conformity can have harmful consequences.

In contrast, I draw on Schien's (1961) work on coercion to describe how corporate leaders may construct a social environment that channels the physical, intellectual and emotional energies of employees towards conformity. I begin by differentiating between coercive persuasion and coercive power – the latter simply relying on the forced compliance of subjects to decreed organizational norms ('come to work on time tomorrow or you are sacked'). Rather, coercive persuasion encourages subjects to internalise dominant cultural norms as their own, subsequently producing individuals deemed to be 'appropriate' by the ruling group (Alvesson and Willmott 2002). It also disguises many of the elements of compulsion that are involved, even from those directly affected (Tompkins and Cheney 1985).

Coercive persuasion is a means of linking surveillance with intense indoctrination. It seeks to convince those at the receiving end that the sincere adoption of the designated belief systems is wholly consistent with their own self-interest. When organizational members embrace, either partially or completely, an ideological orientation sanctioned by powerful leaders it follows that the legitimacy of organizational structures, hierarchies and practices is more clearly established.

When this occurs, those concerned will be more likely to adopt a 'converted' mindset and display zealous behaviours that are aligned with the belief system chosen for them by powerful others. Under these conditions, minimal external surveillance may be required to ensure that behaviours consistent with the belief system are enacted. As Townley (1993: 520) noted, following Foucault, 'power is not associated with a particular institution, but with practices, techniques and procedures'. Such a view avoids the widespread conception of coercion as a process aimed at getting people to do what they would otherwise not want to do. If, by contrast, they can be 'coercively persuaded' by the deployment of various techniques into internalising a given ideology, they will be convinced that behaviours approved of by powerful leaders are actually undertaken of their own volition, rather than by force of command. How might such outcomes be achieved? The answer offered in this chapter begins with Schein's (1961) early analysis of coercive persuasion, which, I argue, still has much relevance for our thinking today.

Schein's techniques of coercive persuasion

The notion of coercive persuasion grew out of Schein's study of US prisoners of war (POWs) detained in Korea in the 1950s. His analysis is strikingly consistent with the contemporaneous work of Lifton (1961), who studied 'thought reform' programmes in China. Lifton also details similar mechanisms devoted to 're-education' through the use of emotional appeals and confession rituals. This greatly influenced contemporary thinking on what are described as cults and which I discussed in Chapter 2. Their Chinese captors successfully convinced many of the POWs to internalise Communist beliefs, adopt an appropriate Communist identity and show intense commitment by adopting proselytising behaviours on behalf of the new belief system. Temporarily, many maintained their new belief system even after they were released from captivity (Taylor 2004). On the basis of this quite remarkable outcome, Schein proposed that:

> if a prisoner was physically restrained from leaving a situation in which learning was the only alternative, they would eventually learn through a process of 'cognitive redefinition'. They would eventually come to understand the point of view of the captor and reframe their own thinking so that the judgment of having been guilty became logical and acceptable. In effect they had undergone what might be called a 'conversion' experience except it did not happen in the sudden way that religious conversions are often described.
>
> (Schein 1961: 165)

This process is reminiscent of what has been dubbed 'the Stockholm syndrome' (Giebels *et al.* 2005) in which kidnap victims come to over-identify with their kidnappers, resist rescue, refuse to testify against them in court or, as with the heiress turned revolutionary Patty Hearst, adopt a new identity in keeping with the kidnappers' value systems (Watkins 1976). Clearly, as with the POWs in Schein's study, kidnap victims are under intense physical and emotional stress. Some identify with their captors to minimise the omnipresent threat of violence. Since it is difficult to achieve any sense of perspective under these conditions, they may also invest the smallest act of kindness by their kidnappers with an importance out of proportion to the act itself. Victims may also see rescue attempts as a threat, since they may be injured or killed during the attempt. This was precisely the fate of 344 civilians during the Beslan school siege in Russia in 2004. Coercive persuasion can reinforce a new group identity that, paradoxically, is shared with people who may previously have appeared to be in a polar opposite position to the victim.

Schein identified a variety of conditions that facilitate such outcomes. I summarise these in Table 3.1 and rearticulate the techniques to express how they can become manifest in today's organizations. I then discuss the techniques in detail, paying particular attention to how these conditions link to contemporary leadership practices within corporate organizations.

1 Reference group affiliation

To reduce anxiety, individuals seek to align themselves with reference groups. The effect of this process is to increase conformity. The development of social groups and knowledge formation are inextricably linked. A great deal of psychological research supports the view that '*individuals' understandings of the world*

Table 3.1 Key techniques of coercive persuasion

Technique	Schein's techniques from POW experiences	Modern organizational translation of technique
1 Reference group affiliation	Prisoners faced an indeterminate sentence. This raised anxiety and created an impetus to affiliate with a new reference group as a means of reducing it.	Environmental changes, new entrants and turnover create organizational anxiety. We seek alignment with reference groups to reduce the anxiety and increase conformity.
2 Role modelling	Prisoners were placed with others who were more advanced in the learning process, who role modelled 'successful' conformity and were rewarded for doing so. Prisoners were tempted to emulate their attitudes and behaviours to secure similar benefits.	Organizations develop systems of role modelling and mentoring so that members learn appropriate behaviour. We learn from and come to emulate those in positions of power over us as we seek to meet their expectations, which increases conformity.
3 Peer pressures	Rewards were given only on a group basis and only if all members of the group embraced the new point of view. This intensified peer pressure to conform.	Focus on teamworking, shared rewards and shared consequences intensifies peer pressure to conform.
4 Alignment of identity	The new point of view was articulated repeatedly and in many forms. Repetition ensured that it eventually acquired a self-evident and eventually unchallengeable status.	Modern workers buy into the firm's strategic vision and shape their behaviours accordingly. Conformity to the vision and values becomes part of our identity.
5 Performance assessment	Written confession and self-criticism became a regular activity, so that prisoners assessed past actions from a new point of view. Problems with the new belief system were viewed as examples of individual rather than systemic weaknesses.	Employees are assessed based on their conformity with strategy and practice, including mechanisms such as 360-degree feedback. As individuals, we are expected to conform and the system is assumed to be correct.
6 Reward systems	Conformity attracted instant rewards. Signs of insincerity or limited understanding were punished. Conformist behaviours therefore increased while dissenting attitudes withered from lack of nourishment.	Conformists are rewarded. Dissent, such as whistleblowing or resistance, is punished.

Table 3.1 Key techniques of coercive persuasion (cont'd)

7 Communication systems	Communications that in any way reinforced the old point of view or that reminded the prisoner of previous attachments were withheld or eliminated entirely. The past became ever more remote; the present acquired heightened power to shape attitudes, emotions and behaviours.	Management and control of communication becomes central to the organization. Companies exert increased control of stakeholder information and management engagement with stakeholders.
8 Physical pressure and work life balance	Physical pressures were constantly applied to weaken the prisoner's physical strength, with sleep deprivation being the most potent of these pressures; 'torture' was only used as a punishment for insincerity or lack of motivation to learn.	Members are expected to work longer hours and expend greater effort as a means of demonstrating conformity and commitment. Individuals are expected to demonstrate fortitude to overcome the physical demands of labour.
9 Psychological safety	Psychological safety was produced for prisoners by fellow prisoners who were further along in their 're-education' and could be supportive of the target prisoner's effort.	Psychological contracts become invested in expectations of conformity. Mutual support creates both psychological safety and conformity.

are held as true to the extent that they can be affirmed by some social group' (Kruglanski and Orehek 2012: 3 [emphasis in the original]). These authors also note the importance of cognitive closure – that is, our need to reduce uncertainty and ambiguity. But when this need is heightened we tend to 'freeze' on available information and adopt readily available judgements, particularly if they are valued by our immediate reference group. Coercive persuasion takes full advantage of these psychological dynamics.

Thus, the POWs' only hope of redemption and release in Schein's study was when they made a confession that their captors judged to be sincere. This was a powerful stimulus for cognitive closure and an equally powerful disincentive for dissent. Clearly, most organizations are not POW camps. Nevertheless, employees frequently face management demands for conformity and the internalisation of belief systems sympathetic to corporate values. An example is Barker's (1993: 431–2) jarring account of forced confession and redemptive acceptance of conformity in peer work groups. Of course, like the POWs, people have the option of concealed resistance – for example, by pretending towards a sincere, penitent and converted mindset. However, performances of this kind contain their own hazards. As Goffman (1959: 28) stressed, 'one finds that the performer can be fully taken in by his own act; he can be sincerely convinced that the impression of reality which he stages is the real reality'. In any event, coercive persuasion seeks to produce a genuine desire for conformity rather than its facsimile. Pressure alone is unlikely to have such an impact. Rather, a process of enculturation is also required. How is this likely to be achieved?

The key lies in the emulation of conformist rituals that are commonplace in organizations. For example, Kunda (1992) demonstrated, in an ethnographic study of a hi-tech American corporation, how such rituals are developed by leaders to inculcate the 'right beliefs' and produce an 'acceptable' organizational identity. Employees may then play along with these rituals, rather than reveal what might be described as a 'bad attitude'. But this also renders employees liable to internalise the values behind the rituals – even if they have initially resisted them. In essence, like a method actor over preparing a part, the person internalises a role to such an extent that they become indistinguishable from their performance. It is likely that many of the POWs in Schein's study embarked on a similar course of action, only to find that their dissimulation gradually eroded pre-existing beliefs and helped install new values and codes of conduct in their place.

2 Organizations develop systems of role modelling and mentoring so that members learn appropriate behaviour

This provides the subjects of coercive persuasion with role models and socially legitimised identities to emulate. In Schein's study, prisoners could also see at first hand the rewards attached to adopting the prescribed organizational identity of 'the good Communist' and demonstrating high commitment through the enthusiastic display of behaviours consistent with their new identity. This dynamic is consistent with social identity theory, which asserts that individuals identify themselves with respect to various group memberships and tend to classify others into one or more categories (for example, 'in-group' and 'out-group') to identify similarities and differences (Bartel *et al.* 2007). It is also seen in Barker's (1993) description of placing new team members with longer-tenured members for 'proper' socialisation. Individuals establish a positive social identity and confirm association by showing preference to members of their own social category. As Jost and Elsbach (2001: 183) argued, 'we derive a great deal of personal value and meaning from our group memberships, so that our self-concepts depend in significant ways upon the ways in which our groups are regarded by ourselves and by others', a point echoed in the organizational identification literature (see, for example, Tompkins and Cheney 1985).

In the case of the POWs, more long-standing members of the group would have appeared as experienced survivors and hence as positive role models. Following Tompkins and Cheney (1985), identification with their behaviours and subsequent internalisation of their attitudes would have been logical survival behaviour, helping to forge a new group identity of considerable value and strength.

More broadly, the power of leaders in so-called 'high-demand' groups increases as a result of the identity-related benefits accruing from conformity that are provided by other group members (Baron *et. al.* 2003). Social identity theory proposes that our self-conception as a group member is a central feature of group life, since such groups so often structure our understanding of who and what we are (Haslam 2004). Building on this, Hogg proposes the notion of uncertainty–identity theory. This theory recognises that:

> People strive to reduce or protect themselves from feelings of uncertainty, particularly uncertainty about and related to themselves, and about their social world and their place within it. People like to know who they are and how to behave and what to think, and who other are and how they might behave and what they might think.
>
> (Hogg 2007: 38)

Thus, acceptance by the members of the group feels gratifying to those joining it, increasing the desire to affiliate. But affiliation is dependent on the acceptance and eventual internalisation of the norms within the group concerned – an acceptance that, in a punitive and disorienting environment, feels attractive because it reduces uncertainty about what to think, feel and do (Hogg 2001).

If we accept that people are attracted by the idea of order, then the embrace of ideological commitment offers many attractions. A comprehensive belief system can appear to explain the world and the place of the individual within it, producing an inflammation of righteousness. Under conditions of stress and uncertainty, ideological totalism of this kind may become more alluring, especially if people's need for security increases (Hogg 2012). Such dynamics reinforce leader power since the leaders define norms of behaviour and ideology and thus set the parameters within which acceptance or exclusion from the valued group is likely to occur. In a similar way, new recruits to corporate organizations are typically predisposed to follow more established employees, whose longevity suggests they are familiar with organizational belief systems and their associated rituals of conformity.

3 Focus on team working, shared rewards and shared consequences intensifies peer pressure to conform

A number of general group theories and empirical studies point toward the potential impact of this technique. As the Milgram (1974) and Asch (1951) experiments demonstrated, we are strongly inclined to act on the basis of authority and to change our behaviours to be more consistent with those of other group members, particularly when members of the group have a higher status than us. In the case of the POWs in Korea, rewards were dependent upon compliance. Those inclined toward compliance were thereby provided with a tremendous incentive to increase their pressure on the rest. Given their already strong tendency to conform to emergent group norms, this additional pressure created an even more powerful context for conversion. It also provided an incentive for at least some group members to engage in the surveillance of their fellows, in an expression of what Foucault (1977, 1982) regarded as *disciplinary power*. Such surveillance enforces norms of behaviour on all parties to a social interaction (Sewell *et al.* 2012), ensuring that alternative forms of being and doing are pushed to the margins of the group's tightly policed activities and consciousness (Lacombe 1996).

In a parallel process, workplace surveillance systems increasingly seek to produce conformist (that is, compliant and pliant) individuals in the workplace. The growing emphasis on teamwork is an important mechanism for unleashing similar dynamics, in the form of peer pressure (Barker 1993). Many such systems use group-based incentives and rewards, as well as other mechanisms, to create powerful systems of peer pressure. In Foucault's terms, these processes illustrate the disciplinary effects of power and identity and the barriers they can create for resistance (McKinlay and Taylor 1996). Corporate culture initiatives (Kunda 1992), performance assessment systems (Townley 1994) and information-gathering systems (Zuboff 1988) have all been explored in ways consistent with this view of coercive persuasion. For example, Mehri's (2006) study of the lean production system at Toyota contrasted the official company rhetoric with a more coercive reality noting that 'Employees are expected to follow all rules and obey the prescribed code of behaviour that exists at the company' (Mehri, 2006: 26). Researchers have argued that such approaches seek to regulate, discipline and control employee selves, while camouflaging such intentions in the more benign rhetoric of family values and empowerment (Martin 1999). Culture, in such contexts, becomes another form of social control (Willmott 1993, 2003), regardless of the emancipatory rhetoric through which it may be expressed.

4 Modern workers buy into the firm's strategic vision, shape their behaviours accordingly and align their identity with that of the dominant group

This is largely accomplished through the repetition of key messages. Repeated presentations give any vision multiple advantages. Firstly, research into influence and persuasion suggests that we are inclined to believe that whatever is repeated is more likely to be true (Cialdini 2009). Secondly, in the example of Korea, when presentations were offered by authority figures in whom the prisoners had some confidence (in particular, by fellow prisoners who were further along in the conversion process), they were even more inclined to give the message undue credence. The perceived expertise and trustworthiness of the person articulating the message added enormously to its potency (Cialdini 2009). Moreover, the message itself was presented as if it articulated a set of self-evident, scientific and unchallengeable truths – much in the same manner as the reality of corporate power often cloaks itself in a rhetoric of personal liberation (see, for example, Peters 1992) and 'the end of history' (Fukuyama 1993) today. Communist ideology was presented to the prisoners in highly selective generalities emphasising human liberation. Such an appeal to a wider social interest is a regularly used means of ensuring that domination acquires the trappings of legitimacy rendering the internalisation of a given ideology much more attractive (Miller 1989).

Likewise, corporate ideology fixes on such questions as competitive success for the company, the notion of unitary interests between corporate owners and employees, and the blissful future which the success of the corporation will ensure for all those fortunate enough to affiliate with it. Within the public sector, also, the growth of managerial authority has sought to claim a unitarist power by stressing the need for 'leadership' to attain objectives that are assumed to be beyond challenge – a discourse that has been described as 'leaderism' (O'Reilly and Reed 2011). As Ford and Harding (2007) ironically put it: 'We are all leaders now'. The internalisation of such messages, should it occur, confers advantages on those who have developed them and whose interests they serve. As Townley (1993: 519) wrote, in applying a Foucauldian perspective to management issues, 'what counts as truth depends on, or is determined by, the conceptual system in operation'. The repeated articulation of what may be viewed as contentious corporate ideologies seeks to reshape the conceptual systems of employees, thereby reinforcing their acceptance of and devotion to particular ideals.

5 *The performance of members is assessed based on their conformity with strategy and practice*

Criticism and self-criticism in a group context is a powerful tool of discipline and conversion (Baron 2000) and was widely used in Korea. Such self-criticism has been extensively and more broadly documented as an approach used by leaders of organizations that emphasise extreme forms of conformity and compliance (Lalich 2004). Group members are bombarded with monotonous and simplified messages, shorn of all ambiguity and uncertainty. Criticism and self-criticism sessions establish that any difficulties perceived with the message, or in its implementation, arise from followers' insufficient compliance and devotion rather than from weaknesses in either the message or the overall social system. This in turn erodes people's confidence in whatever critical perceptions they held before joining the group and increases their dependence on the group and its leader for 'guidance, interpretation, explanation and normative control over activity and choices' (Baron *et. al.* 2003: 173). Approval from such leaders depends on ever-greater levels of conformity.

Even if the belief is not fully internalised, a person hearing nothing but a one-note message is eventually likely to be compelled to draw from it when expressing their own opinions (Tourish 1998). The more public people's statements in support of a new belief become, the more likely it is that their internal views will shift to be consistent with their external behaviours (Cialdini 2009). When our views shift far enough from their starting position, the outcome can be defined as conversion. Moreover, once enough people internalise an 'appropriate' attitude, it may produce organizational contexts reminiscent of what Aldous Huxley described in *Brave New World* as a 'really efficient totalitarian state', that is, one 'in which the all-powerful executive of political bosses and their army of managers controls a population of slaves who do not have to be coerced, because they love their servitude' (Huxley 2004: xxxv).

There are plentiful corporate parallels. Appraisal systems are commonly used not just to monitor performance, but also 'to foster identification with corporate goals and objectives and inculcate organizational standards' (Fairhurst 2007: 83). Individuals are permanently on show and their performance and attitudes are subject to examination. Some appraisal systems go much further and seek to identify 'poor' performers for dismissal (so-called 'rank and yank' systems), thereby activating internal dynamics very similar to the criticism and self-criticism processes identified by Schein (see Chapter 7 for discussion of this dynamic within Enron). Managers are required to identify lots of problems with behaviours, levels of commitment and attitudes. Employees are then required to 'confess' their weaknesses and agree action plans to resolve them, in order to survive the culling process. The focus here also tends to be on individual failings rather than systemic weaknesses – an emphasis which creates further pressure towards conformity and conversion, while minimising the scope for productive dissent.

6 Conformists are rewarded, while dissent is sanctioned strongly

Again, reinforcement theory demonstrates that rewards have a potent effect in shaping behaviour (Dezfouli and Balleine 2012). When people experience rewards for conformity and punishment for resistance, the volume of dissent will likely diminish while the clamour of conformist opinion will increase (Kassing 2011). There is abundant evidence that the penalising of dissent has become an organizational norm, with a consequent increase in ingratiating behaviours by employees (principally, overt, enthusiastic and excessive agreement with the ideas propounded by leaders and managers) used as a means of both surviving and trying to acquire influence over powerful others (see Chapter 5). Evidence also suggests that when the need for cognitive closure is high – for example, through the imposition of time constraints – 'the desire to "freeze" on beliefs and to remain firm in one's knowledge makes any statement questioning the established order potentially unsettling' (Kruglanski and Orehek 2012: 6). Negative perceptions are then formed of the dissenter, while a preference develops for more autocratic group structures. In short, it is increasingly normal within the corporate milieu for people to find their dissenting options significantly restricted while their ingratiating/conformist behaviours are rewarded.

7 Management and control of communication becomes central to the organization

In Korea, the captors' intention was to cut people adrift from previously influential sources of information and to ensure that only information consistent with the new world-view penetrated their social environment. By heightening interaction within the prisoner's new reference group, the potential influence of those within the group on shaping new attitudes was also significantly strengthened.

Generally, in the business world today, the issue of identity construction is 'closely tied up with the ways organizations organize their "world" in terms of communication' (Cheney and Christensen 2001: 241). This emphasis on identity heightens concern with the management of internal and external communication and with controlling the boundaries between them. The management and control of communication is central to the building of organizational culture through the creation of symbols and the performances by which they are transmitted to and then internalised by employees (Weeks and Galunic 2003). Communication, rather than merely 'carrying' information, can thus become viewed as a process which has a power to constitute organizations, rather than merely represent them (Kuhn 2008). It follows that some discourses are typically more privileged than others. Recognising this and the opportunities it affords to constrain and define reality for others, leaders can place restrictions on the communicative activities of employees (for example, by monitoring personal email traffic/internet access), insist on residential training courses during which communication with families and others is discouraged and prohibit attendees from travelling home until the training has been completed.

8 Members are expected to work longer hours and to expend greater effort as a means of demonstrating conformity and commitment, thus coming under intense physical pressure and losing any sense of work–life balance

In the Korean context, this technique deprived POWs of the physical and emotional reserves required for effective resistance. It also heightened tension, thus rendering them more susceptible to messages or a new ideology that prom-ised to relieve them of their growing sense of vulnerability. Such pressure rendered non-compliance costly – a major means by which coercion can shape behaviours, attitudes and emotions (Haugaard 1997). Of course, most employees never face anything quite so dramatic. But they do face the intensification of work brought to an extreme in organizations such as GE, Microsoft and the late, lamented example of Enron, in which 70-hour work weeks and above were common. Although unlikely to be as intense as those felt by the POWs, the psychological effects may nevertheless be similar in kind.

9 Psychological safety becomes dependent on conformity

Ultimately, 'redemption' was depicted to the POWs in Korea as an easy choice. It was rendered all the more attractive by the existence of ready-made role models, who offered support and rewards to those former recalcitrants now embarking on a similar journey to themselves. Above all, surrender was depicted as a capitulation to bliss. This process recalls the climax of George Orwell's (1949) novel, *1984*, in which a tearful Winston Smith finally 'wins' the battle over himself: he now really loves Big Brother.

Again, there are many organizational parallels. Teams are commonly constructed with a mixture of experienced and inexperienced members. One of their key tasks is the socialisation and acculturation of new team members (Pentland 2012). Mentoring is also used to achieve the same effect. Employees with mentors have been found to 'learn the ropes' faster than those without (Wilson and Elman 1990). Of course, in a non-coercive environment this may be entirely benign but, in organizations in which leaders are seeking to impose an all-encompassing ideology and constricting behavioural norms on others, mentoring and teamwork may simply become another means of exercising coercive control.

Coercive persuasion and corporate culturism

The nine techniques derived from Schein's famous study provide a useful mechanism for engaging and assessing the force of coercive persuasion in modern organizations. Below, I apply the framework to explore their manifestation in the growth of corporate culturalism.

As I have been careful to note, the imprisonment of US POWs in Korea clearly does not parallel the context of most contemporary organizations. Their detention is closer to the experience of being confined within what Foucault (1977) termed 'carceral institutions' and Goffman (1968) named as 'total institutions', forms of organization such as prisons or asylums that exist in partitioned space and time separated off from the rest of the world. However, organizations do have considerable influence on our 'personal' time and space. Burrell contended that 'as individuals, we are incarcerated within an organizational world. Thus, whilst we may not live in total institutions, the institutional organization of our lives is total' (Burrell 1988: 232). Exploring the impact of career projects on the lives of UK accountants, Grey (1994) revealed how aspiring and conformist individuals tend to treat all organizational and even personal relations as a means to the end of career progress. As he suggested, the concern with career 'links home and work, leisure, and past, present and future through the vector of the self'. Non-work lives become totally subordinated to the pursuit of career with friends, who are gradually redefined as 'contacts', while social life is reduced to the instrumental activity of 'networking'. Suggesting that career projects construct individuals as highly disciplined subjects, he concluded that 'the project of self-management might be said to consist of the construction of our lives as total institutions' (Grey 1994: 481).

Suffice it to say here that, while I acknowledge significant differences between the case of the POWs in Korea and the experience of working in organizations, I also highlight interesting overlaps between these contexts. Many contemporary organizations now encourage their employees to think of their work as a way of life, a cause, a movement, even 'a religion' and, ultimately, a crusade instead of being merely a job. For leaders and managers who seek to generate employee commitment rather than formal compliance, thought reform (realised by means of coercive persuasion) may seem a highly desirable process. The outcome is likely to be an environment dominated by what has been described as 'bounded choice' (Lalich 2004); that is, one in which the expression of only a limited and tightly regulated repertoire of beliefs, behaviours and emotions is permissible. Paradoxically, employees may embrace such environments in an attempt to reduce uncertainty and anxiety and in pursuit of a heightened sense of greater purpose. But, in the process, they are required to engage in ever more extreme acts of self-renunciation, involving the subordination of important personal norms to those of the group.

Connecting this issue once again to organizational surveillance and the work of Foucault, it is worth recalling his description of the intended effects of the Panopticon. This is a model for a prison, in which the threat of constant and inescapable surveillance is sufficient to condition the behaviour of inmates in 'desirable' directions and so exclusive reliance on rules and bureaucracy. Its aim is:

> to induce in the inmate a state of conscious and permanent visibility that assures the automatic functioning of power. So to arrange things that the surveillance is permanent in its effects, even if it is discontinuous in its action; that the perfection of power should tend to render its actual exercise unnecessary ... in short, that the inmates should be caught up in a power situation of which they themselves are the bearers.
>
> (Foucault 1977: 201)

The techniques of coercive persuasion discussed in this chapter are likely to produce a similar effect, through creating an environment in which an officially sanctioned ideology is internalised by subjects. In such contexts, ideology serves as a source of conscious and permanent scrutiny, functioning as an invisible internal eye, which holds the behaviour of the subject to the ideology's exacting standards and ensures that subjects themselves become the instruments through which their own subordination is exercised. Once values that are deemed appropriate by a ruling élite have been internalised there is no hiding place and no possibility of escape.

Thus, efforts at coercive persuasion start with the articulation of an ideology, which people are required to endorse, enthusiastically, publicly and often. Ideology in corporate organizations is increasingly 'rooted in [a] sense of mission associated with charismatic leadership, developed through traditions and sagas and then reinforced through identifications' (Mintzberg 1989: 223). Cheerleading rituals are crucial to a mission's internalisation by organizational members as is the threat of isolation for defiance. In particular, the increasing interest in strong corporate cultures and in the development of associated 'visions' represents a form of ideological development that underpins contemporary processes of coercive persuasion. Many management development programmes are expressly designed to produce what can be described as conversion on the part of managers, through the adoption of corporate evangelism, to convert people into 'True Believers' in the designated belief system (Turnbull 2001). The rhetoric of self-discovery, faith and commitment (more often associated with religious environments) is often employed to engage people in an emotional quest for a new identity sympathetic to corporate goals. In the context of asymmetrical power relationships, such rhetoric can easily have a coercive undertone.

Accordingly, what has been defined as 'corporate culturism' frequently:

> aspires to extend management control by colonizing the affective domain – the hearts as well as the minds of employees – in an innovative, oppressive and paradoxical manner – by claiming to extend their practical autonomy … The implicit intent of corporate culturism … is to establish monocultures in which choices and decisions are made within a normative framework of core values that are established, or at least sanctioned, by management.
>
> (Willmott 2003: 75)

It is frequently assumed that core organizational values must take priority over all other values. This viewpoint is often expressed in the authoritarian language of those in senior positions, intended to intimidate and reframe individual identity within a narrow corporatist paradigm. Exhibit 3.1 reproduces an email sent by Vadim Ponorovsky, the owner of a New York restaurant, to his staff in 2009.[2] It illustrates these issues particularly well.

Exhibit 3.1 Restaurant owner email to staff

'To All,

Please read this email carefully. This is the last time we will be discussing this.

This weekend, saturday and sunday we had 451 customers. Guess how many emails we collected? 60? 80? 40? No. None of those. We, or more acurately you, collected 2 emails. Thats less than half of one percent. 2 f**king emails.

WHAT THE F**K IS WRONG WITH YOU A**HOLES?!?!?! How many times do we have to tell you how important it is that you collect emails. Everytime we have a slow night and you make no money and you sit there bitching about how you make no money, remember its because youre f**king lazy motherf**kers. YOU SHOULD ALL BE FIRED IMMEDIATELY!!!!! ALL OF YOU, INCLUDING THE HOSTS!!!!

Let me guess, youre probably sitting there saying "Vadim is such a f**king a**hole. How dare he speak to me like this. I dont need this." Youre right, you dont, so why dont you get the f**k out. Any and all of you.

Youre probably sitting there saying "How dare he speak to me like this. How dare he not have respect for me". Youre right there also. I have absolutely no respect for any of you. Why? Because every f**king day, all of you continue to show that you have absolutely no respect for me or Alex. So if you dont respect us enough to do the little that we ask you to do, then GET THE F**K OUT YOU F**KING LAZY DISRESPECTFUL A**HOLES!!!!!

Effective immediately, any server or host who fails to collect at least 20 emails per week, will be fined $100. Anyone failing to collect at least 20 emails for two weeks in a month will be fired immediately. No matter what. No matter who you are.

You dont want to do your job, you dont want to do what we ask, you dont belong at Paradou. Go find another place to work.

How dare you disrespect Alex and me this way. How dare you completely ignore what we ask of you time after time after time.

I am sick of all this s**t, you bunch of f**king children. This is what I have to deal with at 6AM?!?!? I wouldnt tolerate this from my 13 year old, and Im sure as s**t not going to tolerate it from any of you a**holes.

You give no respect, you get 10 times back.'

Ponorovsky subsequently defended his approach. Pressure on staff to work longer and longer hours, to tolerate abuse and endure surveillance illustrates how corporate leaders can coercively persuade employees to privilege (paid) work above everything else (see also Collinson and Collinson 2004). The discourse, in the example given, is clearly one of surveillance, measurement and compulsion – an attempt to construct the leader as a subject of power and employees as its compliant objects. It is also, of course, deeply unpleasant.

Alternative discourses to those of corporate culturism tend to be viewed as deficient and disposable (Willmott 1993). Corporate culturism creates a struggle for a new identity and a conflict with whatever old ones get in the way (du Gay 1991). The ideal state is assumed to be one of employee devotion to corporate goals and values. It has long been clear that one of the main tactics for dealing with people's sense of ambivalence in the face of management power has been to depict corporate life as being much freer than it really is (Hoopes 2003). In this context, the compulsory engagement I am highlighting is often couched in the language of empowerment, and liberation. Fundamentally, this discursive framing represents a '*systematic and totalizing approach to the design and strengthening of the normative framework of work*' (du Gay 1991: 524 [emphasis in the original]).

Coercive persuasion is rooted in the imbalance of power between leaders and non-leaders and is reproduced through the emphasis on followers' identity. In contemporary corporations, coercive persuasion is frequently facilitated by the compelling and 'positive' visions of leaders seeking to attract the enthusiastic support of employees (see, for example, Deal and Kennedy 1982, 1999; Collins and Porras 1995). Visions have been defined as a set of beliefs about how people should act and interact to attain some idealised future state (Strange and Mumford

2002). They are intended to establish cultures that rest on uniform values, beliefs, attitudes and behaviours and in which alternative discourses are marginalised and suppressed. As Maccoby (2003: 229) has written with specific reference to the USA, the public has been 'seduced by the promise of visionary leaders'. Given that people want work with some social meaning or social value, want to feel part of a larger community and want to live and work in an integrated fashion (Pfeffer 2003), their tendency to comply is hardly surprising.

Underlying these positive visions, leaders and managers typically make all-important organizational decisions. In practice, they retain the power to reward and punish, to define strategic direction and to withdraw whatever empowerment initiatives on which they embark. Organizational influence sharing has therefore made remarkably little progress over recent decades. Coercion remains an endemic characteristic of the leader–follower, management–employee relationship.

Moreover, by extending leaders' and managers' power into the affective domain, corporate culturism promotes a monoculture in the workplace (at least as the ideal) and significantly limits dissent. The intent often appears to be to activate intense commitment on the part of employees, as a means of heightening work effort, productivity and profitability.

The extent and the limits of coercive persuasion

Weber (1930) famously characterised rule-based and rational control as an 'iron cage', tightly controlling forms of behaviour. But, as many have pointed out, the notion of a perfect Panopticon developed by Foucault (1977) is illusory – there is always some means of avoiding total surveillance. Resistance to control has been documented in many seemingly all-powerful contexts (Simon 2005). This can go beyond 'the usual suspects'. In addition, Foucault was most concerned by how the process of external observation compelled the adoption of centrally sanctioned behavioural norms, particularly since inmates could never be certain when they were being observed. This uncertainty required consistent conformity as observed 'deviancy' could attract punishment from the unseen observer. Coercive persuasion describes such systems of observation, control, reward and punishment in acute detail.

It is an approach used to manufacture employee conformity and minimise dissent within contemporary organizations. In a sense, I have used Schein's (1961) framework to cast a new light on the subtle but essential and powerful process through which our individual 'I's become functional corporate 'we's (Burke 1937: 140). Given the argument that 'power is relational because it reveals itself in its application with others vis-à-vis specific practices, techniques, or procedures' (Fairhurst 2007: 81), this has illuminated how coercive power can be expressed in organizations, through a series of practices aimed at combining surveillance with the internalisation of particular ideologies deemed to be acceptable and therefore more likely to produce the 'appropriate individual'. Schein's (1961) early work on 'coercive persuasion' is a useful framework from which to identify and assess such persuasion and then explore that contemporary corporate attempts to sustain employee conformity through coercive persuasion are informed by the exercise of particular forms of control that invoke specific (legitimised) identities. In such cases, dissent tends to be defined as disloyalty and punished, while conformity is rewarded. These tensions may be especially pronounced in particular kinds of organizations. As Gordon *et al.* (2009) have noted, such organizations as police forces play a distinctly coercive role in society and many have struggled with the legacy of their quasi-military past. In short, where a tradition of hierarchy and obeying orders is particularly pronounced, those who belong may be attracted to or affected by the articulation of strong cultural values and the mechanisms of coercive persuasion discussed in this chapter.

Nevertheless, the issues discussed here have a much wider application. I have therefore connected the discussion to the literature on organizational surveillance and to Foucault's influential work on disciplinary processes within prisons and, in particular, his discussion of the Panopticon. This literature focuses on 'the few watching the many' (Sewell and Barker 2006: 935) and therefore conceives of organizational control in terms of powerful individuals exerting control over relatively powerless ones. But however insightful much of this literature is, it cannot fully account for all the conformist behaviours that we witness daily in organizations and that occur in the absence of constant surveillance. I have not argued that the techniques of coercive persuasion are likely to achieve such a totalitarian impact either and have acknowledged the forms of resistance that are also found in most organizations. To take one example, some scholars have claimed that call centres could be viewed as instances of perfect panoptic surveillance (Fernie and Metcalf 1999). Yet detailed studies have demonstrated that resistance, both overt and covert, is a daily occurrence (see, for example, Bain and Taylor 2000). I referred in Chapter 1, for example, to a series of uprisings even within Nazi concentration camps. Thus, there is no perfect Panopticon or other form of social control that can infallibly regulate human behaviour.

Despite this, coercive persuasion seeks to combine both explicit forms of surveillance and intense indoctrination to ensure that those at its receiving end are more likely to internalise dominant ideological norms as their own. Such 'thought reform' (Lifton 1961) reduces the need for surveillance since, if people embrace a particular belief system and the norms that are associated with it, they can guide their behaviour in desired directions with minimal external oversight. While Schein studied this phenomenon in a particularly coercive context, these coercive persuasion techniques are still found in a modern corporate context and thus warrant our understanding and critique. Schein (1961) himself drew attention to similarities between the techniques he was exploring and their use in other contexts, such as in religious orders, prisons, educational institutions and mental hospitals. But he also recognised that these methods only achieved an effect in some cases because of the interaction between the techniques and such factors as individual predisposition, innate interest in whatever ideology was being promoted, and social context (Introvigne 2002). Hence, the outcome of compliance and conversion is partially determined by the *content* of the ideology in question as well as by the specific techniques that are employed in its promotion.

The general dominance of and unquestioning attitude towards a managerial or pro-business ideology in today's society would suggest that when techniques of coercive persuasion are employed in a corporate context, they may be operating within a particularly fruitful environment, since the techniques will be building upon attitudes that are already at least partially in place.

The notion of coercive persuasion represents an underused analytic lens through which to study power, conformity and resistance in organizations. The application of the nine techniques in Schein's framework provides a model for engaging and interrogating both the pull toward and the possibility of resistance against (Zoller and Fairhurst 2007) conformity in modern organizations. By focusing on the behavioural aspects embedded in Schein's framework, we can gain a more sophisticated and useful understanding of how coercive persuasion in contemporary organizations can shape and direct subordinate behaviour and identity.

Conclusion

Clearly, all groups and organizations must share some norms of behaviour and have some agreement about the vision they are seeking to achieve or they would be incapable of functioning. However, when the norms and vision in question become all-embracing in their scope and particularly when they prohibit critical discussion, they can facilitate the harmful exercise of manipulative and coercive control by leaders and managers. Coercive persuasion seeks to sidestep the challenge of followers' autonomy and resistance by convincing those in subordinate positions that what is on offer is in their real best interest. Its message is that people should embrace an organizational identity set for them by their leaders, display enthusiastic commitment in support of organizational goals and adopt conformist behaviours that have been centrally sanctioned, while avoiding any behaviour likely to be regarded as 'deviant'.

Yet leaders can lose touch with reality or can view their organizations as vehicles for purely personal gain (Sankar 2003). Such leaders are likely to see the real self-interests of employees as secondary to their own preoccupations. In these contexts, noble-sounding ideals may become just another form of social control, mobilised in support of interests that are different to those implied in the surface declarations of its advocates. Moreover, strong organizational cultures can provide normative support for misconduct by endorsing it, focusing attention on ends without offering ethical guidance as to how they should be reached or by conveying indifference towards any moral issues that may arise (Greve *et al.* 2010). Used as a means of promoting strong organizational cultures, coercive persuasion is rife with the potential to facilitate the kind of misconduct that we saw in Enron (see Chapter 7) and in many other recent business scandals.

Individual identity is a fluid and multifaceted construct formed in the context of conformity and resistance (Collinson 2003). People do not enter organizational life with an immutable identity, which they either uphold in an organic 'pure' form or collapse into whatever shape is dictated to them by powerful others.

Identity is always relational: 'one can only ever be seen to be something in relation to something else' (Clegg 1989: 159). A creative process of struggle, therefore, unfolds in which neither the agents of influence nor their subjects remain fixed in time or space but in which they exert a reciprocal influence on the other (Shamir 2007). Accordingly, it is worth stressing that these processes of coercive persuasion and of employee conformity are themselves characterised by numerous ambiguities, inconsistencies, tensions and contradictions, which in turn can produce counterproductive effects as well as the possibility of organizational change.

Nevertheless, given the constraints imposed on dissent, employee conformity in contemporary organizations is often more evident than resistance. Drawing on Schein's model enables us to critically examine leadership practices designed to reinforce employee conformity via coercive persuasion. Many of these practices have become so widespread and 'normal' as to assume an unchallenged status in the minds of organizational actors. I have highlighted several problems that this 'normality' is likely to create. These problems feature in one form or another throughout this book.

Points for discussion

1. Consider the corporate parallels to Schein's key techniques of coercive persuasion. How many of them have you observed or experienced in various environments?
2. Pressure to conform to behaviours or ideas that we disagree with is common. When were you last aware of experiencing such pressure? When did you last put such pressure on others?
3. Many leaders promote the idea of a 'common culture' in the organizations they lead. What devices do they commonly use to achieve this? What are the dangers that might arise?
4. People value certainty more than uncertainty. To what degree is it healthy for leaders to challenge this, by acknowledging that they do not have all the answers to complex problems? Or do leaders need to appear completely confident of their approach to acquire influence over others?

Notes

1 This chapter is a revised version of work that originally appeared in Tourish, D., Collinson, D. and Barker, J. (2009) Manufacturing conformity: leadership through coercive persuasion in business organizations, *M@n@gement*, 12, 360–83.
2 See http://gawker.com/5409080/new-york-restaurant-owners-turn-evil, for full text [last accessed 16th November 2012].

4 Spirituality and leadership

Using ideology to enhance leaders' power[1]

Introduction

Recent years have witnessed a significant growth of interest in 'spirituality' within the workplace and, in particular, in spirituality oriented management and leadership development. The literature in the area is replete with unresolved paradoxes. These revolve around how spirituality is defined, with advocates variously stressing its religious dimensions, usually from a Christian perspective, and others articulating a more secular approach focusing on non-denominational humanistic values. Much of the literature stresses the value of spirituality as an aid to increasing productivity and so assumes that the values of business leaders reflect unitarist rather than sectional interests. In exploring these contradictions, I argue that spiritual management approaches seek to abolish the distinction between people's work-based lives on the one hand and their personal lives and value systems on the other. Influence is, once more, conceived in unidirectional terms: it flows from 'spiritual' and powerful leaders to more or less compliant followers, deemed to be in need of enlightenment, rather than vice versa. It enhances the influence of leaders over followers, on the assumption that stable, consistent and coherent follower identities can be manufactured, capable of facilitating the achievement of leaders' goals. Despite often being couched in emancipatory terms, I argue that spirituality at work promotes constricting cultural and behavioural norms and seeks to reinforce the power of leaders at the expense of autonomy for their followers. Implications for the constructs of 'leadership' and 'followership' and the need to preserve the distinction between private and public spaces, are considered.

Spirituality in the workplace

Spirituality at work (SAW), together with associated movements promoting spiritual management and leadership development, has grown in significance over the past decade, particularly in the USA. Aburdene (2005) has argued that it constitutes a 'megatrend', likely to dominate much business activity in the years ahead. Indicative of this, articles have appeared in *Newsweek*, *Time*, *Fortune* and *Business Week*. The Academy of Management has a special interest group devoted to the subject with (in 2012) almost 700 members, a development which has created 'legitimacy and support for research and teaching in this newly emerging field' (Neal and Biberman 2003: 363). Special issues of various journals have been produced, including the *Journal of Managerial Psychology*, the *Journal of Organization and Change Management*, the *Journal of Management Education*, *Organization* and *The Leadership Quarterly*. The field now has its own journal (*Journal of Management, Spirituality, and Religion*). A thick handbook has been published, which attracted input from major luminaries in the field of organizational studies, including Stanford's Jeffrey Pfeffer (Giacalone and Jurkiewicz 2003). It is scarcely surprising that some advocates have been able to note with evident satisfaction that 'Spirituality at work ... appears to be an idea whose time has come' (Singhal and Chatterjee 2006: 162).

Efforts are also underway to legitimise the place of spirituality in the business school curriculum. Barnett *et al.* (2000: 563) urge the teaching of spirituality on business courses, to 'engage students in self-discovery about the inner energies of the soul, their connections to personal and professional development, and their contributions to social and economic evolution'. On this principle, albeit in an extreme form, a 'Maharishi University of Management' has been created, in which spirituality is expressed through twice-daily gatherings for meditation and the transmission of cosmic vibes of spiritual energy intended to heal a stress-stricken world (Schmidt-Wilk *et al.* 2000). Its graduates are encouraged to maintain these practices as a staple of their future leadership practice.

Advocates of SAW challenge the notion that work should be a spirit-free zone and assert that organizations and their leaders should facilitate more holistic personal expressions by employees (Lewis and Geroy 2000). Since people now spend most of their waking hours at work, it is claimed that they increasingly look to their organizations 'as a communal centre' (Mirvis 1997: 702), thereby legitimating the concern of leaders with what might previously have been considered to be the private belief systems of their employees. It is argued that SAW is 'changing the fundamental nature of work' (Konz and Ryan 1999: 200), with employees increasingly expecting their leaders to offer meaning in both their work and wider lives (Ashmos and Duchon 2000). The management of meaning is therefore held to be a crucial activity for leaders (Singhal and Chatterjee 2006), which the adoption of SAW related practices will purportedly help them to perform. Fry suggests, without any suggestion of irony, that:

> Companies as diverse as Taco Bell, Pizza Hut, BioGenenex, Aetna International, Big Six accounting's Deloitte and Touche, and Law firms such as New York's Kaye, Scholer, Fierman, Hayes and Haroller are extolling lessons usually doled out in churches, temples and mosques.
>
> (Fry 2003: 702)

There are few limits. Thus, if SAW gains a sufficiently strong purchase on organizational practices, much of the literature asserts that personal, social and global transformation will surely follow – and for the better (Driscoll and Wiebe 2007).

Business leaders, meanwhile, are presented with a vastly expanded range of issues with which to concern themselves, despite their evident difficulties in resolving those that they already confront. In consequence, they are invited to exercise a colonising influence on the deepest recesses of their employees' hitherto private belief and value systems. The assumption that such an approach can succeed is consistent with the longstanding but questionable tendency to treat followers as though they are an undifferentiated collective (Collinson 2006), thereby capable of adhering to a relatively simple normative framework proposed by leaders on their behalf. It is an assumption that is consistent with the ideas of transformational leadership discussed in Chapter 2 and the mechanics of coercive persuasion discussed in Chapter 3 but it is one that I challenge in this chapter.

I apply a critical perspective to SAW, particularly in terms of its implications for the theory and practice of leadership. In line with post-structuralist approaches to leadership, my basic assumption is that:

> relations between leaders and followers are typically characterised by asymmetrical power relations and deeply embedded, historically specific control practices (such that) leaders' hierarchical, power enables them to define situations in ways that suit their purposes, provide rewards, apply sanctions, gain access to expertise, and secure followers' consent.
>
> (Collinson 2008: 311)

Consistent with this premise, my core argument is that SAW has been poorly defined and has attempted to straddle both secularism and a particular stress on religion; however, both secular and explicitly religious manifestations of it seek to extend the power of leaders; nonspiritual, utilitarian and performative notions of productivity underlie much of its advocacy, with the assumption that because such notions are valued by leaders they embody priorities which either are or ought to be shared by their followers; it is presented without sufficient acknowledgement of power differentials in the workplace and therefore ignores the additional power which its practice may cede to a managerial elite; as a result, its claimed emancipatory agenda may serve as a vehicle for the advancement of a more controlling and oppressive leadership agenda than is normally acknowledged or may be intended. In particular, SAW can be employed as yet another means of establishing monocultural workplace environments, in which employee dissent is demonised as the sinful antithesis of pure spiritual values, to which only morally deficient individuals could object and which organizational leaders are uniquely qualified to articulate.

Spirituality at work – a religious or secular paradigm?

A key problem lies with the multiple ways in which SAW has (failed) to define itself. Even proponents of the movement have noted that disagreement on what it is remains endemic to the field (Dent *et al.* 2005). In one sense, the absence of such agreement insulates its proponents from critique. Since SAW is so protean in conception, it can assume whatever form is most likely to help it to escape censure. But, in another sense, both the secular and religious definitions that have abounded share an underlying performative intent. They therefore privilege the values, priorities and concerns of leaders, while affirming to employees that these capture their own immediate and seemingly homogeneous interests. I review some of the contradictions that this reveals and then argue that a common feature of the competing definitions on offer is their tendency to reify organizations and, intentionally or otherwise, promote the desirability of a monocultural environment, in which the power of leaders is intensified and dissent is marginalised.

Religious definitions of spirituality at work

In general, SAW has been defined in terms that imply a deep relationship with the core of what it means to be a human being. It has been described as something that involves ultimate and personal truths (Wong 1998), as the promotion of a relationship with a higher power that effects how one conducts oneself in the world (Armstrong 1995), as being intimately bound up with religion (Dent *et al.* 2005) and as an animating force that inspires one towards purposes beyond oneself and which in turn gives life meaning and direction (McKnight 1984). Mason and Welsh (1994) define it as wonder, play, spontaneity, joy, imagination, celebration, discernment, insight and creativity. This might be a revelation to those who disdain the nomenclature of spirituality and who view such terms as 'joy' and 'spontaneity' from a humanist or secular perspective. In straightforward religious terms, spiritual wellbeing has also been posited as requiring an affirmation of life in a relationship with God and the celebration and nurturing of wholeness (Ellison 1983). Reave argues that:

> Most spiritual teachings urge the appreciation of others as fellow creations of God worthy of respect and praise. Praise of God's creation is widely considered to be a means of prayer, so appreciating others may similarly be considered an expression of gratitude not only to individuals but also to God.
>
> (Reave 2005: 677)

In this view, spirituality and religion are inseparable constructs. Daniels *et al.* (2000) are among those who argue for a specifically Christian approach to management and management education, including an advocacy of the need to model a sense of Christian community on university campuses. Similarly, Cavanagh (1999) argues that spirituality includes acknowledging both God and the importance of prayer.

This overtly religious orientation is also evident in an increasing body of practitioner-oriented literature. Granberg-Michaelson's (2004) text includes chapters with titles such as 'Listening for God's call'. This asserts that:

> Beneath the challenges posed to any leader by temptations arising from money, sex, and power is a more fundamental question: how does one hear God's

'call' for one's life at a particular point in one's journey? ... I have no doubt that God does call us in this way; our problem comes in listening, so that this call can be heard.

(Granberg-Michaelson 2004: 36)

Some organizations have taken significant steps to put such ideas into practice. Bell *et al.* (2012: 429) cite the example of Tyson Foods, based in Arkansas and the 2005 recipient of *Fortune* magazine's 'most admired food company' award. Tyson identifies a number of 'core values' listed on a plastic card carried by employees, and which includes the following:

We strive to be a faith-friendly company.
We strive to honor God and be respectful of each other, our customers, and other stakeholders.

The religious definitions of SAW described above and arguably the explicit faith-based model articulated by organizations such as Tyson, offer a narrow, normative framework of limited appeal when significant numbers of people have abandoned formal church attendance and the rituals of religious commitment. It is nevertheless suggested that leaders can articulate this framework in such a manner that it assumes a wide appeal and so acts as a unifying force within their organizations.

Although these assumptions are a given in the literature, they are deeply problematic. Overt religious symbols are unwelcome in many workplaces, precisely because of their divisive potential – for example, in Northern Ireland (Dickson *et al.* 2008). There are, in addition, a multitude of legal issues around the expression of spirituality in the workplace in the USA (Schley 2008). Such perspectives also confer considerable additional power on leaders, whom it is assumed can and should encourage employees to redefine their views of God and religion in terms determined by powerful others. There is little evidence that such an approach would be welcomed. Attempts to pursue it may be viewed as an effort to create a monocultural environment that, by privileging particular belief systems over others, reproduces a repressive managerial agenda at odds with a claimed emancipatory intent.

Secular definitions of spirituality at work

While this critique can be applied to the overtly religious definitions of spirituality, the more secular notions on offer suffer from similar limitations. With such approaches, a seemingly humanistic approach is to the fore. Duchon and Plowman (2005: 807) assert that 'Workplace spirituality is defined as a workplace that recognises that employees have an inner life that nourishes and is nourished by meaningful work that takes place in the context of community'. SAW is therefore depicted in emancipatory terms, simply intended to 'help' people bring more of themselves to work without incurring sanction or ridicule.

Thus, Mitroff (2003) promotes spirituality as a transcendent force connecting people to the universe, which therefore enables them to bring the deepest essence of themselves to work, while being distinct from religion, particularly of the organized variety. Leaders who champion it are cast in the role of liberators, freeing the human spirit, but also as construction workers, demolishing outmoded barriers between people's identities at work and other important areas of their lives. Consistent with this, Pfeffer (2003) views SAW in secular terms, as that which enables people to learn, develop, have a sense of competence and mastery and live an integrated life in which work roles and personal roles exist in harmony with each other. So framed, this might appear an entirely benign ambition. The problem lies, however, with how it is to be translated into practice within the power-saturated and conflicted organizations where most people work.

Ashmos and Duchon (2000) epitomise the difficulty. They argue that SAW encompasses three major themes: the importance of a person's inner life, the need for meaning at work and the importance of a sense of connection and community within organizations. It is commonly assumed that the promotion of 'connection' and 'community' requires employees to align their values with the organization's larger purpose, as it has been defined by its formal leaders (Milliman *et al.* 2003; Ashforth and Pratt 2003). SAW is therefore advocated as a means of personal rather than organizational transformation. People's attention is directed internally to whatever obstacles block their full engagement with an unproblematic organizational agenda – rather than externally, to those systemic difficulties that might prevent the emergence of more humanistic work organizations. By contrast, a post-structuralist perspective, drawing in particular on the work of Foucault (1977, 1979), would suggest the need to acknowledge that specific regimes of power and knowledge can be inscribed on people, creating individuals who essentially participate in their own subordination through absorbing the value systems of others, which may, in reality, reflect interests contrary to their own. In this way, the social control of leaders over followers becomes more deeply entrenched (Collinson 2006). This process is not necessarily mitigated by a discourse which often asserts its intention to accomplish the opposite.

A managerialist bias

The predominant presumption within the literature is that those at the top will have ultimate say on these issues, and that how leaders view themselves is a key ingredient behind the 'successful' development of SAW. This managerialist bias runs through the literature, with minimal awareness of its complications. For example, a much cited book by Mitroff and Denton (1999) reports on the results of a 'spirituality audit' conducted by them. It is based on a survey of 1,738 people. But all of these were managers. Moreover, they all worked in the USA. This is sufficient for Mitroff (2003: 376) to conclude that 'people want to bring their whole selves to work ... They are extremely frustrated with and tired of having to leave significant parts of themselves at home and pretending that one can do it'. The point is not whether this conclusion is valid; it is simply that it is an unusual research practice to extrapolate from a survey of managers in one country to the workforce of the whole planet. It is also questionable whether, based on their responses, it is then justified to assume that business leaders should have full control over developing a spirituality agenda for their employees, thus extending their power in ever wider directions.

While the tendency towards eroding boundaries between work and non-work domains has been widely noted (see, for example, Perlow 1999; Bell and Taylor 2003) I suggest that something else is also involved in the kind of discourse examined here. In particular, the literature on SAW has the potential to erode the boundaries between leaders and followers, by permitting and encouraging the former to exercise a dominating influence over the most private values and belief systems of the latter. The paradox is clear. On the one hand, since it is asserted that employees bring spiritual values with them to work, it follows that 'the organization is cast neutrally as the provider of opportunities for individual spiritual expression' (Bell and Taylor 2003: 343). But, simultaneously, spiritual values are to be defined, shaped and introduced by managers. It is rarely said that such values are merely there, awaiting discovery. The spiritual leader is cast in quite a different role to that of an explorer, bringing hidden treasures to the surface. Rather, he/she assumes the demeanour of a spiritual engineer, transforming the already existing values of followers. This imperils one of the crucial dimensions of effective followership, which is the extent to which people think independently and critically for themselves (Kelley 1988, 2008). Rather, it is argued that:

> the president or CEO is usually the key person to initiate a process defining an organization's mission and vision, and, as stated, this should be part of his or her job description, but a governing board should be deeply involved in the process, especially in the case of religious and other non-profit institutions. Granted, the process may create new expectations for them and change their role. Similarly, staff must be consulted throughout the process in meaningful ways that take seriously their input but don't place inappropriate expectations on them to ultimately control the outcome.
>
> (Wagner-Marsh and Conley 1999: 107)

Ultimately, it appears that staff must be prepared to internalise all-embracing value systems set for them by others, albeit with the consolation of having been 'consulted' about what these should be.

Thus, it is routinely asserted that spiritual management leadership involves 'creating a vision wherein organization members experience a sense of calling in that their life has meaning and makes a difference' (Fry 2003: 711). Leaders must promote a common vision and achieve value congruence at all organizational levels (Maghroori and Rolland 1997). Much that is ostensibly positive is claimed to flow from this, including improved organizational learning (Bierly *et al.* 2000), unified communities in the workplace (Cavanagh *et al.* 2001), a greater feeling of connection between employees, and between employees and their work (Khanna and Srinivas 2000), increased compassion, wisdom and connectedness (Maxwell 2003) and increased corporate social responsibility – at, incidentally, no cost to key indicators of financial performance (Fry and Cohen 2009). Leaders must therefore aspire to instil a sense of the spiritual realm within individuals, teams, and the organization more widely (Cacioppe 2000). A key proposition is that workplace spirituality is related to the leader's ability to 'enable' the worker's inner life, sense of meaningful work, and community (Duchon and Plowman 2005). Accordingly, a leader who embraces SAW will have a heightened ability to create a definition of what represents a meaningful life, to predefine employees' sense of community in the direction of workplace relationships and to transform their inner life so that it is more consistent with corporate purposes. It is an agenda built on the assumption that organizations have a unitarist nature, thereby ensuring that the extension of leaders' power in ever-wider and more intrusive directions will have a benign effect.

To prepare for such a development, it also follows that leaders require 'development' (that is, training/indoctrination) in its precepts. Spiritual management and leadership development is therefore increasingly offered by providers, who 'claim to enable the release of managers from their socialised selves so they can be liberated from the "negative thoughts," "fears" or "barriers," which impede the development of a successful corporate culture' (Bell and Taylor 2004: 441). In so doing, it reflects a focus on managing identity (and thus ensures compliance through the internalisation of dominant corporate values) rather than old hierarchical structures and simple mechanisms of command and control (Kamoche 2000). The focus is on the need for individuals to adapt everything they possess, body and soul, to the organizational environment in which they find themselves, in pursuit of meaning and solace. The possibility that such a colonisation of people's affective domain might be oppressive, invasive or unwelcome is not generally considered.

Thus, while some texts acknowledge that there is a danger of overly 'enthusiastic' CEOs attempting to impose a particular religious belief system on others (for example, Cavanagh 1999), such writers generally still favour a unitarist view of organizations which privilege a managerial voice above that of other organizational members. Cavanagh (1999: 192) also posits the view that 'If handled well, common religious and spiritual beliefs in an organization can be fruitful. But if not handled well, it can lead to divisiveness and even law suits'. It is simply assumed that an organization must have a 'common' view about such inherently contentious subjects and that, somehow, leaders can become adept at managing whatever tensions inadvertently arise.

A post-structuralist view of identity

In opposition, post-structuralist perspectives assert that identity is 'multiple, fluid, shifting, fragmented, contradictory and nonrational' (Collinson 2008: 312). Paradox, contradiction, ambiguity and inconsistency are endemic to identity construction and maintenance (Schultz *et al.* 2012). In this context, it may thus be that people have many 'spiritual' essences, none of them necessarily in harmony with each other, let alone an overarching organizational purpose, vision or mission. Cavanagh (1999) nevertheless argues in favour of prayer within 'religiously oriented business schools', to bring a sense of 'perspective' to the curriculum. Meanwhile:

> Spirituality enables a businessperson to gain a better perspective on their firm, family, neighbours, community and themselves. Furthermore, acknowledging dependence on God gives the individual manager a more stable and helpful vision. The manager then knows that his/her success also depends on someone beyond themselves, so such a view also lessens stress. Such a vision also enables the manager to integrate their life, so that it is less segmented and compartmentalized.
>
> (Cavanagh 1999: 198)

Whether non-religious employees will be likely to feel the same is not considered.

Consistent with an approach which privileges a managerial voice over issues of personal belief and, hence, which prioritises conformity over dissent, Benefiel (2005) approvingly discusses one US organization, where the organization's founders committed to 'follow the will of God in business decisions, to be determined through prayer and their unanimous agreement'. It is assumed that this is a model way to proceed. Giacalone and Jurkiewicz's (2003: 663) assertion that 'a theory of spiritual leadership would start with the leader's own ethics and integrity' is typical of the literature. Once a leader has clarified such issues to their own satisfaction, their next task is to transmit spiritual insights to their followers, who presumably are little more than empty vessels awaiting a transfusion of integrity from their leaders. However, there is no reason to believe that such a transfusion can be accomplished without evoking dismay, suspicion and resistance.

Again, it is notable that many of the terms used in the literature are much more problematic than is acknowledged. One leader's definition of integrity in decision making (for example, on such issues as downsizing) can be defined as unethical with equal or greater legitimacy by other voices. However, the dominant discourse within the SAW literature does not consider such an approach. Rather, the role of God in spirituality is central; spirituality is generally synonymous with a Christian belief system; organizations have a unitarist nature; employees possess a stable identity and are capable of holding a common set of values and beliefs; and a managerial voice is permitted and encouraged to define core values for everyone within its orbit.

Even assuming that such a discourse is greeted by a receptive audience, we encounter a further problem. Forray and Stork (2002: 507) argue compellingly that an invocation of spirituality involves a retreat from rational thinking, to such an extent that 'in any commitment to spirit, reason is silenced'. It could therefore be suggested that leaders advocating SAW diminish the rational and hence questioning roles of their followers, arousing instead an unreflexive emotional response that is more likely to promote conformity and so further entrench leadership power. Again, this would contradict the emancipatory rhetoric with which most discourse on SAW is infused.

The illusion of inclusivity

Many advocates of SAW, particularly those who place less emphasis on the term's religious connotations, have been keen to stress the inclusive nature of their approach, as a means of addressing these issues. If SAW is inclusive, then it theoretically follows that it cannot be a means of advancing the sectional interests of organizational leaders to the detriment of those of their followers. In line with this approach, Mitroff and Denton (1999) argue that spirituality must be broadly inclusive by definition, since it promotes values that are 'universal and timeless'. SAW is also characterised as 'the ultimate source and provider of meaning and purpose', dealing with 'the sacredness of everything' by exploring 'the deep feeling of interconnectedness of everything'.[2] Ashmos and Duchon argue that:

> spirituality is neither about religion nor about getting people to accept a specific belief system. Rather, it is about employees who understand themselves as spiritual beings at work whose souls need nourishment, a sense of purpose and meaning, and a sense of connectedness to one another and to their workplace community.
>
> (Ashmos and Duchon 2000: 634)

The language seeks to articulate appealing values that lie beyond the domain of one religious world view and which can therefore elide controversy. In line with this, Reave (2005: 655) concludes that 'there is a clear consistency between spiritual values and practices and effective leadership. Values that have long been considered spiritual ideals, such as integrity, honesty, and humility, have been demonstrated to have an effect on leadership success'.

However, many of these statements are deeply ambiguous and contested. For example, what does it mean to say that spirituality is 'universal and timeless'? Arguably, there is no one set of universal values to which all people subscribe – unless humanity has become a much more homogeneous species than previous studies of conflict, power and resistance would lead us to believe. If, however, some 'universal' values can be identified, they may, by definition, be so general in nature as to confer little real meaning on what they ostensibly denote. Thus Daniels *et al.* (2000) cites a magazine article on South-West Airlines in the USA which argues that the organization's culture is based on spiritual values. These are identified as a strong emphasis on community, an (alleged) employee perception that they are part of a cause, a culture of empowerment and an emphasis on emotion and humour. Clearly, the linguistic terms employed can withstand

multiple interpretations – an elasticity of meaning which creates further paradoxes. As Hicks put it:

> if citizens do hold in common a few values, such as freedom, equality, and
> toleration, these values are not 'thick' enough to provide the resources to
> settle morally challenging leadership questions such as what role religion
> should play in the contemporary workplace. Attempts to translate religiously
> particular values into common spiritual or secular values are reductionist at
> best and inaccurate at worst.
>
> (Hicks 2003: 165)

However, followers' identities are complex, conflicted and discursive formations. Recognising this requires us to acknowledge that the definitions of SAW
discussed above suffer from a twofold problem. When couched in religious
terms, they exclude many and are opposed by others. Such definitions are likely
to have a limited and perhaps diminishing appeal. This may not prevent leaders
who have bought into such a philosophy from expending enormous energy in the
pursuit of a monocultural environment that, in reality, is likely to prove elusive.
On the other hand, when SAW assumes an inclusive and secular form, it lacks
real regulatory power, since allegedly universal values are in reality vulnerable to
multiple and contested interpretations and, hence, applications. Again, despite the
effort invested in its advocacy, it would have a limited impact on people's
thoughts, emotions and behaviour – the three main areas where it aspires to have
a normative effect.

The paradoxes of performativity and 'spiritual leadership'

The literature on SAW inherently reifies organizations. It assumes that they have a
taken for granted quality and a unitary nature that precludes multiple and contested
interpretations of either the common good or spirituality. A thinly disguised
performative intent is therefore endemic to most of this discourse (Driscoll and
Wiebe 2007) – that is, the assertion is made that, by embracing spirituality, organizations (that is, senior managers) will improve effectiveness, productivity and
profitability. It is assumed that these are worthwhile outcomes. But, while it may
be obvious that they are appealing to business leaders (particularly those who hold
stock options), it is less clear that they confer unalloyed benefits to employees.

Summarising this position, Giacalone and Jukiewicz argue:

> The scientific study of workplace spirituality must be founded on sound
> theoretical justification of its utility. Researchers must effectively demon-
> strate the utility of spirituality in the workplace by framing it as a question of
> value-added: How does spirituality help us to undertake work processes more
> effectively?
>
> (Giacalone and Jukiewicz 2003: 9–10)

In this 'spirit', spirituality audits have been conducted in many workplaces, with some key spirituality auditors arguing that their research shows how spirituality enhances competitiveness (Mitroff and Denton 1999). It is routinely claimed (albeit, in my view, with minimal supporting empirical evidence) that such workplaces are more productive, flexible and creative (Eisler and Montouori 2003), that they lead to reduced absenteeism and turnover (Giacalone and Jurkiewicz 2003), that SAW enhances individual creativity (Freshman 1999), increases honesty and trust (Wagner-Marsh and Conley 1999), provides employees with an enhanced sense of personal fulfilment (Burack, 1999) and, in general, increases commitment to organizational goals (Delbecq 1999). They will also be better primed for successful implementation and adaptation to 'change' (Heaton *et al.* 2004).

In addition, it is argued that organizations that embrace SAW are inherently more likely to become exemplars of the 'learning organization', in which greater intrinsic as opposed to extrinsic motivation will be unleashed (Fry 2003). Again, profits will rise. Such organizations will, it is claimed, be 'love-led', obsessed with customer/client satisfaction, diverse, flexible, networked and much less hierarchical than in the past, since new normative frameworks will replace the need for previous models of coercion (Ancona *et al.* 1999). For most leaders of corporate organizations, these would be alluring goals and are clearly articulated to attract their attention. To advance this agenda, a spiritual leadership theory (SLT) is posited, as 'a causal leadership theory for organizational transformation designed to create an intrinsically motivated, learning organization' (Fry *et al.* 2005: 835). Since leaders will be enabled by this approach to integrate their personal and professional lives, it is also argued that it will improve their effectiveness (Neal 2001). But not only leaders will gain. Tischler *et al.* (2002) argue that, for similar reasons, individuals who embrace SAW will have greater success at work. Within this unitarist framework, it appears that no one stands to lose. All will have prizes.

Paradoxically, organizations are urged to promote increasingly religious values and require employees to buy into them – to make more money. Spirituality seems to be viewed as another means of asserting that the visions developed by an organization's leaders have been designed to genuinely reflect their followers' interests – as opposed to, say, enhancing shareholder value. Followers should therefore comply, to boost organizational performance. It is merely a coincidence, albeit a happy one, that profits will rise in consequence. Advocates of this approach seem oblivious to the risk that work–life balance mechanisms will be thrown out of kilter, allowing 'spirituality to become another control mechanism for getting individuals to work harder in their paid jobs, often at the expense of other avenues toward meaningful and fulfilled lives such as family and voluntarism' (Lips-Wiesma *et al.* 2009: 291).

This paradox is heightened by the context in which it is occurring. Kinjerski and Skrypnek (2004: 26–7), in noting that downsizing and re-engineering failed to accomplish improvements in organizational performance, characterise SAW as being among efforts to develop 'work environments that foster employees' creativity and personal growth … The assumption is that such environments will

foster more fulfilling lives for employees and positive outcomes for organizations'. Thus, even as the traditional psychological contract is violated, SAW is
deployed in an attempt to increase loyalty (Burack 1999: Cash and Gray 2000).
This is supposed to take place in a context in which the credibility of business
leaders as advocates of humanistic values has been damaged by previous, divisive and discredited fads that they have endorsed.

There are some more cautious voices in the literature. For example, Dehler and
Welsh (2003: 115) acknowledge that:

> The most serious danger may be managerial attempts to exploit the emotional
> side of work by turning it into an instrumentality, that is, embrace people's
> spiritual side because it impacts on the bottom line, rather than treating peo-
> ple as complete human beings as the 'right' thing to do. Inevitably, there will
> be tension in the relationship between workers and their institutions, in part
> as a result of business cycles ... There are ... legitimate concerns about the
> usurpation of first the body, then the mind, and now the heart of workers by
> employers.
>
> (Dehler and Welsh 2003: 115)

Nevertheless, this kind of acknowledgement is rare. For the most part, and as
I have argued here, theorists in the field presume that leaders and followers share
a unitarist interest; that employees, as a relatively undifferentiated mass, should
embrace an identifiable set of core values; that business leaders are well placed
to discover, shape and articulate these values, in the form of SAW; and that
performative ends can therefore be safely attached to what is being proposed.

Performativity also intrudes into the development of a future research agenda.
To date, there has been relatively little empirical research designed to test the
frequent assertions that SAW confers multiple organizational benefits (Dean
2004). While advocates have been compelled to recognise that this is a weakness,
their response may accentuate rather than resolve the issues at stake. Thus,
Milliman *et al.* (1999) acknowledge that many senior managers will only
embrace SAW if they believe that it offers bottom-line benefits. They then argue
that research designed to validate this notion 'is needed if we are to create a paradigm shift in CEOs so that they incorporate spiritual principles into their organizations'. This comes close to determining the findings of empirical research in
advance – an approach which would have more in common with pseudoscience
than genuine academic inquiry.

A focus on enhanced organizational performance as a key driver of SAW is
therefore embedded in the extant literature, even though this would appear to
violate the notion that it should be promoted primarily because of its intrinsic
ethical superiority and emancipatory potential. It is doubtful that leaders pursuing
it for these ends could sustain a credible impression over the long term. Rather,
it may be that such an obvious intent further undercuts the possibility of the
concept taking deep root in people's minds. Instead, it may generate further cynicism about the intentions of leaders in the workplace. However, even if SAW is

not well placed to exercise a colonising impact by leaders on the affective domain of employees, this is clearly its intent.

Abolishing limits on leader power

My critique in this chapter is consistent with the suggestion made by Willmott (1993: 517), to the effect that the emphasis on the importance of a strong corporate culture that was prevalent in the 1980s and 1990s 'aspires to extend management control by colonising the affective domain. It does this by promoting employee commitment to a monolithic structure of feeling and thought'. And, as discussed in Chapter 3, the linking of intense surveillance mechanisms to the articulation of a compelling ideology is central to the notion of coercive persuasion. But, by extending the power of leaders into the affective domain, all forms of dissent and resistance can be deemed to be off limits. Within this world view, it is no longer permissible for employees merely to do a decent job while holding a privately critical attitude towards an organization's goals, its culture or its leaders. Leaders are encouraged to extend their influence into every area of employees' lives, including their most private values and belief systems. The implied goal seems to be that behaviour will be rendered complaisant with the needs of the corporation, always and everywhere. I suggest that if something such as 'spirituality', which sounds inherently positive to many people, can be invoked as the basis of an organization's culture then it may be appropriated for the same ends as were served by the 'excellence' and 'strong cultures' movements that I discussed in Chapters 2 and 3 and perhaps with similar, doleful results. The problem is that the advocates of SAW tend to present the prerogatives of leaders in an unassailable and uncontested light and merely assume that they have a perfectly legitimate right to determine values and beliefs for employees.

Consistent with this, social identity theories of leadership postulate that when people identify strongly with a group, the leader's effectiveness is bound up with their ability to demonstrate that they embody what are deemed to be prototypical properties of the group (Hogg 2007). In this context, an obvious problem is the potential for such leaders, assuming that they succeed in embedding SAW, to so engage their followers that they become overcommitted to the group and its values. But when people become what can be defined as 'true believers' and evince overly zealous commitment, they 'can endow a prototypical leader with overwhelming power to influence' (Hogg 2008: 273). Such influence may be benign – or it may not. In either eventuality, an emphasis on corporate culturism combined with an emerging focus on spirituality management and leadership may unleash precisely this dynamic and so constitute major mechanisms for the deep structural exercise of power and constraint in organizations, albeit couched in emancipatory and humanistic rhetoric.

Thus, Korac-Kakabadse *et al.* (2002: 172) simply assert that 'Spiritual leaders are moral leaders. Moral leaders prefer not to compromise, accommodate or collaborate in areas where core values are at stake. They prefer to challenge opinions and ideas, rather than accommodate them'. An immediately obvious riposte to this is to ask: in how many organizations do followers have an equal right, authority and power to challenge opinions that they find objectionable, particularly when those are held by leaders? How frequently do they have access to the resources necessary to accomplish this? These authors, as with many others, simply take it for granted that leaders have special powers to determine reality for their followers, in ever wider and more personal directions.

Accordingly, it is axiomatic in much of the literature that leaders should seek to mould the organization's culture and, hence, the personality of those who work within it. An organization's culture is viewed as merely another resource, to be defined and moulded by its managerial élite (Smircich 1983). It is assumed that leaders can demonstrate to those lower down the organization how they should perform, think and feel, by a judicious combination of example and exhortation. But those who hold managerial positions are, in turn, expected to take their ideological cue from the CEO at the top and internalise their values accordingly. The challenge is to frame spiritual values so that they are inclusive – but yet capable of exercising a powerful enough normative appeal to constrain behaviour. Management development programmes play a critical role in this effort. The use of programmes which have appropriated much of the rhetoric and ritual of self-discovery, faith and commitment are therefore increasingly common (Ackers and Preston 1997).

Such programmes often just assume that leaders can and indeed should embark on the personal transformation of whatever value systems are held by their employees (for example, Gozdz and Frager 2003; Reave 2005). An environment characterised by 'bounded choice' may then emerge, in which only a limited repertoire of feelings, attitudes and behaviour is permissible (Lalich 2004). This view is consistent with the notion of 'concertive control'. SAW has the potential to become precisely such a form of concertive control. This possibility rather belies the emancipatory rhetoric with which the literature on SAW is saturated. Within this paradigm, it is not too fanciful to see business leaders as a priestly caste, endowed with greater wisdom than other lesser mortals and empowered with the dispensation to impart it unidirectionally to all within their orbit. It is taken for granted that they can frame productivity targets and organizational goals for everyone in a manner that secures the interests of all, that the goals of the organization's formal leaders are intrinsically uncontentious and that these goals can and should be linked to spirituality, in the somewhat Machiavellian calculation that profit driven goals will become more acceptable to employees. The overall implication is that whatever prevents full engagement with the management agenda is a personal weakness to be overcome and that organizations have the right to invade people's internal cognitive space to reshape their values ('We need a new vision around here'), in the unproblematic pursuit of corporate efficiency.

The deal on offer amounts to a Faustian pact. It means that leaders are increasingly liberated to engineer the souls of their employees, who stand to secure approval and career progression if they embrace the new value system. The goal is to abolish any distinction between the public and private spaces in people's lives and between the values of leaders and their employees. Little thought has been given by the advocates of SAW to the potentially negative effects of breaching boundaries between the personal and professional domains of people's lives in this manner. Since it is agued that people want 'soul enriching fulfilment at work' (Dean and Safranski 2008: 359), it is simply assumed that those in charge of organizations have an obligation to provide it. Thus, leaders decide – everything. In the context of asymmetrical power relations in the workplace, it is difficult to see how this agenda could genuinely serve an emancipatory purpose. Whatever the intent, SAW seems well placed to become another repressive project, expressed through the coercive exercise of power.

Yet leaders often lose touch with reality, frequently because employees fail to openly ventilate their disagreement with organizational goals. The distance between leaders and followers is therefore increasingly recognised as a problem (Collinson 2005a). This calls into question the ability of leaders to invariably articulate a compelling vision that is genuinely in the interests of their followers and which is capable of engaging their support. Advocates of SAW are thus likely to encounter a working environment in which leaders have an overly privileged voice in determining the spiritual values to be embraced. Employees, meanwhile, may be reluctant to articulate their true feelings but feel compelled to conceal this reluctance behind public statements and actions that ostensibly embrace the new value system.

Despite the espousal of an emancipatory intent by leaders intent on promoting SAW, such a conflicted stance by their followers is liable to increase the gap between their public and private selves, engendering additional alienation. Collinson's (1999) study of safety on North Sea oil installations demonstrates how adept employees can be at concealing their true values and behaviours when they conflict with official policy and therefore how ubiquitous the phenomenon of 'disguised selves' is in many workplaces. It may be postulated that it would be even more difficult to secure genuine buy-in with spiritual values, when many people traditionally see such issues as beyond the domain of work and as constituting the essence of a highly personalised self. Their promotion at work may therefore exacerbate rather than resolve the tension between people's private and public identities, even as proponents of SAW stress their intent of abolishing it. In such a context, noble-sounding ideals expressed in the language of spirituality can become another form of social control, mobilised in support of interests that are different to those implied in the surface declarations of its advocates. In a context of growing corporate power and the concentration of authority within corporations in the hands of powerful CEOs, it is questionable whether society should cede them the right to abolish the distinction between employees' activities at work and their private values and, hence, legitimise only those aspects of spirituality that can be depicted as serving the bottom line.

Conclusion

Brown (2003: 393) has argued that the overall concept of SAW 'is not so much elusive and intangible as confused and imprecise'. The multiple definitions on offer and the tendency to ignore potential paradoxes also means that the field can be classified as being 'saturated with subjectivity' (Lips-Wiersma 2003: 406) – a subjectivity which enables powerful élites to promote sectional interests while claiming that they embody universal truths and principles. The critique in this chapter has therefore pinpointed the inherently autocratic potential that lies behind what purports to be an emancipatory agenda and has argued that SAW is more likely to extend and deepen the power of leaders than it is to constrain it.

A bald assertion of 'shareholder value' has limited appeal for most people and little potential to inspire greater effort in the workplace – a problem which is increasingly recognised by business leaders. If corporate goals can be couched in more ideologically appealing forms, people may be more likely to shift their attitudes in the direction deemed to be desirable. I have argued that spirituality has increasingly been invoked as the ideological foundation of corporate culturism in an attempt to achieve this, often in the overt pursuit of such unspiritual needs as enhanced profitability. Vague, highly generalised or what Taylor (2004: 28) has characterised as 'ethereal ideas' (such as those offered by many advocates of SAW) have the potential to encourage over conformist behaviour and monoculturism, at least for a period. When this occurs, formal elements of compulsion (for example, one-way communication systems, from top managers to employees rather than vice versa) may appear less intrusive or oppressive than they actually are. Spirituality offers the promise of a coherent ideology that does not question a corporate power that is now so pervasive as to be unremarkable. It may therefore underpin new rituals of commitment and a new language of obedience to whatever goals are deemed acceptable by business leaders and which have a clear performative intent.

Downplaying such issues, advocates of SAW contend that leaders should seek to fill the void in people's lives that has been created by the well-documented decay of wider socials networks. Putnam's (2000) classic study, *Bowling Alone*, is a powerful analysis of this process. In essence, work pressures have appropriated the time that people used to spend on sports, churches or even political parties. Altruism, philanthropy and volunteering have all declined precipitously. But there is no obvious reason to assume that business leaders would be motivated in an endeavour to address these problems by anything other than the performative norms which have been instrumental in creating this void in the first place. In fact, SAW could be employed as a convenient ideological tool to limit dissent, heighten commitment and secure a redoubled focus on profit-oriented goals. This danger is particularly acute when those who advocate such approaches are insensitive to the problem of power and its unequal distribution in most workplaces. However, as Galbraith (1977: 259) wryly noted, 'By pretending that power is not present, we greatly reduce the need to worry about its exercise'. Seemingly unaware of such complications, most advocates of SAW take power differentials for granted and propose measures which would, perhaps ironically, have the effect of strengthening them.

A different approach is required. In particular, I suggest that the workplace is not a useful medium for people to find the deepest meaning in their lives.

Leaders of business organizations are not spiritual engineers or secular priests, charged with responsibility for the human soul, and business organizations are not a suitable forum for exploring such issues. The distinction between private and public spaces is important and worth preserving. The notion that people's private identity or sense of separateness can or should be overcome through forming an emotional attachment to a larger organizational identity is highly questionable and perhaps even delusional (Driver 2005). Work can and should be meaningful but only in its own terms and not as a substitute for the creation of wider social networks, interests, commitments, values and beliefs. To suggest otherwise is to extend the power of leaders in new, inappropriate and dangerous directions. In particular, it inadvertently seeks to abolish vital distinctions between leadership and followership (since it is assumed that followers must imbibe critical, core values articulated by leaders, in pursuit of a unitarist organizational framework). As Case and Gosling (2010: 276) express it: 'The workplace has no special relevance to spirituality; it is simply another site, amongst the multitude of transient phenomena within which subjective spiritual journeys may or may not be pursued'. It follows that distinctions such as those between leadership and followership are vital to people's sense of their authentic inner selves and what it means to be a well-rounded human being. On this basis, we may be better placed to find the path towards true liberation.

Points for discussion

1. Should leaders seek to bring a deeper sense of meaning into the lives of their followers? What are the advantages and disadvantages of such an approach?
2. To what extent is spirituality, either secular or religious, appropriate in the workplace?
3. Can you identify forms of spirituality that you think would be widely accepted in most organizations?
4. Are followers entitled to hold different values to those advocated by their leaders?

Notes

1 Much of this chapter originally appeared in Tourish, D. and Tourish, N. (2010) Spirituality at work, and its implications for leadership and followership: A post-structuralist perspective, *Leadership*, 5, 207–24.
2 All quotations from Mitroff and Denton (1999) here are from pages 23–5 of their book.

5 The dark side of leadership and silence in the workplace[1]

Introduction

One of the most malignant and commonplace symptoms of leadership's dark side is the way in which dissent from powerful leaders is constrained and often eliminated (Kassing 2011). Leaders have the power to articulate a 'vision' and to ensure that others take action to have it implemented. Consequently, much of the literature on employee 'voice' focuses on those forms of expression most calculated to assist in the implementation of goals that, although determined by managers, are assumed to express a unitarist interest (Morrison 2011). Followers are generally expected to obey orders rather than ask questions. In this chapter, I look at how this process is enacted in most organizations. Leaders often do not mean to suppress dissent and most of them imagine that what I think of as 'critical upward communication' is much more prevalent than research suggests that it actually is. My purpose here is to explore the destructive implications of this for how leaders and followers interact – and to suggest what should be done about it.

The problem is that no individual or group makes the right decisions all the time. But here is the paradox. While critical feedback may be indispensable for good decisions (Nutt 2002), most of us react instinctively against it. We then penalise dissenters ('the awkward squad'), thus ensuring that we will hear less from them in the future. Faced with this, a leader's followers quickly realise that the best way to acquire influence and secure their position is to exaggerate how much they agree with the opinions of those in charge. Over time, more and more upward communication becomes flattering rather than critical in nature. This may be gratifying and, indeed, most of us are more vulnerable to the seductive power of flattery than we like to think. But it poses a serious problem. What happens when strategies wrought by an organization's leaders are seriously in error, as many of them inevitably are? When sufficient and timely critical feedback is curtailed or eliminated, such leaders deprive themselves of a crucial means of ascertaining how viable their strategies are. Flattery constitutes a perfumed trap for decision makers. It improves the odds of organizational failure, separates leaders even further from non-leaders, institutionalises dysfunctional power differences and ensures that leaders develop ever more elaborate plans and strategies with which their followers profoundly but silently disagree.

To be personal for a moment, my attention became focused on this problem in the course of conducting assessments of communication practices and climate in numerous companies with a number of colleagues (for example, Tourish and Hargie 1998; Tourish and Robson 2003, 2006). We were invariably struck by the following pattern. The leaders of the organizations concerned generally accepted positive findings uncritically. Indeed, they often claimed that they knew them already. However, they were frequently shocked by negative information. It appeared that the surveys we conducted were often their first opportunity to find out what their people really thought about such issues as the priorities of its senior leaders and their style of communication. Evidently, formal communication channels tend to filter out crucial bits of information, leaving those at the top more out of the loop than they had realised.

Some leaders took data indicating problems as an alarm call and immediately went to work on action plans designed to remedy them. But many bitterly contested the findings. They argued that no one had ever brought such issues to their attention before and that the data must therefore be flawed. Paradoxically, we rarely found that problems of morale or communication were any surprise to those further down the organizational hierarchy. Both middle managers and non-managerial employees had a keener awareness of problems concerning such issues as morale and communication climate. In contrast, top leaders were much more convinced that others could openly speak their minds to them than anybody else we encountered in their organizations. In exploring these issues, I look at the benefits of critical upward communication, the obstacles and practices that prevent it – and what might be done to ensure that we see rather more of this rare beast than we tend to do at present.

The benefits of dissent and upward feedback

Communication is consistently recognised as an integral part of participative processes and its role in these has been widely studied (Seibold and Shea 2001). But most corporate organizations have remained largely autocratic in form. In particular, the need for upward communication that is critical of organizational goals and leadership performance has been little recognised by management practitioners. Paradoxically, it has long been known that feedback is essential to effective performance in any task. The more channels of accurate and helpful feedback to which we have access, the better we are likely to perform. Most companies recognise the importance of obtaining feedback from key markets to assess how their products are being received. They pay particular attention to data indicating problems with product quality or an ebbing of customer confidence. However, in relation to staff communications, many appear to take the view that feedback is only required from the top down. Such a perspective is consistent with the bias in the literature on both strategic management and transformational leadership (see Chapter 2, in particular) which emphasises change as a top-down process.

A double standard is evident. Senior leaders set a strategic direction but do so after a robust process of discussion and debate. Typically, employees are denied similar opportunities – their role is to act as the enthusiastic cheerleaders for decisions already made. They are nevertheless expected to display an understanding, commitment and engagement to strategies similar to that of managers – but without the benefit of a comparable process of debate, dissent and dialogue. In turn, the 'lack of honest upward communication from lower levels (makes) it impossible for top leaders to learn about the limitations of their mental models and the capabilities needed to accomplish strategic objectives' (Beer *et al.* 2005: 453). No wonder that these authors identify the lack of adequate upward communication as one of the 'silent killers' of organizational strategy, contributing as it does to an inadequate alignment in goals and purpose between many of the key people who are essential for success.

Contrary to such a situation, the weight of research evidence suggests that, where they exist, upward feedback, upward communication and open-door policies deliver major organizational benefits (see Box 5.1). However, significant problems have also been reported with the delivery of feedback. In an everyday occurrence, 'people often have to make decisions about whether to speak up or remain silent' (Morrison and Milliken 2003: 1353). They experience a wide range of conflicting emotions in doing so, including fear, anger and anticipated regret (Edwards *et al.* 2009). It appears that fearful emotions when considering dissent are perfectly rational. Nemeth and Goncalo (2012: 29) point out that 'the usual reaction to a dissenter is negative. They are annoying, wrong and unpredictable'. Nor are these critical perceptions confined only to managers. These authors go on to point out that dissenters are also seen as 'not team players', a trait that a recent survey of American workers ranked more highly than whether they had knowledge, skills and ability.

It is little wonder that many people decide not to provide feedback in any form. Eighty-five per cent of respondents in one survey indicated that, on at least one

---

Box 5.1 The impact and benefits of upward feedback

- The promotion of shared leadership and an enhanced willingness by managers to act on employee suggestions.
- A greater tendency by employees to report positive changes in their managers' behaviour.
- Actual rather than perceived improvements in management behaviour following on feedback, beyond what could be attributed to regression to the mean.
- A reduced gap between managers' self-ratings and those of their subordinates.
- The creation of improved forums for obtaining information, garnering suggestions, defusing conflict and facilitating the expression of discontent.
- An enhancement of organizational learning.
- Greater creativity and innovation.
- Better decision making: currently, it is estimated that about half of decision in organizations fail, largely because of insufficient participation and a failure to carry out an unrestricted search for solutions.
- Enhanced participation.

occasion, 'they had felt unable to raise an issue or concern to their bosses even though they felt that the issue was important' (Milliken *et al.* 2003: 1459). More fundamentally, feedback tends to mainly flow from persons in authority to their subordinates, rather than the other way round (Luthans and Larsen 1986). Despite the fact that communication is a central theme in the leadership literature, it is conceived, 'almost exclusively in terms of managers doing the talking. With few exceptions, listening is not addressed in the literature' (Alvesson and Sveningsson 2003: 1439). Moreover, where upward feedback occurs it tends to be more positive than critical in nature (Baron 1996). We are therefore left with a paradox. On the one hand, it is increasingly recognised that organizations now suffer from information overload, sometimes termed *infoglut* or *data smog* (Edmunds and Morris 2000). On the other hand, motivating truthful upward communication, and so ensuring more of it, is widely recognised as a serious problem (Chow *et al.* 2000).

Such findings are consistent with the view that organizations are best viewed as information-processing entities (Putnam and Nicotera 2009). From this standpoint, research has long suggested that people are more likely to be committed to a course of action if they are involved in the decision-making process that gives rise to it. The articulation of the employee voice is therefore a vital, if often underrealised, ingredient of efforts at empowerment and involvement (Garner, 2012). People cannot be viewed as passive recipients for information. They are active and questioning agents in the process of decision making. To ignore this, as a display of leader power, is to violate one of the most fundamental traits of our being. Paradoxically, this is more likely to undermine the status of an organization's leaders than it is to strengthen their position. Research has shown that when managers openly solicit and accept negative feedback they gain a more accurate picture of their actual performance and are rated more favourably by employees. But when they look for positive feedback they acquire no extra insight into their true performance and are viewed less favourably by others (Ashford and Tsui 1991).

Despite this, many leaders deny the existence of problems and discourage critical feedback. To deny fault and avert the possibility of blame, they sometimes conceal negative organizational outcomes, suppress information, cover up negative financial data, deny failure and often 'launch propaganda campaigns that deny the existence of crises' (Starbuck *et al.* 1978: 118). Given that they also appear to receive little in the way of critical upward feedback from followers, it is pertinent to identify the obstacles that get in the way.

Barriers to upward feedback

Fear of feedback

Most of us have a tendency to prefer feedback that is supportive of our behaviour, in both our personal and professional lives. Negative feedback can be personally upsetting and may also impact adversely upon one's public image. Feedback to the effect that a cherished course of action is failing or lacks support is bound to be unwelcome. Seeking critical feedback may even be feared as denoting weakness. It is not surprising therefore that people at all organizational levels are often hesitant about seeking feedback on their performance or on the quality of their decisions; managers are no different (Morrison 2002).

Followers who are less compliant will be more likely to deliver upward and critical feedback. But many leaders value compliance more than dissent and will be more likely to fire dissidents than to applaud them. Examples abound. Notably, there is evidence that in the run-up to the banking crisis in 2008 senior executives from the Halifax Bank of Scotland in the UK actively discouraged feedback and took punitive action against their own risk advisers who suggested that problems loomed (Collinson 2012). The result was the biggest corporate bankruptcy in UK history.

Problems of ingratiation

One of the most potent explanations for difficulties with upward feedback can be found in ingratiation theory. This proposes that those with a lower level of status habitually exaggerate the extent to which they agree with the opinions and actions of higher status people as a means of acquiring influence with them (Jones 1990; Tourish 2007). Studies indicate that decreased power among subordinates is accompanied by an increased tendency on their part to employ some form of ingratiation and an increased use of 'politeness' strategies (Baxter 1984). The business consequences can be severe. A study of 451 CEOs looked at the impact on them of more intense and frequent flattery (such as offering exaggerated compliments) and opinion conformity (such as an expression of agreement even when people do not agree) (Park *et al.* 2011). The study found that flattery and opinion conformity were linked to CEOs having more favourable evaluations of their own strategic judgements and leadership skills than was warranted, being less likely to make strategic changes when firm performance suffered and being more prone to lead firms that suffered persistently poor performance.

Similarly, British Prime Minister Tony Blair became convinced that Iraq possessed weapons of mass destruction and took the country to war on the premise that they could be deployed against the UK within 45 minutes. Exhaustive searches after the invasion showed that Iraq had none of these weapons. It appears that any evidence inconsistent with his instincts was critiqued or ignored. However, a flawed dossier culled from an old PhD thesis was accepted, as the evidence it appeared to offer was consistent with the Prime Minister's instincts. In effect, different standards of proof were demanded for positions depending on how supportive or critical they were of the decisions preferred by those at the top. Officials involved in policy and strategy development learned to muffle their views. However, as Kets de Vries (2001: 94) has noted in a different situation: 'Effective organizational functioning demands that people have a healthy disrespect for their boss, feel free to express emotions and opinions openly, and are comfortable engaging in banter and give and take'.

Self-efficacy biases

Most of us imagine that we are better on various crucial dimensions of behaviour than we actually are. As an interesting illustration of this, a survey of more than 800 British drivers by the road safety charity Brake (2011) found that more than two-thirds of drivers worried about being killed when driving. However, only one per cent believed that their driving was worse than average; 98 per cent thought that they were safer than, or as safe, as the average driver. It is little wonder that researchers have generally found that managers view the defective and uncritical feedback they receive from subordinates as accurate, sincere and well meant – it is in line with their self-efficacy biases. Inclining to the view that the inaccurate and ingratiating feedback they receive daily is accurate, they grow even less inclined to seek mechanisms that institutionalise critical upward feedback into the decision-making process. Both peripheral and close range vision become tainted and lead to increasingly poor decisions.

Implicit voice constructs

Detert and Edmondson (2011) found that employees often confront the challenge of upward communication to powerful leaders with semiconscious or unconscious beliefs about what is appropriate – what they characterise as 'implicit voice theories'. These include the view that one needs solid data or solutions to speak up; that it is inappropriate to bypass a boss to go above them with feedback; that one should not embarrass a boss in public, even if only for self-preservation; that you need to be an expert to speak up (which you should not do anyway in front of clients or customers); and that violating any of these strictures will be career damaging. In their entirety, these beliefs form huge roadblocks to open communication between leaders and followers, creating what has been termed 'the hierarchical mum effect' (Biesel *et al.* 2012). And, as my next obstacle shows, leaders often blithely do a great deal to reinforce them.

Power differentials and the co-construction of leader and follower identities

The powerful positions held by leaders structure the decisions that employees make on upward communication in several ways. For example, fostering a culture of silence about issues that non-leaders deem to be important can promote cynicism, a rejection of 'official' voice structures and an embrace of alternative forums for ventilating views and emotions, such as trade unions (Donaghey *et al.* 2011). Secondly, power and status differentials fuel ingratiation practices – as we have seen, awareness of status differences discourages those with lower status from expressing their real feelings to those deemed to be 'above' them. It strengthens the implicit voices that tell people that upward communication is a very bad idea indeed. Clearly, some imbalances of power are unavoidable. But counterbalancing mechanisms are essential. Otherwise, the communication climate will deteriorate and those at the receiving end of whatever information is transmitted will find it harder, through the fog, to retain a clear perception of reality.

In addition, See *et al.* (2011) found that the more power leaders have the less inclined they are to take advice, largely because confidence in their own judgement becomes so elevated. This finding is not unique. Flyvbjerg's (1998) detailed study of town planning in Denmark demonstrated that, the greater the power held by individuals or groups, the less they feel the need to assemble evidence or consider means-end justifications. The overall effect, again, is to limit the scope for upward feedback to important decision makers – an absence that contributes significantly to poor decisions.

However, power flows in both directions. It has been suggested that, in most organizations, 'moments of contestation are precluded by power imbalances' (Deetz and McClellan 2009: 446). But to stress only this aspect of power relationships misses crucial processes of co-construction that also occur. For example, ingratiating behaviour by followers, in which they exaggerate how much they agree with the opinions of leaders, contributes to exaggerated self-belief, narcissism and the adoption of ultimately destructive forms of leader action (Tourish and Robson 2006). We can see here that the identity (and fates) of leaders as leaders and that of followers as followers is the result of a mutually constitutive interaction between the two. For followers, the decision not to offer critical feedback is a demonstration of agency manifest in silence, based on an often justified calculation of self-interest. But silence remains a form of communication and, hence, has a co-constructive impact on its recipients in formal positions of leadership. Organizational actors can never fully relinquish the power to manage meaning, since any attempt to abstain from communication itself becomes a form of communication. In Fairhurst's (2007) terms, drawing on a Foucauldian perspective, this would recast leaders as the subjects of influence attempts by others, rather than, for example, 'change masters' who make things happen to other people. In essence, this approach suggests that organizational phenomena, including leadership, are regarded 'as (re)created through interacting agents embedded in sociomaterial practices, whose actions are mediated by institutional, linguistic, and objectual artefacts' (Langley and Tsoukas 2010: 9). The overall effect, however, is to minimise vital forms of upward communication.

Groupthink

Problems with upward feedback have consistently been shown to be a key part of what is known as groupthink. This proposes that groups insulated from critical outside feedback develop illusions as to their own invulnerability, excessive self-confidence in the quality of their decision making and an exaggerated sense of their distinctiveness from other groups. Furthermore, they deny or distort facts, offer rationalisations for their activities, use myth and humour to exaggerate their sense of worth and attribute the failure of their decisions to external factors rather than the quality of their own decision making. It follows that such groups will also disparage criticism from outside their own ranks, since it is more likely to conflict with the group's ideal self-image, departs from its well-entrenched norms and comes from sources outside the high status few that belong to the inner circle of key players (Janis 1972; Mayo Wilson *et al.* 2012). Ironically, while 'companies of all sizes increasingly recognise that ideas are their most precious commodity and employees who produce them are sought after resources' (Andriopoulos 2003: 375) the evidence suggests that the welcoming embrace accorded new ideas stops short of those that are critical of organizational orthodoxy. Moreover, those attempting to offer feedback are more likely to respond to such a reaction by minimising much needed future critical feedback. In turn, this is likely to reinforce the conviction of those at the top that, rogue indicators aside, things are much better than they are and additional outside input is not required.

These pressures are exacerbated when a group puts itself under time pressure to reach decisions quickly – a familiar phenomenon in the organizational world. Psychological experiments have found that, when they are under relatively little time pressure, groups are likely to evaluate deviant opinions positively. But, once pressure is applied to decide something quickly, precisely the same opinions are downgraded and evaluated negatively. The person expressing them is also more likely to be disliked (Kruglanski and Webster 1991). Under such conditions, we rapidly learn to stay quiet, while groupthink becomes even more intense.

Narcissism and group identity

Critical upward feedback is often systematically distorted, constrained and eliminated. When this occurs, and consistent with the data on groupthink, a narcissistic group identity may result, characterised by such ego-defence mechanisms as 'denial, rationalisation, attributional egotism, sense of entitlement and ego aggrandisement' (Brown 1997: 643). People have a need to nurture a positive sense of self and they embrace ego-defensive behaviour to maintain self-esteem. Eliminating or disparaging critical feedback is one obvious means of accomplishing this.

An example may be in order. My colleague, Paul Robson, and I worked with one senior management team (SMT) in the health sector who insisted that they wanted to empower their staff to take decisions and free them to transmit upward feedback (see Tourish and Robson 2003, for a full case study). They complained, however, that people resisted their efforts to accomplish these goals and that rather than take decision-making power into their hands they continued to 'delegate it upwards'. Narcissism implies a tendency to blame others for whatever problems are admitted, rather than owning one's own contribution to their creation – what could be described as a process of 'blame realignment'. In line with this, the SMT explained all communication problems as the responsibility of the next tier of general managers immediately below themselves. They were held to be uniformly incompetent and failing in all aspects of their job. Unfortunately, close scrutiny of the SMT's behaviour, as opposed to its avowed intentions, found that these same managers had themselves appointed this management layer in the previous 18 months; that they had then eliminated two dissenters from the ranks of the SMT and thus had acquired a reputation for penalising dissent; that even their direct reports were afraid to openly express critical views; and that transparent mechanisms to facilitate upward communication were absent.

In general, the danger is that managers deprived of sufficient critical feedback can develop a mindset similar to that found among rock stars who surround themselves with a sycophantic entourage. A narcissistic self-image results, in which all success is credited to the wisdom of a select few and all problems are blamed on the frailties of others. Such managers eventually find themselves deceived by their own publicity. The solution requires experimentation with power sharing and a downsizing of entourages. I use the word 'experimentation' deliberately, since it is clear that letting go means someone else taking many decisions for which managers may still be held responsible. Given that all humans are fallible, the results may be occasionally unedifying. But most organizations have erred in precisely the opposite direction. They have a long way to go before there is a realistic possibility of over-empowered employees running amok in the boardroom.

How leaders exaggerate the frequency of critical feedback

Irrational belief systems ensure that leaders often have an imbalanced view of communication between themselves and their followers, an exaggerated impression of how much upward feedback they receive and an insufficient awareness of the need for more robust systems to facilitate communications between themselves and others. These unfounded assumptions about the nature of the physical and social world are often adopted because they confer certainty in an uncertain or ambiguous world (Hutson 2012). In particular, it appears that unusual events stand out in our minds and, in the process of retelling, acquire an added vividness. Even though the event was actually atypical, perversely, those involved in the discourse gradually become convinced that what they are describing is more typical of the category than is actually the case. This is a good illustration of what has been termed the availability error – information that is more readily available to us (such as an unusual or recent event) influences our perceptions much more than information that is harder to access (Kahneman 2011). Doctors, for example, may make a diagnosis because a patient's case looks very much like other similar ones that have been seen recently and the diagnosis comes easily to mind (Connor 2011). The effect, however, is that implausible stories become widely circulated, more available to our minds and hence more deeply believed.

Thus, on the relatively rare occasions when leaders, particularly those in senior positions, do receive critical upward feedback, they experience it as a striking and, hence, memorable event. They are likely to pay it special attention – it remains vividly in their memory and so convinces them that it is more typical an event than it actually is. Thus, one research project found that positive upward feedback is a more common occurrence than negative upward feedback (Baron 1996). However, this study also showed that the managers concerned perceived many more instances of negative feedback than their subordinates but both managers and subordinates perceived the same frequency of positive feedback. In essence, each instance of negative feedback acquired a heightened sense of

vividness for its recipient. Managers then assumed that their heightened awareness of the event rendered it more typical of the feedback category than was the
case. Hence, they are less likely to appreciate the need for more of it.

Moreover, how leaders respond to critical feedback largely determines how much
of it they will receive in the future. For most of us, critical feedback is less accepted
and is perceived as less accurate than positive feedback. People are especially sensitive to negative input – what has been termed the automatic vigilance effect (Pratto
and John 1991). In general, it generates an angry response. (Try telling your friends
that their new dress, suit or hairstyle is a disastrous mistake and then calculate the
ratio of welcoming and outraged responses you receive!) For example, Burris (2012)
explored different management reactions to employees speaking up in a 'challenging' or 'supportive' manner. As might be expected, they responded well to the latter.
But those employees perceived as offering a challenging voice were viewed as 'poor
performers', while their ideas were also less likely to be endorsed. In the work
context, intentionally or otherwise, it is clear that the generally less-than-enthusiastic
response of managers to critical feedback discourages it. When this happens, the
opportunity to grapple with problems recedes ever further into the mist.

I offer an example here from the health sector SMT discussed earlier. During
feedback to the team, some mildly critical data were reported which indicated
lower-than-ideal levels of staff trust in information received from senior managers.
A number of positive issues were also highlighted, including trusting relationships between lower level managers and their direct immediate subordinates. The
SMT responded in two markedly different ways. Firstly, they enthusiastically
accepted the data indicating strengths in the communication climate but they
rejected outright any feedback that implied weaknesses in their performance,
although it was derived from the same methods. Moreover, they invited a trained
statistician to interrogate the data, with a view to exposing its shortcomings.
In meetings on the issue, their efforts were completely devoted to rejecting critical
data, rather than developing an action plan to address the problems that it illuminated. In short, the data were simultaneously regarded as prescient but fatally
flawed. The process suggests that top leaders have a tendency to overcritique
negative feedback, while instantly agreeing with positive feedback.

Two results are likely to flow from this. Firstly, most people at the receiving
end of negative responses to their input will minimise further efforts at conveying
what they really feel (Richardson and Taylor 2012). The organizational climate
is perceived as punitive. In essence, this suggests that senior leaders engage too
readily in a process of unconscious feedback distortion. For example, it has been
found that some subordinates who had experienced extremely negative emotional
encounters with their supervisors edited future communications to make them
more formal, superficial, task-oriented and devoid of personal messages (for
example, self-disclosures) (Waldron and Krone 1991). Thus, motivating truthful
upward communication is widely recognised as a serious problem.

Secondly, when senior managers put themselves in the position of encouraging
only the feedback that they like and penalising that which they dislike, they
acquire an imbalanced view of the climate in their own companies. I suspect that

this dynamic underlies a problem is often encountered – the tendency for senior managers to be the only ones surprised by data offering a critical diagnosis of the climate in their companies. The challenge, clearly, is to adopt an equally rigorous approach to both positive and negative feedback.

Characteristics of top teams and communication networks

As organizations grow larger, so do distances between team members, between teams and between teams and senior leaders. This creates an obvious problem with the emergence of rich communication networks. The 'law of N-squared' proposes that, with more and more people in a given organization, the number of potential links in a network organization increases geometrically and can rapidly exceed everyone's capacity for communicative action (Krackhardt 1994). The law of propinquity also recognises that the probability of two people communicating is inversely proportional to the distance between them. The number of communication options, as well as obligations, combined with such prosaic matters as physical distance renders contact between senior leaders and those further down the hierarchy increasingly elusive. Although initiatives can be taken to compensate for these difficulties, it is unlikely that much will happen if senior leaders themselves do not recognise the absence of upward communication as a problem.

Such problems are compounded by autocratic models of the leadership process. Research has long shown that new group members or those with low status initially acquire influence within a group by overconforming to its emergent norms; that is, so as not to offend key players, they minimise the amount of critical feedback that they are prepared to offer. If they are perceived not to be 'fitting in', they are penalised, usually through the withdrawal of valued social rewards (Packer 2011). I recently worked in one company that exemplified the resultant mindset. Employees reported the existence of an unofficial culture which revolved around the motion that people were expected to *'fit in, or f*** off.'*

Overconformity means that followers comply with destructive forms of action, to ingratiate themselves with their leaders. In fact, it puts leaders at risk. The leader takes the absence of overt dissent as assent and, moreover, views it as supplementary evidence – as consensual validation – that the given course of action is correct. They march into battle, armoured by their greater status, authority and power. This fails to recognise that the structure which gives them these advantages also deprives them of critical reaction from followers, thus leaving the leader fatally out of touch with reality and bereft of sufficient followers on the battlefield. Thus, the most successful leaders are liable to be those with the least compliant followers, 'for when leaders err – and they always do – the leader with compliant followers will fail' (Grint 2000: 420).

The consequences of such defects are clear. They include the elimination of dissent, an insufficient flow of critical upward communication, the accumulation of power at the centre, a failure to sufficiently consider alternative sources of action and a growing belief on the leader's part that s/he is indispensable for the organization's success.

Ten commandments for improving upward communication

There is no 'magic bullet' on this issue and no substitute for a patient and persistent approach. Moreover, whatever we do, some status and power differentials are bound to remain. However, their negative impact can at least be minimised. With those caveats, the following 'ten commandments' may form a modest starting point. They are discussed in detail below and – having inevitably less authority than a Biblical edict – are committed to paper rather than stone as Box 5.2.

Box 5.2 Improving critical upward communication:
the ten commandments

1 **Experiment with both upward and 360-degree appraisal.**
Can lead to further self-development but requires patience, determination and a supportive atmosphere.
2 **Leaders should familiarise themselves with the basics of ingratiation theory.**
Appreciate that no one is impervious to flattery – including and especially you!
3 **Positive feedback should be subject to the same or greater scrutiny than negative feedback.**
Seek a balance between positive and negative feedback. Instinctively mistrust positive feedback and concentrate on problems and criticisms, their validity and solution.
4 **Managers should seek out opportunities for regular formal and informal contact with staff at all levels.**
Seek honest, two-way communication by establishing informal contact with staff at subordinate levels of your organization.
5 **Promote systems for greater participation in decision making.**
A suggestion scheme should be first base – something more systematic can follow.
6 **Create 'red flag' mechanisms for the upward transmission of information that cannot be ignored.**
There must be some mechanism to ensure that important or urgent problems are flagged up to the highest level. Whistle blowing is evidence of the complete failure of upward communication. But unless you make functioning upward communication channels available, it is likely to occur – with disastrous public relations consequences.
7 **Existing communication processes should be reviewed to ensure that they include requirements to produce critical feedback.**
Communication systems should allow information to travel in both directions and should enable responsive action. They should be constantly reviewed, to ensure critical as well as positive feedback reaches the top.
8 **Train people to be open, receptive and responsive to dissent.**
Give them the vital communication tools, encourage them to do the job and reward them when they do.

9 **Power and status differentials should be eliminated or, where that is impossible, at least reduced.**
Open upward communication cannot coexist with penal appraisal systems and will be discouraged by a culture in which status differentials are overtly displayed.

10 **The CEO, in particular, needs to openly model a different approach to the receipt of critical communication and ensure that senior colleagues emulate this openness.**
The CEO must 'walk the talk' and personify what s/he wishes to foster.

1 Experiment with both upward and 360-degree appraisal

Such practices are no longer regarded as revolutionary and are commonly employed in many leading corporations, including AT&T, the Bank of America, Caterpillar, GTE and General Electric. They are a powerful means of institutionalising useful feedback. Moreover, there is growing evidence to suggest that they genuinely stimulate more focused self-development activities (Mabey 2001). It is, of course, vital that the underlying organizational culture is genuinely supportive and that the feedback obtained is used to shape changes in behaviour. Otherwise, both sides grow discouraged and give up on their relationship. Disappointment is more likely to occur when such efforts are freighted with over-optimistic expectations and the need to transform the wider organizational culture is not recognised. But, implemented with a realistic grasp of what can be achieved and a determination to tackle whatever obstacles arise, both upward and 360-degree appraisal can make a major contribution to the creation of a more open and honest communication climate.

2 Leaders should familiarise themselves with the basics of ingratiation theory

I have found that most top teams readily accept the notion of ingratiation. During workshops, many have swapped amusing anecdotes that vividly describe the process in action. But, in line with the great deal that is now known of self-efficacy biases, they then mostly go on to assume that they themselves are immune to its effects. In reality, they almost never are. The more senior a leader is in any organization, the more they should recognise that they will be on the receiving end of too much feedback that is positive and too little that is critical, whatever their intentions. Moreover, they are just as susceptible to the effects of ingratiating behaviours as anyone else. While increased awareness never solves a problem by itself, it is an essential first step. Leaders at all levels need to become more aware of ingratiation dynamics, of their own susceptibility to their effects and of the most effective responses to adopt in dealing with it. Such awareness forms part of the ABC of emotional literacy. Leaders without it risk building catastrophically imbalanced relationships with their people.

3   *Positive feedback should be subject to the same or greater scrutiny than negative feedback*

Without such scrutiny, positive feedback will come to predominate; leaders will give it undue attention and they will then go on to develop a dangerously rose-tinted view of the climate within their own organizations. In turn, this means that key problems remain off the agenda and will therefore grow worse. Leaders should adopt a thoroughly questioning attitude to all feedback from those with a lower status and should treat feedback that is unremittingly positive in tone with considerable scepticism. Perhaps Jonathan Swift, author of *Gulliver's Travels*, offered the most instructive advice on how to react: 'The only benefit of flattery is that by hearing what we are not, we may be instructed what we ought to be'. Management meetings should combat the tendency to bask in positive feedback and, instead, should focus on a regular agenda of questions such as:

- What problems have come to our attention recently?
- What criticisms have we received about the decisions we are taking?
- Are the criticisms valid, partially or completely? What should we change in response to them?
- How can we get more critical feedback into our decision-making processes?

As in all things, balance is critical. A focus only on critical feedback would be as detrimental as its opposite, even though, in the present climate, there is little danger of this occurring. As Kassing (2011: 178) points out, many safeguards are now in place to protect whistleblowers. This can occasionally get out of hand, with 'some employees ... bringing frivolous legal cases and suing their employers on a number of grounds. Organizations frequently end up settling regardless of a claim's merit, because it is the quickest and most efficient way to appease dissenters'. Kassing provides the example of a lecturer at a UK university, a serial litigant, who filed complaints against three universities in 2002, nine in 2001 and seven in the year 2000.

I am not advocating this kind of nonsense. Rather, my suggestion is that both positive and critical feedback should be probed to ascertain its accuracy. In particular, the motivation of the person or persons engaged in flattery should be considered. Flattery is best thought of as a non-monetary bribe. It preys on similar weaknesses. Leaders should therefore ask themselves: What does this person have to gain by flattering me? And also: What they have to lose by disagreeing with me?

4   *Managers should seek out opportunities for regular formal and informal contact with staff at all levels*

This should replace reliance on official reports, written communiqués or communication mediated through various management layers. Informal interaction is more likely to facilitate honest two-way communication, to provide managers with a more accurate impression of life and opinions at all levels of their organization and to open up new opportunities for both managers and staff to influence each other. 'Back to the floor' initiatives, in which senior leaders work alongside front line staff, are increasingly recognised as a useful means of achieving this. A key focus during such contact should be the search for critical feedback. By contrast, royal tours and flying visits yield nothing in the way of useful feedback. There are many other means by which managers can put more distance between themselves and head office and less distance between themselves and non-managerial employees. As a rule of thumb, the more reliant a manager is on official channels of communication, the more likely it is that s/he will be out of touch with the mood of his or her people.

5 Promote systems for greater participation in decision making

Participation involves the creation of structures that empower people and which enable them to collaborate in activities that go beyond the minimum coordination efforts characteristic of much work practice (Wilkinson *et al.* 2010). In general, people should be encouraged to take more decisions on their own. Open, information-based tactics are critical for success. Nevertheless, on this crucial issue, many communication efforts remain rudimentary. In working with senior managers, I have frequently been astonished by how many admit that their organizations do not have even a formal suggestion scheme in place. Its benefits have been documented over several decades yet one survey of members of the Institute of Management in the UK found that no more than 42 per cent of them made significant use of what is an elementary practice (O'Creevy 2001). As with all systems developed to address this issue, suggestion schemes have their limitations. In my experience, the biggest predictors of failure are:

- a reluctance on the part of managers to take them seriously;
- a tendency, in the face of initial setbacks or a lacklustre employee response, to give up rather than to persevere;
- an expectation of revolutionary new employee initiatives to start flowing immediately;
- a slowness to respond to whatever ideas employees do produce, combined with a criticism that more has not been forthcoming;
- the absence of even minimal rewards; as an example, a large aerospace company with which I worked had a longstanding and modestly successful suggestion scheme. Suggestions implemented attracted a small cash reward. Senior managers decided to eliminate the reward, since 'it is employees' job to provide suggestions, and they are paid for it already'. Employees felt that their input was no longer appreciated and the flow of suggestions dried up. Managers, meanwhile, concluded that employees were not interested in 'the bigger picture'.

A more systematic, creative and persistent focus on this issue is clearly required. It is important that employees are fully involved in such efforts, rather than simply being presented with senior management's vision of the systems that it thinks are required to produce it. Lessons can be drawn from General Electric's famous 'Work Out' programme, which brought together people from various cross sections of its business units to tackle bureaucracy and speed up decision making (Mintzberg 2011). The programme was a pivotal element in the company's transformation. Its techniques could usefully be adapted to address the feedback issues identified in this article.

6 Create 'red flag' mechanisms for the upward transmission of information that cannot be ignored

Organizations rarely fail because they have inadequate information but they will fail if vital information either does not reach the top or is ignored when it gets there. Readers may recall that, in 2008, the CEOs of Ford, General Motors and Chrysler flew to a meeting of the House Financial Services Committee in Washington to request bail-out money in view of their parlous financial positions. But all three hired private jets to do so. One Democratic Representative, Gary Ackerman, observed tartly that 'There is a delicious irony in seeing private luxury jets flying into Washington, DC, and people coming off of them with tin cups in their hand, saying that they're going to be trimming down and streamlining their businesses' (Levs 2008). It is inconceivable that nobody within these organizations anticipated this kind of reaction. But either they said nothing or their feedback was ignored by those at the top when it reached them. The result was a major public relations disaster for these companies, precisely when goodwill was required more than ever. Red flag mechanisms are needed to ensure that important information is transmitted and acted upon rather than ignored. These do not have to be complex.

NASA offers one example of a communication system that achieved its aim of facilitating clear upward communication and thus ensured that important information reached the ears or desks it needed to reach. Tompkins (2005) interviewed engineers at Marshall Space Flight Centre in the 1960s, when Werner von Braun was its director. Repeatedly, people told him that the communication device that worked best was 'The Monday notes'. This referred to a practice that had sprung up when von Braun had asked 24 key managers across several units to send him a one-page memo every Monday morning, in which they described the preceding week's progress and problems. Von Braun read their comments, initialled them and added his own questions, suggestions and praise. The collected notes were then arranged in the order of the authors' names and returned as a package to all contributors. Closer investigation showed that the key managers involved had compiled their own Monday notes by asking their direct reports for a 'Friday report' about their activities. Some of them even organized meetings to gather the required information. Many of them also circulated von Braun's eventual report back down the line. In short, a simple request had triggered a robust mechanism for the transmission of information and ensured that whatever was contained in the Monday notes was acted upon rather than ignored. Organizations need to develop similar mechanisms, appropriate for their own circumstances, and pursue their implementation rigorously.

In a cautionary coda, subsequent research into NASA has suggested that many of its later problems, including the catastrophic Challenger and Colombia explosions, partly resulted from systems such as the Monday notes falling into disuse (Roberto 2005). A culture appears to have developed in which senior managers were dismissive of critical feedback and flatly discouraged it. They then developed overoptimistic views of what could be achieved and ignored problems that at least some employees attempted to bring to their attention. This heightened levels of risk, with disastrous consequences, most obviously for those who died but also for NASA's reputation.

7 Existing communication processes should be reviewed to ensure that they include requirements to produce critical feedback

With few exceptions, team briefings emphasise the transmission of information from the top to the bottom. This is akin to installing an elevator capable of travelling only in one direction – downwards. Team briefings should also include a specific requirement that problems and criticisms be reported up. Again, balance is vital. As already noted, exclusively critical feedback may end up as damaging as exclusively positive feedback and create a fearful climate dominated by the expectation of imminent catastrophe. No one can innovate, or work with even minimal effectiveness, if they confidently expect the imminent arrival of the Four Horsemen of the Apocalypse. Nevertheless, with that proviso in mind, most organizations are a long way from having to worry about the risk of too much critical feedback disturbing the tranquillity of those in top positions.

Targets should be set for critical feedback and closely monitored. A culture change is required. In particular, managers who tell their people 'Don't bring me problems, bring me solutions' need to reengineer their vocabulary – they are generating blackouts rather than illumination.

8 Train people to be open, receptive and responsive to dissent

When leaders behave in such a manner they are signalling receptiveness to entire workgroups. However, training in the appropriate skills is often lacking. As with many other vital communication skills, it is frequently just assumed that everyone has access to the right toolkit. This optimistic assumption is unwarranted. Even if people have some notion of which tools are available to them, training is required so that they select the right one for each task. Otherwise, those trained only in how to use a hammer may instinctively reach out for it, even when a screwdriver is more appropriate for the job in hand. The lack of appropriate communication skills on the part of top leaders is one of the main reasons for the disconnect so frequently noted between the inspiring rhetoric of strategic visions and the mundane operational reality.

9 Power and status differentials should be eliminated or, where that is impossible, at least reduced

Status differentials can be reduced by blitzing some of the most visible symbols of privilege, such as reserved parking, executive dining rooms and percentage salary increases far in excess of those obtained by other employees. A growing body of research suggests that excessive and highly visible signs of executive privilege undermine organizational cohesion and effectiveness. In particular, it promotes an 'us versus them' mentality rather than one of 'us against the competition' (Pfeffer and Sutton 2006). The risks with addressing this question are few but the potential gains are immense.

10 The CEO, in particular, needs to openly model a different approach to the receipt of critical communication and ensure that senior colleagues emulate this openness

As Mahatma Ghandi once asserted, 'You must become the change that you want to see in the world' and many studies have shown that, when people are asked to gauge the efficacy of communication in general and the role of senior managers in particular, they personalise the issue into the role of the CEO. Organizations that take communication seriously have leaders who take communication seriously. Those that are defensive, uncertain, closed to feedback and dismissive of contrary opinions may indeed get their way – in the short term. At the very least, they will be gratified by effusive public statements of compliance. But coerced compliance is usually combined with private defiance. Ultimately, it produces a fractious relationship between senior managers and their staff and organizations where managers and employees are at war with each other, rather than with the competition, cannot conquer new markets. Without a clear lead at the level of an organization's top leaders, particularly the CEO, it is unlikely that progress on the issues discussed in this chapter will be made.

Conclusions

The issues raised in this chapter are fundamental to any discussion of the perils inherent to leader power. No one individual or any one group has a mastery of all the problems in any organization. The world is too complex. Information from many sources is needed if effective decisions are to be made (Morrison and Rothman 2009). Yet, given the constraints on the feedback they receive, many managers in fact have a poor grasp of their organization's problems. Winston Churchill, reflecting on lessons from the Battle of the Somme in World War One, put it well:

> The temptation to tell a Chief in a great position the things he most likes to hear is one of the commonest explanations of mistaken policy. Thus the outlook of the leader on whose decision fateful events depend is usually far more sanguine than the brutal facts admit.

> (Churchill 1931: 666)

It is self-evident that this is not good for organizations. It is also increasingly clear that it is not good for leaders either. Park *et al.* (2011) found compelling evidence that poor performance, resulting from the behaviour of CEOs who have internalised the overly positive feedback delivered by their followers, increases the likelihood of them being fired. The dynamics discussed in this chapter are widespread but it seems that few people really gain from them, other than in developing a gargantuan sense of personal power that is ultimately self-destructive.

In the diverse and pluralistic organizations of today, it is never possible to reach full agreement on important strategic issues. The only organizational context everyone always agrees with everyone else on all vital issues is a cemetery. Inevitable debates and disagreements on strategy are best brought into the open, where they can be engaged by leaders, rather than repressed, denied or ignored. The dialogic organization will always be involved in discussion about strategic direction, including after decisions have been reached. Critical feedback, despite its frustrations, consistently offers fresh opportunities for evaluation. Such discussions sometimes expose differences that may appear insoluble. But the point is that such disagreements exist anyway. There seems little point in attempting to prohibit something that will proceed with or without the encouragement of managers. Rather, decision making and implementation will be improved if the inevitable debates that occur are brought into the open rather than concealed from the view of senior leaders.

The prize that lies within our grasp is better organizations, better leaders and more fulfilled followers.

Points for discussion

1. Consider the dynamics of ingratiation between leaders and followers. When did you last offer ingratiating feedback to someone who had more power than you?
2. When did you last receive ingratiating feedback from someone? How difficult is it to recognise this when it occurs?
3. How do leaders suppress critical upward communication in organizations?
4. Apart from the suggestions in this chapter, what else do you think organizations could do to ensure that more honest upward communication takes place?

Note

1 Many of these ideas were originally published as Tourish, D. and Robson, P. (2006) Sensemaking and the distortion of critical upward communication in organizations. *Journal of Management Studies,* 43: 711–30; and also in Tourish, D. (2005) Critical upward communication: ten commandments for improving strategy and decision making. *Long Range Planning,* 38: 485–503.

6 The folly and the dangers of leadership education in business schools[1]

Introduction

As we have seen in Chapter 2, much of the literature on leadership in the popular, practitioner and business press and in academic journals stresses the notion of leaders as heroes and charismatic visionaries. Leaders are routinely depicted as 'change masters' (Kanter 1985), heroes and saviours (see Hatch *et al.* 2005), and miracle workers (see Slater, 1999, for a hagiography of Jack Welch's leadership of General Electric). Rather than 'the Great Recession' calling such notions into question, it largely continues to be assumed that 'better' or more refined models of leadership are needed to enable renewed growth and prosperity (Kellerman 2012). Common to all of these depictions of leaders is the notion that leadership is transformational. Leaders exist to 'change things'. They render organizations as something different. They help organizations to transform for the better – to find heretofore unknown meaning, to articulate and advance common goals and effect (allegedly) outstanding performance. Thus, good leadership is depicted as the font of all good things that happen in organizations and society and bad leadership is the font of all the bad things that happen.

Business schools have not been immune to these ideas. In their research and teaching, they have increasingly emphasised the role of heroic individuals and sought to recruit people into their MBA programmes with the promise that they will not only study transformational leaders but become ones themselves. However, this has occurred in a context where agency theories – emphasising self-interest – have also had a powerful impact on the wider business school curriculum. These theories also have leadership implications, some of them in conflict with the nostrums of transformational leadership theory. It is these fundamental dynamics and contradictions that this chapter addresses. My purpose is to look at how leading business schools teach leadership, slavishly worship the claimed accomplishments of top business leaders such as Jack Welch, and also promote agency theories that stress the selfishness of people and the consequent need for regimes of intense control.

In that spirit, this chapter argues that the dominant approach to the teaching of leadership in business schools contributes to leader narcissism, legitimises the overconcentration of power in leader hands and promotes rigid control mechanisms without which the dark side of leadership would be much weakened. I look at the promises made to students on major business school websites and consider the implications for the content of their curriculum. I also examine how they often bring in outside 'superstar' CEO leaders, presenting their 'accomplishments' in a wholly uncritical light. Presentations by Jack Welch at Sloan School of Management, Massachusetts Institute of Technology (MIT) and Stanford University in 2005 are used as a case study. We cannot separate the practice of leadership from how it is taught. I therefore also offer some suggestions intended to transform how business schools approach this all-too-critical issue.

Impact of leadership theory on practice

The idea that theories can influence human behaviour is well documented. For example, it has been found that, after studying economics, however briefly, students become greedier. They then develop positive views of their own greedy behaviour (Wang *et al.* 2011). Ghoshal (2005) argued that the teaching of 'bad' theories on management – such as, in his view, transaction cost economics – also has a damaging macro impact and claimed that 'Business schools do not need to do a great deal more to help prevent future Enrons: they need only to stop doing a lot they currently do' (Ghoshal 2005: 75).

Developing this critique, I suggest that theories which privilege the agency of those who hold formal, hierarchically based leadership positions above that of other organizational actors will likely have an intuitive appeal for many business students. In turn, the theory and the practice can become mutually constitutive. The theory finds traction because it legitimises dominant power relations, which is appealing to those who either hold power or covet it and those relations in turn further legitimise and promote a theory which appears to simply describe 'what is' and that therefore (surely?) must lie beyond interrogation. Mautner (2010) explores this process well, in terms of the intrusion of the language of the marketplace into more and more spheres of life. She argues that the increased dominance of market terminology in universities, public services, religion and even in terms of what is sometimes described as 'your own personal brand' seeks to achieve a form of 'discursive closure,' in which alternatives are not only not discussed, but in an Orwellian sense become unthinkable. The dominant focus on leadership in business schools can be viewed in the same light, rendering unimaginable the notion of communities of people jointly participating in decision making (and any leadership theory which describes it). Rather, leader power is naturalised in a manner that is appealing to those holding leadership positions but which is devoid of emancipatory potential and which may, by legitimising the concentration of power in élite hands, contribute to ongoing crisis in society.

Leadership teaching in business schools

Business schools and MBA curricula have been subject to sustained criticism from some prominent figures in the business school academy (see, for example,

Pfeffer and Fong 2002; Mintzberg 2004; Gosling and Mintzberg 2006). A slew of critical books has appeared, collectively challenging the curriculum content, overall purpose and the underpinning philosophies promulgated in business schools (for example, Amann *et al.* 2011; Locke and Spender 2011; Durand and Dameron 2011). It has been suggested that business schools need to do much more to focus students' attention less on 'profit mongering' and more on such issues as social justice (Toubiana 2012). This is consistent with the view that public interest schools of management should be constructed that put a wider interest than that of shareholder value at the core of their missions and pedagogy (Ferlie *et al.* 2010). Within this debate, there has been considerable critical discussion of the effectiveness of leadership teaching in business schools (Barker 1997; Morrison *et al.* 2003; Hay and Hodgkinson 2006; Burrell 2006). MBA programmes have been flayed for 'failing to impart useful skills, failing to prepare leaders, failing to instil norms of ethical behaviour – and even failing to lead graduates to good corporate jobs' (Bennis and O'Toole 2005: 96).

My core argument is that much of the leadership teaching takes leader power for granted and is likely to encourage hubris and narcissism on the part of students. The *Harvard Business Review* (HBR), required reading in most MBA programmes, illustrates this very well. HBR regularly runs flattering interviews with top leaders. One such interview in 1998 with Michael Dell of Dell Computers (Magretta 1998) commences with the question: 'How do you create a $12 billion company in just 13 years?'. The implication is that this achievement was accomplished single-handedly by the interviewee. Another article went so far as to announce in its title: 'The CEO is the company' (Webber 1987). Partly influenced by such approaches, as one study into CEO succession has noted, 'even strong insider candidates are now routinely dismissed as unequal to the role of corporate saviour ... a figure now seen as the key to reviving troubled companies' (Khurana 2002: 51). Thus, both the theory and practice of leadership has come to fixate on the key role of heroic individuals, blessed with exceptional powers and enacting roles in which they unidirectionally change the behaviours, attitudes and emotions of others (Haigh 2003), with the more prominent among them seemingly attaining the stature of a 'legend'.

It is presumed that leadership resides in individuals rather than social systems; that leadership is hierarchically based and linked to office; that leadership occurs when leaders do things to followers; that leadership makes a crucial difference to organizational performance; and, that leaders differ from other people (Simkins 2005). Such attitudes are fostered by a tendency to praise, rather than analyse, leadership practice. As one review of leadership research concluded:

> most leadership studies have explored only the positive relationships and outcomes of leader actions, ignoring those behaviours that may be harmful to subordinates and organizations ... there has been little investigation of leader errors and how those errors impact organizational success or failure.
>
> (Hunter *et al.* 2007: 438)

Moreover, a study of international MBA students in the UK concluded that leadership in UK programmes is taught with a US-based corpus, the universality of which is simply assumed (Mellahi 2000).

Thus, the predominant approach to leadership education is unitarist and uncritical. Generally, leadership is conceptualised as a unidirectional process, in which powerful actors (leaders) exercise control and influence over relatively passive subjects (followers). The 'right' of leaders to impose their wishes on subordinates is rarely questioned. There seems to be tacit acceptance that leaders have the power to reframe private belief systems of employees and render their behaviour consistent with the needs of the corporation, always and everywhere. This is particularly evident in such notions as spirituality leadership theory, discussed in Chapter 4. A more critical focus on how power is acquired by leaders and enacted by them in organizational relationships would be a useful antidote to such potentially totalitarian developments. In particular, a critical focus would stress how noise, deviance and resistance also constitute organizations.

In addition to its unitarist assumptions, the implicit model that is routinely presented to students assumes that the practice of leadership is an extraordinary phenomenon, which can only be mastered by a 'new breed of change agents' (Morrison 2003: 4). Typically, there is little mention of greed, shame, duplicity, stupidity, hubris, soaring CEO salaries, power and lack of democracy/employee involvement: that is, there is no mention of most of the emotional and political issues that frequently preoccupy 'real' people in 'real' organizations. In effect, the implied mental model of leadership is one-dimensional and blinkered.

Thus, much leadership teaching presumes a top-down hierarchy, sets some level of organizational performance (such as an earnings per share target) as a goal to be achieved and 'focuses on bureaucratic efficiencies ... center[s] on self-interest ... is founded in materialism ... is male (or male characteristic) dominated ... uses utilitarian ethics ... and ... uses quantitative methods to solve rational/technocratic problems' (Rost and Barker 2000: 4). Business schools also have made increasing use of the case study method, originally derived from Harvard Business School. However, as Starkey and Tiratsoo (2007) have pointed out, the primary sources for material to be included in these studies is usually drawn from the managers of the organizations being studied. Their voice is privileged above all others. Starkey and Tiratsoo's analysis of award-winning case studies over a nine-year period found that out of 183 quotations attributable to individuals, 107 were drawn from senior managers. Followers are rendered largely mute, their perspectives subordinated to those of their leaders.

It is worth dwelling a little on the approach adopted by Harvard Business School, widely ranked as the leading business school in the world. Delves Broughton's (2010) account of his two years as an MBA student there documents in fine detail how students are persistently assured of their élite status as future business leaders who will transform the world. Many of them arrive already primed with this conviction. The Harvard Business School approach seems likely to elevate their self-belief to even greater heights and so to penalise humility – arguably, a key requirement for more participatory and effective styles of decision making.

Nor is this emphasis on leadership unique to the institution's Business School. Kellerman (2012), herself a Harvard University academic, notes that the words 'leader' and 'leadership' feature prominently in the mission statements of almost all its professional schools. She challenges this emphasis by, for example, the University's Law School, pointedly asking: 'Why is Harvard Law School so insistent on educating leaders? Does it no longer suffice to excel at what you do?' (Kellerman 2012: 156). This stress is all the more remarkable given the volume of work that has documented the prevalence of hubristic leadership practices and chronicled its effects on individuals (for example, Hopfl 2005; Schilling 2009; Aasland *et al.* 2010), whole organizations (see Chapter 7) and wider economic systems (Kerr and Robinson 2011, 2012). It is difficult to reconcile such work with the mainstream emphasis on unbounded leader agency, generally regarded in an unproblematic manner. Moreover, when inflated expectations of agency collide with the messy reality of a complex world that refuses to conform to the norms of HBS case studies, the strain for stressed followers and anxious leaders is likely to be considerable.

Consistent with such criticism, a study of key textbooks used in teaching leadership in US business schools concluded that 'leadership, as presented in the selected texts, is a collection of control theories that ignores essential aspects of the leadership concept' (Nirenberg 1998: 82). For example, Nelson and Quick (1995: 358) define leadership as 'the process of guiding and directing the behaviour of people in the work environment'. Widely prescribed MBA texts typically assume that leadership exists because of a leader's 'superior' position over 'subordinates'; that this relationship is relatively unproblematic and uncontested; and that a unity of interest prevails between leaders and followers. As a result, many issues are largely unexplored – including dissent, disagreement, disengagement, envy and most of the difficult human emotions that are endemic in leader–follower relationships. We can see these weaknesses at work when we consider how 'celebrity' CEOs are often presented to business students.

Jack Welch as a study in paradox

Many leading business schools regularly invite 'celebrity' CEOs to make presentations to students or to be interviewed by a senior academic or others in the presence of a student audience. Here, I focus on two such encounters featuring Jack Welch, former CEO of General Electric (GE): one at the Sloan School of Management at the MIT and the other at Stanford University in 2005. For most of the 1980s and 1990s, he was revered as a charismatic and exemplary CEO. Welch was viewed by media commentators as the best CEO of his generation and depicted in several hagiographies as a master transformer of a business (for example, Slater 1999), lionised as 'the incarnation of a corporate chieftain' (Hegele and Kieser 2001: 298), revered in academic journals (Greiner 2002) and lauded because he 'set a new, contemporary paradigm for the corporation that is the model for the 21st century' (Byrne 1998: 90, citing Tichy, a long-time GE observer). In 1999, *Fortune* magazine named him the manager of the century.

The general tone that prevails on such occasions was reflected by the introduction of Welch by the dean of the Sloan School:

> He became the company's eighth chairman and CEO in 1981. During the 20 years as CEO he transformed the company into a dynamic and innovative powerhouse and grew the market value from 13 billion to over 500 billion. He became one of the most influential and respected executives in the world, I would say one of the few rock stars in the business world. It is an absolute delight to welcome him here today and to hear his thoughts on leadership and some of the lessons he has learned in over 40 years building one of the most successful companies in the world. Ladies and gentlemen – Jack Welch. [Applause]

The introduction implies that most of the credit for GE's claimed success should be attributed to its CEO – an echo of HBR's fawning interview with the CEO of Dell. There is no acknowledgement that even the most able of CEOs relies on a vast number of followers to achieve his or her goals. Nor, incidentally, did Welch make any effort to correct this impression during his presentation. Consistent with the view that managerial rhetoric plays an important part in determining organizational culture and effectiveness (Hogler *et al.* 2008), I suggest that the rhetoric of business school deans and faculty is important, precisely because it is likely to play an influential part in shaping the behaviours of students. The leadership model promoted by the dean in this excerpt appears to be one of a 'genius' atop the organizational pyramid, surrounded by a multitude of marvelling minions.[2] This hagiographic approach and uncritical atmosphere is maintained with the preface to the dean's first 'question', in which he refers to Welch's then recently published (2005) book: 'Let me start the ball rolling with the first question. This is a terrific book'.

The innate 'transformational' and hierarchical dynamic that characterises the ensuing discourse is best illustrated by focusing on Welch's justification for what he terms 'differentiation'. Welch argues that leaders should classify employees annually into one of three groups: an *élite* highly performing few who are to be given huge rewards; a *middle* grouping who are 'encouraged' to improve and a '*bottom*' ten per cent who should be compelled to leave. Welch's ideas on this issue have been very influential. For example, a survey of 562 chairmen, CEOs and managing directors in the UK found that three-quarters of the respondents were willing to conduct an annual cull of staff with the aim of raising productivity (Hudson 2007). One in six thought that they could get rid of 20 per cent of employees without damaging performance or morale. Half reckoned that firing up to five per cent a year would be a good idea.

This emerges as the major single issue raised by Welch in his presentations at Stanford and MIT. But it goes largely unquestioned by the audiences and senior facilitators at the schools concerned. Indeed, the dean of the Sloan Management School supports Welch by drawing parallels with the tenure review process found in US universities, noting that, 'The way the university is run, about 25% of the new faculty get tenure. The others either leave or get cancelled. So it is quite similar'.

The mindsets on play here reveal much about how the roles of top leaders are conceptualised in leading business schools. The following quotations from Welch's presentation illustrate the point:

> The evaluation processes aren't frequent enough. We get this, 'I'm too kind to evaluate my team.'... It's sort of frightening that people are sitting in an organization and don't feel that people are laying it on straight and telling you how it is ... My view is take care of the top twenty ... make them feel loved; hug them, give them cash, give them rewards in the soul and the wallet; do everything for them. That middle seventy, show them what they need to do to get in the top twenty, and that bottom ten, tell them ... why they basically should move on and don't do it in a guillotine job; have a conversation that goes over a year or so about what their shortfalls are; tell them they're in the bottom ten; don't give them a raise of any kind; don't give them two or three per cent, that's a fake raise, keeps people hanging around longer, cut off the salary issues and then ask them to leave and say, 'Let's over the next several months work together to get you in the right place ... If you have responsibility, if you lead people, they should know where they stand'.

Explicit in Welch's view is that it is the job of the leader to evaluate, grade, reward and punish subordinates. He further argues: 'You will become managers and everything and everyone who becomes a leader has an obligation to let everyone who works for them know where they stand. That is an absolute obligation. So I came up with this differentiation thing'.

It is not made clear precisely how leaders are expected to accomplish this 'differentiation thing'. Rather, it is assumed that they will have accurate, objective and valid mental ready reckoners that enable them to pronounce on the performances of their subordinates. However, a vast literature on appraisal processes calls this core assumption into question (see, for example, Tourish 2006). Leaders bring their own biases to bear in evaluating subordinates. Indeed, since the occupation of management has itself been 'downsized' and 'de-layered', much of it at the instigation of Jack Welch, many managers have ever larger numbers of subordinates, thereby compounding the difficulties of forming reliable impressions of how well these subordinates perform. The distance between leaders and followers is therefore a growing and problematic phenomenon (Collinson 2005a).

The potential impact of the manner in which Welch is presented to his student audience can be understood using a 'romance of leadership' (ROL) theory perspective, in which leadership is viewed as a largely attributional phenomenon (Meindl 1993; Meindl *et al.* 1985). Leaders are romanticised and their contribution to organizational outcomes is exaggerated, owing to their phenomenological significance to organizational actors. Leaders become important because of what they represent in the minds of subordinates. As Mayo and Pastor (2007: 98) suggest 'followers construe their leaders from information that is available in their social environments ... thus, the key element in this social constructionist view of leadership in the organization is the network of contacts that bring organizational actors together'.

When a CEO such as Jack Welch is introduced glowingly as a 'rock star', his charismatic status and views are enhanced in the minds of the audience. Celebrity is not renowned for evoking a critical response in its audience. Also, the hierarchical underpinning of transformational leadership models is further strengthened in the minds of the audience. It is highly debatable whether such endorsement of hierarchical models is justified and accords with empirical evidence on the nature of leadership, the role of individual leaders and the promotion of acceptable leader behaviours in our society.

Building the self image of business students – the lure of hubris and narcissism

The problems discussed so far are likely to be intensified by the promotional materials and pedagogical philosophy that underpin much of the content found on business school leadership programmes. To explore this, I downloaded leadership education information from the websites of those business schools identified by the *Financial Times* in 2007 as offering the top 21 MBA programmes in the world. Box 6.1 lists a selection of the common promises found on these.

Box 6.1 Transformational leadership promises made by business schools

1 'When you enter one of Wharton's classrooms, you join an élite group of executives. Whether it's a senior manager being groomed for the top seat or a CEO ready to leave his mark, everyone who comes here is focused on developing the skills to leave an impact on their organizations and shape the business world of tomorrow. The Wharton Executive Education experience has had an impact on many Fortune 500 companies, including AT&T, Boeing, Coca-Cola, Fujitsu, and Microsoft. What's more, the wide variety of industries represented – from financial services to pharmaceuticals, technology to transportation – allows for a cross-disciplinary collaboration with the best minds in business.'

(Wharton)

2 'Columbia MBA students are extremely attractive to corporate recruiters, who actively recruit on behalf of as many as 600 employers on campus each year, holding thousands of interviews. The 2003 Forbes ranking, based on return on investment, placed Columbia Business School No. 2. The survey measured the pre-MBA and post-graduate income of the class of 1998. An article accompanying the magazine's previous survey was titled 'The Whiz Kids' and singled out the class of 1969 as one of the most successful classes ever to graduate from a business school.'

(Columbia)

3 'Organizational leadership is a noble pursuit. Effective leaders have a greater potential for influence than ever before in human history. If your passion is to lead teams and organizations that change the world, we want to hear from you.'

(Stanford)

---

4 'The study of leadership is a very important component of the Sloan Program. In addition to reading and discussions in the Sloan leadership seminars, you will hear from leaders of major organizations about their personal experiences and views on what it means to be a leader. You will visit some of these men and women in their offices. Others will come to the Sloan classroom to meet you in an informal setting.'

(Sloan, MIT)

5 'Wise leaders recognize that people are a source of corporate wealth. A potent leader co-creates with his or her people to push the company ahead of the competition. But before a leader can assume this role and responsibility, they must be willing to engage in their own developmental journey. In this course, we take leadership out of the box by studying the lives of extraordinary leaders while engaging in our own self-exploration ... Leadership ... is the ability to inspire others to strive and enable them to accomplish great things. The program ensures that Tuck students graduate empowered to do just that—and to feel responsible for being a leader in the world.'

(Tuck, Dartmouth)

6 'In academic discussions of leadership over the past thirty years, there has been too much emphasis on 'leaders as equals among equals'. This emphasis is misleading and dangerous. Actually, leaders must show the way to others... The IMD Executive MBA takes you beyond the basics to a true understanding of the forces that will be shaping business in the future. It prepares you for senior management challenges and responsibilities – a rigorous modular MBA for fast-rising global business leaders.'

(IMD)

7 'Revolutionize the way you think, and results will follow. This seminar offers a unique approach for maximizing your leadership performance – looking beyond two-dimensional maps for increasing productivity to a more holistic view of leadership. During this program you will complete an intensive analysis of your motivations, behaviors, and goals for leadership improvement.'

(Kellogg, Northwestern)

8 'The magic of the Cambridge Leadership Seminars exists in the personal interaction between speakers of the very highest calibre and our diverse group of exceptional MBA students, who are themselves future leaders in business and society.'

(Judge Business School, Cambridge University)

There were 12 programmes in the USA, five in Continental Europe, one in China and three in the UK. The resulting document, totalling 46,943 words, was carefully analysed, with two key issues in mind: to determine the extent to which the marketing materials of the schools draw upon the rhetoric of transformational leadership to indicate that they will produce graduates capable of its practice; and to explore the extent to which the websites disclosed an underlying pedagogic philosophy that might (or might not) be characterised by assumptions consistent with transformational leadership theory.

The website promotional material of the UCLA's Anderson School seems unabashed in its claims to offer 'unparalleled expertise in management education' such that 'the world's business community turns to [it] as a center of influence for the ideas, innovations, strategies, and talent that will shape the future'. Dartmouth's Tuck College is slightly less restrained. Its students are assured of enjoying 'genuine relationships with accomplished, brilliant professors, classmates, alumni, and colleagues from around the world … [and] without question … a collaborative, intellectual environment [that] will help [them] become a stronger leader and a more valuable team player'.

There are persistent, flattering suggestions that those who participate in the programmes concerned are exceptional individuals. Students in these business schools are portrayed as engaged in a 'noble pursuit' (Stanford). They are 'an élite group of executives' (Wharton), who are 'extremely attractive to corporate recruiters' (Columbia). They are said to appeal to leaders who 'push the company ahead of the competition' (Dartmouth); and to be people whose 'passion is to lead teams and change the world' (Stanford). Among those listed by Cambridge University as presenters at its seminars are the Chairman of Barclay's Bank (presumably, before his resignation for his role in fixing interest rates in 2012; see Chapter 1), the CEO of Shamrock Holdings, its own vice chancellor and a former governor of the Bank of England. It describes the seminars as 'magic', available to MBA students who are described as 'exceptional' and 'themselves future leaders in business and society'.

Likewise, a transformational agenda is explicit. Those who emerge from these programmes will 'shape the business world of tomorrow' (Wharton) and be empowered 'to accomplish great things' (Dartmouth); 'have a greater potential for influence than ever before in human history' (Stanford), will develop 'their employees in order to get the very best productivity' (Dartmouth); will 'show the way to others' (IMD); and will develop a 'more holistic view of leadership' (Kellogg). There is rarely any suggestion that leaders should learn from others, including their followers. Also conspicuously absent is any suggestion of the benefits to leaders and leadership of humility, dissent or follower input. Rather, the preponderant assumption is that those who emerge from a business school education will unidirectionally influence the behaviours of others. But overstatement is not the preserve of US schools. Cambridge University's website asserts that the University has 'set the standards for learning around the world [and it is] a name recognized in every country [for] blazing trails in innovation, science, technology, law and business'.

Overall, these are messages that seem almost tailormade to encourage hubris and narcissism – two of the chief perils confronting powerful leaders in large corporations. There are reasonable grounds to presume that most CEOs exhibit some narcissistic tendencies. Kets de Vries (2004: 188) argued that 'a solid dose of narcissism is a prerequisite for anyone who hopes to rise to the top of an organization'. This proposition is consistent with Lubit's (2002: 127) argument that 'certain personality traits commonly but not exclusively found in destructive narcissism help people to rise within management structures … [such traits include] high levels of expressed self-confidence, magnetic enthusiasm, and unrelenting drive to attain prestige and power'. While all humans show some signs of narcissistic behaviour (Kets de Vries and Miller 1985), it is important to acknowledge that 'it is the danger of excess, particularly in the case of leaders, which gives narcissism its often derogatory connotations' (Kets de Vries 1994: 84). It seems prudent for business school pedagogy to not enable the attraction and development of such excessive forms of dysfunction.

To help to cope with the potential problems that can arise from narcissism, corporate stakeholders should be alerted to the need to monitor the discourse of those modern business school graduates who progress to become CEOs, for narcissist-like signs (Amernic and Craig 2007). Perhaps even more importantly from a preventive perspective, business school promotional material about leadership pedagogy should avoid such narrow, perverse marketing messages regarding leadership and should better reflect the breadth and nuance of leadership in action.

Box 6.2 also contains examples of the pedagogical philosophy underpinning such approaches. Both explicitly and implicitly, a transformational agenda is again strongly entrenched. Explicitly, we are regaled with statements to the effect that 'Leaders ... decide what needs to be done' (INSEAD) and that leaders 'create conditions that enable organization members to accomplish great things, and that lead them to act in the organization's best interest' (Dartmouth). We are reminded of the need to 'explore strategies for building a team of strong individuals who will support each other, deal with tough problems in an efficient manner, and take accountability for results' (Stanford). The model is one in which powerful ('strong') individuals exert influence on others. But this model's neglect of followership is subject to increasing criticism. It is also one in which a unitary interest is presumed – the organization is assumed to have a clear, unclouded 'best interest', to which leaders, using their influencing skills, can unproblematically secure employee commitment. The possibility that leaders may use this idea as a cover for advancing sectional interests of their own is not considered. But it is precisely this possibility that arises when we consider the weight often given to agency theory elsewhere in the business school curriculum.

Transformational leadership and agency theory: a marriage of inconvenience?

The problems noted above are compounded by the prominence of agency theory, particularly in economics (for example, Friedman 2002) and cognate disciplines such as finance and accounting (for example, Watts and Zimmerman 1986). Despite the invocation of common goals on the part of transformational leaders, agency theory assumes that self-interest is the guiding principle of human behaviour (Sen 1977). This is defined as an intense individual human motivation to satisfy the person's own desires, irrespective of their effects in others (Adams and Maine 1998). In particular, agency theory focuses on relationships in which one party, the principal, determines and guides the work of another, the agent (Jensen and Meckling 1976). Mirroring the theory X and theory Y view of management (McGregor 1960), it assumes that agents are shirkers, with a self-interest incentive to avoid work. Individuals in all walks of life are viewed as 'resourceful, evaluative

Box 6.2 Pedagogic approaches to leadership

'Managers get things done efficiently. Leaders, in turn, decide what needs to be done. Aware of changes affecting their industry, their market and their competences, they welcome such changes as an opportunity to outpace competition. It is the role of leaders to turn a group of disconnected people into a strong motivated team: they shape a collective ambition and infuse values into the firm.'

INSEAD

'This course focuses on the skills sets needed to elicit high commitment and productivity from people and groups. Awareness of one's own values, beliefs, decision-making tendencies and behaviours is seen as a crucial first step in becoming a leader. Thus, a significant portion of the course consists of activities designed to enhance students' self-awareness. The course provides students with the interpersonal skills needed to motivate key actors in the workplace and to manage group dynamics so as to create synergy among group members. Methods of instruction include individualized feedback, cases, role-plays and experiential exercises.'

Columbia

'The goal of HBS is to prepare students for the challenges of leadership. We believe that the case method is by far the most powerful way to learn the skills required to manage, and to lead. The case method forces students to grapple with exactly the kinds of decisions and dilemmas managers confront every day. In doing so, it redefines the traditional educational dynamic in which the professor dispenses knowledge and students passively receive it.'

Harvard

'The Executive Program in Leadership is designed to help participants put effective, collaborative methods of leadership to work in their organizations and leverage the leadership potential of all members of their teams. Participants focus on developing their own leadership skills and personal influence, as well as explore strategies for building a team of strong individuals who will support each other, deal with tough problems in an efficient manner, and take accountability for results.'

Stanford

'Chicago GSB's unique Leadership Effectiveness and Development (LEAD) Program is about maximizing success in business. LEAD is a laboratory class where students practice and perfect key communication skills such as negotiation, team-building, and giving feedback. We consider these skills so critical to success in business that we require all full-time campus and International MBA students to complete the class.'

Chicago

'Though there are countless different styles of leadership, all effective leaders must accomplish one objective: create conditions that enable organization members to accomplish great things, and that lead them to act in the organization's best interests.'

Tuck, Dartmouth

maximizers' (Jensen 1994: 1), pursuing money, respect, honour, love and whatever else is in their interests.

For example, transaction cost economics (Williamson 1975) assumes that whatever promises people make will be quickly broken if a greater advantage accrues to them for doing something other than honour their commitments. Departures from self-interest are depicted as irrational, aberrational and, ultimately, inexplicable. Shirking is therefore inevitable (Rocha and Ghoshal 2006). On the other hand, the principal is motivated to ensure that no shirking occurs (Ross 1973). But it is often the case that the principal cannot be sure if agents have applied maximum effort in pursuit of the goals and tasks to which they have been directed by the principal (Holstrom 1979). It follows that intense surveillance and tight supervision is required. An indispensable element of such monitoring is a complex incentive and performance management system which makes full use of hierarchical authority (Ghoshal 2005) and is based largely on monitoring often-reductionist performance measures such as the primacy of shareholder value (Morsing and Rovira 2011).

Agency theory's assumption of individualistic interest is quite explicit. Thus, it is asserted that 'most organizations are simply legal fictions which serve as a nexus for a set of contracting relationships among individuals' (Jensen and Meckling 1976: 310). While classic agency theory has therefore been criticised as 'an organizational theory without organizations' (Kiser 1999: 150), the problem is that the theory has had real impacts on existing organizations and on business school curricula. Shapiro (2005: 269) noted how agency theory had percolated into 'the management literature, specialised academic and applied practitioner journals, the business press, even corporate proxy statements'. In particular, it had become the dominant logic of work on corporate governance (Zajac and Westphal 2004). Consistent with this, agency approaches assume that the only (or chief) goal of a firm is profit maximisation, an end to which all strategy and leadership practice is geared (Friedman 2002; Grant 2000).

Leadership, founded on these kinds of assumptions, will inevitably be self-serving in its intent and practice, irrespective of any inclusive rhetoric leaders have been exposed to in dedicated MBA leadership modules. Moreover, the rhetoric of inclusivity, empowerment and a unitarist interest that are found in at least some transformational leadership theory are, in any event, undermined by persistent suggestions that leaders are exceptional individuals; and that they should make key decisions which unidirectionally influence the actions of others, in pursuit of what is deemed to be a higher corporate good. Leaders with such an orientation will be likely to have an instrumentalist view of their relationships with employees – that is, to view employees as a resource, to be employed or discarded purely on the basis of profit and loss calculations. This mindset appears to influence much leadership practice.

Logically, leaders with an instrumentalist orientation are more likely to act primarily in their own self-interest – rather than in the interests of their followers, the wider organization or other stakeholders. Ever more lavish CEO compensation packages are one manifestation of this type of mindset. Jack Welch's leadership is a prime example. He is alleged to have earned more than US$16 million in compensation in his last year with GE. But a retirement agreement that eventually aroused great public controversy included an annual pension of more than US$9 million a year. It also permitted him to continue as a consultant to GE, earning US$86,535 a day for his first 30 days of work each year, plus US$17,307 for each additional day. Other perks included access to a GE-owned luxury apartment at the Trump International Hotel and Towers in New York City, unlimited use of a corporate jet (with an estimated monthly running cost of US$291,869), a grand tier box at the Metropolitan Opera, membership at country clubs, box seats at Yankee Stadium, prime tickets to the French Open, US Open and Wimbledon tennis tournaments, VIP tickets to all Olympic events and a great deal more (Borrus 2004). Perhaps the notion of Welch as a rock star is not so far-fetched, after all.

Indeed, Jensen and Meckling (1976) argue that the dominant 'want' among economically active people is money – something which at least appears to largely define the life of Jack Welch. Furthermore, agency theory indicates a distrustful attitude towards the behaviours of followers; it presumes that individual (rather than collective) interests govern the behaviour of all organizational actors. Thus, the norm of reciprocity, which postulates an inherent inclination for people to mirror the behaviour that others display towards them (Cialdini 2009), suggests that self-serving behaviours by managers will evoke a similar behaviour in employees. It is unlikely that employees who have been alienated by instrumentalist management behaviours, such as downsizing, would respond positively to future management 'visions' which stress the common interests of management and staff and posit an exciting future state to which all can subscribe. Yet such visions and messages would be precisely what transformational leadership theories in particular would encourage leaders to provide.

However, agency notions sit uneasily with some of the core precepts articulated in the literature on transformational leadership. This is particularly the case with assumptions of a collective interest, which often make emotive and moral appeals in support of this interest. Leaders are prone to finding themselves uncomfortably bestriding two contradictory theoretical paradigms. In one, *self-interest* is held to predominate. Incentive and organizational surveillance systems are designed with this in mind. They are buttressed by aspects of transformational leadership theory which assert hierarchical principles and notions of a unidirectional influence from leaders to followers. The other paradigm, drawing from a different aspect of leadership theory, is characterised by rhetorical appeals to universal needs, higher moral purposes and a *common interest*. It is as though much of the more inclusive language of transformational leadership has been appropriated by advocates of agency theory to serve instrumental and self-centred ends that conflict with some core precepts of transformational leadership theory. This process is likely to be intensified by overemphasis on leadership as a factor in organizational success and the narcissistic self-image that the marketing materials of prominent business schools induces in students. It can mean that people emerge with self-delusions of charisma, produced by a leadership theory and business school environment that nurtures inflated, inaccurate self-images.

Business school graduates often then proceed to apply the command and control assumptions implicit to agency theory in their managerial actions. The resultant brew is likely to be unpalatable.

Reflections on the way forward

The leadership literature, although vast, is 'often contradictory, confusing and lacks cohesion' (Rost 1991: 145). I have argued here that this confusion is manifest in business school curricula in multiple, contrary and damaging forms. Business school educators should be less keen to uncritically exaggerate the contributions that leaders make to business success and reproduce largely make-believe stories which chronicle how powerful and charismatic leaders routinely rescue organizations from the precipice of failure. Such practice seems likely to encourage business students to develop inflated notions of their own leadership potential and likely future role, invoke leadership theories which overstate the directive role of leaders and underestimate the potential role of followership. In accord with Hunter *et al.* (2007), I urge that more critical studies of leadership be conducted and be reflected more often in the business school curriculum. These studies should explore the negative effects of leadership, leader errors and leader misbehaviour in general.

In addition, there is a conflict between those aspects of transformational leadership theory which extol the benefits of a collective organizational interest and the self-interestedness of human behaviour found in agency theory. Rather than an idyllic blend, I suggest that these two perspectives represent a marriage of inconvenience, in which each undercuts the other, without ever acknowledging that this is the case. Business graduates, like a conclave of cardinals torn between virtue and vice (before determining to embrace both), may therefore find themselves marrying two contradictory theoretical frameworks in their leadership practice. On the one hand, teachers of transformational leadership expound the need for common organizational goals and propound the notion of a unity of interest between the goals of management and the needs of employees, and make moral appeals as they do so. On the other hand, they advocate the adoption of performance management systems which assume that people are motivated only by self-interest and that they must be monitored closely to avoid them damaging the organization's interests. I do not question the value of exposing students to different and even conflicting theoretical paradigms. However, the point is that the intrinsic paradoxes in the areas discussed here should be acknowledged and explored, to produce more reflective practitioners.

With a view to improving the teaching of leadership in business schools, I offer the following proposals for discussion and debate.

1 Recognise that leadership is a co-constructed phenomenon between leaders and followers, replete with attributional biases

In a major sense, leadership is an iterative and discursive phenomenon, born of language 'games' between leaders and followers (Fairhurst 2007). The search for its 'essence', often expressed in competency frameworks and instruction manuals, therefore has severe limitations. A more critical awareness of the language used by leaders to legitimise their authority and to depict it as a naturally occurring phenomenon (rather than one that is socially constructed by human interaction) would demystify leadership practice (Amernic *et al.* 2007). It would enable a more fruitful debate about the actual contribution of leadership to organizational outcomes. It would also recognise the abundant evidence that transformational leadership is neither straightforward to implement, nor necessarily the most effective leadership approach in all organizational contexts (Currie *et al.* 2005). Some studies even suggest that charisma, in particular, does not influence firm performance, beyond the share price and the level of compensation won by CEOs (Tosi *et al.* 2004).

2 Provide a more critical evaluation of leadership practice in which individual leaders (such as Jack Welch) are not depicted largely as paragons of effectiveness, to be admired and emulated uncritically

I do not question the value of business leaders addressing students. But I do question the value of introducing them as 'rock stars' and 'legends' and of suggesting that academics and students can do little more than learn lessons from what such leaders have done, as though their behaviour is bereft of error, self-interest or malign intent. For example, although criticism of Jack Welch has been muted, he is also alleged to have been a 'dark' schemer who perfected the insidious art of 'global management by stress' (Weissman 2001). He has been described as ruthless, impatient and intimidating; as possessing an 'unbridled passion for winning'; and as having the attitude of a 'take-no-prisoners tough guy who gets results at any cost' (Byrne 1998: 90). A teaching and research agenda which also explores the negative consequences of such leadership behaviour would investigate the damaging effects of overconformity to destructive behavioural norms, the promotion of monocultures that stifle critical feedback and 'executive hubris' (Hayward 2007). This would have a significant educational benefit and be more consistent with the role of the university in society. It would not take the self-proclaimed goals of leaders as unproblematic. Rather, it would seek to explore the purposes of leadership and question who is most likely to benefit from the attainment of their goals (Sinclair 2007). Indeed, if an important function of the university is, as Alfred North Whitehead contended almost 80 years ago, 'to civilize business' (Whitehead [1929] 1957), the pedagogy of leadership in business schools deserves a more critical perspective than what is presently on offer.

3 Rebalance the notion of 'leadership' and that of 'followership'

We need to focus more fully on what constitutes effective follower behaviours and explore how leaders can encourage more of it (Chaleff 2003; Seteroff 2003). For example, how might some of the command and control mechanisms that flow from agency theory impede effective follower behaviours, thus distorting the leadership function? This suggests that the detailed study of such management control structures and processes, particularly (but not exclusively) compensation schemes, is an important aspect of the study of leadership. How can destructive control mechanisms be dismantled? What stops many leaders from implementing even elementary mechanisms to institute follower involvement, such as suggestion schemes? In an inversion of normal protocols, we might conceive the follower as a teacher to the leader (Grint 2005), rather than the other way round.

4 Provide more focus on assessing the merits of frank, open and critical two-way communication between leaders and followers

Much leadership education promotes a notion of leadership as a process that can be used to shape the attitudes of others and to secure compliance with centrally sanctioned goals. There is very little focus on the benefits of dissent, which is often dismissed as resistance to be overcome, rather than as useful feedback (see Chapter 5). Potentially, a focus on the value of dissent would also have the salutary effect of reducing the need for 'resistance strategies' of the less powerful in organizations (Mumby 2005).

5 Openly consider the limitations of agency theory

This would include a consideration of agency theory's capacity to encourage strategies of over-control, the unleashing of self-centred leader behaviours and of how such theory is used as a source of legitimation for the concentration of power in the hands of a select few. More critical theories of leadership which challenge the notion that monetary self-interest invariably guides the behaviour of leaders and followers could be developed and could be incorporated into the business school curriculum.

Conclusion

In many business schools, leadership is taught too simplistically (formally, in courses, and informally, in the manner in which CEO visiting speakers are provided an ideologically unexamined platform and in the messages conveyed on business school websites). It is taught without due care for how it conflicts with the agency perspectives underpinning much of the rest of the curriculum. Neither society nor its organizations have benefited. Rather, heroic models of leadership have legitimised an overconcentration of power, created hubris rather than humility, helped to disempower employees and played a significant part in business scandals. Existing theories and pedagogic methods are part of the problem rather than the solution. It is time to rethink. Business schools should – with urgency – adopt approaches to leadership education that are more critical, relational and reflective.

Points for discussion

1. Which aspects of agency theory might be in most conflict with theories of transformational leadership?
2. To what problems for the practice of leadership might this give rise?
3. How well do you think that business schools prepare students for the challenges of leadership in organizations?
4. Should business students be encouraged to develop a greater sense of humility in their leadership practice? Or do you think that the risks of hubris and narcissism discussed in this chapter are overstated?
5. What ideas do you have to improve the study of leadership in business schools?

Notes

1 An earlier version of this work appeared as Tourish, D., Craig, R. and Amernic, J. (2010) Transformational leadership education and agency perspectives in business school pedagogy: a marriage of inconvenience? *British Journal of Management*, 21: S40–59.
2 I am indebted to my colleague, Russell Craig, for this wonderfully evocative phrase.

Part II
Case studies

7   The dark side of leadership in corporate America

Enron revisited[1]

Introduction

Enron's bankruptcy in 2001 was the largest in US corporate history, until the demise of Lehmans in 2008.[2] Barely a year earlier, Enron had declared its intention to become 'the world's leading company'. At that stage, by some measures of turnover, it was the seventh largest company in the USA and was at one point valued at US\$70 billion by the stock exchange. Its huge ambition on the eve of disaster thus had some credibility. But its subsequent demise ensures instead that its fate is to become one of the most analysed case studies of failure in business history. Enron, essentially, is now 'a representative anecdote ... for corporate greed and corruption' (Turnage 2010: 2).

Enron traced its origins to 1985, when it was born as a result of a merger between two energy companies. Ken Lay, whose name looms large in these annals, was its founding chairman and CEO. The company diversified repeatedly during its history. Eventually, Jeffrey Skilling, a Harvard Business School MBA graduate and former top consultant with the giant consulting firm McKinsey, ended up as its CEO at the time of its bankruptcy. Under his leadership, Enron entered ever more deeply into trading and finance. Eventually, it was trading in metals, plastics, paper, coal, pulp, weather derivatives and bandwidth capacity – and had ambitions for still more.

It was not to be. Bankruptcy took place in 2001, after ever more complex 'creative accounting' arrangements unravelled to reveal that most of Enron's 'success' was based on fraud. Skilling was jailed in 2006 for 24 years, on charges that included conspiracy, securities fraud, false statement and insider trading. He is not scheduled for release until 2028, by which time he will be 74 years old. Andy Fastow, Enron's Chief Finance Officer, was more fortunate. After plea bargaining, he was sentenced to ten years in prison in 2006. Ken Lay was found guilty on ten counts of securities fraud and related charges and faced 20–30 years in prison. He only avoided this by dying of a heart attack before he could be sentenced on 26 October 2006. The effects of the scandal were incalculable. Thousands of employees lost their jobs, countless numbers of savers saw their money disappear, never to be retrieved, and trust in business leaders plummeted.

The 2002 Sarbanes-Oxley Act was passed largely as a direct result of the debacle, requiring a number of structural changes in publicly owned companies that it was hoped would avert such scandals in the future. There was at least one fatality. An Enron manager, 43-year-old Cliff Baxter, committed suicide. He shot himself in the head, after leaving the following despairing note to his wife:

> Carol, I am so sorry for this. I feel I just can't go on. I have always tried to do the right thing but where there was once great pride now it's gone. I love you and the children so much. I just can't be any good to you or myself. The pain is overwhelming. Please try to forgive me. Cliff.

This chapter does not recapitulate in detail the now familiar story of Enron's meteoric rise and spectacular fall. Rather, it addresses a major omission in the literature. While it has been noted that the Enron scandal highlights 'a recurring communication dysfunction within the organizational structure of the corporation itself' (Cohan 2002: 276), relatively little attention has been focused on what the culture of the organization demonstrates about the dark side of charismatic leadership. A partial exception is the work of Stein (2007) and Stein and Pinto (2011), who employ a psychoanalytic perspective to explore its destructive leadership and group dynamics. But although *The Economist* astutely suggested in June 2000, in an article entitled 'The Energetic Messiah', that if you 'Spend long enough around top Enron people ... you feel you are in the midst of some sort of evangelical cult' (Economist 2000), the idea has not been systematically explored in the academic literature. I therefore consider the extent to which the role of Enron's leaders was consistent or otherwise with the major characteristics of cults and of transformational leadership discussed at repeated points in this book. Finally, the discussion is located in the context of the changing roles of CEOs more generally and the extent to which what can be defined as corporate cultism is becoming a more common characteristic of organizational life.

Information on Enron is derived from the vast archive of material now published on the organization – in particular, on the key accounts of former employees, as exemplified by Cruver (2003), Swartz and Watkins (2003) and Watkins (2003a,b).[3] Other accounts have proliferated in the mass media and business press and are broadly consistent with the sources highlighted in this analysis. I apply a conceptual framework drawn from the general literature on both cultic organizations and transformational leadership and analyse the narrative constructs of others to ascertain to what extent their accounts of facts, intention and agency can be better understood from within that particular analytic framework. This is a voyage around the dark side where many knowledgeable guides can be called upon to accompany us.

Enron is too complex a story to avail of one single explanation for its rise and fall. With that caveat, I highlight an important but still under explored aspect of the Enron saga and one that has wider implications for the role of leadership in most business organizations.

Charismatic leadership and cults

In Chapter 2, I suggested that both transformational leadership and dysfunctional organizations generally known as cults share many common traits. In particular, there is a stress on charismatic leadership. Leaders deemed to be charismatic are encouraged to articulate a compelling vision to offer their followers intellectual stimulation. But all this leads to a common culture characterised by extreme degrees of conformity and a high concentration of power in the hands of a few leaders. Many of them feel liberated from the constraints that apply to others and adopt leadership practices that advance their own interest at a terrible cost to their followers.

I now consider the extent to which dysfunctional aspects of transformational leadership and cults were at play within the Enron organization. The dominant traits of cults were summarised in Chapter 2, in Table 2.1. Readers may find it useful to refer back to this table. In what follows, I consider the extent to which Enron's internal cultural dynamics operated in parallel to the traits identified there.

1 Charismatic leadership, dissent and leadership privileges

The importance of 'vision' has been increasingly stressed in the business world, in a growing volume of largely uncritical practitioner and academic literature. These theories highlight such effects as emotional attachment to the leader on the part of followers, greater emotional and motivational arousal, increased follower commitment to the mission articulated by the leader and enhanced confidence in the leader. Leaders therefore often build their charismatic reputation around the energetic communication of a vision, designed to solicit ever higher levels of compliance from followers.

There is ample evidence that Enron's leadership aimed at creating an aura of charisma around themselves along these lines. They unburdened themselves of humility to embrace hubris. The following quotation from a *Fortune* magazine article published in April 2000 is typical of how Enron leaders saw and projected themselves:

> Imagine a country-club dinner dance, with a bunch of old fogies and their wives shuffling around half-heartedly to the not-so-stirring sounds of Guy Lombardo and his All-Tuxedo Orchestra. Suddenly young Elvis comes crashing through the skylight, complete with gold-lame suit, shiny guitar, and gyrating hips ... In the staid world of regulated utilities and energy companies, Enron Corp. is that gate-crashing Elvis.
>
> (quoted in Sherman 2002: 23)

Consistent with their image in the business press, Enron's leaders engaged in ever more dramatic forms of self-promotion. It may be a stretch to imagine Kenneth Lay, a portly middle-aged businessman, as a latter day Elvis, let alone as

Che Guevara. Nevertheless, he was described by *Fortune* magazine as a 'revolutionary'. Jeffrey Skilling was equally adept at promoting a charismatic self-image. Consistent with a company wide dramaturgical predilection for *Star Wars* analogies, Cruver (2003: 10) recounts that he was known internally as Darth Vader:

> a master of the energy universe who had the ability to control people's minds. He was at the peak of his strength, and he intimidated everyone. He had been lured over to the Dark Side from McKinsey & Company in 1990. He dressed for the part at company gatherings, referred to his traders as 'Storm Troopers' and decorated his home in a style sympathetic to the Darth Vader image.
>
> (Schwartz 2002)

Skilling was also sometimes known as 'The Prince', after Machiavelli. New recruits were instructed to read *The Prince* from beginning to end or be eaten alive (Boje *et al.* 2004). Dramatic nomenclatures were not uncommon. Another senior executive, Rebecca Mark, became known as 'Mark the Shark', with all its attendant overtones of predatory aggression and greater competitive power (Frey 2002).

This tone appears to be typical of the unusually charismatic and extremely powerful image that Lay and Skilling, in particular, attempted to promulgate at every opportunity. It was clearly part of an intense dramaturgical effort designed to project an unusually alluring spectacle and thereby convince people that they belonged to a cause far greater than merely being part of a business or working for a living. Hagiographic accounts of their accomplishments were correspondingly widespread, including in an influential book by Hamel (2000), entitled appropriately enough *Leading the Revolution*. Faculty at the prestigious Harvard Business School produced 11 case studies into Enron, uniformly lauding its 'successes' and commending its business model to others. All of them have since been discreetly withdrawn.

Within cults, leaders tend to enjoy extraordinary wealth – a disparity which is used to reinforce the impression that the people concerned have extraordinary abilities, insight and charisma. Opulence certainly characterised the lifestyle enjoyed by Enron's top executives. For example, Kenneth Lay had Enron pay US$7.1 million for a penthouse apartment, which he and his wife converted into a Venetian palace, with dark woods, deep velvets, period statuary and a vaulted brick ceiling in the kitchen. The implication was that others could some day hope to obtain similar privileges for themselves – provided that they embraced the value system and vision articulated by the leaders, emulated their behaviours and suppressed whatever critical internal voices occasionally threatened to surface. It thus became a further means of enforcing conformity with the vision of the charismatic leader and obtaining enthusiastic demonstrations of support for whatever the general direction of the organization was proclaimed to be.

2 Compelling vision – intellectual stimulation

Enron's vision was secular in nature but, within that framework, became all encompassing. In essence, it promised people heaven on Earth. If the company were to achieve its goals, unimagined wealth and happiness would be the lot of those fortunate enough to be employees at the time. This frequently led to hubris. The company's annual report for 2000 typified the tone of fantasy increasingly emanating from those at the top:

> We believe wholesale gas and power in North America, Europe and Japan will grow from a $660 billion market to a $1.7 trillion market over the next several years. Retail energy services in the United States and Europe have the potential to grow from $180 billion to $765 billion in the not-so-distant future. Broadband's prospective global growth is huge – it should increase from just $17 billion today to $1.4 trillion within five years. Taken together, these markets present a £3.9 trillion opportunity for Enron, and we have just scratched the surface.
>
> (cited by Cruver 2003, p.45)

At around this time, Enron draped a huge banner at its entrance, proclaiming its latest vision – 'FROM THE WORLD'S LEADING ENERGY COMPANY – TO THE WORLD'S LEADING COMPANY'. Such hyperbole was a normal part of Enron's discourse. Craig and Amernic (2004) have highlighted numerous examples of its presence in letters to shareholders, which as they point out also made use of the language of war, sport and extremism, to reinforce the potency of what was a compelling and totalistic vision of the most dramatic kind. Extraordinary goals, set by the leaders, encourage group members to regard their group as being particularly special and engender a sense of privilege and uniqueness among those who belong (Lalich 2004), as do images of the organization being at war with everyone else.

The wealth that could be made within Enron further encouraged feelings among employees that they faced a much more exalted destiny than that of people who worked for other companies. For those who achieved their goals, huge bonuses were available – to such an extent that Houston's luxury car dealers habitually visited Enron to exhibit their products every bonus period (Prentice 2003). Largesse was also extended to employees' families. The prevailing philosophy, as Cruver (2003: 191) summarised it, was that 'If you were smart enough and tough enough to work at Enron, you deserved to live like last year's Oscar winner'. The consistent message to employees was that they were the brightest and the best, that they were greatly favoured by being selected to work at Enron and that they were now charged with an evangelical mission of transforming how business conducted itself in the world. All accounts describe it as an intensely stimulating environment – to the point where many wondered how they could ever bear to work anywhere else again (for example, Cruver 2003). For those who bought into such messages, it followed that extraordinary levels of commitment were required.

Work regimes of up to 80 hours a week came to be regarded as normal. Employees sacrificed their today in the hope of a better tomorrow. But, given the demands:

> Skilling hired people who were very young, because very young people did not insist on coming in at nine or leaving at five, or on keeping things as they had always been, or, for that matter, on questioning authority once they had signed on with him.
>
> (Swartz and Watkins 2003: 58)

As with other organizations that could be regarded as cults, a totalistic vision may offer plentiful intellectual stimulation but such visions also imply high levels of social control. As Lalich observed:

> In identifying with the group, members find meaning and purpose and a sense of belonging. This is experienced as a type of personal freedom and self-fulfilment. Yet that freedom is predicated on a decrease in personal autonomy, manifested in continuous acts of ever-increasing self-renunciation.
>
> (Lalich 2004: 18)

Those affected experience a diminished capacity for critical reflection. Specifically, in the context of Enron, Swartz and Watkins (2003: 58) comment on the widely held belief that hard work now might buy a liberated future: 'That the single-minded pursuit of money might be self-limiting in other, psychic ways was not really considered'. The problem is that unbounded commitment to career development encourages people to 'treat all organizational, social and even personal relations as instrumental to career progress' (Collinson 2003: 537). In essence, their sense of who and what they are becomes indistinguishable from the corporate environment and the priorities decreed by its leaders – a personality transformation, it should be noted, that is greatly valued by cult gurus of all persuasions. It is also a mindset which is increasingly promoted by corporate leaders and one that leaves those who adopt it much more liable to escalate their commitment beyond any point of rationality.

3 Individual consideration, 'love bombing' and the process of conversion

Recruitment is clearly vital for cults, since the expansion of their influence requires a growing army of enthusiastic disciples. The problem is that the prospective recruit's resistance is likely to be at its highest immediately before they join. They have yet to buy into the belief system, invest much energy in pursuit of the group's goals or acquire unreasoning faith in its leaders and they still have plentiful other choices. The challenge is to recruit and initiate people into the group, engage a process of conversion and then reinforce it with indoctrination. How is this accomplished and to what extent did similar practices prevail at Enron?

Recruitment and initiation

Cults usually recruit people through a two-pronged process characterised by intense and emotionally draining recruitment rituals on the one hand and what I noted in Chapter 2 has been described as 'love bombing' on the other. In terms of rituals, a process is engaged that may stretch over several days, which exposes the would-be recruit to powerful messages from the leader, which requires them to express ever-greater levels of support for the leader's insights and which may involve the person adopting behaviours that might otherwise seem irksome and certainly strange. The process can be likened to a rollercoaster, with potential recruits soaring to emotional highs and then experiencing mood collapses which, in total, leave them ever more vulnerable to the messages of its leaders. Research into group dynamics has long established that, when we endure particular initiation rituals or experience discomfort to join, we are then more inclined to exaggerate the benefits of group membership and to intensify our sense of commitment as a means of establishing that we belong to the group (Aronson and Mills 1959). Emotionally debilitating recruitment rituals, assuming that the potential recruit has some intrinsic motivation for looking positively on the group, are likely to have precisely this effect.

However, pressure alone does not suffice. Love bombing is also crucial, with the implied promise that that, if the recruit merely accedes to the high demands of the group, they will receive the beneficent regard of the leader and other members of the organization. Thus, cult leaders make great ceremony of showing individual consideration for their members – at least, immediately before and after they join. Prospective recruits are showered with attention, which expands to affection and then often grows into a simulation of love. This is the courtship phase of the recruitment ritual. The leader wishes to seduce the new recruit into the organization's embrace, gradually habituating them to its rituals and belief systems. Individual consideration overcomes moods of resistance, by blurring distinctions between personal relationships, theoretical constructs and bizarre behaviours.

Consistent with this, recruitment at Enron was a particularly gruelling procedure. Fusaro and Miller reported that job candidates:

> had to demonstrate that they could maintain high levels of work intensity over an extended period of time. Some have compared the work environment and high employee intensity at Enron to that of a top law firm, which is typically filled with brilliant young associates willing to do whatever it takes to make partner.
>
> (Fusaro and Miller 2002: 49)

It was clear that those selected would be required to devote most of their waking hours to their new life as Enron employees. In this regard, as has already been highlighted, Enron certainly delivered on expectations. After the initial interview, they then attended a second interview on one of three to five 'Super Saturdays' that were held at Enron's Houston office. Candidates were interviewed for 50 minutes by eight different interviewers in succession with one ten-minute break – an emotionally intense experience for all.

Initially, prospective employees may have staged a dramatic performance designed to convince the recruiter that they viewed the company's vision with the mindset of True Believers, even if they felt doubts – a normal aspect of impression management during selection interviews. However, prolonged performance of this kind has hazards. As Goffman (1959: 28) stressed, 'one finds that the performer can be fully taken in by his own act; he can be sincerely convinced that the impression of reality which he stages is the real reality'. I discussed similar dynamics as a key aspect of coercive persuasion in Chapter 3. The further emulation of organizational rituals heightens the effect. Within Enron, there was intense pressure to participate in a whole variety of rituals – including those associated with ostentatious consumption – and which had precisely these effects.

Conversion

It is thus likely that, within Enron, the dramaturgically focused selection process and subsequent induction into a high-performance work environment initiated a process analogous to cultic conversion, in which prospective employees:

- needed overwhelming levels of intrinsic motivation to persevere;
- found themselves joining a high-demand environment, in which it was made clear that they would be required to display further levels of inordinate commitment;
- were exposed to the notion that membership of the Enron team represented a particular privilege but also imposed unusually high obligations;
- were presented with the 'vision' proclaimed by Enron's leaders and required to frequently express their solidarity with a dominant and centrally ordained corporate philosophy.

All this was reinforced by various versions of love bombing – once the person was selected and agreed to join the organization. As many have noted, Enronians were frequently told and came to believe that they were the brightest and best employees in the world. They were certainly well rewarded and were the eager recipients of a great deal of company largesse. For example, many had access to company credit cards, on which they were encouraged to charge their prostitution expenses (Fusaro and Miller 2002). Provided that they performed to a high standard, they could count on an unlimited benevolent attitude from Enron's leaders. Seeking to hold on to such approval and the benefits that flowed from it, attitudes shifted further and further from whatever their original starting point had been. The Enron way seemed increasingly natural: it was, after all, 'the way of the world'. At some point, those so seduced would look in the mirror and see only an Enronian staring back at them.

Indoctrination

Once established, the convert mentality is reinforced by a process of indoctrination. Indoctrination occurs through the one-way transmission of intense messages from leaders to followers that require ever greater levels of devotion to the group ideal and which are designed to instil into the recruit a feeling that being accepted into the group is a particular privilege that makes him or her a member of a special élite. Thus, recruitment and initiation, conversion and indoctrination are all vital stages in the cultic experience and are sustained through the impression of individual consideration by the group's leaders.

What can be viewed as indoctrination, flowing from the organization's leaders, became a normal part of life throughout the employee's Enron career. The further one ascended the hierarchy, the more one was exposed to it. A typical example can be found in the company's 1999 management conference, as described by Swartz and Watkins. They reported that the then CEO, Jeffrey Skilling, turned the event into:

> a grim tutorial on "growing earnings" or, in layman's terms, boosting prof-
> its ... the Hyatt's ballroom felt like a reeducation camp, as every speaker
> stressed the new corporate dogma, which was that Enron's hard assets could
> no longer be depended on to keep the stock price rising at Skilling's desired
> rate of 20 percent a year ... Enron's mandate was to become more nimble,
> more flexible, more innovative – or else. The speakers ... had droned on
> about that mission for hours. Most of that day, Skilling prowled the perimeter
> of the ballroom, making sure that his acolytes were, in his words, "getting it".
> (Swartz and Watkins 2003: 7)

In this, and other accounts of Enron, communication emerges as essentially one way – from the organization's top leaders to those at the bottom. Its purpose was to reinforce the demanding goals set by Enron's leaders. Corrective feedback was not sought. In fact, it was stifled. The purpose of communication, Enron style, was simply to transmit a highly demanding company vision and to ensure its rapid implementation. People were expected to escalate their commitment and transform their attitudes to be ever more consistent with the needs of the organization's leaders.

4 Promoting a common culture

I suggested earlier in this book that much of the most influential management literature in the last three decades has sold the notion of what amounts to a mono- lithic organizational culture, to be determined exclusively by senior managers, as the key to overall success. The importance of this resides in the notion that organizational cultures consist of cognitive systems explaining how people think, reason and make decisions (Pettigrew 1979, 1990). If cultures can therefore be controlled by those at the top, the overall impact on people is likely to be enor- mous. In such schemas, the views of non-managerial employees, women and/or minorities are unlikely to be considered (Martin 1992, 1999).

A further paradox within cults is that individual consideration shifts from being positive to critical in nature. Once the recruit has been 'won over' and has made an intense commitment, the group seeks to ensure the further embrace of its norms by a relentless process of criticism and attack. Individual consideration of a positive kind (Dr Jekyll) alternates with its alter ego (Mr Hyde). Relentless criticism gradually erodes people's confidence in their own perceptions (Tourish and Wohlforth 2000), creating a form of learned helplessness (Seligman 1975). 'Love' – always dependent on the unconditional expression of enthusiasm for the goals of the group's leaders – alternates with abuse, in a disorienting cycle that leaves recipients feeling fearful and powerless. Context is crucial. Having made an initial commitment, possibly of a dramatic kind, recruits are motivated to engage in further behaviours consistent with the commitment originally made – the principle of commitment and consistency. When this blends with learned helplessness, it reinforces even further people's already strong inclination to over-identify with the norms that have been decreed by the group's leaders. The leaders, meanwhile, have adorned themselves in the garb of omniscience and infallibility. Paradoxically, and provided that it has come after a period of love bombing, criticism from such sources reinforces the person's attachment to the group's belief system and their sense of loyalty to its leaders.

Moreover, abuse generates multiple insecurities, further strengthening leadership power. Whatever its precise content, insecurity reinforces 'the construction of workplace selves and the reproduction of organizational power relations' (Collinson 2003: 530). In particular, it seems likely that, when people are insecure about their self-identity and their status, the nominal freedom of their position (after all, they retain the choice to leave) will be experienced as a form of existential angst, intensifying their sense of vulnerability. If they are rendered fearful in the manner described here and when the most modest expression of dissent attracts punitive attention from those above, it seems even more likely that people 'might try to find shelter in the perceived security of being told what to do and what to think, viewing this as a less threatening alternative to the responsibility of making decisions and choices for themselves' (Collinson 2003: 531). When the group environment assumes that all change must start at the top, the leader knows best, the leader must have a compelling vision and that one unifying culture is a precondition of effectiveness, inherently cult-like dynamics of the kind described here may be unleashed. It is clear that many of these assumptions are now standard features of the leadership culture in many corporate organizations.

The case of Enron: 'rank and yank' and the elimination of dissent

Side by side with largesse and ego stroking, a punitive internal culture was established, in which all that had been so painstakingly gained could be withdrawn at the whim of senior managers. As Fusaro and Miller (2003: 51) remarked: 'Despite all the effort that Enron expended in selecting the right people to hire into the company, it was quick to fire them'. The most striking illustration of this was in the organization's appraisal system, known as 'rank and yank'. Its practice within Enron was close to the approach of 'differentiation' advocated by General

Electric's Jack Welch and which I discuss and criticise in Chapter 6. An internal performance review committee rated employees twice a year (Gladwell 2002). They were graded on a scale of one to five on ten separate criteria and then divided into one of three groups – 'A's, who were to be challenged and given large rewards; 'B's, who were to be encouraged and affirmed; and 'C's, who were told to shape up or ship out. Those in the top category were referred to internally as 'water walkers' (Swartz and Watkins 2003). Those in the bottom category were given until their next review to improve. In practice, however, with another 15 per cent category emerging within six months sufficient improvement was almost impossible and they tended to leave quickly. Furthermore, those in category two were also now in a position where they too faced the strong possibility of being 'yanked' within the next year. A cut-throat culture was created. The overall, and distinctly cultic, impact is well summarised by Fusaro and Miller:

> It is clear that Enron's management regarded kindness as a show of weakness. The same rigors that Enron faced in the marketplace were brought into the company in a way that destroyed morale and internal cohesion. In the process of trying to quickly and efficiently separate from the company those employees who were not carrying their weight, Enron created an environment where employees were afraid to express their opinions or to question unethical and potentially illegal business practices. Because the rank-and-yank system was both arbitrary and subjective, it was easily used by managers to reward blind loyalty and quash brewing dissent.
>
> (Fusaro and Miller 2003: 52)

Ultimately, cults and their leaders thrive on internal aggression. Intense criticism aimed at individuals stresses the imagined weaknesses of the person at the receiving end rather than, for example, difficulties with the wider organization. The punitive internal atmosphere that results reminds members of the fate that awaits them should they dissent or deliver performance below the high goals set for them by the group's leaders. In addition, by keeping members fearful of each other, their attention is further diverted from the behaviour of the group's leaders. Within Enron, it appears that the tyrannisation personified by the rank-and-yank system unleashed what has been described, in other contexts, as the 'identification with the aggressor syndrome' (Kets de Vries 2001). This postulates that, to feel safer, those at the receiving end of aggression assume an aggressive posture themselves. They move from being threatened to being threatening. The catch is that 'all they accomplish is to become aggressors themselves, thus increasing the total organizational aggression' (Kets de Vries 2001: 81).

The rank-and-yank system therefore pitted employees against each other. It was clearly in every individual's interest that someone other than themselves received a poor rating. This created a strong incentive to provide poor evaluations for others while simultaneously seeking positive evaluations for oneself. Backroom deals, shifting alliances and broken promises were the norm. It also provided an incentive to conformity and a disincentive to the articulation of a dissenting voice. But there was no escaping the relentless logic of the bottom line. Whatever they did, 15 per cent of all employees would find themselves in the lowest category twice a year, where they faced the daunting prospect of being yanked.

Clearly, the switch from affirmation to punishment within Enron meant that employees regularly received mixed messages. On the one hand, they were the cleverest and best in the world – a form of positive reinforcement or love bombing that it would be hard to better. On the other, they could be branded as 'losers' (a favourite term of abuse, for those who fell at the performance review committee hurdle) and fired at any time. The overall effect was disorientation, an erosion of one's confidence in one's own perceptions and, most crucially, a further compliance with the group's leaders that strengthened conformist behaviour in general.

Mixed messages within cults are a standard means of projecting 'the illusion of choice' (Lalich 2004: 190), while actually intensifying control by the group's leaders. Such messages also constrain topics of discussion, further reinforcing conformist behaviours. As Werther (2003: 69) expressed it, the ambiguities and inconsistencies of mixed messages became undiscussable within Enron. But the prevailing culture rendered 'the undiscussability of the undiscussable also undiscussable'. There were no forums where employees could communicate about such concerns, beyond whatever informal grapevines managed to survive in such a hostile climate.

It was clear to all that dissent would not be tolerated. As Salter (2008: 5) summarises it, there was a widespread 'intolerance of internal dissent regarding the company's controversial financial strategies'. Anyone who queried accountancy practices was likely, at best, to be reassigned or lose a bonus. A 1995 survey of employees found that many were uncomfortable about voicing their feelings and 'telling it like it is at Enron' (Swartz and Watkins 2003: 76). The example of Sherron Watkins illustrates the mindset. Watkins was a senior employee who worked with Enron's Chief Financial Officer, Andy Fastow. When she realised that the company's losses would become apparent sometime in 2003 or 2004, an insight that obviously erred in the direction of optimism, she drew her concerns to the attention of Ken Lay, who had stepped back into the role of CEO. Support was not forthcoming from other senior executives, who evidently feared that to acknowledge the problems would damage their careers at Enron. Lay's own response suggests that these fears were well founded. Within days of meeting with Watkins, he contacted the organization's lawyers to inquire if grounds could be found for firing her (Watkins 2003a,b). It should be noted that the intrinsically modest act of approaching the CEO to voice concerns is amongst the most notable acts of resistance currently on record within Enron. It is also notable that its impact was negligible. Enron's collapse was precipitated when it was compelled to knock US$1.2 billion off shareholder equity, rather than because of a widespread refusal to go along with its fraudulent practices or destructive internal culture.

Thus, processes of co-construction were constantly at work. Dissent, while present, was minimal. The outlandish visions and corrupt business practices of

Enron's leaders received the vindication of endorsement and enactment, encouraging them to further develop risky business models increasingly constructed from fantasy. Among participants in this fiction was the company's board, which 'perpetuated outmoded board processes. They ratified and were subject to an inflated stock-based compensation plan that made it increasingly difficult for them to challenge management' (Salter 2008: 179). Moreover, they waived the company's code of ethics in certain circumstances (Knottnerus *et al.* 2006). It is easy to see why this was the case. Board members benefited from the fraud that was going on and did little to probe beneath the surface of the glowing accounts that Lay, Skilling and Fastow presented to them. When the organization crashed, so did the reputations, livelihoods and liberties of its leaders – the identities and fates of leaders and followers were co-constructed and destructively intertwined.

This reading resists an account of Enron's failure simply in terms of the agency of its leaders, for this agency drew considerable strength from the agency of others. Indeed, leader agency would be neutered without an accompanying social context in which dissent is muted and/or active endorsement is offered by significant numbers of other organizational actors. Consistent with structuration perspectives on agency, agents within Enron can therefore be said to have drawn extensively upon their knowledge of the structural context in which they operated (including their knowledge of established rules, precedents and modes of legitimation) when they engaged in purposeful action, or inaction (Stones 2005). Their use of such knowledge reinforced the social structures and power relationships from which they were derived, in another instance of co-construction at work. Thus, the dark side of leadership achieves much of its effect by implicating non-leaders in its dynamics. It is a contagion to which few are immune. In the case of Enron, resistance would have been career suicide. There were few volunteers.

A company of 'believers'?

In 1997, employees were interviewed about their attitudes and, perhaps inevitably, a 'vision' was adopted in response (Swartz and Watkins 2003).[4] The process and its outcome illustrate particularly well the extent of a common but totalistic culture within the organization and a widespread overreliance on the supposedly superior insights of the organization's leaders. An advertising agency was charged with developing the new vision, a choice of firm that is itself bizarre. It concluded that Enron was a company of 'believers'. In particular, employees had intense faith in Ken Lay and Jeff Skilling. They were also convinced – naturally – that Enron employees were the best and the brightest in the world and they believed that they were doing good by opening new markets and creating new products and services. As a result, an advertising campaign was launched, around a concept called 'What We Believe'. Those beliefs included 'the wisdom of open markets' and 'being a laboratory for innovation'. A new 'vision and values' team was created, which declared that 'Everything we do is about change'.

From an outside perspective, the slogans may appear rather vacuous, as indeed are those of more well-known and non-corporate cults. However, this may also be their strength. Slogans bereft of real content often enable people to read into them whatever meanings they wish and thus ensure a much wider buy in. A video was also produced, entitled *What we Believe*, for company-wide dissemination (RealTimeLiveTV 2009). In it, Lay proclaimed that his main objective was 'to create an environment where our employees can come in here and realize their potential'. He did not specify whether this ambition extended only to those who survived the 'rank-and-yank' system. Lay also said:

> Enron is a company that treats everyone with absolute integrity. We stand by our word. We mean what we say, we say what we mean. We want people to leave a transaction with Enron thinking that they've been dealt with in the highest possible way.
>
> (RealTimeLiveTV 2009)

As Swartz and Watkins observed:

> The whole campaign was not unlike a religious tract from a New Age mega-church, but instead of directing disciples to God, Enron hopes its congregation would be inspired to join its mission to make itself The World's Leading Energy Company.
>
> (Swartz and Watkins 2003: 103)

Language was crucial to the process. Again, the testimony of Swartz and Watkins is typical. They describe language within Enron as follows:

> No one at Enron would ever 'build consensus,' they would 'come to shore,' as in 'We have to come to shore on this,' or 'Are you ready to come to shore on this?' One week somebody used the word 'metrics' to mean the numbers in a deal, as in 'We've got to massage the metrics!' Pretty soon, everyone was using the term 'metrics' and anyone who used the term 'numbers' or 'calculations' was a 'loser,' the most popular Enron label of all.
>
> (Swartz and Watkins 2003: 193)

Such constricted language, often baffling to outsiders, is typical of totalistic environments and has been observed in a huge variety of cults. As Hardy and Phillips (2004: 299) argue, power and discourse are mutually constitutive: discourse can 'shape the system that exists in a particular context by holding in place the categories and identities upon which it rests'. Control of language within Enron, in the manner described here, played precisely this function. It engineered a uniform definition of reality, consistent with a managerially sanctioned vision of the truth. In turn, this established an increasingly conformist culture in which the possibility of dissent and debate retreated ever further from the organization's practice.

Deception and the control of information

Typically, cult leaders have extraordinary authority, privileged access to informa-tion and a hidden agenda of self-aggrandisement that is concealed behind more idealistic statements. The dominant culture is maintained because ordinary followers are denied full information about the organization's goals or practices, while a carefully contrived public display of righteousness by the leaders prevents detailed scrutiny of actual behaviour as opposed to avowed intentions. Consistent with this dynamic, information emanating from the top within Enron was also distorted in nature. As Lalich (2004: 235) noted, in her comprehensive compari-son of two cults: 'the vast majority of members did not know such things as where the money went or how overall strategic decisions were made. Strict poli-cies controlled and contained information'.

Information flow within Enron was indeed tightly regulated in this manner. The intended effect was to reinforce the authority of Enron's leaders. People assumed that at least the leaders knew what was happening and that they had their followers' overall best interests at heart. Given what is known as the false consen-sus effect, which causes honest people to impute their honest motives to others (Prentice 2003), it is not surprising that Enron employees tended to assume that such people as Kenneth Lay were abiding by normal accounting procedures. In reality, 'there was misrepresentation of hard data, that is, concealment of debt, lying about accounting results, as well as about the stream of earnings and the distortion of the company's future prospects' (Cohan 2002: 280).

A particularly ironic example of misinformation, deception and double stand-ards within Enron can be found in its heavily promoted code of ethics, known as 'RICE' – an acronym standing for 'respect, integrity, communication and excel-lence'. A 64-page booklet was produced, explaining the code in depth (Enron 2000).[5] Kenneth Lay issued a foreword to the code in July 2000, barely 18 months before Enron declared bankruptcy, in which he concluded that 'We want to be proud of Enron and to know it enjoys a reputation for fairness and honesty and that it is respected … Let's keep that reputation high'. As is now known, Enron's leaders disregarded the code in their daily practice – to such an extent that, to take but one of many examples, a 166-page report was published in 1999 entitled *The Enron Corporation: Corporate Complicity in Human Rights Violations*. It documented, among much else, how Enron executives paid local law enforcement officers to suppress legitimate and peaceful opposition to its power plant near Mumbai in India (Human Rights Watch 2002). The code of ethics was thus a dramaturgical device, whose theatrical display cultivated the illusion of noble ideals and generated a convincing spectacle of ethical practice for both the organization's internal and external audiences (Boje *et al.* 2004). It also helped to douse whatever suspicions people may have been nurturing about the behaviour of the organization's leaders.

The RICE code suggests that Enron was engaged essentially in the production and trading of illusions. The dominant illusion, of course, was one of high profit-ability. Skilling, for example, secured approval from the Securities Exchange

Commission (SEC) – after lobbying in conjunction with the doomed accountancy firm, Arthur Anderson – to use an accountancy system known as 'mark-to-market' accounting. This enabled Enron to report ever-rising profits even though the cash concerned would not be earned for many years. But this triggered lucrative bonuses for Skilling himself, since these depended on the perceived overall value of the company (Salter 2008).

The main spectacle was sustained, at a deep structural level, by a myriad of other theatrical discourses. In this instance, the RICE code suggested that the organization's activities were underpinned by a strong ethical code. The cultivation of such a belief was intended to facilitate intense belief, compliance, over-identification with the group's goals and leaders and heightened dedication to the pursuit of declared ideals. The presentation of an image at odds with a malignant reality is a standard leadership tactic in most documented cults. It is now clear that the architects of the Enron story also made ample use of drama, spectacle, and the projection of financial illusions in their daily practice.

Producing the 'appropriate' individual

Overall, it appears that Enron's leaders inculcated a powerful set of cultural norms in its employees. These specified acceptable business dress, how people talked to each other and to what values they were supposed to subscribe. The culture attempted to regulate people's identities – an increasingly common process and one which has the effect of reinforcing organizational control, through producing individuals deemed appropriate by the ruling group (Alvesson and Willmott 2002). It is a dynamic consistent with the role of culture within cults, particular in terms of its role in defining a narrow range of acceptable behaviours, attitudes and emotions.

Paradoxically, even from Enron's own perspective, the ultimate effect was dysfunctional – after all, the organization expired. This suggests that, although the methods analysed here may temporarily strengthen leadership control in small groups, they are incompatible with long-term growth and success. Thus, Enron maintained a façade of teamwork. But behind the façade lurked the ruthless self-interest of its leaders – a self-interest that others then felt compelled to emulate. As Swartz and Watkins (2003: 192) noted:

> There was so much infighting over who got financial credit for a deal in the Performance Review Committee that the total amount credited to individuals far exceeded the total company income for the year. Even so, everyone felt obliged to quibble over the smallest points, because if you didn't, you got a reputation as a chump.
>
> (Swartz and Watkins 2003: 192)

Those deemed to be 'chumps' were thought to be exhibiting a purely personal weakness, rather than demonstrating any systemic difficulties with the organization. Such a fate and set of labels again mirrors those directed against dissenters in all variety of cults. They had the effect of reinforcing the power of Enron's leaders. Other employees manoeuvred and conspired to avoid joining those in the category of 'losers' or 'chumps'. Most critically, with so much effort invested in face saving and self-enhancement, the destructive practices of Enron's leadership remained unchallenged, while a destructive corporate culture took deeper root. The end result was disaster, disgrace, impoverishment, jail, suicide and a legacy of corporate criminality that will demand attention for many years to come.

Conclusion

I have argued that many of the dynamics found within Enron resemble those of organizations generally regarded as cults. In particular, I have described the existence and the downsides of charismatic leadership, the development of a compelling and totalistic vision, intellectual stimulation aimed at transforming employees' goals while subordinating their ethical sense to the needs of the corporation, individual consideration designed to shape behaviour and the promotion of a common culture which was increasingly maintained by punitive means.

The one exception is that, as the general literature testifies, cult members donate most of their money and possessions to their chosen cause. They endure great hardship. Enronians, by contrast, were well paid, with the promise of much greater wealth to come. On the other hand, most saw their retirement savings wiped out in Enron's collapse; they lost everything they had invested in its shares and received nothing more than a US$4,000 severance payment when it filed for bankruptcy, while top managers were paid exceptionally generous retention bonuses (Watkins 2003b). Overall, the organizational culture strongly resembles that of many well-known cults, as does the behaviour of Enron's leaders.

There were many attempts at the time of its demise to portray the Enron scandal as a one-off or at least rare occurrence. In particular, President Bush characterised it as the product of poor behaviour by a few 'bad apples' and therefore as an exceptional event (Conrad 2003). Others have noted that many business commentators used Enron as a 'scapegoat', standing as a surrogate for a wider corporate malaise that was hence denied (Hensmans 2003). In even more optimistic vein, as Deakin and Konzelmann (2003) have critically observed, the exposure and then collapse of Enron was used by some to argue that we can be more confident in corporate America and its regulatory regimes. It is a line of argument heard less often since 2008 and the revelation of just how self-interested and unregulated the behaviour of many banking leaders proved to be.

In particular, recent years have witnessed an extraordinary growth in the power of CEOs, while the power of employees has declined. But a corollary of great power is the anticipation of miraculous results. Imperial CEOs, all too aware of the limited opportunity they are now afforded by the stock market to make a dramatic difference, may be tempted to resort to the theatrical approaches typical of cult leaders, which were certainly the norm at Enron. In the process, they encourage conformity and penalise dissent. Yet the evidence indicates that effective leaders need to do the opposite and, in particular, should encourage constructive dissent, rather than destructive consent (see Chapter 5). Enron suggests that many, if not most, leaders have yet to grasp this point, with potentially catastrophic results for their organizations – and, in many cases, themselves.

Thus, more leaders are attempting to bind employees to the corporate ideal, while curtailing forums for debate. They project an image of charismatic leadership, stress a compelling vision, depict their companies as a surrogate family and attempt to blur any perceived difference between the interests of managers and non-managers. Such approaches seek to re-engineer the most intimate beliefs of employees, so that they are aligned with whatever the leader deems is helpful to the corporate enterprise. I suggest in Chapter 4 that the spirituality at work movement is a good example of an approach which has this potential. It makes it even less likely that employees will ask awkward questions of their leaders and so be capable of correcting their inevitable misjudgements. These may constitute fertile conditions for the emergence of other Enrons in the future.

The dangers are considerable. Once people overalign themselves with a company and invest excessive faith in the wisdom of its leaders, they are liable to lose their original sense of identity, tolerate ethical lapses they would have previously deplored, find a new and possibly corrosive value system taking root and leave themselves vulnerable to manipulation by the leaders of the organization, to whom they have mistakenly entrusted many of their vital interests. Human beings need to believe in something. They are frequently naïve in where they choose to invest their belief and are vulnerable to dramaturgical spectacles designed to engage their loyalty. Enron's leaders 'traded' on the desire of many people to believe that ever increasing profits could be manufactured by means of accountancy conjuring tricks, by an organization that was also serving a greater good – a secular miracle. In that context, it may bequeath a cultural legacy that other business leaders increasingly seek to emulate. The phenomenon of corporate cultism, too easily facilitated by theories of transformational leadership, may thus become more widespread and may require much closer study than it has merited to date.

Points for discussion

1. To what extent do you think that the leadership style of Kenneth Lay and Jeffrey Skilling contributed to Enron's collapse?
2. Which leadership behaviours within Enron are most consistent with the suggestion that it was a corporate cult? How widespread a problem do you think corporate cultism is?
3. Consider Enron's policy of 'rank and yank'. What do you think its effects were on critical upward communication? What are the wider leadership implications that this raises?
4. Enron had an exemplary code of ethics but did not live up to them in practice. What does this suggest for the practice of ethical leadership in business organizations?

Notes

1 Much of this analysis originally appeared as follows: Tourish, D. and Vatcha, N. (2005) Charismatic leadership and corporate cultism at Enron: the elimination of dissent, the promotion of conformity and organizational collapse, *Leadership*, 1, 455–80.

2 Events leading up to the collapse of Lehman's are vividly described by Ward (2010), in a book evocatively entitled *The Devil's Casino*.

3 In 2005, an excellent documentary was also produced. It is entitled *Enron: The Smartest Guys in the Room*. This is available in DVD format and also in full on Youtube, at http://www.youtube.com/watch?v=_xIO731MAO4. Last accessed 20 November 2012.

4 The following discussion of Enron's 1997 re-visioning is taken from the account of Swartz and Watkins (2003). All quotations used here can be found in their original form in their text, on pages 103–5.

5 A complete copy of this remarkable document can be found at the following link: http://bobsutton.typepad.com/files/enron-ethics.pdf. Last accessed 20 November 2012.

8 The Militant Tendency's long march to oblivion

Conformity and authoritarian leadership on the left[1]

Introduction

Cultic leadership in politics has attracted relatively little attention. I have chosen this as a case for several reasons. Firstly, and in defiance of the irrelevance that normally attaches, limpet like, to fratricidal far-left groups, the Militant Tendency acquired significant influence in the 1980s and early 1990s. It was also known as the Committee for a Workers International (CWI), a term that I will use in the rest of this chapter for the sake of brevity. The CWI led a major local authority in Liverpool, from which position it launched a prolonged struggle against the then Tory Government. CWI members controlled the mainstream Labour Party's youth section, the Young Socialists. Three Labour Members of Parliament were well known CWI activists. It helped split the Labour Party asunder for much of the 1980s. It therefore arguably made an important contribution to ensuring that the Conservative Party remained in power for 17 years. At its peak, the organization had around 8,000 members and over 200 full time workers – more than the Labour Party employed. It occupied a spacious international headquarters in London and published a 16-page weekly newspaper, *Militant*, from which it derived the name by which it was best known. In short, the CWI became probably the most successful Trotskyist organization in the world since the 1930s. In addition, it played a leading role in the mass movements against a proposed government tax (the 'Poll Tax') in the early 1990s and therefore had an important role in the growing unpopularity of Prime Minister Margret Thatcher, who eventually resigned. Whether this balances out helping to sustain her in power for so long in the first place is a matter for political scientists and activists to debate. While the CWI may be destined to be a footnote in British political history, it is a rather large one. This alone makes it an important object for study.

The influence I have described proved transitory. In short order, members of the CWI found themselves at war with each other. Denunciations, expulsions and splits, as inevitable in such organizations as snow during an Arctic winter, duly ensued. My interest here is in the leadership dynamics that were implicated in its rise and all too predictable fall. This chapter is not therefore a detailed history of its ups and downs, splits, struggles, occasional victories and more frequent defeats. Rather, it is a study of the CWI's leadership practices, in an attempt to understand dysfunctional leadership more widely. The coercive influence processes that I will describe are not unique to the CWI or, for that matter, the broader Trotskyist tradition. They are uncannily similar to the Communist parties that at one time had tens of thousands of members in many countries, including the USA, and millions of supporters in Europe. As economic conditions deteriorate, it is not excluded that many may find themselves attracted to such ideas, in their Communist or Trotskyist variants, once again. The rise and collapse of the CWI is an excellent role model for them – but as a dreadful warning, rather than a good example.

I draw on previously published accounts (including my own), many documents intended only for CWI members that have come my way, interviews with former members and comments drawn from publicly accessible online discussion groups in which ex-members have participated to draw out the destructive leadership practices which ultimately led it to ruin. I suggest that the rise and fall of the CWI can be understood in terms of Lifton's (1961) notion of 'ideological totalism', discussed briefly in Chapter 2. Lifton defined this as 'the coming together of immoderate ideology with equally immoderate individual character traits – an extremist meeting ground between people and ideas' (Lifton 1961: 477). He made it clear that the potential for such ideological totalism is present within everyone, in that extreme conformity exists at one end of a continuum, consisting at the other end of extreme dissent. However, totalistic convictions are:

> most likely to occur with those ideologies which are most sweeping in their content and most ambitious – or messianic – in their claims, whether religious, political or scientific. And where totalism exists, a religion, a political movement, or even a scientific organization becomes little more than an exclusive cult.
>
> (Lifton 1961: 477)

Trotskyist and similarly inclined organizations adhere to what could only be described as such an ambitious and messianic ideology, thereby holding an enormously exalted view of their role in society. The case history of the CWI suggests that conformity, the concentration of power in the hands of a few increasingly deluded leaders, the banning of dissent, intense activism and ultimate collapse are inevitable features of such a political landscape. It shows us much about leadership generally, helps us identify what social change movements should avoid doing and implicitly points to at least some leadership practices that are less likely to end in catastrophic failure.

The CWI and cultism

The CWI traces its origins to South Africa. It was there, in 1913, that Isaak Blanck was born. An unusual adolescent, whose only known non-political interests in later life were cowboy movies, gobstoppers and table tennis, Isaak had become a convinced Marxist by the age of 15. In the 1930s, hopeful that a more fertile field for activity could be found elsewhere, he departed for Britain, detouring long enough in France to meet with the charismatic and dedicated Leon Sedov, Trotsky's son, who, in 1938, died at the hands one of Stalin's agents. En route, Isaak Blanck became Ted Grant. It was a name he retained for the rest of his long political life, until his death in 2006 at the age of 93.

Many years of fractious and largely fruitless activity followed Grant's arrival in Britain. It would be pointless to document this in any detail. His story, and ours, only really meshes in the 1960s, by which stage Grant was instrumental in creating the newspaper, *Militant*, and had entrenched himself and his still small forces within one of the country's main political parties, the Labour Party. It was a policy originating with Trotsky himself in the 1930s and known as 'entrism'. In a move that may not have appeared significant at the time but which assumes importance later, a young Liverpool clerical officer named Peter Taaffe joined Grant's organization in the late 1950s/early 1960s, rapidly assuming a key role as an organizer – an area of expertise which always eluded the chronically disorganized, dishevelled and chaotic Ted Grant.

Also, beginning in the early 1970s, the CWI built small groups of supporters internationally, including within the USA. However, a huge dispute erupted within its ranks in Britain during 1991 over whether to remain inside the Labour Party and similar social democratic parties elsewhere in the world. This led to a split in early 1992, during which the organization's original founder, Ted Grant (alongside another key CWI leader, Alan Woods) and many others were expelled.[2] They instantly set up a new Trotskyist international, still committed to entrism, and later naming itself the 'International Marxist Tendency' (IMT). Bombast has never been in short supply within these circles. The CWI reconstituted itself as a new 'open' party named 'Militant Labour,' relaunched as the 'Socialist Party' in early 1997. This was now led by Peter Taaffe, who had become the organization's General Secretary in 1964, and who at the time of writing still holds this post in his 70s. His tenure rivals that of Fidel Castro. It tells much about the bizarre internal regimes found in such organizations. Tolbert and Hiatt (2009) suggest that the long-term entrenchment in office of a leader or leading group helps to insulate them from control by the rank and file and thus promotes forms of oligarchy. In the case of the CWI, top and semi-permanent leaders have tended to assume unchallengeable guru status over their largely unquestioning followers. They swiftly dispatch any who have the temerity to challenge them. Both the CWI and IMT, and the now numerous fragments that have since issued from them, have blazed a trail on the outer fringes of obscurity ever since the bitter split of 1992.

Here, I assess the CWI's theoretical beliefs, organizational and leadership practices and the 1992 split in terms of what they tell us about cultic leadership practices, an issue first visited in Chapter 2. In particular, the data on the CWI are viewed from the standpoint of Lifton's (1961) suggested criteria for 'ideological totalism'. Finally, the implications for the ideological underpinnings and organizational cultures of political organizations (particularly those on the left) are examined.

Traits of political cults

While extensive data is now available on the extent to which cultic methods have been used in a variety of settings, it is limited in its application to political cults in general and left-wing cults in particular. The main case study material hitherto available concerns a Marxist-Leninist party (the Democratic Workers Party, DWP) based in California from 1974 to 1985 (Siegel *et al.* 1987; Lalich 1992, 1993, 2004). There has also been a voluminous, fascinating and appalling memoir literature on the part of former Communist Party members in many countries (for example, Koestler 1949; Barmine 1954; Hyde 1958; Fast 1958, 1990; Valtin 1988; MacLeod 1997; Schrank 1998). While none of this draws on the literature on cultism, it offers invaluable primary testimony on precisely that phenomenon. Stein (2002) has also chronicled her own experiences in a little-known Minneapolis political cult of Maoist orientation. Despite their mutual antipathy, it is striking how closely the leadership and other practices in the Communist/Maoist environment parallel what we repeatedly find in Trotskyist and other left currents. More recently, Rudd (2009) has produced a riveting personal memoir of his experiences as a leading radical student activist in late 1960s America and subsequent involvement with the leftist terrorist group 'the Weathermen' in the 1970s, responsible for a series of bombings in protest against the Vietnam war.

These accounts, building on the definitions of cults discussed in Chapter Two, suggest that political cults tend to be characterised by the presence of the following traits:

1 A rigid belief system

In the case of left-wing political cults, this suggests that all social, natural, scientific, political, economic, historical and philosophical issues can only be analysed correctly from within the group's theoretical paradigm – one which therefore claims a privileged and all-embracing insight. As a CWI exemplar of this, there have been many online discussions of its history over the years in which ex-members participated. During one discussion of its failure to anticipate such seismic events as the return of capitalism in the Soviet Union, one former leader remarked: 'After all, we regarded ourselves as the most advanced theoretical current on the planet'. The view that the group's belief system explains everything eliminates the need for fresh or independent thought and removes the need to seek intellectual sustenance outside the group's own ideological fortress. All such thinking is dismissed as contaminated by the impure ideology of bourgeois society.

2 The group's beliefs are immune to falsification

No test can be devised or suggested which might have the effect of inducing a reappraisal. The all-embracing quality of the dominant ideology precludes re-evaluation, since it implies both omniscience and infallibility, particularly on the part of the group's leaders. Methods of analysis which set themselves more modest explanatory goals are viewed as intrinsically inferior. Those who question any aspect of the group's analysis are branded as deviationists bending to the 'pressures of capitalism,' and are driven from the ranks as heretics.

3 An authoritarian inner party regime is maintained

Decision making is concentrated in elite hands, which gradually dismantles or ignores all formal controls on its activities. Members are excluded from participation in determining policy, calling leaders to account or expressing dissent. This is combined with persistent assurances about the essentially democratic nature of the organization and the existence of exemplary democratic controls – on paper.

4 There is a growing tendency for the leaders to act in an arbitrary way, accrue personal power, perhaps engage in wealth accumulation from group members or in the procuring of sexual favours

Activities that would provoke censure if engaged in by rank and file members (for example, having a reasonable standard of living, enjoying time off, using the organization's funds for personal purposes) are tolerated when they apply to leaders.

5 Leader figures, alive or dead, are deified

In the first place, this tends to centre on Marx, Trotsky or other significant historical figures. It also increasingly transfers to existing leaders, who represent themselves as defending the historical continuity of the work of 'the great Marxist teachers'. In effect, the new leaders are depicted, in their unbending devotion to the founders' ideals, as the reincarnation of Lenin, Trotsky, Guevara or whoever. There is a tendency to settle arguments by referring constantly to the sayings of the wise leaders (past or present), rather than by developing an independent analysis. Even banal observations are usually buttressed by the use of supporting quotations from sanctified sources.

6 There is an intense level of activism, leaving little or no time for outside interests

Social life and personal 'friendships' revolve exclusively around the group, although such friendships are conditional on the maintenance of uncritical enthusiasm for the party line. Members acquire a specialised vocabulary. They call each other 'comrade'; many become archives of trivia from the misunderstood history of Bolshevism and pepper their dialogue with anecdotes about what Martov or Plekhanov allegedly did in 1903; others inject specious dialectical jargon into everyday conversation. This reinforces a sense of distance and difference from those outside their ranks. It also repels those who are not to some extent already attracted to the group's ideas, thereby ensuring that members turn inwards all the more. The group becomes central to their personal identity and they find it more and more difficult if not impossible to imagine a life outside their organization.

I will now explore the most salient features of the CWI's guiding ideology and leadership practice, to assess the extent to which they match the criteria suggested above.

The concept of a 'vanguard' party and its effect on conformity

A central tenet of Trotskyist politics and (with no small irony) its Communist rivals in their heyday has been its insistence that a 'vanguard party' is required to guide the working class to power. This is conceived as an organization of professional revolutionaries, steeped in Marxist ideology, tightly organized and determined to win the leadership of the working class. The idea was most forcefully advanced by Lenin at the turn of the last century and justified by reference to the particular needs of a revolutionary movement operating under an autocratic regime.

From the perspective of the discussion in this book a number of important consequences follow. Firstly, the notion of a vanguard party inherently predisposes its adherents, and its leaders in particular, to view themselves as the pivot on which world history is destined to turn. Revolution is seen as the only route by which humanity can avoid annihilation but revolution is only possible if a mass party is built around a group of 'cadres'; that is, devotees of the party with a particularly deep insight into its ideology. Thus, Trotskyists are possessed of a tremendous sense of urgency and a powerful conviction of their group's unique role in bringing about the transformation of the world. They develop delusions of historical grandeur. This approach leads to the belief that the leaders of the self-designated vanguard party have a level of insight into society's problem unmatched by anyone else. There are many instances of such a conviction in the CWI's publications. The following quotation from one of its internal documents is typical of the mind-set:

> What guarantees the superiority of our tendency... from all others inside and outside the labour movement is our understanding of all the myriad factors which determine the attitudes and moods of the workers at each stage. Not only the objective but the subjective ones too.

This insistence on the superior insight of the organization extended into all intellectual spheres, an example of what Lifton characterised as 'mystical manipulation'. He argues that: 'Included in this mystique is a sense of 'higher purpose', of 'having directly perceived some imminent law of social development', of being themselves the vanguard of this development' (Lifton 1961: 480).

Thus, the expelled Alan Woods and Ted Grant self-published a book on science, which attempted to apply a Marxist understanding to the origins of the universe, chaos theory, Einstein's theory of relativity, geology, evolutionary theory and much else (Woods and Grant 1995). The discussion here shows the extent to which the claim of privileged insight is central to the appeal of Trotskyist organizations and is ritually invoked to encourage supporters into binges of party building. Again ironically, such unfounded intellectual pretensions were common within the official Communist movement and are well documented in Kraditor's (1988) fascinating account of the mental life of Communist Party members in the USA in the period from 1930 to 1958.

This conviction of superiority is combined with contempt for all other organizations on the left. The closer such organizations are to the group's own ideological lineage, the more likely they are to be the targets of abuse. A CWI International Bulletin in 1975 declaims: 'we consider that our organizations are alone in upholding the banner of Marxism... we repudiate every sectarian fragment appropriating the name of the Fourth International'.[3]

One interviewee (David) told me:

> We were taught to absolutely hate every other political organization that there was. Anybody on the left who wasn't a Marxist were called left reformists, and we were absolutely convinced that they didn't have a clue. We looked on them as hopeless people. People outside left politics at all were dismissed as 'liberals', but we probably hated them more than extreme right wingers – we used the word liberal as a sort of political swear word. But other Trotskyist groupings were the worst. We just laughed at them in internal meetings. We called them 'the sects' and took the view that they were incapable of any development at all. They were good for a laugh at best, but really the attitude towards anybody else claiming to be Trotskyist was that they were the complete enemy of everything we stood for. If we ever had taken power God knows what we would have done to them.

This approach is useful for promoting in-group favouritism while stigmatising 'out-groups' and enhancing the authority of those leaders who are keepers of the sacred flame. However, an additional feature of Lenin's conception of a vanguard party is that it was to be governed by the principles of what he termed democratic centralism. It would not be a loose federation but a tightly integrated fighting force with a powerful central committee and a rule that all members publicly defend the agreed positions of the party, whatever opinions they might hold to the contrary in private. Between conferences the party's leading bodies would have extraordinary authority to manage the party's affairs, arbitrate in internal disputes, update doctrine and decide the party's response to fresh political events.

As Lenin expressed it:

> The principle of democratic centralism and autonomy for local party organizations implies universal and full freedom to criticise, so long as this does not

disturb the unity of a defined action; it rules out all criticism which disrupts or makes difficult unity of action decided upon by the party.

(Lenin 1977: 433)

This approach is almost certainly destined to prevent genuine internal discussion and to concentrate all real power in the hands of a tiny number of leaders. Firstly, it is not at all clear when 'full freedom to criticise' can actually be said to disturb the unity of a defined action. The norms of democratic centralism confer all power between conferences on to a central committee, allowing it to become the arbiter of when a dissident viewpoint is in danger of creating such a disturbance, normally presumed to be lethal. The history of the CWI suggests that they are strongly minded to view *any* dissent as precisely such a disruption and to respond by demanding that the dissident ceases their action on pain of expulsion from the party. It should be borne in mind that the leadership of Trotskyist groupings views itself as the infallible interpreter of sacred texts that are essential for the success of world revolution, which in turn is seen as vital if the world is to be saved from complete barbarism. This 'all or nothing' approach to political analysis reinforces the tendency to view dissent as something which automatically imperils the future of the planet and a justification of whatever measures are required to restore the illusion of unanimity. Critical upward communication is notable only by its absence. The following quotation, from a document written by those members expelled in 1992, suggests that such unanimity was endemic to the CWI method of working:[4]

> The immense authority of the leadership created an enormous degree of trust... In reality, the leadership of this tendency enjoyed more than trust. It had virtually a blank cheque (even in the most literal sense of the word) to do what it liked, without any real check or control. No leadership, no matter how honest or politically correct, should have that amount of 'trust'... we built a *politically homogeneous tendency*. Up to the recent period there did not appear to be any serious political disagreements. In fact, there have been disagreements on all kinds of political and organizational matters, but these were never allowed to reach even the level of the CC (Central Committee) or IEC (International Executive Committee). Nothing was permitted to indicate the slightest disagreement in the leadership ... There was uniformity, which at times came dangerously close to conformism ... The tendency became unused to genuine discussion and debate. To be frank, many comrades (including 'leading comrades') simply stopped thinking. It was sufficient just to *accept* the line of the leadership ... We have a situation where the leadership enjoys such trust that it amounts to a blank cheque; where there is uniformity of ideas, in which all dissent is automatically presented as disloyalty; where the leadership is allowed to function with virtually no checks or accountability, under conditions of complete secrecy from the rank-and-file. [emphasis in the original]

The points made here are not invalidated by the fact their authors went on to replicate precisely the habits they were criticising in their new organization, the IMT. It supports the view that intense fear of real debate and discussion was a defining characteristic of the CWI. This can be read as an example of what Lifton (1961: 483) described as the *demand for purity*, in which 'the experiential world is sharply divided into the pure and the impure, into the absolutely good and the absolutely evil'. Thus, internal debate was effectively squashed for most of the CWI's history, since ideas which challenged orthodoxy could be beaten off as tainted by 'the pressures of capitalism'. But, when the organization experienced significant setbacks in the late 1980s, internal debate became unavoidable, particularly since an opposition was declared by several of the most prominent leaders. However, this rapidly led to the formation of factions, uproar and expulsions, with each side to the dispute claiming (a) complete fidelity to sacred traditions and (b) that opponents were in some way capitulating to 'the pressures of capitalism'. Similar ructions have occurred at regular intervals within both of these groups ever since, most recently within the IMT in 2010, when a new set of sceptics and dissenters received their marching orders. The 'demand for purity' is thus central to Trotskyist practice but is inimical to the norms of democratic debate.

The CWI was by no means the worst in this respect. The Workers Revolutionary Party in Britain achieved notoriety in the 1970s and 1980s largely because it attracted such thespian luminaries as Vanessa Redgrave to its ranks. The group's leader, Gerry Healy (expelled in 1986 for the sexual abuse of female members, in an act of regicide that completely destroyed the organization), was in a constant state of high alert for heresy. He excommunicated anyone suspected of harbouring dissident views, no matter how flimsy the evidence that this was genuinely the case. The purity of the belief system always took precedence over influence in the outside world.

How debate was suppressed

Within the CWI, all resolutions at party conferences would traditionally come from the leadership or be completely supportive of its position. On those rare occasions when members submitted resolutions that were insufficiently enthusiastic about the general line, CWI leaders exerted enormous pressure for them to be withdrawn. They almost invariably were. The leading role in the elimination of dissent appears to have been played by the CWI's General Secretary, Peter Taaffe. A gifted organizer and a good speaker (by the standards of the CWI), he was also intellectually insecure, arrogant, ambitious and easy to antagonise. The 'oppositionist' document already quoted above recounts on this issue that:

> To cross the General Secretary would result in a tantrum or some kind of outburst. Comrades became fearful of initiative without the sanctions of the General Secretary. Incredibly, even the opening of a window during an EC

(Executive Committee) meeting would not go ahead without a nod from him! Under these conditions, the idea of 'collective leadership' is a nonsense ... The EC as a whole – which is supposed to be a sub-committee of the CC – is out of control. In 99% of cases the CC is simply a rubber stamp for the EC.

The picture that emerges is of elected bodies usurping the normal democratic rights of members and becoming increasingly removed from formal controls. It also appears that power continued to flow upwards to Peter Taaffe and the full-time staff that he had ample scope to mould in his image. The oppositionist document quoted above recounts:

no decisions of any significance are taken without the full knowledge and consent of the General Secretary, and that the great majority of them are taken, either on his initiative, or at least with his active participation ... The full-timers tend to order and bully the comrades, instead of convincing them. They rely upon the political authority of the leadership handed down from the past, in order to get their way. If you do not accept the targets handed down by the full-timer, you are 'not a good comrade', you are 'conservative', and so on.

All of these problems were exacerbated by the split of 1992. Power was centralised still further, in a process characteristic of all cult organizations. Taaffe had plainly come to believe that he was indispensable to the success of his organization in Britain and beyond – a variant, one interviewee joked to us, of 'founder's syndrome'. Another former leader told me that, in the middle of one discussion, Taaffe had leaned across the table and declared: 'The success of the British revolution rests on my shoulders'. He had determined that his destiny was to become the Lenin of modern-day Britain. This conviction began to guide the whole internal life of the organization.

Nor did this stop at formal meetings. Those CWI full timers at the London headquarters who had an athletic disposition usually retired to a local park at lunch time for a football match. Taaffe invariably captained one of the teams and again used his power of selection to signal who was in and out of favour. Parallels with the Byzantine power struggles in Stalin's Russia are unmistakable.

The now tired remnants of the organization embarked on yet another ferocious internal dispute in 1996, this time about whether to retain the title 'Militant Labour' or call itself 'the Socialist Party'. The then editor of the *Militant* newspaper, Nick Wrack, opposed the name change. Hitherto, he had been a loyal ally to Peter Taaffe and was usually selected by him as his vice-captain for the lunch-time football matches. This stopped as soon as the 'debate' broke out. Wrack was a broken man. Others who had shared his views made cringing apologies to the central committee, renouncing their 'errors'. Wrack himself resigned later in the year, complaining bitterly that Taaffe no longer even spoke to him when they passed in the corridor.

The gospel of catastrophism

Apocalyptic images pervade the ideology of cultic groups. Cultic religious group-ings routinely predict the end of the world. What some writers have termed 'catastrophism' also pervades the ideology of Trotskyist groupings (Callaghan 1984, 1987). A 1980 document produced in Northern Ireland was written by Peter Hadden, the taciturn son of a Church of Ireland minister who entertained a penchant for death analogies in his prose. He anticipated the closing decades of the twentieth century in the following terms:

> On a world scale capitalist economies not only find themselves in a crisis, they find themselves ensnared in an epoch of crisis, stagnation and decline ... short-lived half-hearted booms, followed by downturn and recession in an ever tightening cycle – these are the characteristics of the new period of general decline of world capitalism ... the search for lasting concessions and lasting reforms is now as futile as the search for flesh on an ancient skeleton.

It is further held that this economic contingency will have enormous political repercussions. In particular, it is argued that it poses a 'black and white' choice for society, in that there will be either a triumph for socialism or the planet will be engulfed by unprecedented barbarism. A CWI internal document from 1975 proclaims that the period of upheaval inaugurated by the 1973 oil crisis will:

> end either in the greatest victory of the working class achieving power and the overthrow of the rule of capital with the installation of workers democ-racy or we will have a military police dictatorship which will destroy the labour movement and kill millions of advanced workers, shop stewards, ward secretaries, Labour youth, trade union branch secretaries and even individual members of the Labour movement.

Such a toxic perspective poisons the internal atmosphere of the organization concerned. Firstly, it tends to black-and-white thinking in terms of prognosis, combined with a straining sense of urgency. Mutually exclusive and totalistic options for the future are assured. *Either* there will be a completely new form of society, hitherto unknown in human history, *or* there will be a relapse into forms of Nazism, this time threatening global nuclear destruction. No other options are available.

It is hard to imagine any better mechanism for escalating commitment. This may be one reason why catastrophism in one form or another permeates a wide variety of cultic organizations, in politics, religion, new age movements, psycho-therapy and elsewhere. I offer particularly striking examples of it in Chapter 9. Moreover, it puts such organizations in the bizarre position where they eagerly look forward to the prospect of disaster, the midwife of revolution, and express disappointment when it is averted. Leaders of catastrophist groups often resemble a man joyously dancing on the edge of a volcano. Peter Taaffe offers a typical example of this mindset. In the late 1980s, Ted Grant had raised the possibility of a 1929-style slump and suggested that this was likely to happen within one year. Taaffe and his supporters rejected this. Taaffe later wrote: 'If it should not come to pass, as was likely, we argued, a mood of disappointment, if not dejection, could set in amongst Militant supporters'.[5] It is unlikely that those spared destitution would see such an outcome in the same disconsolate fashion.

Secondly, such a perspective is a classic cult means of extracting maximum involvement from people alongside a minimum critique of the positions argued by the group's leaders. The future is presented as a choice between imminent salvation or eternal damnation and one which hinges on every action that members take. It is a dichotomy that imbues the organization's routine activities with a sense of colossal urgency, purpose and conviction that normal politics can never hope to match. This reinforces a belief on the part of members that they are destined to play a more vital and indispensable role than any previous group in human history. In the process, they grow ever less inclined to challenge the visions of their leaders – no matter how unsavoury they look to outsiders.

Loading the language

Lifton described what he termed 'loading the language' as a key ingredient of ideological totalism. This manifests as the extensive use of what he termed 'the thought-terminating cliché', used as 'interpretive short-cuts' (Lifton 1961: 488). Repetitive phrases are regularly invoked to describe all situations and prevent further analysis. Lifton describes the overall effects thus:

> For an individual person, the effect of the language of ideological totalism can be summed up in one word: constriction. He is ... linguistically deprived; and since language is so central to all human experience, his capacities for thinking and feeling are immensely narrowed.
>
> (Lifton 1961: 489)

This is observable in the CWI's documents and is evident in some of the quotations in this chapter. The writings of CWI leaders are a narcoleptic anthology of clichés – 'dazzling' prospects are always said to exist in the immediate future; 'colossal' opportunities to 'build' are identified in every situation; the years ahead are invariably referred to as 'the coming period'; the group's prognoses are frequently signalled by the tautological expression 'we predict, in advance'. The spectacle is one of thought attempting flight, only to find, in mid-motion, that all its moving parts have been superglued together.

The impoverishment of language used by these groupings, in which historical analysis regularly gives way to hysterical analysis, is clearly a major reason for the members' inability to grasp either the repetitious nature of its leadership's perspectives or the derivative nature of their analysis. Linguistic asphyxiation leads to intellectual paralysis. By narrowing the range of thought, it also hinders falsification. Members lack the information required to compare their leaders' predictions with reality, to distinguish between evidence and assertion and eventually to think.

Power dynamics and life within the CWI

The question arises at this point: what did life within the CWI under such a regime feel like to the average member? How were they recruited and how was their compliance and then conformity to the ideology advocated by their leaders obtained? The following comments on these issues from one interviewee is typical of the accounts gained from many former CWI members. One told me that, when meeting other former members, he felt that they had all been through a shared religious experience together. Ronnie spent a number of years working full time for the CWI. Here, he describes what daily life to a member could look like:

> 6/7 day weeks for activists were common, particularly those full time. We nominally had a day off, but I can remember another leader saying to me proudly of another that 'he uses his day off to prepare his lead-offs (introductory lectures) for meetings'. Full timers were also kept in poverty. Wages were virtually non-existent, and I found out recently that from 1985 to 1991 they got no pay rise at all!
>
> When we worked, the pressure was awful. Key committees often met Saturday and Sunday 9 to 5, on top of your normal week's work. There would be different sessions, with a leader making an hour long introduction which laid out the line. Everyone else then would come in and agree. The more you agreed with the leader the more he or she cited your contribution in a 15–20 minute summing up at the end. If you disagreed, your contribution would be unpicked, but if it wasn't sufficiently enthusiastic about the line it would – even worse – be ignored. In this way you soon knew who was in and who was out. There was a distinct tendency to promote the most conformist comrades to key positions, even if they were also the most bland.
>
> High membership subscriptions were extracted from members. A certain minimum sub per week was set, which at several pounds a week was far in excess of what normal parties extract. But people were 'encouraged' to go beyond this. At big meetings a speech would be made asking for money. Normally, some comrade would have been approached beforehand and would have agreed to make a particularly high donation – say £500. The speaker would then start off asking for £500, its donation would produce an immense ovation and people would then be pressurised to follow suit.
>
> Everything was also run by committees, and we had plenty of those. Branches had branch committees which met in advance of branch meetings to allocate all sorts of work, this went on to districts, areas and nationally and internationally. Very often it was the same people on these committees wearing different hats! But nothing moved without the committees' say-so. This was accompanied by persistent demands for people to take more initiatives, but in practice there was no mechanism for this to happen. Also, at national conferences, leaders were elected by a slate system – i.e. the CC proposed a full list of names for CC membership. If you opposed it you theoretically

stood up to propose a full list of new names, but needless to say no one ever did. New members were regarded as 'contact members' and allocated a more experienced comrade who was supposed to have weekly discussions as part of the 'political education'.

I do remember feeling absolutely terrified when I first left – what was there for me now, what would I do, where did I start? I eventually managed to get my life together, but it was a hard slog.

Milieu control

Such accounts are consistent with what Lifton described as 'milieu control', a key aspect of ideological totalism. As Lifton postulated it, this is primarily the use of techniques to dominate the person's contact with the outside world but also their communication with themselves. People are 'deprived of the combination of external information and inner reflection which anyone requires to test the realities of his environment and to maintain a measure of identity separate from it' (Lifton 1961: 479).

Within the CWI, intense activism of the kind described by Ronnie meant that the party environment came to dominate every aspect of the members' lives, particularly those who worked for it full time. In a sense, they can be regarded as a cult within a cult. They were bombarded with CWI propaganda, in endless meetings, through reading official literature and by virtue of the fact that there was little time to read anything else. Most points of contact with the external world became drastically curtailed. In Chapter 9, I discuss the career of Jim Jones, whose isolated supporters committed mass suicide in the remote jungles of Guyana in 1978, with those who resisted being murdered – one of the grimmest examples of this dynamic in action. Within the CWI relations with the external world were often reduced to set-piece interaction with potential members ('contact work'), involvement in strikes or similar struggles ('interventions') or limited participation in other organizations' events in the hope that more 'contacts' could be found. Milieu control can thus be more subtle than in its most blatant cultic manifestations, while still exercising a profound influence on those affected.

Thus, escalating pressure began with the recruitment process. Given the CWI's secret existence within the Labour Party, people who came into contact with it would not have immediately known that it was an organization, with its own annual conference, full-time officials and central committee. Potential sympathisers encountered CWI members in such normal environments as the Labour Party or trade unions. Once their left-wing credentials were established they would be asked to buy the CWI newspaper, make a small donation and support CWI motions at other meetings – a process of escalating commitment. Only after a series of such tests had been passed would the person be initiated into the secret of the CWI's existence and provided with further internal documents detailing aspects of its programme. As many ex-members have testified, the effect of this was to create a feeling that the potential recruit was gaining privileged information and being invited to participate in the transformation of history. Furthermore, they could only access more of this knowledge by escalating their involvement with the group. The excitement at this stage was considerable.

Again, this is something the Trotskyist tradition has in common with its Communist rivals. In the 1930s, Keith Woods joined the Communist Party after attending a congress in Paris. He wrote a revealing letter to his wife, attempting to convert her to the cause. The letter perfectly captures the messianic mood I am describing here, and flags the presence of a cultic belief system:

> I am fired with a new zeal and I am going to pass it on to you or die in the attempt ... Just think what a difference it would make to have something in life to strive for that was bigger than you, bigger than me, bigger than both of us, something that burns down deep in your bones, that gives you strength and imagination and the courage of which you never thought you were capable, which gives a meaning to life where before there was nothing but a selfish search for pleasure, that helps you to feel in true relationship not only to present history but to all history. Can't you feel it pulsating within me, the hope and the certainty that if the millions of ordinary people like you and me would only take fate by the throat and strangle it, we can literally change the world?[6]

In the 1970s, before the CWI grew to any significant size, the mystical aura around joining was heightened by the formality with which it was concluded. New recruits travelled to London, where they were personally vetted by the organization's founders and current leaders. When this became impractical they were formally welcomed 'in' by the nearest member of the Central Committee – an exercise close to 'the laying on of hands' found in baptism ceremonies. Tremendous feelings of loyalty were engendered by this process and fused together a group which saw itself as intensely cohesive and blessed with the evangelical mission of leading the world revolution. Research suggests that merely being a member of a group encourages the development of shared norms, beliefs systems, conformity and compliance (Haidt 2012). Belonging to a group with such a deep and all embracing belief system as that offered by the CWI encourages this process all the more.

The dispensing of existence

Once someone had joined the CWI more and more demands were placed on them. In particular, they were expected to contribute between 10 and 15 per cent of their income to the CWI, buy the weekly newspaper, contribute to special press fund collections, subscribe to irregular levies (perhaps to the extent of a week's income), recruit new members and raise money from sympathizers. The pressure was at its most intense for those who worked for it full time. They worked exhausting hours for pitiful wages and on minimal expenses, a level of exploitation that outrivalled the capitalist abuses they so loudly denounced in their press.

Tobias and Lalich (1994) suggest that cults have only two real purposes: recruiting other members and raising money. These certainly emerge as central preoccupations of the CWI. Crick (1986: 178) cites a former member as follows on some of these issues:

> A lot of it boiled down to selling papers. The pace didn't bother me, but one day I suddenly realised that after a year my social circle had totally drifted. I had only political friends left, simply because of the lack of time. There'd be the ... branch meeting on Monday evening, the Young Socialists meeting another evening, 'contact' work on Friday night, selling papers on Sunday afternoon, and on top of that, to prove to the local Labour Party we were good party members, we went canvassing for them every week and worked like hell in the local elections.

Such a level of activity could be physically and emotionally ruinous and required members to redefine their entire existence in terms of their membership of the CWI. It is consistent with Lifton's (1961) notion of 'the dispensing of existence', where it is assumed that only those in the group devoted to its ideology are fully good or fully human. It follows that the group and its activities should monopolise their time. Crick cites another interviewee as recalling:

> The most abiding memories ... are filled with the sheer strain of it all. If you were even moderately active, you would be asked to attend up to six or seven boring meetings in one week.
>   You built up an alternative set of social contacts as much as political activity. It can easily take over people's lives. It became obsessive. They were almost inventing meetings to attend. There was a ridiculous number of meetings held to discuss such a small amount of work. Even if you didn't have a meeting one evening, you'd end up drinking with them.
>   The kind of commitment ... required was bundled together in the form of highly alienating personal relationships. You had to make sure your subscriptions were paid and your papers sold so as not to feel guilty when you chatted to other members. The only way out seemed to be 'family commitment' and the unspoken truth that as soon as a young ... member got a girlfriend he either recruited her or left.
>
>   (Crick 1986: 182)

Recruitment, and much of CWI life, consisted of hearing the same basic ideas endlessly repeated: there might be variations but they would be variations around a minimalist theme. As Scheflin and Opton (1978) pointed out, paraphrasing no less an expert on mind control than Charles Manson, such repetition, combined with the exclusion of any competing doctrine, is a powerful tool of conversion. Even if the belief is not fully internalised a person hearing nothing but a one-note message will eventually be compelled to draw from it in expressing their own opinions. But once inside the CWI, this became akin to spending every night listening to an orchestra playing the same piece over and over again. However well accoutred the musicians and no matter how superb their performances, boredom, tiredness and cynicism inevitably set in.

The recruitment process can also be interpreted as a means of indoctrinating new recruits by presenting them with an escalating series of challenges or ordeals. Wexler and Fraser (1995) have argued that this is an important method of establishing the cohesiveness of decision élites within cults, thereby activating the extreme conformity of groupthink. It seems that such methods were used within the CWI on all new recruits to embroil them more deeply in the organization's activities. Thus, the prospective recruit first expressed private agreement with some CWI ideas. They were then required to advance this agreement publicly at Labour Party or trade union meetings, contribute money (followed by more money), buy literature and sell newspapers on the street. This continued until their entire life revolved around the CWI. The process seems to be one of *extracting commitment and then forcing a decision*. The full extent of the group's organization and programme would not be immediately made clear and, given the secretiveness of the CWI about its very existence, would not be readily known via the media, at least until the mid-1980s. Nevertheless, a commitment to some form of activity was obtained and sounded on first hearing to have nothing in common with a life-transforming commitment. Another interviewee told me:

> We would routinely lie to recruits about what their membership would involve. They would ask what level of activity we expected, and we would talk mostly about the weekly branch meeting and tell them that they could pick and choose what else to do, if anything. But once they were inside there would be systematic pressure to do more and more. Once they were in, very few could resist. But we knew that if we told them in advance all that was involved they would never join. I remember telling a full-timer once that I thought this new recruit we had met didn't have any friends. He looked absolutely delighted, and told me that meant we would at least get plenty of work out of him!

Recruits soon found their initial levels of activity rising: 'come to one more meeting', 'attend one more conference', 'read an extra pamphlet this week'. Whether they had consciously decided anything became irrelevant: a real commitment had been made to the organization. They then found that their attitudes changed to come into line with escalating levels of commitment and eventually reached such an intense pitch that a formal decision (if it needed to be made at all) was only a small final step – a classic demonstration of cognitive dissonance theory (Festinger 1957).

Doctrine over person

The primacy given to doctrine over person – a key element of ideological totalism – reinforced such dissonance all the more. Essentially, Lifton argues that historical myths are engendered by ideologically totalist groups as a means of reinforcing its black-and-white morality and in the process of escalating its members' feeling of commitment. Then:

> when the myth becomes fused with the totalist sacred science, the resulting 'logic' can be so compelling and coercive that it simply replaces the realities of individual experience ... past historical events are retrospectively altered, wholly rewritten, or ignored, to make them consistent with the doctrinal logic.
> (Lifton 1961: 490)

Trotskyist organizations have no shortage of such historical myths but the one which is most doggedly advanced concerns the 1917 Russian Revolution – often simply referred to in CWI circles as 'October'. The objective then becomes one of repeating this glorious chapter under modern conditions. Countless subsidiary myths are woven around the primary myth of October. For example, a document by those expelled from the CWI describes the Bolshevik Party as 'the most democratic party in the history of the world working class'. There are also frequent references to the lonely but allegedly indispensable role of the CWI in maintaining the 'sacred science' of Trotskyism in the post-war period. Historical myths console members for their present-day impotence, provide a ready made historical schema to impose on the complex realities of modern politics and – principally – act as a straitjacket on innovative thought.

The evidence therefore suggests that, until the mid-1980s, the CWI was a growing political force, with several thousand predominantly young and enthusiastic members. Prospects seemed limitless. Members were certainly encouraged to believe that what their leaders described as 'the world revolution' would develop within a 10–15 year period and that their organization would play a decisive role in history's most crucial turning point. It was at this point, with pride at its peak, that everything began to go wrong.

Collapse and disintegration

The steady growth that the CWI experienced in the late 1970s and 1980s, particularly in Britain, created the twofold illusion that the organization's entire programme had been confirmed and that permanent expansion was assured – if everyone merely redoubled their already incredible work rates. New members were recruited without the period of lengthy indoctrination which had hitherto been a major condition of CWI membership. Consequently, their loyalty, conformity and respect for the methods of work advocated by the CWI's leaders were much less pronounced. Simultaneously, the Labour Party began to take action against its members, expelling them in large numbers. In addition, a year-long miners' strike ended in defeat in the mid-1980s, while the Liverpool Council's conflict with Margaret Thatcher's government also unravelled in disastrous fashion. These circumstances created the first ripples of doubt concerning the organization's rationale for its existence.

Fundamentally, the CWI was hoping to remain a highly cohesive grouping but with a mass membership: in essence, it was attempting to design a round square. Given an influx of new members not prepared to devote all their energies to party building, nor to avoid challenging CWI leaders when their predictions failed to materialise, this proved impossible. For many, after a short period of time, applause gave way to a slow handclap. After 1987, the numbers of CWI members began to fall precipitously, reaching a turnover level of 38 per cent in 1990. By then, less than 1,100 people were regularly attending branch meetings, including 200 full-time organizers. The CWI has continued to decline ever since. Peter Taaffe's (1995) gloriously turgid official history of the organization boasts of increased membership figures up until the late 1980s, when it seems to have peaked at around 8,000. Thereafter, no figures are claimed. It lost its three Members of Parliament, positions in trade unions and a great deal of money. Its headquarters building was sold to sustain some more modest level of activity. Moreover, Ted Grant and his eventual successor, Alan Woods, rapidly reproduced within the newly minted IMT the regime they had criticised when they belonged to the CWI. Ruin all round ensued. In the 2010 UK general election, the CWI stood in alliance with a few other grouplets as 'the Trade Unionist and Socialist Coalition'. Its candidates secured an average of 370 votes, or 0.9 per cent of votes cast in each constituency. The IMT in Britain gathered fewer than 100 members for its annual conference in 2012, its largest, it announced, for 20 years. It pronounced this a great success. The glowing future which its leaders anticipated in the glory days of the 1980s is by now well behind it.

Conclusion

This chapter has explored the techniques used by the leaders of some groups on the left to maintain high levels of conformity, activism and intolerance on the part of their members. None of this necessarily implies that radical movements to change society are inherently destined to become obscure cults or that a radical critique of society is inappropriate. In the final analysis, the condition of society is a vitally important issue and it requires a political rather than a psychological analysis. However, the evidence plainly suggests that a number of traditional Leninist or Trotskyist assumptions endanger internal democracy, political thinking and what must be a central goal of any movement seeking wider influence – the regular updating of ideas to retain relevance.

In particular, their conception of the role of 'the revolutionary party' has become transmuted into a rationale for the creation of tyrannical fiefdoms locked into a spiral of irrelevance, fragmentation and ideological petrifaction. Rigid adherence to 'democratic centralism', a term which appears to be an oxymoron, reflects an excessive veneration for 'October', which in turn prevents them from developing an updated historical analysis of the 1917 Revolution and its disastrous aftermath. Accordingly, the Leninist tradition eschews innovation. Those marooned in its static preoccupations find themselves condemned to an ever greater isolation, in which the search for other footprints in the sand is always in vain. This is combined with a catastrophist political analysis that, despite its frequent falsification by events, acts a spur to such intense activism that the energy, time and confidence required for political reflection is consumed by party building. Such 'party building' is generally signified by the presence of innumerable fragments and factions – and the absence of a party.

Those interested in movements which set themselves ambitious goals of social, moral or economic regeneration need to temper enthusiasm for change with a stronger awareness of the techniques of social influence and a greater scepticism towards totalistic philosophies of social change. Without such an approach, individuals who have submerged themselves in such organizations only to emerge blinking into real life face lifelong disillusion with any form of political action. Cult leaders prey upon our aversion to uncertainty. They offer certainty about issues that are objectively uncertain, a shining light in the blackest of nights. In reality, they only illuminate the darkness with burnt-out candles. The disillusionment they cause becomes an enormous waste of democratic energy. In learning from leadership practice in organizations such as the CWI, it may be more possible to strengthen people's willingness to engage in forms of action which genuinely liberates their thinking and thereby contributes to positive change in our society.

Points for discussion

1. How was the power of CWI leaders over their followers established and then maintained?
2. What are the major defining characteristics of ideological totalism, as defined by Lifton? How common are at least some of them in organizations that you know?
3. The CWI had an approach to politics that this chapter describes as 'catastrophism'. What are the likely effects of catastrophism on people's level of certainty in a particular belief system?
4. What are the major implications of the CWI case study for the practice of leadership within politics?

Notes

1 Some of the material in this chapter is derived from Tourish, D. (1998) Ideological intransigence, democratic centralism and cultism: a case study from the political left. *Cultic Studies Journal*, 15: 33–67.
2 Interestingly, there is disagreement even on whether Grant and Woods left voluntarily or were expelled. The CWI's leadership insists that they left of their own volition. Grant and Woods claimed that they were expelled. Either variant testifies to a culture among the members of its top leadership that was deeply suspicious of internal dissent. Absolute agreement or civil war followed by separation was the norm.
3 The Fourth International was founded by Trotsky in 1938, who had concluded that there was no longer any possibility of moving the Stalin-dominated Communist International (Comintern) in a Trotskyist direction. The CWI argued that the Fourth International 'degenerated' after Trotsky's assassination in 1940 and the upheavals of the Second

World War. Both it and the IMT now assert that it only lives on, at least as a tradition, in their respective organizations.

4 The full text of this document, *Against Bureaucratic Centralism*, can be found on the IMT's website at http://www.marxist.com/against-bureaucratic-centralism.htm. Last accessed 20 November 2012. While it is completely lacking in self-awareness or any sense of responsibility for the problems it discusses, it offers invaluable insights into the internal and usually hidden life of the CWI.

5 This quotation can be found in the online version of Taaffe (1995), an 'official' history of the organization, available at http://www.socialistparty.org.uk/militant/ and last accessed 20 November 2012. Nor was this a casual mis-statement. Taaffe repeats the point almost verbatim in a 2002 polemic against Grant and Woods.

6 This letter is cited in a study of children growing up in Communist homes in Britain during the cold war (Cohen 1997: 152).

9 Leadership, group suicide and mass murder

Jonestown and Heaven's Gate through the looking glass

Many thousands of words have now been written about Jonestown and Heaven's Gate, and even more tears have been shed. In 1978 909 people who were living a communal existence in a People's Temple agricultural project perished by poisoning in the remote jungles of Guyana, at the behest of their leader, Jim Jones. Two hundred and eighty-seven of them were children. Those reluctant to commit suicide had it forced on them by others. How many died in this fashion is unclear. An audiotape exists of the final mass gathering. It begins with Jones saying: 'How very much I have loved you'. He sounds exhausted. His words are sometimes slurred. Other voices are heard but the last statement on the tape is from Jones: 'Take our life from us. We laid it down. We got tired. We didn't commit suicide, we committed an act of revolutionary suicide protesting the conditions of an inhumane world'.[1]

In the intervening minutes, death was unleashed on a scarcely imaginable scale. Jones himself was among the dead, shot in the head by persons unknown, how voluntarily or otherwise we can never say. Nor was the carnage restricted to Jonestown. Earlier that day, two planes prepared to depart from a nearby airport with a small number of 'defectors'. They were attacked by Jonestown gunmen. US Congressman Leo Ryan, who had spent the previous day in Jonestown talking to members, was killed, together with an NBC cameraman and three others. Nine people were seriously injured. Some few seconds of the shooting survive on video-tape. On a lesser scale, but equally tragic for those involved and their families, 39 devotees of Heaven's Gate died in California in March 1997. They had also consumed poison and left behind upbeat videos, proclaiming their devotion to the group's ideals and leader, and affirming their faith in the better life awaiting them at 'the level above human'.

These events are a grotesque challenge to notions of human dignity and the benefits that have often been attributed to leadership. In both cases, all-powerful leaders assumed total control over every aspect of their followers' lives. People submitted to what they regarded as the beneficent and all-knowing insights of their leaders. The reality was far different. Behind the ideals on offer were leaders with a self-destructive streak who increasingly fantasised about their followers sharing in a grand gesture of self-immolation. In both cases, care was taken to present this as an act of redemption that would help to purify an impure world. The legacy of grief has been profound.

I do not intend to provide a detailed account of the history of these groups in this chapter. Excellent book length histories and memoirs already exist – in the case of Jonestown, primarily Layton (1999) and Reitermann (2008).[2] Lalich (2004) provides a book-length comparison between Heaven's Gate and a Californian political cult, while an edited text also offers a useful variety of theoretical perspectives on Heaven's Gate (Chryssides 2011). I will outline here the main events in their life stories, to bring the leadership dynamics within each to the fore. The dark side of leadership, as I have noted throughout this book, takes many forms, varies greatly in its intensity and can be looked at from numerous theoretical perspectives. In these two parallel cases, its malignancy is revealed in chemically pure form. There is much that these stories can teach us. Learning such lessons is some small recompense for the sufferings of the victims and their families in each group.

Beginnings

It is tempting to see the history of any destructive group through its end rather than its beginnings. This is a false prism. No leader would attract much influence or retain many followers without offering something that, on the surface, has considerable appeal. So it also is with Jim Jones. His career as a leader started in the mid-west of America in the 1950s (Richardson 1980). Friends from the early days report that Jones, born in 1931, showed a precocious fascination with religion and death that included holding Bible readings for other children and conducting funerals for dead pets. By the 1950s he was ready for challenges in the adult world. There is some evidence that this initially took the form of joining the Communist Party, before Jones realised that presenting his beliefs in a religious form might enable him to acquire greater influence. At this early stage, his approach was not obviously destructive. Jones stood against racism at a time when it was far from popular to do so, and he developed an interracial egalitarian church. This gradually became 'The People's Temple'. While its actual membership probably never exceeded 3,000, it has been estimated that between 50,000 and 100,000 people heard Jones speak over the years (Galanter 1999). He was charismatic, persuasive and offered hope to the poor, the despairing and the spiritually forlorn.

The People's Temple became an unusual fusion of religion and politics. Bible readings increasingly gave way to a stress on social issues and the explicit advocacy of 'socialism'. On several occasions, particularly in later years, Jones denied any belief in God. A former Temple member, Hue Fortson, quotes Jones as follows:

> What you need to believe in is what you can see ... If you see me as your friend, I'll be your friend. As you see me as your father, I'll be your father ... If you see me as your saviour, I'll be your saviour. If you see me as your God, I'll be your God.[3]

Jones also informed a select few that he was the reincarnation of Lenin, the leader of the 1917 Russian Revolution, here to repeat the act in modern America. In the last days of Jonestown in Guyana, he preached at length on the virtues of North Korea and held out some hope that his followers could find sanctuary in what was then still the Soviet Union. It is important to stress that this was a gradual process. Most of those who stumbled into his orbit were looking for spiritual answers, hope and a sense of community. Jones was not averse to offering all of this and more, in whatever form he thought people would follow.

There was never much pretence of democracy within the organization. Jones was, from its inception, the ultimate authority on all issues. A second tier of between 15 and 20 people, often known as 'the angels', helped him to carry the burden of leadership. They tended to be attractive, tall, white women. Although married, and with his wife Marceline playing a key role in the Temple, Jones enjoyed promiscuous sexual relationships with many of his followers, male and female. He always did so with the assurance that 'I am doing this for you'. Beneath 'the angels' sat a 'planning commission', responsible for taking disciplinary action against dissenters, doubters and defectors. Again, this was mostly white in composition. It was an organizational structure designed to facilitate control by the group's supreme leader.

Heaven's Gate had an altogether different genesis.[4] By most accounts, it began with a meeting between Bonnie Nettles and Marshall Applewhite in 1972. Both were then in their early 40s. She was a registered nurse, married with four children. Applewhite had been married and had fathered two children but this relationship was over long before he met Nettles. He had worked as a music teacher at the University of Alabama and elsewhere. All reports suggest that he was gay and struggled throughout his life with this realisation. He met Nettles shortly after having a breakdown partly induced by these conflicts. Nettles, long interested in New Age ideas, was perhaps not the most fortuitous individual to encounter in such circumstances. She convinced Applewhite that they were soul mates and that he in particular was on a divine mission. Together, they would work out what this was. While the group's ultimate fate in 1997 is indelibly associated with Applewhite, since Nettles had died in 1985, it was always clear that she was the group's main leader. Members continued to view her in this light even after her death.

For some time after their meeting, they operated small but unsuccessful bookstores selling New Age paraphernalia. Gradually they lost all contact with previous friends and family, becoming ever more absorbed in each other and their developing philosophy. From 1973 onwards, they travelled America looking for converts. By this stage, they were certain that they had known each other in past lives and also had developed the view that they had been sent here from another planetary existence that they called 'the Next Level'. Followers proved elusive until 1975, when Nettles and Applewhite were invited to a meeting in Los Angeles organized by another New Age teacher named Clarence King. They now called themselves 'The Two' and asked this group to renounce their material possessions and the trappings of their previous lives to follow them. It was by all accounts a bravura performance. It seems that about two dozen people, including

King, did so. They embarked on a nomadic existence whose main purpose was to recruit more adherents.

While Jim Jones preached a mixture of Christianity and Marxism, Heaven's Gate's belief system was rooted in the New Age mysticism then popular in America and elsewhere. Members believed that the planet Earth had irremediably degenerated and was about to be 'recycled'. The only chance of survival was to leave it immediately. To do this, members were instructed to detest what the world had become and also to rise above and thus renounce many traits of being human. This included sexual desire. Nettles and Applewhite, for example, maintained a platonic relationship throughout their time together. As the belief system evolved the two of them, eventually known only as Ti and Do, asserted that they were the spirits of beings from an alien planet. They argued that humans emerged from the seeds planted by aliens millions of years ago, who would now return in flying saucers to save those who had shown they were enlightened enough to be worthy of it. This salvation would be restricted to members of Heaven's Gate. In the cult's final phase, Applewhite went further, insisting that the spiritual being within him had been here 2,000 years earlier, when he was known as Jesus Christ. He had now returned to complete his work.

Why people were attracted

It is useful at this point to consider what attracted people to such visions. Goldstein and Cialdini (2007: 170) point out that 'people … maintain positive self-evaluations by identifying with and conforming to valued groups'. For devotees of Jonestown and Heaven's Gate, the norms, beliefs and leaders of both groups were clearly valued. The question is: why?

Layton (1999) offers some useful background on her own experience as a People's Temple member who became one of Jones's most trusted aides. Typical of many, she had a troubled childhood. Members of her family had fled Germany in the pre-war period, as persecuted Jews. This bequeathed a legacy of anxiety and confused parenting, against which she rebelled. After an unsuccessful stint at rehabilitation in an English boarding school she returned to the USA. By then, her brother, Larry, had joined the People's Temple. He raised the possibility that here at last was a leader and an organization that could offer a sense of direction previously missing in her life. Jones was by now criticising the war in Vietnam, racism and social injustice more widely – all popular messages for alienated youth in the late 1960s. The establishment, personified by President Richard ('I am not a crook') Nixon, had little appeal. Layton travelled from San Francisco in 1970 to Ukiah in Northern California to meet Jones and reunite with her brother. She was instantly bombarded with messages stressing that Jones was 'the Prophet' or 'Father' and offered a true path to salvation for the world. She was also exposed to recruitment rituals familiar in all manner of cults. These involved three hour long sermons, promises of a special destiny awaiting her if she committed, noble objectives boldly articulated and moving displays of personal devotion on the part of many in attendance at Temple events.

This was deeply attractive. Tim Carter, a Vietnam war veteran, was one of the few to survive the final conflagration in 1978. He recalled his first encounter with the organization as follows: 'As soon as I walked into the San Francisco Temple, I was home'. Surviving footage of Temple services shows highly talented choirs singing, people dancing and rousing oratory from Jones. The emotion generated was intense enough to silence the spirit of critical inquiry in many. Impressed by Jones's rhetoric and personal attention, Layton became a convert at the age of 17. To those lost and looking for answers, idealism in almost any form can be alluring. Debbie Layton would not be the first or the last to fall for the charms of a charismatic leader at a moment of acute vulnerability in her life. As the years passed, Jones became ever more adept at managing this process. He staged miraculous healings, in which Temple members previously assigned the role would pretend to be incapacitated or suffering from cancer, only to be miraculously cured by him at Church gatherings. The rationale was always that such minor acts of deception were aimed at a greater good – bringing more people to the realisation that they needed to join a common struggle for a better society. In short, the ends justified the means.

Within Heaven's Gate, Lalich (2004) highlights the importance of the New Age movement as a force of attraction. The idea that the world was sick and needed to be healed was popular. It was also a moral imperative of a compelling nature. Nor was it difficult to obtain evidence in its favour. Then, as now, potential members had only to turn on their news bulletins each evening. But, as Lalich explains:

> The moral imperative was guided not by a political vision but a cosmic one that held to a belief that a person could – and should – transcend daily life by tapping into the universal mind, the oneness of all existence. In so doing, the mundane realities of mainstream ways would be superseded by a grand cosmic interconnectedness that would do away with war, suffering, and earthly spoils.
> (Lalich 2004: 32)

Once more, global transformation of some kind would take place. Special insights into oneself and the deeper meaning of life could be accessed only through membership of the group. This necessitated absolute personal change. Inevitably difficult, such change required the subordination of oneself to a particular group and, above all, to the edicts of its leaders. Surrender of the self was a capitulation to insight, security and redemption. For at least some of those who saw themselves as 'seekers' and who were conversant with New Age ideologies it seemed a prospect worth pursuing. The problem is that once the journey had begun, even if it was only one of tentative inquiry, a great deal of social pressure was exerted to ensure that it did not end.

Manufacturing conformity

Lalich's (2004) indispensable analysis of Heaven's Gate and a Californian political cult, the Democratic Workers Party, highlights two key processes – that of conversion (or, as she prefers to term it, a 'worldview shift') and how people's initial idealistic commitment is gradually escalated out of control. Eventually, cult members find themselves in an environment where most of their thoughts, feelings and behaviours are prescribed for them by powerful leaders. In short, their daily life consists of 'bounded choice'. She defines conversion as a transformational process that changes values, standards, attitudes and emotions:

> The outcome of a successful conversion is a firm believer, a new person. In part, this adoption of and adherence to a newly found, all-consuming worldview is the binding matter that makes it difficult to leave totalistic groups or give up cultic thinking, in spite of the moral and emotional conflicts that arise within some if not most believers from time to time.
>
> (Lalich 2004: 15)

There is an extensive use of emotional appeals, rituals, instruction, self-examination, confession and rejection to produce this effect. People lose confidence in their own perceptions of reality but acquire over-confidence in the perceptions of their leader. In essence, the cultic environment became 'a self-sealing system'. Disconfirming evidence is hidden from view, while dissident opinions perish under a heavy bombardment of criticism from the group's leaders.

The charismatic authority of leaders, of the kind I described in Chapter 2, is crucial to the process. A deep emotional bond is gradually formed between leaders and followers. The leader presents themselves as the font of all wisdom. The job of followers is to obey. Whatever difficulties arise in reaching the group's ever elusive goals are invariably blamed on the limited commitment of the members, rather than on the feebleness of the group's leaders or the weaknesses of its ideology. All of this is starkly evident in both Heaven's Gate and Jonestown.

The problem faced by many members of both groups was that, having made an initial commitment (often involving the loss of contact with family and friends, the giving up of careers or the surrender of all money to the group), the cost of reconsidering the new belief system appeared to be too high. In line with cognitive dissonance theory, many opted to escalate their commitment – the second key dynamic to which Lalich pays particular attention. The outcome in both cases proved fatal.

Thus, in both groups, regimentation increased with the years. Heaven's Gate exposed its members to bizarre diets and exercise regimes. Every aspect of life was regulated. This included precisely how the male members were expected to shave (down, not up) and how meals were to be prepared. There were detailed guidelines on how long a pancake was to be cooked on both sides, how high the gas should be, its precise shape and size and the exact blend of ingredients that went into it. Each member had a 'check partner' whose role was to ensure that these protocols, written down for easy reference, were strictly followed. As one former member later testified:

> It was designed for a person not to think for themselves. It was designed that you give your will over to what appeared to be a benevolent being

who was taking you through a process that would help you come out the other side.[5]

Members were sometimes forbidden to talk. They now spoke of their bodies as 'the vehicle', distancing themselves from its needs. Eight of the men, including Applewhite, took this to the extent of having themselves castrated, the better to combat sexual urges. Increasingly Ti and Do presented themselves as 'The Second Coming'. Submission to their authority was stressed with greater frequency. Members were taught that they could only escape planet Earth and its impending destruction ('the recycling') if accompanied by 'a Representative of the Next Level'. This meant staying with Ti and Do. Moreover, since the final crisis was imminent there was no opportunity for further reflection or hesitation. But staying with The Two was insufficient. Members must also model all aspects of their behaviour after them and show complete respect for their directives. This was a blatant appeal to emotion rather than thought, intended to silence reason.

Always, and in line with my discussion of coercive persuasion in Chapter 3, there was the reassurance of other members behaving in a conformist way. We readily identify the norms that exist within the groups to which we belong and conform to them in the interests of maintaining our group membership. Deviancy attracts sanction. Sensitive to this possibility, we rapidly adjust our actions to those that will find favour within whatever groups we value. Normally, brakes on extreme conformity exist. In many groups, what counts as normal can be hard to determine, while there are unlikely to be heavy sanctions for those who deviate from them (Jetten *et al.* 2012: 120). But in groups such as Jonestown and Heaven's Gate, care is taken by the leader(s) to ensure that everyone has a clear insight into the norms of the group – principally, compliance and obedience. The penalties for dissent (chiefly, the possibility of excommunication from the group, and consequent loss of the opportunity of salvation) are also rendered obvious. In particular, the fate that has befallen previous dissenters serves as a stark reminder to anyone tempted to follow their example. The arousal of fear is a potent means of persuasion, since all that is valuable becomes bound up with membership of the group in its members' eyes. To be outcast is to share the fate of the damned.

Effective resistance and dissent appears to require the formation of viable subgroup identities (Haslam and Reicher 2012a). In both Jonestown and Heaven's Gate, care was taken to maintain a cohesive overall group identity. Those belonging to Heaven's Gate were tasked with developing what they termed 'crew-mindedness', in which only the one overarching group identity was permissible. Within Jonestown, all communication to and from the outside world flowed through Jones. There was no TV and the only 'radio' broadcasts were endless sermons from Jim Jones. These usually portrayed the USA as a capitalist and imperialist villain and cast leaders such as North Korean leader Kim Il-Sung, Robert Mugabe and Joseph Stalin in a positive light. While, as Galanter (1999) notes, feedback 'from the outside world can also be helpful in moderating a leader's deviant views', very little such feedback existed in the People's Temple. The only source of information and form of authority permitted was the Word of

Jim Jones. As this Word became more deranged, so did the regime being constructed in Jonestown.

Zimbardo's prison experiment

Many of our ideas on conformity and the adoption of destructive identities derive from Zimbardo's infamous prison experiment of 1971 (Zimbardo 2007). It is worth considering its relevance in the context of Jonestown and Heaven's Gate. Twenty-four male students were randomly assigned roles of prisoners and guards in a mock prison in the basement of Stanford University's psychology department. Those in the role of prisoners were 'arrested' at home by the police, handcuffed, finger printed, charged and deposited in the 'prison'. Guards – in reality, other students – awaited them. These enforced authoritarian measures that came to include, in Zimbardo's view, psychological torture. Prisoners also fell into the role of learned helplessness, while collaborating with some of the extreme measures employed. Increasingly concerned, including by his own behaviour, Zimbardo terminated the experiment after six days, more than a week early. Ever since, it has been cited as strong evidence for the impact of social situation on human behaviour and of our tendency to conform to bizarre behaviours that violate all norms of reason and ethical behaviour. Arguably, if model students of the kind who participated in Zimbardo's experiment could behave in such ways, it is absolutely no surprise to find members of high-commitment and high-control groups such as Jonestown and Heaven's Gate also departing from behavioural norms that include respect for human life, above all their own.

This view has been criticised by some psychologists involved in a replication of Zimbardo's study for BBC television in the UK. In this case, there was prisoner resistance and many fewer instances of guard brutality. As a result, Turner has argued:

> Those of us who have never found the SPE (Stanford Prison Experiment) picture at all plausible as a historical or political story can now point to the BBC study and say 'look, when one gives people a chance to act reasonably naturally, with choice, as they might in reality, over time, then there are instances when far from conforming to imposed rules they reject or change the roles, they reject and change the social structure.
>
> (Turner 2006: 42)

Possibly. But the point here is that in Jonestown, Heaven's Gate and groups of a similar kind, opportunities to engage in 'reasonable' behaviour were systematically dismantled. Jonestown, in particular, became a prison that replicated many features of Zimbardo's study rather than the more liberal regime found in the BBC version. Moreover, even critical commentaries on Zimbardo's work have acknowledged that when people identify with a particular group they are more likely to take on the roles – good or bad – that are associated with membership of the group concerned (Haslam and Reicher 2012b). Over-identification with group norms was clearly a key dynamic within Heaven's Gate and Jonestown. The constraining effect on dissent is all the more evident when we consider the rituals of confession and the promotion of fear that prevailed within both groups.

Rituals of confession and the promotion of fear

In Chapter 3, I discussed how rituals of confession are a standard part of coercive persuasion. Jim Jones adapted this practice for members of the People's Temple. Layton (1999) records how Temple members were taped making bizarre confessions of the worst things they had allegedly ever done. Many of these were fantasies, intended to win Jones's approval and set an example for others. But they were used to blackmail those who showed a desire to leave. The sense of confusion this engendered was enormous. As Layton (1999: 69) later recalled:

> It's hard to explain why I didn't realize something was seriously wrong; why I stayed deaf to the warning calls ringing in my ears. I ignored my doubts and my conscience because I believed that I could not be wrong, not that wrong.
>
> (Layton 1999: 69)

This is a good example of Cialdini's (2009) principle of commitment and consistency (Chapter 3), this time with lethal consequences for many.

Members also wrote regular testimonials, affirming their love for Jones and their dedication to his cause. One typical such text, titled 'for Dad's Eyes Only', and signed by 'Cliff G' reads in part:

> If you were to die tonight of a natural death and your wishes were to follow the leader who you appoint, I would give my life as I would at any moment for the cause – Unless there was total anarchy – I would proceed on my own to subdue as many enemies as I could get hold of – also killing myself.
>
> (Ulman and Abse 1983: 655)

Galanter cites yet another letter as follows:

> I will endure until I am dead … I shall not let this movement down. I shall not beg for mercy either in that last moment. I shall proudly die for proud reason. You can count on me even if all desert you. I shall be by your side whether it be tangible or in spirit. If, suddenly, a U.S. vessel or plane will come to get us all to take us back with promises of all the luxury and benefits if we would sell you out, I would not go on board because I am attracted to your goodness as magnets attract one another … Nothing will ever break your pull.
>
> (Galanter 1999: 116)

These testimonials reaffirmed Jones's own sense of power, reinforced the commitment of those writing them and strengthened patterns of conformist behaviour that others then felt compelled to emulate.

Conformity was also ensured by more brutal methods, particularly once members had relocated to Jonestown. Punishment was used against anyone suspected of violating group norms. This included spending stints in a plywood box that resembled a coffin. Recalcitrant children were sometimes confined overnight at the bottom of a well. Jones had long excelled in involving his followers in such practices, thereby implicating them in his regime and further removing the possibility of them contemplating the possibility of a different life. Layton recalls her own experience before the final move to Jonestown. A member who had allegedly abused a child was beaten with a rubber hose. Layton was forced to watch and was then photographed holding the hose in question. As she notes, this 'paralysed my questioning inner voice' (Layton 1999: 61) – presumably, the intent.

By 1977, the compound at Jonestown was also ringed by a security fence and a watchtower was in place. If anyone attempted to escape, drugs such as Demerol and Valium were administered. Armed guards patrolled the area, ostensibly because it was under threat from the CIA and others, but in reality to ensure that no one could leave without Jones's approval. Fear of the outside became matched by fear of the inside. The overall effect was a paralysis of hope and a growing expectation of disaster – unless, somehow, Jones could offer a last-minute route to salvation, a final miracle. Meanwhile, the spectre of outside enemies was used to arouse vigilance for any accomplices on the inside, spreading fear, obedience and atomisation. Layton (1999: 151) again vividly summarises the effect:

> Once you were in, it didn't take long to learn the ropes: keep your head down and don't talk unless it's absolutely necessary. For each person showing weakness by speaking of his or her fears, another would become more trusted for reporting it. There were no enduring friendships – members soon learned that it was just too dangerous to run the risk of public confrontation or public beating and not being trusted.
>
> (Layton 1999: 151)

Family ties weakened. Children were cared for communally. They called Jones 'Dad' and at times saw their parents for only a short time at night. Safety, it seemed, lay exclusively in conformity and obedience. Jonestown had become Zimbardo's prison experiment on steroids. But there was a twist. Everyone was both a guard and a prisoner, the hunter and the hunted.

Within Heaven's Gate, confession rituals were embedded in a daily routine devoted to listening to Ti and Do. Their 'lessons' revolved around exploring their journeys and those of the classmates. With everything regarded as a lesson, examples were regularly drawn from 'errors' that the students made, presented as of instructive significance to the rest of the group. Privacy was abolished. Everything was out in the open, minutely scrutinised, evaluated and publicly commented upon. In particular, Lalich reports that:

> Progress was monitored at 'slippage' meetings, where students' errors were reviewed. The shame engendered by 'slippage' was sufficient to keep students'

behaviour in check. Nothing was secret. Applewhite and Nettles knew every-thing, demanded everything. That was their right as the Older Members.

(Lalich 2004: 74)

Particular attention was paid to any sign of members readopting human habits. This included highlighting and criticising such commonplace practices as doodling on scraps of paper. As Balch and Taylor (2002: 216) noted: 'So eager were students to change that they often called meetings themselves'. A former female member recalled: 'We used to joke in the class that we were the cult of cults. We weren't here to be programmed or brainwashed. We were here to *beg* to be brainwashed'.

By comparison with Jonestown, the use of fear within the group was restrained. Given the potency of the vision, members were terrified of losing their group membership and, in their terms, then being cast into the outer darkness of the nonbelievers, where they would miss out on 'the next level'. Applewhite height-ened this anxiety by instigating a membership purge in 1976, ridding the group of those 'weaker' members (sceptics) who were judged to be bringing the others down. The effect was to heighten the commitment of those who survived the cull, while reinforcing their faith in the judgement of their leader. But, so far as we know, he never enacted the regime of punishment that characterised Jonestown and his followers seemed to retain genuine feelings of affection for him through-out the group's lifetime.

Seclusion of followers

Heaven's Gate

Heaven's Gate had a revolving membership, a phenomenon typical of cultic organizations. Turnover is usually at its highest in the early days of people's membership (Barker 1995), although the level of turnover falls significantly after two or three years, when various commitment mechanisms exert a greater hold (Zablocki 2001). Membership of Heaven's Gate seems never to have reached beyond 100. It was in every sense a smaller operation than the People's Temple. But some similarities are obvious. Followers lived communally. They pooled whatever money they had. While they sometimes worked at outside jobs to finance their activities, as much time as possible was spent proselytising, at least in the early days. From 1976 until 1992, the group essentially went underground, engaged in little attempt at recruitment and spent most of its time in group rituals depicted as study. The effect was that members 'bonded into a closed, unified, self-sealing group' (Lalich 2004: 93). Contact with families was lost. As many of these have since testified, the distress was enormous. Everyone waited eagerly for 'The Demonstration' – that is, the arrival of the space ships that would take them to 'the next level'.

Seclusion and increased leader control became more apparent. The group now earned most of its money from computer work and web design, minimising the need for its members to work elsewhere and so to socialise with other people. The Two were described as the 'The Teachers', while the followers referred to themselves as 'classmates'. Each was given a new name – three letters followed by 'ody'. One long standing member, for example, was known as 'Stlody'. This amounted to a renunciation of members' previous lives and any identity associated with it. It signified rebirth into a new life. The further depiction of members as akin to children at school ('classmates') and the continued elevation of Ti and Do, who allegedly knew everything, further infantilised them, undermined whatever independent judgments they could still form and heightened their devotion to the belief system. Moreover, their system of communal living involved frequent moves, often at short notice. This ensured that permanent community bonds would not be formed outside the group. Once more, the effects included heightening the power of Ti and Do. But time was passing, without the longed for ascension to 'the next level'. By the 1990s, there were less than three dozen people still involved, increasingly aged and desperate for the fulfilment of The Two's prophecy. When would it happen, and would they be ready?

Jonestown

By 1977, Jones's activities were attracting greater and more critical, press attention. He had already purchased land in Guyana, now of use under these conditions. More and more followers moved to what Jones described as 'The Promised Land', where they cleared the forest, built homes and planted crops. He painted an increasingly lurid picture of imminent threat at home in the United States, from the press, CIA and myriad other enemies, compared with the salvation that awaited them in Guyana. Layton arrived in December 1977 with her mother, now also in the People's Temple and suffering from cancer. Unknown to everyone, there was less than a year of the story left to run.

Jones himself also moved there in 1977 to take full charge. His arrival changed life irrevocably and for the worse. Jonestown became like a military compound. The Soviet Embassy happily supplied Jones with propaganda films about the joys of life within the USSR. These became compulsory viewing, alongside other films documenting such aspects of American life as the return of scarred and disillusioned Vietnam veterans and the problems facing elderly Americans. There were more lectures and classes, focusing on enemies, revolution and the need for socialism. Members worked six days a week from 6.30 in the morning until 6 in the evening. This was then followed by endless hours of 'classes' in Jonestown's main pavilion. There, Jones often read news he obtained from such sources as Radio Moscow and Radio Havana, invariably painting a bleak picture of the outside world. This heightened members' anxiety about what would befall them should they leave. In any event, exhausted, they had little time for the reflection needed to carve out a fresh path. Those who, like Debbie Layton, could see that Jonestown was a primitive jungle work camp rather than a paradise in the making dared not share this insight with others, who were likely to report such heresy straight to Jones. One father made the mistake of confiding to his small son that he thought he had found a way out. Imagining this was a 'test', the boy reported him to Jones. The father was separated from his family and confined to a labour intensive work unit. All perished in the final nightmare. Layton only escaped by being allowed to travel on an important 'mission' to Guyana's capital, Georgetown, from where she made contact with the US Embassy and then got back to California. It is impossible to estimate how many shared her misgivings but were too fearful of Jones's vengeance to share them. An almost perfect totalitarian system had been created in miniature.

For Jones, on the other hand, things looked at least temporarily better. As Reitermann (2008: 350) put it: 'At last, he had people where he wanted them – on another continent, in a jungle with no law except his own. Their isolation was complete. Events in the world – and reality itself – would be filtered exclusively through him'. For the time being, the rituals of obedience continued. But, unbeknown to Jones, the end was already in sight.

Endings

Pause for a moment and put yourself in the position of members of Heaven's Gate in the mid-1990s or those whose belief systems still survived in Jonestown in early 1978. What is about to happen will look crazy to everyone outside your ranks but it all feels different to you. Fear has been stoked. In the case of Jonestown, it is fear of the CIA and countless other intelligence agencies. In Heaven's Gate, people feel fearful of missing out on the only opportunity for ascension to the next life that they will ever have. Your senses are on fire. Everything has been committed to this group. In many cases, family and friends have not been heard from in years. What happened before you joined is hazy. Life is a blur of activity, leaving you no time to even try to recall the past. Careers have been abandoned, educations terminated. There is no stash of money in a safe haven to cushion any return to the outside world. What you do now may be decisive for all of humanity as well as yourself. You shiver under the weight of responsibility but resolve to be its equal. Others may weaken but you will rise to the demands of history. You are marooned in an oasis of certainty from which you contemplate a baffling outside world that looks back at you with equal disdain and incomprehension. You only know other members of the group. They are, it seems, your soul mates. Without them, you are lost. Even more importantly, you have a leader who cares about you, who understands your deepest desires, who has wisdom beyond comprehension and in whose decisions you have learned to place absolute faith. You are ready for whatever happens next.

Jonestown

Catastrophe often happens in stages. Jim Jones diligently habituated his followers to the idea of a looming end. He regularly organized what came to be known as 'White Nights'. During these, members were presented with a number of options. But, increasingly, the only one on the table was that of 'revolutionary suicide'.

On many occasions, this was enacted. Debbie Layton described one such event in an affidavit, made shortly after she managed to escape from Jonestown in June 1978:

> Everyone, including the children, was told to line up. As we passed through the line, we were given a small glass of red liquid to drink. We were told that the liquid contained poison and that we would die within 45 minutes. We all did as we were told. When the time came when we should have dropped dead, Rev. Jones explained that the poison was not real and that we had just been through a loyalty test. He warned us that the time was not far off when it would become necessary for us to die by our own hands.[6]

Events outside Jonestown ushered this tragic end closer. From late 1977, some families of People's Temple members made increased contact with each other. Calling themselves 'Concerned Relatives', they publicly urged an investigation into Jones's activities and lobbied various media outlets and government officials. Debbie Layton's affidavit in June 1978 also fuelled the growing concern. Among those who responded positively was Congressman Leo Ryan. It was an interest that cost him his life. He travelled to Georgetown, Guyana, on 14 November 1978, bringing 18 people with him. They were a mixture of government officials, media representatives that included an NBC camera crew and some of those involved with the Concerned Relatives group. This was a seismic event in the history of Jonestown. As Galanter (1999: 118) puts it: 'The arrival of Congressman Ryan and his entourage portended the imminent disruption of the group's *control over its boundary*, and thereby precipitated the final events at Jonestown'. For Jones, what was at stake was his absolute control over the group. Any intrusion of this kind threatened to weaken it.

Ryan and some of his delegation managed to reach Jonestown on 17 November. That night, they attended a carefully stage-managed reception in the pavilion. People's Temple members sang, danced and performed as if all was well. But the strain on Jones was immense. Despite the surface ebullience, filmed by the accompanying NBC crew, several of Jones's followers, their loyalty in shreds, covertly passed notes to Ryan or members of his entourage affirming that they wanted to leave. The stakes were steadily being raised.

And so the last day, 18 November, arrived. Those leaving were distraught, as were those staying. Mutual appeals ensued between both sides. One Temple member attacked Ryan with a knife but was prevented from injuring him. Eventually, they left for the airport at Port Kaitumna. Fourteen People's Temple members had opted to leave. As everyone eventually began to board one of the two planes that had been hired, a tractor with a trailer attached approached. It was driven by armed members of the Temple's Red Brigade security squad. A few seconds of the shooting that ensued were captured on film by NBC cameraman Bob Brown. When it was over, Congressman Ryan and four others, including Bob Brown and one defector, were dead. Nine others were injured, some seriously.

Jonestown itself now rushed to catch up. Ominously, as Tim Carter later recalled: 'Literally, out of nowhere, this storm came blowing in. The sky turned black. The wind came up and it just – torrential rain. But what I personally felt was that evil itself blew into Jonestown'. By 5 p.m. that evening, the final 'white night' had begun. A metal vat filled with Kool Aid and laced with a lethal cocktail of poisonous drugs had been prepared. Events now followed the pattern of previous such occasions. The difference this time was that the poison was real. Jones urged the end in rambling, apocalyptic terms, presenting the only alternative as a fate worse than death:

> Of what's going to happen here in a matter of a few minutes, is that one of the few on that plane is gonna shoot the pilot. I know that. I didn't plan it, but I know it's gonna happen. They're gonna shoot that pilot, and down comes that plane into the jungle and we had better not have any of our children left when it's over, 'cause they'll parachute in here on us. I'm telling you just as plain as I know how to tell you, I've never lied to you ... I never have lied to you. I know that's what's gonna happen, that's what he intends to do and he will do it. He'll do it. What's there being so bewildered with many, many pressures on my brain, seeing all these people behave so treasonous, it is just too much for me to put together, but, I now know what he was telling me and it'll happen. If the plane gets in the air even. So my opinion is that we be kind to children and be kind to seniors and take the potion like they used to take in ancient Greece, and step over quietly because we are not committing suicide. It's a revolutionary act. We can't go back. They won't leave us alone. They're now going back to tell more lies which means more congressmen. And there's no way, no way we can survive.

One follower, Christine Miller, stood insistently against Jones, repeatedly suggesting that the children had a right to life. She argued that other options, such as escaping to Russia, should be considered:

> *Christine*: But I look at all the babies and I think they deserve to live ...
> *Jones*: I agree ...
> *Christine*: You know ...
> *Jones*: But also they deserve ... what's more they deserve peace.
> *Christine*: We all came here for peace ...
> *Jones*: And we, have we had it?
> *Christine and crowd*: No ...

Others affirmed their debt to 'Dad', believing that without him life was not worth living. There is repeated crying and the dreadful noise of children screaming. The dying had begun. Firstly, poison was administered to some of the children – an irrevocable step that sapped the souls of those remaining. The adults watching this were then expected to do likewise. Those who refused were threatened at gunpoint by Jones's armed security guard. Individual choices were subordinated to the collective will. Pain, doubt and protest are evident through-out, as shown in the following excerpt:

> Jones: Die with respect, die with a degree of dignity. Lay down your life with dignity. Don't lay down with tears and agony ... Don't, don't be this way. Stop this hysterics ... This is not the way for people who are socialistic Communists to die ... no way for us to die. We must die with some dignity.

Much later, an unsigned note was found, left behind by one of the dead. It reads as follows:

> To whomever finds this note. Collect all the tapes, all the writing, all the history. The story of this movement, this action, must be examined over and over. We did not want this kind of ending. We wanted to live, to shine, to bring light to a world that is dying for a little bit of love. There's quiet as we leave this world. The sky is gray. People file by us slowly and take the some-what bitter drink. Many more must drink. A teeny kitten sits next to me watching. A dog barks. The birds gather on the telephone wires. Let all the story of this Peoples Temple be told. If nobody understands, it matters not. I am ready to die now. Darkness settles over Jonestown on its last day on Earth.

A handful managed to survive, by escaping into the jungle. They included Tim Carter, who had earlier watched his wife and small son die. But gradually every-thing subsides. By the time of Jones's last words only the dismal echo of funereal music in the background remains. Jonestown was over.

Heaven's Gate

The end for Heaven's Gate also arrived in stages. Records are fewer, since the end was not recorded and nobody who was there managed to survive. But we do know that Bonnie Nettles died in 1985, most probably from liver cancer. This shook Applewhite to his core. Members of the group, above all its leaders, were not supposed to physically die but would rather ascend in some form to the Next Level. He went through a profound crisis of faith in the group's belief system as a result of this but was talked into continuing by his followers. For many of them, the bridge back to real life had long been dynamited. What else could they do but continue and adapt to changed circumstances? In consequence, only one member dropped out during this traumatic time (Balch and Taylor 2002).

While there is no real indication of significant upset in the group's belief system, some details changed. Applewhite now suggested that Nettles would assume an angelic new body, returning at a later stage to collect the others. In the meantime, she would send communications that only he could interpret. Increasingly the view emerged that they would reach the next level by leaving 'the vehicle' of their old bodies behind. This would be made possible because a small group of people had received a deposit 'in the form of a special soul from benevolent extra-terrestrials. Those in this category, who would thus be able to connect with this "deposit", would eventually be saved by the extra-terrestrials from this imminent Doomsday' (Introvigne 2002: 216). Applewhite's behaviour grew stranger. From 1985 onwards, he sat in front of the group with a vacant chair beside him, denoting Nettles' presence. He aged rapidly and acquired the shaven head and staring eyes now familiar from the group's final videos. The question became how they could leave their bodies behind and complete the journey begun back in 1972.

One conclusion was that further attempts at recruitment should be made. This is consistent with the view, originating in cognitive dissonance theory, that, when major prophecies fail, those who have invested much in their fulfilment are more likely to escalate their commitment to the group that has pronounced them, rather than re-evaluate their belief system (Festinger 1957). In a final attempt to attract more followers, Heaven's Gate created a sophisticated website. They then waited in hope. But only two people joined, six months before the end. They were a married couple who left behind four children and renounced their sexual relationship to do so. He left after three months, wrongly anticipating that she would soon follow him out. In the event, their last recruit stayed to the end and joined the veterans in their final suicide. Members concluded from this recruitment failure that 'the harvest' was finished. Here was further evidence of the Earth's imminent end time. Now it was time to seriously consider leaving the planet. In March 1997, for the first time, Applewhite taped himself speaking of mass suicide. He suggested that only this could complete the group's mission. Eventually, he and his 38 remaining followers became convinced that that a spacecraft was trailing the comet Hale-Bopp. It was thought that their souls could ascend and board the craft by committing suicide. This decided, the 'students' and Do went to a local restaurant for a last public supper together two days before the first suicides. Witnesses saw nothing to arouse anxiety. They then returned home to prepare for the end.

Farewell videos were made. That of 'Stlody' is typical.[7] Evidently filmed in the garden of the group's rented mansion, against a backdrop of lush vegetation and sunshine, he looks like someone preparing for the vacation of a lifetime rather than death. His testimony lasts no more than six minutes. Like the others, it is labelled 'Students of Heaven's Gate expressing their thoughts before exit'. He recounts meeting Ti and Do in 1975, testifies to the power of their message and reaffirms his conviction that it provided him with the purpose in life he always sought. He talks movingly of the 'goodness' he had found inside Ti and Do, their dedication to the cause and of being 'honoured' at being part of their 'mission'. When mentioning the beliefs that Ti and Do had brought to the group, Stlody invariably calls it 'the information', as though it represented established truths beyond challenge. There is no sign of hesitation or regret, only immense pride in those with whom he has shared this journey and boundless faith in the future that awaits them all.

The group's last recruit also left behind an 'exit statement'. In it, she speaks of her preparations to 'separate' from 'the vehicle' and 'leave it all behind'. She adds: 'There is nothing here for me. I want to look forward and keep my eye on Ti and Do. That's my path'.[8]

The 38 Heaven's Gate members, plus group leader Applewhite, were found dead in the home they rented on 26 March 1997. They were all lying in their bunk beds. Their ages ranged from 26 to 72. Each body was covered by a purple cloth. For some inexplicable reason, each carried a five-dollar bill, as if some form of cash were needed at the Next Level. All wore identical black shirts and sweat pants, athletic shoes and armband patches that read 'Heaven's Gate Away Team'. *Star Trek*-inspired terminology was common, and 'Stlody' had used it in his farewell video when referring to the group. It is believed that they died in three groups over three days. Applewhite was among the last to die. A framed picture of an imagined alien being rested on the mantelpiece of his room. The dead included Thomas Nichols, the brother of actress Nichelle Nichols who played Uhura in the original *Star Trek* television series. Autopsies found cyanide, arsenic and alcohol in their bodies. Yet this was not quite the end. Two former members, Wayne Cooke and Charlie Humphreys, committed suicide, in May 1997 and February 1998, respectively. The force of Applewhite's ideology had reached beyond the grave. One senses that it would not have displeased him.

Leadership lessons

An obvious question arises. To what extent did Jones or Nettles and Applewhite have a genuine belief in the ideologies they advocated? It is a question frequently posed when considering cultic groups of all persuasions. The beliefs in question depart so far from the mainstream that common sense suggests – surely – that the leaders at least must have known they were all nonsense. I do not think so. Writing of Heaven's Gate, Lalich (2004: 52) insightfully suggests: 'The extent to which they believed the myth they created about themselves can never be known, but it seems likely that they were motivated by a mixture of belief and the desire to control and manipulate'. Human motivation is rarely one-dimensional. It is possible to seek complete power but to justify this with the thought that it will serve noble ends.

Consider also the group dynamics to which such leaders are themselves subject. They expend enormous energy attempting to convince others of their belief system. This engages them in a process of self-persuasion, since such efforts to convince others involves a relentless focus only on the positive aspects of the belief system and ensures that they end up reconvincing themselves (Briñol *et al.* 2012). What is real and what is imagined can become blurred by the act of performance. Moreover, such leaders receive constant reinforcement from their followers, who affirm to them the validity of the belief system in question. The co-construction of leader and follower identities is always at play. There can be few deadlier examples than that of how Applewhite's own crisis of faith in 1985 was resolved, through the encouragement of those he had himself recruited. This process can also be read as an example of 'consensual validation' or 'social proof': the spectacle of others enthusiastically advocating our chosen ideology convinces us, quite irrationally, that it must be true (Cialdini 2009). While leaders of all hues expend much energy in attempting to shape the cognitions of their followers, the compliance of followers, when it is achieved, in turn shapes the cognitions of leaders. It is likely, I think, that whatever doubts each of them may have occasionally entertained diminished steadily over the years, leaving only faint echoes behind.

A key lesson for potential followers of leaders stands out. It is that the sincerity and passion with which a belief system is articulated does not constitute evidence of its correctness. We should be more attracted to doubt than certainty. We should welcome openness instead of closure. Leaders who promise all-encompassing answers to the complex problems that afflict the world are to be distrusted. Those who invite us to suspend our critical faculties and embrace a belief system determined for us by others are to be doubly distrusted. Linked to this, we need to be sceptical of leaders who make far-reaching claims but who do so with minimal supporting empirical evidence. Bold claims require a substantial body of evidence. In the case of both Heaven's Gate and Jonestown this was entirely lacking.

High-activity groups are particularly worthy of suspicion. There is no idea so outlandish that people cannot come to believe it, provided that they are in the process of escalating their commitment to a high-activity group that talks only or mainly to itself. Layton sums it up with unsurpassed insight:

> When our own thoughts are forbidden, when our questions are not allowed and our doubts punished, when contacts and friendships outside of the organization are censored, we are being abused for an end that never justifies its means. When our heart aches knowing we have made friendships and secret attachments that will be forever forbidden if we leave, we are in danger. When we consider staying in a group because we cannot bear the loss, disappointment, and sorrow our leaving will cause for ourselves and those we have come to love, we are in a cult.
>
> (Layton 1999: 299)

Layton's wisdom came at a high cost. In departing Jonestown, she had to leave her dying mother behind. She never saw her again. Her brother was convicted in 1987 of participation in the attack on Leo Ryan and his entourage and jailed until 2002. The lives of those lucky enough to survive had to be rebuilt from scratch. It behoves the rest of us to learn from such dearly bought experience.

But here we also find an important lesson for leaders. By the end, Marshall Applewhite was a shadow of his formal self. Greatly aged but still seemingly sure of his chosen path, it is clear from the final videos of Heaven's Gate that his mental health had deteriorated. Post-mortem investigations also showed that he suffered severe heart disease and could have died at any moment. The strain of leading his group had taken a terrible toll. For similar reasons, Jim Jones had also seriously declined by the end of 1978. He was illicitly ingesting vast amounts of drugs, many of them filched from People's Temple members, who needed them for medical conditions. Those deprived of medication included Debbie Layton's cancer stricken mother, who died in agony ten days before the final massacre. The end may, in part, have been induced by a growing feeling that he could not go on any longer. Thus, whatever the superficial attractions of absolute power over others, the effort of holding on to it is often mutually destructive.

Moreover, such power is usually limited in its reach. A leader may be able to exert great control over a relatively small number of followers but, unless they have obtained state power, will struggle to extend similar control over larger groups of followers. It is possible to maintain intense surveillance over a few but hard to do so over the many. Thus, for all the efforts expended to ensure compliance and recruit more members, cult leaders, as with Jonestown and Heaven's Gate, find that their power has limitations. When freed from stringent oversight people debate, dissent and many leave.

This realisation should not promote complacency about the cultic phenomenon. Despite the difficulties posed, it is possible for some such groups to acquire significant influence and to hold it for lengthy periods of time. For example, various writers have noted that Nazism relied on a central charismatic figure, exploited a crisis situation to gain power and employed major theatrical group events to maintain its hold on followers (Kerr 2008). Cults have also sometimes acquired wider influence through front organizations and various public activities. Nevertheless, there are difficulties in this occurring and, outside of a context of social upheaval, it appears that most cultic leaders struggle to achieve a large following and lasting influence. Such influence requires different leadership models, more open to debate, difference and shared responsibility. The challenge is to close the distance between leaders and followers, rather than – as is the case within many organizations – to exacerbate it (Collinson 2005a). A more careful and reflexive approach to follower engagement is necessary. This may also keep a leader sane. As the examples of Jim Jones and Marshall Applewhite attest, those with absolute power are unlikely to ever be absolutely rational.

Following the wrong kind of leader can get you killed. A spirit of independence, self-awareness and a willingness to dissent are among the traits that leaders such as Jim Jones and Marshall Applewhite attempt to eradicate, as one would attack an outbreak of pestilence in a city. But it is precisely these qualities that we need if we are to ensure a healthy relationship between leaders and followers. The alternative is a subordination to the will of others that may well end in catastrophe.

Points for discussion

1. Can Jim Jones and Marshall Applewhite be considered 'transformational leaders?' What behaviours did they display that convince you they either were or were not transformational leaders?
2. How precisely did the leaders of both groups establish and maintain conformist behaviours on the part of their followers?
3. To what extent do you think it is important for followers to always maintain some sense of independence and distance from their leaders?
4. Jonestown, in particular, is described in this chapter as a miniature totalitarian system. Do you think this is a valid characterisation and on what grounds would you agree or disagree with it?
5. What are the implications that arise from both these groups for the practice of leadership more widely?

Notes

1 The full text of this tape can be found at: http://jonestown.sdsu.edu/AboutJonestown/Tapes/Tapes/DeathTape/Q042fbi.html. Last accessed 21 November 2012. The audio recording itself can be heard on YouTube, at the following URL: http://www.youtube.com/watch?v=OkookcrAnSE&feature=related. Last accessed 21 November 2012.
2 Numerous documentaries have featured the Jonestown tragedy. These include *Jonestown: The Life and Death of Peoples Temple*, released in 2006 and then on DVD in 2009. It is of particular note for the numerous first-hand testimonies that it contains. This documentary is also available in full on YouTube, at http://www.youtube.com/watch?v=iQYoHiM-Uko. Last accessed 21 November 2012.
3 Unless otherwise specified, quotations from former People's Temple members are transcribed from the documentary, *Jonestown: The Life and Death of Peoples Temple*.
4 Heaven's Gate has also featured in many television programmes about cults. Of particular note is a BBC *Inside Story* documentary, available to view on YouTube at http://www.youtube.com/watch?v=nAx2KAQcqqM. Last accessed 21 November 2012.
5 Unless otherwise indicated, quotations from former members are transcribed from the *Inside Story* documentary, *Heaven's Gate*. See http://www.youtube.com/watch?v=nAx2KAQcqqM. Last accessed 21 November 2012.
6 The full text of this affidavit can be viewed at http://www.rickross.com/reference/jonestown/jonestown12.html. Last accessed 21 November 2012.
7 This video is available to view on YouTube and can be accessed at http://www.youtube.com/watch?v=ZKQ2a7tQLd4. Last accessed 21 November 2012.
8 This is available to view on YouTube at http://www.youtube.com/watch?v=k-s1oqIIfN4&feature=related. Last accessed 21 November 2012.

10 Accounting for failure

Bankers in the spotlight[1]

Introduction

In Chapter 1, I suggested that the banking crisis which began in 2008 has become a crisis in the practice of leadership and the theories that have sustained it. This uncomfortable insight has not escaped the attention of senior bankers. Pilloried in the media, scorned by the public, micro-analysed by academics and attacked by politicians, they have been keen to shore up their tattered reputations and to ensure that they retain their ability to lead banks in a manner as close to the way they have traditionally done as possible. They resemble a man with a hangover looking forward to his next drink rather than resolving to mend his ways. Their approach tells us much about the dark side of leadership and points to dangers ahead. In particular, how leaders account for failure has a major bearing on whether lessons will be learned for the future. The extent to which leaders are willing to accept responsibility for their actions is also a litmus test for integrity. The dark side of leadership reveals itself in many shades between white and black. Bankers are not demons, nor are they saints. But they are powerful leaders who have brought many of us to the brink of disaster and whose explanations for why this has happened illustrate much about the practice of leadership far beyond the esoteric world of credit default swaps, collateralised debt obligations and sub-prime mortgages.

Before the crisis, bankers had been widely praised for their contribution to prosperity, including by many who were later keen to distance themselves from them. To take one example, the then UK Chancellor and future Prime Minister, Gordon Brown, made a speech in June 2007 where he declared:

> Over the ten years that I have had the privilege of addressing you as Chancellor, I have been able year by year to record how the City of London has risen by your efforts, ingenuity and creativity to become a new world leader ... I congratulate ... the City of London on these remarkable achievements, an era that history will record as the beginning of a new golden age for the City of London. And I believe the lesson we learn from the success of the City has ramifications far beyond the City itself – that we are leading because we are first in putting to work exactly that set of qualities that is needed for global success.[2]

With praise like this ringing in their ears, it was perhaps inevitable that banking leaders began to believe in the myth of their own infallibility. But it was a myth soon shattered by events.

Alongside such acclaim, top bankers had been well rewarded for their leadership roles. Fred Goodwin, the man once in charge of the Royal Bank of Scotland (RBS), serves as the best known example. He retired with a pension pot of over £16 million. His resignation meant that, at the age of 50, he was entitled to benefits which he would only have been able to claim at the age of 60 had he remained in work. He could therefore draw an annual income of over £700,000 – a generous reward for failure. In 2009, it was revealed that, although Goodwin joined RBS when he was 40, the bank treated him as having joined when he was 20, thereby inflating his pension. It would be difficult to think of starker status differentials between leaders and followers than the exceptional generosity he enjoyed. Such differentials are one of the main means by which the dark side of leadership is most manifest. It amplified the volume of public criticism that they experienced after the crisis in 2008 and ramped up the tension that was evident when they tried to account for their actions. It is these accounts that I analyse in this chapter.

I draw here on one major data set. On Tuesday 10 February 2009, four senior bankers from major banking corporations in the UK were called to give evidence to the Banking Crisis Inquiry of the Treasury Committee of the UK House of Commons. They were Sir Tom McKillop, former Chairman of RBS Group plc, Sir Fred Goodwin, former Chief Executive of RBS Group plc, Lord Stevenson, former Chairman of Halifax Bank of Scotland plc (HBOS), and Mr Andy Hornby, former Chief Executive of HBOS plc. Goodwin received his knighthood in 2004 for services to banking. It was 'cancelled and annulled' in February 2012. At the time he appeared before this committee, he was still Sir Fred. The crisis the system faced was immense. RBS alone had recorded an annual loss of £24.1 billion for the previous year, the largest in UK corporate history, and had effectively been nationalised by the Government. The transcript of this Inquiry was posted on the House of Commons Treasury Committee (2009a) website and runs to 31,725 words. I look at how the bankers attempted to explain the crisis and their role within it. Here, we see powerful leaders under scrutiny in a manner that has until recently been rare. There is much that it reveals – for the most part, unintentionally.

Under scrutiny but not in retreat – bankers on the offensive

It is obvious that the bankers' public image as competent and successful leaders was under unprecedented threat. They were keen to avoid being held responsible for the crisis but, at the same time, anxious to assert that they were moral, trustworthy and effective individuals. Stapleton and Hargie (2011: 267) note that this created an almost irresolvable tension 'between moral or ethical integrity on the one hand, and professional credibility on the other'. They term this quandary a 'double-bind accountability dilemma' – or D-BAD. This captures a situation in which given actors seek to avoid conflict but find that every option open to them appears to have negative consequences. In this case:

> If the bankers claimed to have lacked the knowledge or ability to predict the crisis, they would produce a threat to their personal identity, specifically, the extent to which they can be perceived to have been competent and credible within their roles as senior executives. On the other hand, if they presented themselves as having been competent and in control of the situation, this would pose a challenge to their moral integrity (to the extent that they knowingly allowed the crisis to occur).
>
> (Stapleton and Hargie 2011: 272)

Flowing from this notion, it is clear that the bankers' discourse was characterised by four overarching themes by which they sought to explain the crisis and mitigate their role in it. The themes are, firstly, that the crisis was the product of the wisdom of the crowd. Secondly, and flowing from the first, they also sought to present themselves as relatively passive observers rather than as agents who had been confronted by overwhelming market forces. Thirdly, they repeatedly suggested that they also shared in the problems which had arisen and were therefore, to some extent, its victims. Fourthly, they depicted themselves as penitent learners, bound by the inherent limitations faced by everyone. The overall spectacle is of people attempting to minimise their responsibility for what had occurred, particularly in the suggestion that whatever mistaken perceptions they had held were widely shared and were therefore in some way excusable. I now explore each of these themes in detail, and consider their implications for the practice of leadership.

The wisdom of the crowd

During their testimony, the bankers argued that their unfolding perception of events had been widely shared throughout the previous period. For example, Fred Goodwin stated:

> I do not think anyone saw. I do not think, in fairness even to the Bank of England, that they really saw that it was going to turn this quickly … I think is the part which has just caught everyone out.
>
> (Ev 222)[3]

Here, he refers to authority by asserting that not even the Bank of England foresaw what was about to happen and this is why it just caught everyone out. He further responded as follows in the face of questioning about the wisdom of his bank's takeover of ABN Amro, which contributed significantly to its losses:

> Our shareholders approved the transaction in August of 2007. Barclays' shareholders approved it in the middle of September 2007. After the Barclays

shareholders approved it – and Barclays stayed in the fight to get ABN Amro right to the end and revised their bid terms up ... that may seem hard to believe now, but at the time that fitted into the context.

(Ev 226)

Goodwin's argument here is that all of the best experts thought as they did (*our shareholders, Barclays, ABN Amro*) and it would therefore have been irrational to question the prevailing wisdom of the crowd. The fact that the acquisition received a favourable market reaction reinforces this line of argument:

There was due diligence done earlier in the year on ABN Amro. These were statements that were made to the public market. We raised funds for the ABN Amro transaction in late September – they were eight times oversubscribed. So the view at the time, and we could only work based on the view at the time.

(Ev 226, 227)

Here, the consensus effect is invoked, by emphasising that so many people were willing to buy shares (*eight times oversubscribed*), to strengthen his argument that this particular acquisition made sense, at least at the time when it took place. This approach therefore minimises responsibility and legitimises their actions, depicting the bankers as one small part of a 'herd' making judgment calls that unfortunately proved to be wrong. However, this opened up other problems. Those questioning the bankers were keen to discuss how well they managed risk and the bankers, in turn, were anxious to convey the impression that everything which could be done on this front had been done, as the following excerpt shows:

Lord Stevenson of Coddenham: I would say HBOS had very elaborate systems of risk management and stress testing, worked out over the years and, it is not too much to say, hand-in-hand with our regulator, who was present all the time ... I do think we will not be the only bank in the world which had very elaborate risk management systems, where indeed the Board was involved heavily (which is the thrust of your point), but where in truth we failed to consider some of the extreme scenarios that have actually happened.

(Ev 227)

Once more, responsibility for events is distributed throughout the system – in this case encompassing all those involved in risk management and scenario planning. The acceptance of responsibility for how the crisis was managed, or the detailed business models that provoked it, is excluded by the suggestion that everyone had throughout the build-up to the crisis thought in identical terms to the bankers. Thus, Tom McKillop asserted:

Securitisation, the originate and distribute model, was seen as a stabilising influence in the financial systems. It has been discussed in many forums that I have participated in. This was distributing risk. This was making the whole system more stable. It has not turned out that way. It has turned out completely the opposite to expectations. Everyone has been surprised about that, the regulators, the companies and the banks involved in it.

(Ev 240, 241)

It is here suggested that whatever happened was in spite of the bankers' best efforts; they did what they could; they had elaborate systems in place to forestall crisis; they merely failed to consider some 'extreme scenarios' that by definition lay beyond any rational expectation of occurrence and for which the collective wisdom of the crowd was inadequate. Agency is simultaneously affirmed and denied. That is, it is affirmed in terms of a stress on sound processes and rational decisions but excluded in terms of acknowledging responsibility for the outcomes that derived from these processes and decisions. In terms of Stapleton and Hargie's (2011) notion of D-BAD, this can be viewed as an attempt to claim that the bankers had acted both ethically and with professional credibility. They had, after all, done their best under difficult conditions that 'surprised' everyone. How successful this effort at impression management was is a different matter.

Moreover, invoking the wisdom of the crowd implies that any damaging behaviour that the bankers had sanctioned emerged directly from the pressure of others. McKillop, in particular, drew attention to the pressure applied by institutional investors for greater returns. Lord Stevenson expressed this most clearly, at an early stage of the inquiry's deliberations, in response to a question exploring whether the bankers had thought low interest rates, low inflation and easy access to credit would endure indefinitely:

Lord Stevenson of Coddenham: The question is: did we believe the view which came out not so much of Ben Bernanke but Mr Greenspan and indeed, let us face it, most people throughout the world, that we were in a permanent state of cheap money, and everything was the best in the best of all possible worlds? I have to say, speaking for myself, of course you take note of what the major regulators say and what the opinion leaders say and, yes, that period of a decade, where the supposed Chinese deflation lowered rates of interest et cetera, that was quite a compelling argument. I would not want you to think, however, that we slavishly worshipped that doctrine. If I take you back three years, or thereabouts, for example, we took a decision which was widely criticised at the time on all sides to lower our share of the housing market from 30% to 20% just when the views you have summarised were prevailing, and we took that out of good countercyclical caution; and there have been a number of other decisions of that kind. I think I referred in our memorandum to the fact that about five years ago we deliberately took a P&L hit so as to lengthen the maturity in wholesale markets: but yes, Chairman, the prevailing views best exemplified by Mr Greenspan's testimony on the Hill, which I remember watching regularly, is bound to have an influence on us and most other people in the world.

(Ev 221, 222)

Interestingly, the spectre of a herd mentality is invoked throughout this exchange. Furthermore, world authorities, such as Mr Greenspan, as well as *major regulators, opinion leaders* and, indeed, *most other people in the world* were all running with the herd. While it is acknowledged that these *prevailing views* must impact on the bankers' own thought processes, care is also taken to suggest that, on some level, they began to question it. A religious metaphor is used to underline the fact that due care was being paid to events: *I would not want you to think, however, that we slavishly worshipped that doctrine*. Thus, agency is both affirmed and denied, in a manner that stresses the bankers' insight rather than any analytical deficiencies they may have displayed.

Leaders as passive spectators

The bankers depicted themselves as, at crucial periods, passive spectators, when faced with rapidly cascading events beyond anyone's control. At these times, they were forced to become observers of events caused by the actions of others. Mention is made right at the outset of the bankers' testimony of the phrase *turn of events* to indicate that what occurred was sudden, unpredictable and overwhelming. When asked by the Chairman if they would apologise for their role in the banking collapse, Lord Stevenson of Coddenham replies: 'we are profoundly and, I think I would say, unreservedly sorry *at the turn of events*'. When Hornby responds to the same question, he uses exactly the same phrase: 'we are extremely sorry for *the turn of events* that has brought it about'. Whittle and Mueller (2012: 127) point out that the phrase 'turn of events' also relies on a device known as externalisation or 'out-there-ness'. Externalisation refers to the process by which actions and events are presented as out of the control of the actor, simply part of the 'world out there'. Thus, the bankers avoid acknowledging any link between the current situation and their own actions, a reversal of the active, purposeful and commanding agency they are normally keen to claim and by which leaders are normally depicted in the leadership literature, and in practitioner journals such as *Harvard Business Review*. Note also that the bankers do not apologise for their actions. They were sorry for what happened, rather than what they did. Personal responsibility is therefore avoided. The *turn of events* appears to have arisen in no way from any action by the bankers – rather it was a situation beyond their control and one that could not have been predicted (Hargie *et al.* 2010).

In addition, the phrase 'turn of events' implies an element of unexpectedness, which suggests that, as well as being unable to control or influence events, the bankers could not reasonably be expected to have *foreseen* the crisis. Of relevance here is Scott and Lyman's (1968) typology of accounts, which identifies excuses and justifications as two primary account types. Excuses can be built around appeals to accidents ('The other car crashed into me'), biological drives ('I couldn't help doing it') and 'scapegoating' ('It was all your fault'). Within this frame, then, the banking crisis was an accident caused by the impersonal interplay of market forces rather than by the conscious decisions of the bankers themselves – it was an 'accident'. It is interesting to reflect on what alternative excuses might have looked like. A 'biological' excuse may have necessitated an admission such as 'We were greedy and careless', which is scarcely a face-saving rhetorical device. On the other hand, a scapegoating excuse may have taken such forms as 'Weak government regulation was at fault' or 'Borrowers really caused the crisis by being reckless'. Again, however, this may have stoked even wider public resentment, since, in effect, people who were suffering most from the crisis and/or whose actions had saved the banks from ruin would have found themselves being stigmatised by already unpopular senior bankers. In seeking to deflect agency but by projecting it to accidental causes, the bankers were clearly trying to minimise their personal culpability but also to avoid causing further offence and outrage.

This analysis is consistent with the work of Van Langenhove and Harre (1999) on what they call positioning. As they argue:

> Offering an excuse by way of explanation is not just a way of resisting an accusation of guilt, but is also an act of self-positioning through which one adopts the position of one who is helpless and has a right to special treatment.
> (Van Langenhove and Harre 1999: 26)

While the bankers clearly do not argue that they deserve special treatment, they explicitly place themselves in the role of people who were helpless in the face of what the politicians questioning them frequently and obligingly described as a 'financial tsunami'.

The image of passivity was evident throughout their testimony. At an early stage in proceedings, the Chairman of the Treasury Committee, John McFall, cited the *Oxford English Dictionary* definition of a bank as 'an organization offering financial services, especially the safe keeping of customers' money until required and making loans at interest'. He wanted to know whether the bankers felt they had sufficiently lived up to this. The response from Lord Stevenson was: 'We certainly aspired to. As our evidence to you made clear, we got hit by ... ' (Ev 222).

His response was immediately interrupted by the chairman but the suggestion of being *hit by* implies that the crisis occurred because of events over which they had no control. This seeks to mitigate the notion that they were active agents in the developing crisis. It depicts the bankers as the passive subjects of processes for which they had no personal responsibility. Passive metaphors were used by Sir Fred Goodwin in response to a question about why his bank had to access public funds:

> the spotlight shone on us for that very key moment at the beginning of December when we saw the share price come down and when rumours did leak about banks being supported in the UK, and our line was that we were going to need to support, the spotlight fell on us and our share price dropped 60% or so in two days.
> (Ev 222)

Here, Goodwin asserts that the spotlight *fell on us* and our share price *dropped*. He also represents the bankers as observers of outside events – *we saw the share price come down*. There is no account of who or what caused the share price to fall or an acknowledgment that this might have been related to, or in part caused by, the actions of the bankers. Hornby also uses passive language in his description of events: 'the difficulty that HBOS encountered was significant reduction in availability of wholesale funding from August 2007 onwards, and it got much steeper ... and following the collapse of Lehmans we found those wholesale markets even harder to satisfy' (Ev 227).

The reductions in funding *got much steeper* and Lehmans eventually *collapsed*. It was outside forces that resulted in the markets becoming *harder to satisfy*. There is no explanation for why the wholesale markets became harder to satisfy or for how the actions of the bankers may have been involved. Goodwin makes a similar response when asked about his role at RBS:

> I would imagine that there are others out there who think, 'There but for the grace of God'. It was a fact, and all the more numbing, that after a rights issue, right through until the middle of September, we were moving forward positively. It was post-Lehman's that the collapse in confidence, the collapse in markets, just came round and hit us and we were caught at that point. It was very sudden and very sharp. It could have happened to others.
>
> (Ev 228)

Again, the fact is underlined that they were powerless to do anything about it – *it could have happened to others*, who are now thinking *'There but for the grace of God'*. The bankers also represented themselves as at times being the passive recipients of practices which had largely originated elsewhere. The following quotation from Goodwin, responding to the suggestion that the heavy use of bonuses by the banks exacerbated the urge to take too much risk, illustrates the point:

> Many of the remuneration practices have been imported from the United States. As London has emerged as more and more of a global financial services centre ... It is very difficult for an individual institution to make a change unilaterally.
>
> (Ev 225)

While people and organizations generally decide to import products and services, here the act of importing is described in passive, reactive terms – for example, the remuneration practices *have been imported from the United States*. The bankers had no choice but to go along with somewhat 'foreign' practices originating elsewhere, in the interests of remaining competitive, as it was *very difficult for an individual institution to make a change*. This approach is consistent with a recurring theme of diminished agency – a theme that clashes with the stress on leader agency which they were normally happy to accept and which is reinforced by most mainstream commentaries on leadership.

Alongside this, sat the notion that the bankers had done their best to provide for every logical contingency. For example, some of RBS's major problems arose from the purchase of ABN Amro at hugely inflated prices. McKillop dealt with this as follows:

> We had a plan. When we acquired ABN Amro there was a capital plan and a funding plan in place. The problem was, no sooner had we acquired ABN Amro then the world changed dramatically and we were unable to implement that plan.
>
> (Ev 226)

Thus, while asserting that they had formulated a plan, he asserts that *the world changed dramatically* so that they were not able to implement this plan. In this way, the crisis is described as something that is happening to the bankers rather than as being caused by them. Again, their behaviours are framed as a series of reactions to fast moving and deteriorating processes which no one could have been expected to anticipate, and which by their rapidity pre-empted the possibility of preventive action. Leadership agency is thus excluded as an explanatory variable, in favor of a model of passivity.

The paradox of agency and power

Accounts of organizational success by leaders, in contrast, are characterised by a stress on agency and power. For example, Amernic *et al.*'s (2007) analysis of root metaphors in Jack Welch's annual letters to shareholders when in charge of General Electric show that he frequently resorted to those depicting himself as a pedagogue, physician, architect, commander and saint. However, the bankers had little difficulty in resorting to radically different metaphorical constructs when placed in a context of difficulty. This is particularly evident in the following excerpt, where I highlight particularly important parts of the exchange:

> *Sir Fred Goodwin*: I think of necessity this was all happening at an extremely rapid rate. The *rate of deterioration which took place* – and you will have heard from many other witnesses about the *impact of Lehmans on 15 September and the catalogue of failures which came after that* – by the time we got through into that week, Monday 6 October, the 6th and 7th *saw a collapse in bank share price, a collapse in our price, a collapse in the FTSE, and a real collapse in confidence.* Leading up to that over the preceding three weeks or so there has been an increasingly frequent interaction between the banks generally and the tripartite authorities, and the banks collectively and the tripartite authorities as *people were becoming more concerned about how the market was developing*, and in that week *it just tipped over the edge.* I think in a perfect world *the tripartite authority would have liked a little bit longer* to pull the plan together, but it was very clear to everyone that it had to happen there and then and *there was an enormous amount of effort put into it.*
>
> (Ev 230–1)

Goodwin portrays himself as an observer of seismic events, where in essence the financial world was forced to watch a market growing out of control with a *rapid rate of deterioration* – they *saw a collapse* of a market that eventually *tipped over the edge*. In fact, there was a collapse of almost everything – bank share price, their share price, the FTSE and confidence. There is the suggestion that the bankers had worked incredibly hard, with others, to avert what occurred – *there was an enormous amount of effort put into it*. Whatever went wrong was outside of their control and despite their best efforts. Thus, the bankers themselves invested a great deal of effort in mitigating its effects, in the process sharing the pain of the wider community since, by that stage, *people were becoming more concerned about how the market was developing*. Goodwin here depicts himself as at times being forced to be passive (the victim of circumstances) but also, where possible, engaged and active (attempting to avert total meltdown). There is denial of individual agency for negative outcomes and a diffusion of responsibility by invoking third parties – *the banks collectively* and *the tripartite authority* – as the decision-making bodies.

This approach can be usefully looked at from the perspective of how public figures attempt to repair their image following some kind of negative event. Schutz (1998) identified six defensive strategies commonly employed in such circumstances. These include 'dissociation' – that is, accepting that something happened but denying responsibility for it. This denial of agency permeates the testimony analysed here. It is part of a consistent pattern, in which the bankers are keen to establish that the crisis was extraordinary and unanticipated, that it created a collective sense of confusion and that even extraordinary efforts by competent and well-meaning people, such as themselves, were incapable of resolving it.

Bankers as victims

Not only were the bankers somehow passive in the face of overwhelming events but they also sought to represent themselves as amongst its victims. The strategy of 'victimage' (pointing out that the speaker has been a victim and has suffered as well and so can understand and share the pain) is one that is often used in attempts to restore reputation following a crisis (Coombs 2007). As the reputation of the bankers was under severe threat in this Public Inquiry, it is no surprise that they would invoke victimage. This theme was established very early in the proceedings when, in his third question, the Chairman asks Sir Fred Goodwin if he thinks that the crisis has affected ordinary people and Goodwin replies, 'It has affected everyone'. His implication, which they later expand upon, is that the bankers have also suffered. This can be seen in Goodwin's response to a question (Q820) about the pension of over £8 million that he had just received, when he points out:

> I have lost a lot of money. Between the end of 2007 and now I would esti-
> mate I have lost somewhere in the region of over £5 million in the decline in

value on shares that I have put into the company. I bought shares on the day we completed the ABN Amro transaction – more than a year's salary. So the decline in share price in RBS has affected me. I am not complaining but it is highly germane to this conversation.

(Ev 229)

Here, he aligns himself with the victims, by portraying himself as a casualty too, who has personally suffered considerably from the catastrophic events that occurred, having lost *in the region of over £5 million*. Furthermore, the picture he paints is one of a brave victim, since although he has suffered substantial personal losses he is *not complaining*. As a further instance of this, consider the response of Nick Hornby to a question about bank bonuses:

executive directors were encouraged to take all of their cash bonuses in shares. To put it in perspective, in the two years that I have been Chief Executive I have lost considerably more money in my shares than I have been paid. I think that is showing I have been aligned with shareholders' interests.

(Ev 223)

Thus, while his interests were *aligned with shareholders' interests*, who had also shared in the expectation of ongoing prosperity, in the course of doing their best for shareholders the bankers had lost substantially (Hornby says he *lost considerably more money in my shares than I have been paid*), thereby rendering them also victims of a crisis that no one could have been expected to predict. Victims normally merit sympathy rather than reproach. This particular approach may thus be seen as part of an attempt to frame the public's response in this way, by excluding the possibility that the bankers were substantially the agents of the economic misfortunes being discussed. In fact, one of the Panel members recognised this tactic, leading to the following exchange:

Mr Todd: You are presenting yourselves gently as victims in this process?

Lord Stevenson of Coddenham: No. What can be quite plain, the denial, absolutely not. What is, is what is.

(Ev 242)

Although Lord Stevenson denies that the bankers were portraying themselves as victims, the text illustrates that Mr Todd was, in fact, correct. Indeed, in the report into the banking crisis (House of Commons Treasury Committee 2009b), the conclusion is reached that: 'These witnesses betrayed a degree of self-pity, portraying themselves as the unlucky victims of external circumstances' (p. 49). Furthermore, this aspect of deliberate image portrayal was raised by the Chairman during the hearing:

Q837 Chairman: Could I just pick up a point Andy Hornby made to John Mann. You said, "I don't feel I am particularly personally culpable".

What exactly are you apologising for? We have been told that you have coached extensively, meticulously by PR people and lots of money has been spent. The papers tell us that, Sir Tom. Are you expressing sympathy because your PR advisers advise you to do so?

Mr Hornby: No, let me just stress, I have already apologised several times on behalf of myself and the whole Board for what has happened. The precise question I was asked of whether I felt purely personally culpable, I think we all take responsibility for what has happened in the two years I have been running the company. I fully accept my own role within all of that.

(Ev 230)

Thus, Hornby placed himself in the position of apologising *for what had happened* (to him and to his colleagues), rather than *for what he and his colleagues had done*. While accepting his *own role*, he declines to spell this out in any detail. The dominant suggestion remains one of well-intentioned people who were victims of events beyond their control but sufficiently moved to apologise for the effects of a crisis which had also gripped them (they, too, were its victims). Furthermore, a third party entity, *the board*, was centrally responsible for the key decisions.

Bankers as penitent learners

The bankers' testimony sought to represent the bankers as penitent and indeed chastened learners, willing to acknowledge gaps in knowledge but determined to learn and improve. This is evident in the following excerpt, where Sir Fred Goodwin points out that they have carefully re-examined the events that occurred in an attempt to understand the causes: 'We have looked back at that very specific issue and obviously we have done a lot of work to try and understand what happened, how it happened and why it happened' (Ev 224).

Similarly, Lord Stevenson, in the following instances, acknowledges the need for improvement and assures the Committee that he personally has invested the time to achieve this: 'We must improve' (Ev 224) ... 'I would like to think I have invested the time to go up the learning curve' (Ev 248).

In response to the issue of bank bonuses, Nick Hornby portrayed himself as someone who had already learned definite lessons from his experience. In the following excerpt, he acknowledges errors in the previous system of paying short-term bonuses and the need to link bonuses to share ownership over a longer period:

There is no doubt that the bonus systems in many banks around the world have been proven to be wrong in the last 24 months, in that if people are ... paid very substantial short-term cash bonuses without it being clear whether those decisions over the next three to five years have been proven to be correct, that is not rewarding the right type of behaviour ... that should be a philosophy generally and that some way of making sure that annual cash bonuses are not paid in isolation but are tied into share ownership over the next three to five years.

(Ev 223)

Later in the proceedings, he is further pressed about his role, in the following exchange:

Mr Breed: But that was all too late. If you had taken notice of what was being said to you a couple of years earlier you might not have got into that position.

Mr Hornby: ... when I took over as CEO, we did try and preserve capital, we stopped the buyback programme, we reduced asset growth and we pulled back on mortgage market share. Of course, looking back, I would have liked to have done even more ... I believe there are very few people in the world who foresaw the complete collapse and I regret that because clearly I would have tried to pull back even more.

(Ev 233)

Here, while he again raises the point that, although what happened was impossible to foresee, he stresses that he did make efforts to mitigate the consequences – they *did try and preserve capital, stopped the buyback programme, reduced asset growth* and *pulled back on mortgage market share*. However, he also recognises that he would have liked to have done even more and expresses *regret* for this failure. Thus, although mistakes were made, lessons have been learned to rectify these in the future.

Learners are likely to be accorded less blame than powerful pedagogues for errors and misjudgements. Moreover, it is less reasonable to expect them to have full knowledge or provide a comprehensive account of whatever has occurred. This reading is consistent with the observation above that, while key organizational actors appear willing to claim agency in times of success and employ powerful metaphors to assist this (such as the notion of the leader as pedagogue), times of crisis produce much more passive metaphors that frame accounts of failure in terms of diminished agency.

Overall, we see here a clear narrative structure and explanatory framework, guided by the overall imperative to offer an explanation of the events in question but to do so in a manner that helped to restore the bankers' somewhat tarnished reputations by minimising their culpability for what had occurred. The first imperative was to offer some kind of explanation for the crisis. The notion of the wisdom of the crowd does this but it also distributes responsibility among many other significant individuals, groups and institutions. The second imperative was therefore to suggest that there was a certain inevitability to the crisis, in that, once it began (despite concerted efforts to avert its worst effects), events moved so rapidly that the situation was beyond anyone's control. Like most of those centrally involved, the bankers therefore became at times passive observers engulfed in an overwhelming crisis. Thirdly, the notion of bankers as victims suggests that they too had suffered and so should therefore be viewed in a suitably sympathetic light. Of equal importance, fourthly, it was necessary for the bankers to show that they had learned valuable lessons from the crisis, captured in the image of themselves as willing and penitent learners.

These approaches to explaining failure appear to have persisted among banking leaders beyond the immediate crisis of 2008. In Chapter 1, I offered the example of Barclays Bank and how its traders fixed crucial interest rates. In July 2012, its newly departed CEO, Bob Diamond, appeared before the Treasury Select Committee – by now, a well-trodden path for custodians of Britain's banks.[4] While he confirmed that he knew of unethical and probably criminal practices in other banks, he claimed to have been ignorant of them within Barclays. Moreover, he argued that his efforts to expose such practices elsewhere were ignored by government and regulators. But he also suggested that it did not occur to him or his senior colleagues to check whether what they knew to be a widespread practice elsewhere was occurring within their own organization. Rather, Diamond argued that the exposure of wrongdoing and Barclay's rapid acknowledgement of it confirmed that it had a robust culture to ensure ethical behaviour. There is no suggestion that the organization's leaders contributed to the issue that the Committee was investigating, had major lessons to learn from it or had been slow to take appropriate action. One MP, John Mann, commented drily that 'You have spent two hours telling us (Barclays) is doing so well – in fact, from what you have told us, doing so well that I wondered why you had not received an extra bonus rather than the sack' (p. 47). The House of Commons Treasury Select Committee's (2012: 78) eventual report concluded, in words that should make it impossible for Diamond to hold a senior role within the UK ever again, that 'Select committees are entitled to expect candour and frankness from witnesses before them. Mr Diamond's evidence, in the Committee's view, fell well short of the standard that Parliament expects'. This had been Diamond's second appearance before the Select Committee. His first, in January 2011, also attracted widespread coverage and criticism. On that occasion, Diamond recognised 'that there was a period of remorse and apology for banks'. He then added: 'I think that period needs to be over'.[5]

Thus, a leadership culture in which leaders are eager to claim credit for success but keen to evade responsibility for failure seems to have weathered the worst of the Great Recession intact. Leaders it seems can only be held responsible for miracles but, since they must be praised for success and absolved from blame for failure, it follows that they deserve to be richly rewarded under all conditions. This is not a culture consistent with long-term leadership effectiveness or the good of society and its institutions.

Learning from failure – a crucial role for leadership

The accounts provided by the bankers of their role in the crisis tells us much about the dark side of leadership. In boom times they were keen to take full credit for success but when circumstances took a turn for the worse their eagerness to take responsibility evaporated. Failure stood orphaned. Above all, the bankers' sense of agency emphasises intensive efforts to manage risk and concerted attempts to resolve problems once they had arisen. It is well documented that attempts to diminish responsibility and shift blame to others are common strategies in the face of crises, even when it is unlikely to succeed or may inflict further reputational damage. Conrad (2011) offers the example of Boston's Cardinal Bernard Law. Faced with the problem of sexual abuse of children by priests, Law asserted in a court deposition that parents must bear some of the responsibility for leaving their children with priests. Consistent with this, the bankers conveyed the view that the perceptions they held of unfolding events were widely shared by other key actors in the drama – *the wisdom of the crowd*. This, in turn, mitigates their personal responsibility: if everyone of significance shared a common world view, then it would be difficult to allocate the bankers a particular culpability for what happened. This was complemented by related attempts to portray themselves as passive observers and victims of the crisis. It is supplemented by the notion that they are learners rather than pedagogues, and are willing to improve.

The bankers' explanations are consistent with research on self-serving biases, which shows that most of us exaggerate our contribution to organizational success while minimising our responsibility for failure (Rogoff *et al.* 2004). It would appear that leaders are far from exempt from this process. They also align with findings pertaining to the fundamental attribution error. This proposes that, when explaining personal failure, we tend to highlight the significance of situational factors and downplay the role of dispositional causes (Ross 1977). As noted by Fairhurst (2011), in an organizational context, this involves senior executives frequently constructing the realities to which they then portray themselves as being forced to respond. Whittle and Mueller (2012: 129) argue that the bankers were determined to show that:

> Neither the system nor the agent should be blamed or punished. Quite simply, system failures are *very rare* ('once in a lifetime'); therefore we should retain our faith in the system. Thus, a rare nature-like disaster (like a plague or hurricane) was constructed to play the role of the villain in the story and 'explain' the financial crisis.

Attributions of this kind enable individuals to rationalise, interpret and explain their behaviour in ways that are favourable to themselves and continue to protect their self-interest (Winkler 2010).

This analysis challenges those accounts of organizational action which frame success in terms of leader action and volition. It is difficult to see how people can depict themselves as powerful at one conjuncture of events but as simultaneously powerless when dealing with challenges that have arisen in close proximity to other periods of triumph. However, this attempt at what can be termed 'blame realignment' seems to have largely failed. The eventual report of the Treasury Committee unequivocally held bankers responsible for the crisis, asserting that they 'have made an astonishing mess of the financial system' and that 'some of the banks have been the principal authors of their own demise' (House of Commons Treasury Committee 2009c: 3). This conclusion was mirrored in a report by the main UK regulatory agency responsible for overseeing the financial sector, which highlighted 'the errors of judgement and execution made by RBS executive and management' (Financial Services Authority 2011: 8) as key ingredients in the collapse of RBS. Equally scathing conclusions were drawn by this body about the collapse of the Bank of Scotland, when it concluded that the bank had contravened regulatory requirements and issued a formal notice of censure (Financial Services Authority 2012).

This has implications beyond the immediate situation. In terms of failure, Cannon and Edmondson (2005) suggest that learning from it requires that we identify its occurrence, analyse what produced it and experiment with failure, so we can learn appropriate lessons and improve future practice. The ongoing and highly publicised debate about huge bonuses still being paid by banks (including RBS) to senior executives for mediocre performance indicates that bankers are continuing to behave as they have done for over 30 years, despite the financial meltdown (Bones 2012). The dominant themes identified in this chapter constitute obstacles to learning. If failure is framed in terms of a collective group mindset, with those in key leadership positions viewing themselves as passive observers to an overwhelming event or as victims of an (in retrospect) mistaken wisdom of the crowd, they are less likely to seriously consider how they could improve their practice in the future. Their approach may therefore be considered as one means by which what has been described as 'voluntary organizational forgetting' (de Holan 2011) occurs; that is, categories of meaning that are/could be readily available become excluded from consideration and therefore prevent knowledge accumulation, organizational learning and changed behaviour. While the bankers do not claim that everything was for the best in the best of all possible worlds, neither do they express a strong desire for remedial action. Further failure, in part facilitated by explanations for failure, may thus lie in prospect.

Leadership lessons

All told, there are numerous lessons for the future practice of leadership. In particular, greater care is required with performance related pay (PRP). The evidence on its effectiveness is mixed, with almost all such systems having both advantages and disadvantages. Based on his review of the evidence, Pfeffer (1998) argues strongly that:

> Individual incentive pay ... undermines performance – of both the individual and the organization. Many studies strongly suggest that this form of reward undermines teamwork, encourages a short-term focus, and leads people to believe that pay is not related to performance at all but to having the 'right' relationships and an ingratiating personality.
>
> (Pfeffer 1998:4)

Such systems, particularly in the form of stock options, also incentivise risk-taking behaviour (Sanders and Hambrick 2007) and creates the temptation to manipulate company results (Zhang *et al.* 2008).

In the case of the banks, the rewards for success were great while the prospect of failure seemed remote. Recall the idea of self-efficacy biases, which suggests that most of us exaggerate our proficiency at various tasks (such as decision making) that are deemed to be important. It is unlikely that well paid bankers would see their own ability as less than average. Correspondingly, they were inclined to imagine that their business plans rested on sounder foundations than proved to be the case. Their testimony analysed here bears indirectly on these problems. They received individual levels of remuneration far in excess of other employees and in a form that bore no relationship to long-term performance. Moreover, the confidence they displayed in their ability to manage risk appears to have been uncontaminated by deep reflection on any failures that occurred. I suggest that high levels of PRP linked to short-term performance measures helps to explain this. It reinforced their sense of certainty and entitlement and blinded them to the longer-term consequences of actions taken with an eye only on the short term. Research suggests that PRP, if it is introduced at all, should be related to long-term measures of performance, recognise such intangibles as a willingness to cooperate with others alongside traditional bottom line indicators and consider rewarding groups rather than individuals when teamwork is important for success (Rynes *et al.* 2005). More balanced and less self-focused attitudes to leadership are likely to result.

The bankers' testimony also shows that powerful leaders are often reluctant to admit error and change their practice. As we have seen, they are keen to invoke dispositional factors in times of success ('I am a good leader') but attribute failure to situational factors ('Events were beyond my control'). This does not facilitate learning and necessary changes in leadership practice. A shift in mindset is necessary. We should be less inclined to attribute both success and failure to the behaviour of a few leaders and look more deeply at the systems which produce risk-taking behaviour, over-reward those at the top and operate without sufficient public scrutiny. Light-touch regulation of leader behaviour encourages hubris. Checks and balances on leader power are as necessary in business as they are in politics or any other walk of life. Without this, the dark side of leadership is too readily unleashed.

But here, too, balance is required. Vanderbroeck's fascinating analysis of parallels between crises in Ancient Rome and today points out:

> Roman courts and regulation proved ineffective in preventing corruption, fraud and mismanagement. Although the absence of a monitoring and auditing function contributed to that failure, collusion and conflicts of interest between regulators and executives seem to be the primary culprits. It was a matter of 'Quis custodiet ipsos custodes?' or 'Who guards the guardians?'

> (Vanderbroeck 2012: 122)

The attempted solution of the Romans – ever more regulation – led to a proliferating and self-serving bureaucracy that stifled entrepreneurial initiative. Ultimately, the Empire collapsed. All change has unintended as well as intended consequences. In attempting to resolve leadership problems within the banking sector there is no once and for all solution, bereft of risk. Too much regulation may be as damaging as too little. Vigilance alone can offer hope. That said, we have a long way to go before we have a serious prospect of overpowered regulators incapacitating the leaders of major banks: the chief danger lies in the opposite direction.

Issues of upward communication are also raised. Senior RBS officials have testified that Fred Goodwin had a practice of Monday morning meetings with senior managers in the bank.[6] These were known as 'the Monday meetings'. Goodwin, notorious for his pugilistic style of leadership, regularly used these to pick on an individual manager and publicly berate him or her for their alleged weaknesses. The Monday meetings became known as 'the Monday beatings'. People learned to keep quiet, in the hope that the storm would settle on someone else. It is obvious that such a culture is incompatible with the kind of critical upward communication discussed in Chapter 5.

Such problems in banking are far from new or limited to Fred Goodwin. McCabe (2007) provides us with a rich, ethnographic study of a change initiative within a UK high-street bank that he identifies only as 'The T Corporation'. It is a complex picture, consisting mostly of compliance but some resistance, engagement and disengagement and with some aspects of the organization's avowed strategy achieved while others failed. Plentiful opportunities for involving people in decision making were passed up. McCabe concludes:

> There are too many hierarchical layers that allow for a separation between the staff and leaders and an absence of forums for an open exchange of ideas and experience. I am not referring to 'talking shops' but arenas for taking into account various voices and serving multiple interests whilst not being able to entirely satisfy all.
>
> (McCabe 2007: 224)

He goes on to note that, in this organization 'Decisions were taken before "consultation" with the trade unions and misleading information was passed to them'.

Leaders who systematically distort the communication climate in this way are unlikely to create circumstances where they will readily acknowledge failure, accept responsibility and then change their behaviour. It is not conducive to reflexivity, notable in the testimony of the bankers only by its absence. A lack of critical upward communication is thus a crucial indicator of thunderstorms and shipwreck ahead.

The bankers' testimony analysed in this chapter is instructive. Unregulated power was concentrated in the hands of an élite few. It produced risk taking on an epic scale and brought the world's financial system to the brink of collapse.

Stein (2011) has argued that this reflected what he terms a 'culture of mania', consisting of four aspects, namely: denial, omnipotence, triumphalism and over-activity. The myths of heroic leadership associated with this have not served us well, as Gordon Brown, among many, has learned to his cost. Humility and a willingness to learn from failure have been in short supply but it is precisely these attitudes, amongst others, that we now need in our leaders. I consider approaches to the theory and practice of leadership that are more likely to produce them, in the final chapter of this book.

Points for discussion

1. How convincing or otherwise do you find the bankers' accounts of the banking crisis and their role in it?
2. If their accounts are accepted, what are the implications for the future of leadership in the banking industry?
3. What, if anything, does this case study tell us about the theory and practice of transformational leadership?
4. What additional constraints on the power of banking leaders are justified, if any?

Notes

1 I draw here particularly on material from Tourish, D. and Hargie, O. (2012) Metaphors of failure and the failures of metaphor: a critical study of metaphors used by bankers in explaining the banking crisis. *Organization Studies*, 33, 1044–68, and also from Hargie, O., Stapleton, K. and Tourish, D. (2010) Making sense of CEO public apologies for the banking crisis: attributions of blame and avoidance of responsibility. *Organization*, 17, 721–42.
2 The full text of this speech is available online at http://ukingermany.fco.gov.uk/en/news/?view=Speech&id=4616377. Last accessed on 21 November 2012.
3 Throughout this chapter, I follow here the numbering format found in the Treasury Committee's publication of all the evidence that it heard. Thus, each page is numbered with 'Ev' before the relevant numeral (see House of Commons Treasury Committee 2009a).
4 The uncorrected transcript of Diamond's testimony is over 29,000 words long. It can be accessed online on the Treasury Select Committee website, at the following URL: http://www.parliament.uk/documents/commons-committees/treasury/Treasury_Committee_04_July_12_Bob_Diamond.pdf. Last accessed 22 November 2012.
5 Diamond's full testimony can be accessed at: http://www.publications.parliament.uk/pa/cm201011/cmselect/cmtreasy/uc612-vi/uc61201.htm. Last accessed 21 November 2012.
6 This testimony appeared in a BBC documentary on RBS, entitled: *RBS: Inside The Bank That Ran Out Of Money*, broadcast on 5 December 2011. Information on the programme can be accessed on the BBC website at http://www.bbc.co.uk/programmes/b01690y5. The full programme is also available on YouTube at http://www.youtube.com/watch?v=st40Gps08KI. Both last accessed 21 November 2012.

Part III
Conclusion

11 Reimagining leadership and followership

A processual, communication perspective

I have suggested throughout this book that leadership, as traditionally envisaged, is a key part of the problems we now face, rather than the solution. This is particularly true of transformational leadership, in its various guises. Such theories legitimise the concentration of power in élite hands, whatever the intentions of their advocates. Following Alvesson and Sandberg's (2011) suggested approach to theory development, I have sought to problematise the idea of such leadership – that is, to challenge its fundamental premises in a significant way and scrutinise its contradictions. By contrast, most researchers into transformational leadership take its basic postulates for granted. They focus their efforts on identifying how its allegedly positive effects can be better measured or in exploring what seems to determine them. I took three recent papers at random, finding that they dealt with such issues as the impact of a rater's personality on perceptions of transformational leadership (Bono *et al.* 2012); the impact of perceived androgyny on leader effectiveness (Kark *et al.* 2012); and how transformational leadership impacts on positive emotions and levels of customer service (Chuang *et al.* 2012). These may be worthy questions. But they simply take transformational leadership theory for granted, focus their efforts on resolving 'gaps' in incidental aspects of its theory and completely miss the larger issues of power, domination, and control.

As the case study chapters in Part 2 show, the potential for abuse that results from the unreflexive application of approaches sanctioned by advocates of transformational leadership is great – far too great, I suggest, to countenance. This is consistent with social constructionist critiques, which:

> eschew a leader-centric approach in which the leader's personality, style and/ or behaviour are the primary (read, only) determining influences on follower's thoughts and actions. When leaders are the primary symbolizing agents, followers putatively surrender their right to make meanings by virtue of their employment contract with the organization.
>
> (Fairhurst and Grant 2010: 175)

Overall, the faith that many continue to place in such overwhelming models of leadership may be viewed as another instance of *The God That Failed* – the title of a volume of memoirs of former Communist Party members and sympathizers published in 1949, which I referenced in Chapter 2 (Crossman 1949).

In this conclusion, I attempt to outline a different and more emancipatory perspective for both theory and practice. Drawing on process (Langley 2009; Langley and Tsoukas 2010) and communication-based theories of organization (Putnam and Nicotera 2009, 2010; Bencherki and Cooren 2011), I argue that we need to move on from models that put 'the leader' at the centre of more or less solid hierarchies and stable networks in which greater agency is attached to the leader than to followers. Such models reaffirm the power of leaders to declare where the boundaries should be imposed around such concepts as participation and organizational justice, although they sometimes suggest that employees and other followers might be 'consulted' about these issues. Differential power relations between leaders and followers are legitimised, confirming the concentration of decision making and its associated privileges in the hands of leadership élites.

One might imagine that we would have become resistant to the appeal of such approaches, after numerous catastrophic experiences with dysfunctional leaders throughout human history. This book provides ample evidence that this is not the case. Despite much previous experience, as Fryer (2011a: 1) has aptly noted, 'Our faith in the capacity of leaders to make a difference verges on the cultish'. We often think of this faith in terms 'the romance of leadership' (see Chapter 2), normally viewed as describing an infatuation with positively inclined leaders, who woo us with grand visions, noble ideals and at least superficially attractive organizational practices. Maybe so. But it seems clear to me that there is also such a phenomenon as the *romance of authoritarian leadership*. Consider some of the cultic organizations described in Part 2 of this book. In Chapter 8, in particular, I highlighted the loyalty and devotion that many thousands of people, including intellectuals, writers, painters and scientists displayed over many decades to Stalinist-dominated communist parties throughout the world. This idolatry, for many, survived the terror of early Soviet Russia, the horror of the Great Purges in the 1930s, the Gulag and countless other atrocities.

On the other side of the political spectrum, numerous neo-Nazi groups attempt to rehabilitate the memory of Hitler. In the USA, a right-wing race-hate and militia movement mushroomed in the 1990s, declining only after one of its devotees, Timothy McVeigh, killed 168 people in Oklahoma in 1995 – the deadliest attack ever committed in the USA by domestic terrorists. But a report by the Southern Poverty Law Centre (2009) noted that the number of race-based hate groups in the USA was growing once more, up from 602 in 2000 to 926 in 2008. Their renewed lease of life was powered by economic uncertainty and the spectacle of a black man in the White House. Within such groups, wild theories abound. According to one speaker at a gathering of anti-government 'Patriots', who also happened to be a retired FBI agent, the US Government had already set up 1,000 internment camps and stored 30,000 guillotines and half a million caskets in Atlanta for the pending mass detention and execution of white patriots.

There is nothing new in people following leaders who offer bold propositions without evidence. Supreme confidence is more inspiring than doubt. We are attracted to those who promise us certainty. They offer a simplified road map through a world of chaos, intrigue and fear. The notion that someone else can do our thinking for us is alluring. As the writer Saul Bellow (1977: 162) once remarked: 'A great deal of intelligence can be invested in ignorance when the need for illusion is deep'.

In addition, the more we view the world as a 'dangerous' or 'threatening' place, the more likely we are to seek cognitive closure (Federico and Deason 2012), thereby rendering ourselves vulnerable to the persuasive efforts of supposedly all-knowing leaders who appear to offer definite answers. The desire for such closure is often increased, particularly during a collectively experienced crisis. But this predisposes us towards more extreme viewpoints, particularly if we have a latent predisposition towards what might be deemed 'authoritarian' or 'totalistic' attitudes (Merolla *et al.* 2012). Such viewpoints 'are clear cut and unambiguous; by glossing over nuances and intricacies they afford sweeping generalizations that permit certainty and assurance' (Kruglanski and Orehek 2012: 13). The dangers of such processes are considerable and include the potential for a swing to authoritarian forms of leadership in both organizations and wider societies.

The question is whether we can develop models of leadership that refuse to pander to our need for simplified visions of the world, that require us to think for ourselves and that give us the opportunity to genuinely engage with whatever organizations we either join or work for.

The liberating potential of followership?

One response to the leadership tensions that I raise here has been an increased focus on the notion of 'followership'. However, there is little conceptual clarity in most of the literature on what this means and how it might offset excessive leader agency in organizations. While there has been some suggestion that followership is consistent with the notion of 'participants' or 'collaborators' (Uhl-Bien 2006), the term remains little more than a synonym for 'subordinate' in most of its usage (Crossman and Crossman 2011). Subordinates are conceived as those 'who have less power, authority and influence than do their superiors and who therefore usually, but not invariably, fall into line' (Kellerman 2008: xix). Thus, scholars frequently invoke the term 'followership' but do so in a manner that continues to reify and naturalise hierarchy, thereby reaffirming leader agency. Accordingly, 'Followership is a relational role in which followers have the ability to influence leaders and contribute to the improvement and attainment of group and organizational objectives. It is primarily a hierarchically upwards influence' (Carsten *et al.* 2010: 559). Here, asymmetrical power is taken for granted. It is simply assumed that 'group' and 'organizational', as opposed to sectional, objectives exist and that leaders are the prime arbiters of what they should be – albeit while remaining open to an unspecified degree of influence. Moreover, followership is viewed as being what *assists* in the 'improvement' and 'attainment' of such objectives, rather than what might fundamentally interrogate them. It follows that dissent and resistance, of the kind I discussed in Chapter 5, are likely to be dysfunctional and are somehow incompatible with the notion of 'good' followership.

This approach is particularly evident in the following definition, from a military perspective:

> Followership can be defined as a process in which subordinates recognise their responsibility to comply with the orders of leaders and take appropriate action consistent with the situation to carry out these orders to the best of their ability. In the absence of orders they estimate the proper action to contribute to mission performance and take that action.
>
> (Townsend and Gebhardt 1997: 52)

Even in military terms, of course, this notion has contextual limitations. Notoriously, what has become known as 'the Nuremburg defence' ('I was only following orders') has been decreed invalid when the orders in question violate international law (Schabas 2011). Unquestioning follower obedience is, it seems, conducive to positive outcomes less often than is commonly imagined.

However, a tendency to downplay the value of dissent remains deeply ingrained. For example, Agho (2009) explored the perspective of senior business directors on what they thought would be desirable behaviours for followers and leaders. While they found that honesty and competence were highly valued for both, they also found that the directors felt that it was even more important for followers to show dependability, loyalty and cooperation. This is a typically subordinate conception of followership, with it evidently being viewed in terms of how well people translate the visions-orders of leaders into practice. Notions of challenge and independent follower agency are, once more, conspicuous by their absence.

There is a wholly imbalanced view in this literature of the nature of agency. On the one hand, leader agency is assumed to be absolute. On the other hand, 'follower' action is robbed of much of its agentic potential. Rather, the behaviour of followers is viewed as wholly dependent on the structural constraints that are determined by leaders. In contrast, a process-oriented perspective challenges the traditional separation in the literature between leaders and followers (Collinson 2006). It offers a more dynamic view of leadership that is rooted in social context, that places more emphasis on the interplay of influence between leaders and followers and that recognises that excessive agency vested in the hands of a few is unlikely to be used in the interests of the many.

Other leadership theories purport to have a more emancipatory intent and, presumably therefore, to escape or diminish the over-emphasis on leader agency discussed throughout this book. I discussed one such approach, spirituality leadership, in Chapter 4. Two further brief examples may suffice to problematise their promise of (relative) emancipation. I argue that a processual, communication perspective has more potential to liberate our thinking on the vexed topic of leadership.

Authentic leadership theory

Authentic leadership theory suggests that 'Authentic leaders … retain their distinctiveness as individuals, yet they know how to win acceptance in strong corporate and social cultures and how to use elements of those cultures as a basis for radical change' (Goffee and Jones 2005: 88). Here, strong corporate and social cultures are presented as unproblematic. The authentic leader has the (legitimate) power and, hence, the unidirectional agency to ensure that change proceeds in a manner consistent with 'strong' organizational cultures and which purportedly feels liberating to multiple organizational actors. Such cultures are presumed to be authentic manifestations of the private values and beliefs of those in non-leadership positions.

But it is also assumed that the imagined 'authenticity' of the leader will be free of any contradiction between whatever their inner values happen to be and the imperatives of organizational life and a managerial role (Avolio *et al.* 2004). Such leaders will, on internal inspection, see values that are both inherently positive and wholly consistent with those of the organization (Algera and Lips-Wiersma 2012). In this way, they will accomplish the remarkable feat of being 'relatively immune to situational pressures' (Gardner *et al.* 2009: 468). Authentic leaders are depicted as evangelists preaching the benefits of virtue, who are themselves incapable of sin. Moreover, followers will be equally expected to attain a balance between their inner values and those of the organization. This abolition of the barriers between public and private spaces is depicted in beneficent terms. But, as Ford and Harding put it, this means that there is:

> little possibility of freedom of speech or thought: if the model was successfully implemented then to demand such things would result in being seen as inauthentic and thus unsuitable for the organization ... Only the leader, and thus the follower ... who mimics the organization and its demands will be acceptable.
>
> (Ford and Harding 2011: 476)

There is little co-construction in such approaches. Rather, it is possible to read the idea of authentic leadership as a means whereby organizational élites are enabled to further 'shape and reshape the hybridized forms of organizational power and control prevalent in advanced capitalist political economies and societies' (Reed 2012: 207). The overall effect is to place leaders in a position where they demonstrate agency over followers, increasingly encouraged in so doing to exercise a colonising influence over their affective domain. The role of agency, so overpowering in its transformational guise, is reformulated, relabelled and rebranded. But its aroma remains instantly recognisable. Authentic leadership is, in essence, a decaffeinated form of transformational leadership. It is one that is likely to leave a bitter after taste.

Servant leadership theory

As conceived by Greenleaf:

> The Servant-Leader is servant first ... It begins with the natural feeling that one wants to serve, to serve first. Then conscious choice brings one to aspire

to lead… The best test, and difficult to administer, is this: Do those served grow as persons? Do they, while being served, become healthier, wiser, freer, more autonomous, and more likely themselves to become servants? And, what is the effect on the least privileged in society? Will they benefit, or at least not further be harmed?

(Greenleaf 1977: 7)

The construct itself, like much theorising in leadership studies, has inclined to the vague. While Spears (1995) suggested that servant leadership had ten major characteristics, a recent review suggests that this has now grown to 44 (van Dierendonck 2011). These include courage, vision, the ability to exercise transforming influence (while empowering others) and humility. This poses implementation challenges. Attending to 44 characteristics in one's leadership practice suggests levels of sagacity rarely found outside Mount Olympus. That aside, the pattern again is one of dominant leader agency and an implicit assumption of superiority over followers. It is assumed that leaders can determine the growth needs of others and in a manner that will be unlikely to inflict harm. There is little consideration of people's right to determine their own growth needs or indeed to decide whether they wish to grow at all. Rather than non-leaders being allowed to think of such issues for themselves, the servant leader will decide such weighty matters for them.

Little seems to have changed since Hopfl (1992: 24) was able to highlight, within leadership theory, the guiding assumption 'that whilst there may be a plurality of interpretations available to leaders, subordinates and others, it is the prerogative of leaders to manage the meaning of events … and therefore, by implication, to frame the experiences of others'. A radical new perspective is needed. I suggest that what can be viewed as a processual, communication perspective offers a useful starting point.

Towards a process and communication perspective of leadership

Process perspectives suggest that 'the organization is constituted by the interaction processes among its members' (Langley and Tsoukas 2010: 4). Consequently, organizations can be viewed as simultaneously differentiated and integrated, on a number of dimensions. As Cooren and colleagues express it:

organization emerges in the interplay of two interrelated spaces: the textual-conceptual world of ideas and interpretations and the practical world of an object-oriented conversation directed to action… The resulting image of organizational interaction is of an essentially fluid and open-ended process of organizing, in which inherited positions of strength are exploited creatively by the participants.

(Cooren *et al.* 2006: 2–3)

Consistent with this view, some communication theorists have suggested that we replace the notion of organization as a single entity by one in which it is constituted 'by its emergence as an actor in the texts of the people for whom it is a present interpreted reality' (Robichaud *et al.* 2004: 630). Organizations emerge as 'ongoing and precarious accomplishments, experienced, and identified primarily ... in communication processes' (Cooren *et al.* 2011). Interlocking patterns of communication can therefore be viewed as the driving force behind many organizational phenomena, including leadership. Yet leadership is not conventionally theorised in this manner. Rather, we continue to have a stress on solid entities ('the organization'), stable procedures, determinate causal outcomes ('the impact of leader A on organization B') and the downplaying of follower agency in favour of that of leaders.

The recognition that sense making, agency and the processes whereby co-orientation between organizational actors is mediated through language means to acknowledge that organizing is 'an act of juggling between co-evolutionary loops of discursive phenomena' (Guney 2006: 34). Organizations therefore struggle to create shared meanings between organizational actors. Blaschke *et al.* (2012: 882) conclude from this that 'It is only through communication that organization is created and sustained'. But it is also through communication that organizational systems are contested and sometimes dismantled (Deetz 1992). Whereas functionalist perspectives on leadership seek to indicate how leaders can use communication to ensure support for whatever strategies they have predetermined, a processual communication approach puts more stress on how communication both realises and frustrates leader intent and resists the tendency to give leader voice a privileged position in organizational discourse. I have argued throughout this book that doing so gives leaders too much power, disempowers followers and is more likely to wreak organizational and societal havoc.

The communicative constitution of leadership

There are significant implications of this view for the theory and practice of leadership. It challenges the view of leadership as having a taken for granted existence, separate and apart from its discursive constructions (Westwood and Linstead 2001; Gergen 2000). Rather, the organizational world can be depicted as a plenum of agencies (Cooren 2006). Thus, what has been termed the 'communicative constitution of organization' (McPhee and Iverson 2009: 49) in turn means the communicative constitution of leadership. 'Leadership' therefore emerges through the interaction of organizational actors and has a contested, fluid meaning for all of them, in a given social situation for determinate amount of time. It is fundamentally an ongoing process, whereby meaning is constructed between those in leadership positions and those that they lead (Smircich and Morgan 1982; Fairhurst 2007), rather than a discrete phenomenon with easily observable causal relationships, inherently powerful and charismatic leaders, measurable outcomes and clear demarcations between categories of meaning. As Ospina and Uhl-Bien (2012: xix) put it: 'both leaders and followers are "relational beings" who constitute each other as such – leaders and followers – in an unfolding, dynamic relationship'.

Our perspective on leadership shifts, once we view an organization as dealing with how 'socially constructed institutions are reproduced and transformed by the accounting activities of people in interdependent (joint) action as they make sense of what they do together' (Varey 2006: p.191). It means accepting that 'communication generates, not merely expresses, key organizational realities' (Ashcraft *et al.* 2009: 2). Accordingly, the reputations of powerful leaders, particularly CEOs, emerges as a phenomenon that is co-produced and co-reproduced (within certain limits) by the discursive interactions between organizational actors (Sinha *et al.* 2012). This perspective draws attention to what has been described as 'the dance between leader and led and its language of connectedness, temporalness, and embeddedness' (Fairhurst 2007: 24).

Consider again the discussion of the psychology of power in Chapter 1 and the studies cited that show how easily a sense of power and powerlessness can be induced in people. This included attaching such seemingly innocuous labels as 'timer' or 'boss' to people when they were engaged in precisely the same task. These studies support the conclusions reached by Ashcraft *et al.* (2009: 4), who draw attention to how a 'communication constitutes organization' model explains how communication 'defines key realities of the situation (like power relationships, or the capacity to speak and be heard) before interaction even begins'. While they focus their discussion on how this works in such everyday organizational contexts as performance reviews, the point applies with equal force to the broader practices and discourses of leadership. The case study chapters in Part 2 of this book show how the language of leaders and their mobilisation of ancillary symbols of agency and power seek to constitute themselves as overwhelming authorities with (in many cases) power of attorney over all aspects of their followers' lives. Their power does not, for the most part, reside in formal structures, intrinsic charisma or even in having objectively convincing answers for compelling problems. Rather, it was a communicatively constituted accomplishment between leaders and followers, in which mutual projection, wish fulfilment, deception and self-deception worked hand in hand to socially construct the illusion of effective leadership, beneficent organizations and liberated followers. In the case of both Jonestown and Heaven's Gate (Chapter 9), the need of some leaders for power found a soulmate in the need of followers for a comprehensive belief system capable of eliminating uncertainty, thereby soothing their troubled minds and providing an overarching sense of purpose. Eventually, this transmogrified into a relationship where they were told in minute detail what to think, feel and do – a date with destiny that proved lethal.

Here, I wish to consider how this stress on constitutive interaction and co-construction between leaders and non-leaders can be further refined by considering the work of Habermas on communication. I do so because of Habermas's theoretical focus on communication and because other leadership theorists have suggested that his approach can resolve some of the problems that I discuss in this book. As argued below, this is not a conclusion I would share.

The contribution of Habermas

Drawing on Habermas's theory of communicative action, Fryer (2011b) has suggested that it offers a means of envisaging what he terms a less 'impositional' and more a facilitative model of leadership. The question arises here of the degree to which a process perspective informed by a more critical reading of Habermas might facilitate a fresh approach to the problem of agency in leadership studies.

In key writings, Habermas has focused on communicative action and discourse ethics, developing such notions as 'ideal speech acts' and considering how these might promote more rational human behaviour and forms of communication. What he saw as 'the autonomy of the individual, with the elimination of suffering and the furthering of concrete happiness' (Habermas 1974: 254) was central to this preoccupation and became even more manifest in his later work on communicative action (Habermas 1984, 1987). For Habermas, communication is bound up with attempts to create the shared understandings and cooperative relationships that underpin enduring forms of social organization.

His notion of *communicative action* is particularly pertinent for this discussion. Central to this is the idea of what Habermas (1984, 1987) termed the ideal speech situation. This puts a particular stress on how validity claims are raised and the degree to which they may be challenged. All 'speech acts' invite a listener to accept a person's authority to raise issues, to put some trust in the accuracy of the speaker's content and to have some concept of what the speaker hopes to achieve by it. But it also means that people have the right to query such claims. In leadership terms, shared understanding could be envisaged as a goal of collaborative action. This will only be achieved to the degree that followers respect the speech acts of leaders in the terms described here. It follows that they also have the right to query the validity content of a leader's communication, thereby embarking on a process of negotiation to construct some kind of shared meaning. From this perspective, a leader's 'vision' is there to be openly challenged rather than blindly acclaimed (Clifton 2012). Habermas would acknowledge that disagreement inevitably results from such debate but then assumes that it will be mediated constructively through the normal processes of human communication. Critically:

> Rationality carries with it connotations based ultimately on the central experience of the unconstrained, unifying, consensus-bringing force of argumentative speech in which different participants overcome their merely subjective views and, owing to the mutuality of rationally motivated conviction, assure themselves of both the unity of the objective world and the intersubjectivity of their life world.
>
> (Habermas 1984: 10)

Thus, the normative legitimacy of leadership (or anything else) does not derive from the existence of absolute moral standards or universally agreed definitions of right and wrong. Rather, it is determined by the degree to which all organizational actors are able to advance and challenge the validity claims of others – in

Habermas's terms (1984: 115), on the degree to which we have 'reciprocally raised validity claims'. The challenge to notions of leadership which put undue stress on leader agency is obvious. In Habermas's (1990) terminology, what he describes as a normatively legitimating speech act occurs when:

> Every subject with the competence to speak and act is allowed to take part in the discourse.
> Everyone is allowed to question any assertion whatever.
> Everyone is allowed to introduce any assertion whatever into the discourse.
> Everyone is allowed to express his attitudes, desires and needs.
>
> (Habermas 1990)

Relating this notion to what he terms facilitative leadership, Fryer asserts that such leadership:

> would include active processes for individual and collective self-determination, critical self-reflection and associated self-transformation ... the status of a leader should not be taken for granted ... Habermasian ideal speech offers more than a framework for organizational decision-making; it also offers a constitutional procedure by which a leader's right to occupy their roles needs to be justified.
>
> (Fryer 2011b: 31:32)

Accordingly, followers should be able to challenge, and perhaps even disobey, the commandments of their leaders.

However, applying Habermas to the context of leadership also needs to be problematised. The difficulty lies in the asymmetrical power relations that characterise most if not all organizational contexts. It may be that some form of domination – among much else – is inherent to any leader–follower relationship or indeed to any human relationship at all. In an absolute sense, it may be difficult or even impossible to enact ideal speech acts as proposed by Habermas. Thus, Fryer (2011b: 37), echoing Habermas, suggests that facilitative leadership should seek to promote situations in which, for example, 'all are able to introduce any assertion whatsoever into organizational discourse'. Most actors in most organizational situations would hesitate before taking this proposition at face value. Indeed, most human interaction – from parenting, to work, to civil partnership, to marriage – might become problematic were this injunction to be indiscriminately applied. As the discussion of critical upward communication in Chapter 5 has argued, the constrained communicative actions of those in lower-status positions in organizations is partially induced by leader positions of dominancy but also (in a dialectical sense) by followers' own interests in ingratiating with authority and therefore in avoiding overt challenges to managerial power. Silence as a form of followership can thus be viewed as one means of avoiding responsibility for organizational decisions (Grint 2010) – a conscious positional choice, in pursuit of perceived self-benefit.

Such communicative hesitations could be regarded as examples of what Habermas referred to as '*systematically distorted communication*' (his emphasis). He goes on to argue that:

> Such communication pathologies can be conceived of as the result of a confusion between actions oriented to reaching understanding and actions oriented to success. In situations of concealed strategic action, at least one of the parties behaves with an orientation to success, but leaves others to believe that all the presuppositions of communicative action are satisfied.
>
> (Habermas 1984: 332)

However, even when leaders and followers have a primary purpose of reaching understanding, the inherent complexity of their role will most likely continue to frustrate the full accomplishment of ideal speech acts. This can only be regarded as distorted communication if one ignores the perceived self-interests of leaders and followers in sustaining these patterns of communication and the benefits that both believe flow from it – that is, if one abstracts theories of communication from any context in which it ever occurs. The 'ideal' is always distorted when it encounters actually occurring leader–non-leader interaction. As the poet TS Eliot once wrote, 'Between the idea/And the reality/ Between the motion/And the act/ Falls the Shadow' (Eliot [1925] 2007).

Upward communication serves, once more, as a good instance. It is hard to see the reluctance of employees to be openly critical of leader action as irrational, in that it is often a display of perceived self-interest. This is particularly so in the kinds of totalist groups that I discuss in Chapter 9 of this book but the problem is found further afield. I discussed in Chapter 10 how senior executives from HBOS in the UK discouraged feedback and took action against their own risk advisers who suggested that problems loomed. From an organizational and societal standpoint, this illustrates how constraints on dissent can prevent learning from mistakes or crisis, thereby facilitating other crises in the future. But from the standpoint of HBOS employees, a decision not to express dissent may be viewed as a rational decision to prioritise self-preservation. Deciding not to contest the validity claims of organizational actors who possess considerable powers of sanction is thus often a display of power and agency, albeit one that violates what Habermas would see as the conditions needed for an ideal speech act.

This is all the more apparent if we acknowledge Fleming's (2012) argument to the effect that widespread disillusionment with many of the cultural norms of working life has created what he describes as a form of 'post-recognition politics' within organizations. A key feature of such politics is a sense of withdrawal and an increased attachment to people's roles far removed from work. Thus, more often, they 'do not implore to be seen, heard and counted in corporate-sponsored debates' (Fleming 2012). It is manifestation of what Collinson (1994: 37) described as 'resistance through distance', where workers seek 'to deny any involvement in or responsibility for the running of the organization'. In such a context, an insistence on the contestation of the validity claims of more powerful organizational actors can easily become another form of imposition ('You must always tell me what you really think'), once more couched in emancipatory terms.

From my perspective, some attempted emancipatory models of leadership (for example, servant leadership) have suffered from attempting to envisage a model of leadership practice that is free of this kind of contradiction. They therefore offer prescriptions that are 'ideal' in the sense of failing to describe leadership practice in any recognisable organizational world. Their inadequate conceptualisation of leader *and* follower agency is also a significant shortcoming. A processual, communication perspective can ameliorate some of these problems if, rather than aspire in the first instance to the creation of fresh normative conceptions of leadership, we focus on capturing leadership dynamics in a more fluid, contested and multifaceted manner than has so far been seen.

This means, amongst much else, drawing on Habermas to further understand leadership dynamics rather than to seek definitive prescriptions for leadership practice. A dialectical view would recognise that contradiction is inherent to all forms of communication and leadership. This is often manifest in unequal power relations that are resistant to consensus. Ideal speech acts as the foundation of more facilitative forms of leadership are therefore beside the point. While Habermas's emphasis on the role of validity claims and his criticism of any assumption that some communicative actors should have privileged rights in making such claims is useful, a dialectical approach would problematise his emphasis on agreement as a precondition for rationality or the basis for the construction of less contested forms of leadership. It would see the mutual contestation of validity claims as an enduring feature of leader/follower relations, rather than a prelude to resolution. Where, then, does that leave leadership?

Leadership as a dialectical nexus of fluid relationships

A communication and process perspective recognises what Collinson has described as the:

> deep-seated asymmetrical power relations of leadership dynamics ... From this perspective, control and resistance are viewed as mutually reinforcing, ambiguous, potentially contradictory processes. Followers' resistance is one such unintended outcome. In its various forms, dissent constitutes a crucially important feature of leadership dialectics, requiring detailed examination by researchers.
>
> (Collinson 2005b: 1435)

Leadership is less one person doing something to another (with their more or less willing compliance). Rather, it is a process whereby leaders and non-leaders accomplish each other through dynamics of interaction in which mutual influence is always present. For example, authority, a crucial element of leadership, is manifest through talk, conversation, and the 'presentification' of the self, as well as from such factors as a person's formal position within an organization (Benoit-Barne and

Cooren 2009). It follows that accounts of leadership, including those that attempt to ascribe causality, need to be embedded in deeper process studies of preceding and succeeding events, mediated through linguistic and non-linguistic artefacts.

This standpoint offers a dynamic conception of power dynamics, since from a communication perspective:

> power is conceptualised primarily as a struggle over meaning: the group that is best able to 'fix' meaning and articulate it to its own interests is the one that will be best able to maintain and reproduce relations of power.
>
> (Mumby 2001: 601)

Much leadership research is still focused on finding the 'essence' of leadership, with an insufficient consideration of power and as though it were an enduring construct embedded in stable, hierarchical organizational structures. This means that it exaggerates the extent of agency on the part of leaders as a variable that determines organizational outcomes. I advocate a more nuanced view of leadership, in which leader agency is acknowledged to exist but in which it is balanced by a view which takes fuller account of the agency of other organizational actors and the degree to which this agency is complicit in the construction of leader agency and action. Leadership is thus conceived as 'multi-level phenomena, where societal and organizational cultures and discourses are key elements (that) produce regulatory ideals for doing leadership – as leaders and followers – to which individuals and groups adapt, vary, and improvise' (Alvesson and Sveningsson 2012: 209). Greater attention is therefore placed on the positive value of dissent and resistance and on the notion of followers as knowledgeable and proactive agents with multiple prospects for action and deep vestiges of power at their disposal. A purely Habermassian perspective risks becoming another search for the essence of leadership, this time in prescriptions for ideal/idealised discourse contexts that are completely different from what we find in actually occurring organizations and actually observable (or possible) leader–follower interactions.

The view of leadership that emerges from a processual communication perspective is therefore more inclined to see it as an unstable, continuously evolving social construction embedded in what Gergen (2010: 57) has characterised as 'turbulent streams or conversational flows'. As Capra (1982: 305) argued: 'most living systems exhibit multileveled patterns of organization characterized by many intricate and nonlinear pathways along which signals of information and transaction propagate between all levels, ascending as well as descending'. While he goes on to discuss this in terms of traditional representations of hierarchy as a pyramid, I suggest that, if we read his text with the word 'leadership' in mind, the applicability of his alternative depiction in the context of this discussion is readily apparent. Thus:

> That is why I have turned the pyramid around and transformed it into a tree, a more appropriate symbol for the ecological nature of stratification in

living systems. As a real tree takes its nourishment through both its roots and its leaves, so the power in a system tree flows in both directions, with neither end dominating the other and all levels interacting in interdependent harmony to support the functioning of the whole.

(Capra 1982: 305)

Once leadership is conceived in these terms, it ceases to be a discrete 'event', an observable interaction within organizational structures or a unidirectional flow of influence in which A has a causal impact on B. Rather, it is a communicatively organized, fluid process of co-orientation and co-construction between myriad organizational actors, whose 'essence' varies of necessity between each occasion of its occurrence. This is reminiscent of Gabriel *et al.*'s (2000: 2) depiction of the organization as a moving river and consequent emphasis on the experiences and narratives 'of those people who actually know and understand the river well'. It acknowledges the creative potential of *difference* within the theory and practice of leadership. As Boje (2001) has pointed out, there is rarely any one particular narrative of organization that is not heavily contested and earlier competing narratives usually exist for every fresh narrative that an individual or organizational group proposes.

For my purposes here, this means that there is no essence of leadership waiting to be discovered and then summarised in formal definitions or lists of competencies or desired behaviours that are torn from particular social, organizational and temporal contexts and which afford a privileged position to particular organizational actors. As Grint (2000: 3) argued: 'what counts as a "situation" and what counts as the "appropriate" way of leading in that situation are interpretive and contestable issues, not issues that can be decided by objective criteria'. It follows that discursive closure is neither a desirable outcome of leadership practice nor of leadership theorising. Theories and research methods (such as laboratory experiments) that seek intense precision in their approach can become so constrained by the need for 'tightness' in the specification of dependent and independent variables that they may be blindsided to leadership's most distinctive feature of all: it is inherently protean.

This suggests that leadership theories and practices which have an emancipatory intent should place more stress on the promotion of dissent, difference and the facilitation of alternative viewpoints than the achievement of consensus or the promotion of an organizational view wholly originating in the perspectives and values of formal leaders. In turn, followership is conceived in terms of differentiation and alternative positioning, while leadership is seen as those practices that facilitate such creative expression. This resists Habermas's emphasis on rationality as a process of evolution from difference/dissent and towards consensus. Rather, overt consensus is likely to mark covert dissent, since it is unlikely that followers will ever feel completely free to express the full range of their disagreements with leaders. The illusion of such consensus can therefore be held to denote leadership practices that are insufficiently sensitive to follower feedback, rather than a rational endpoint of healthy information exchange processes. While leadership actions that only facilitate the creative expression of divergent viewpoints would be likely to undermine cohesion in a manner at least as destructive as that delivered by excessive conformity, the approach outlined here simply argues that leadership should be rebalanced so that more (but not exclusive) emphasis is placed on communication processes that validate dissent. This would help to 'promote empathy for differing ideas, opinions, and worldviews' (Eisenberg 1994: 282). Eisenberg goes on to suggest that 'Perhaps the greatest obstacle to progress in most organizations is the stubborn belief on the part of those in power that their view of organizational reality is the one, correct view'. I would argue here that this view of the 'correctness' of a particular organizational view is also often found among non-leaders and that the invitation to embrace dissent and show empathy needs to encompass actors at all points of the power-powerless continuum.

Implications for practice

Among the major implications for practice of this approach, I would highlight the following key points:

- The context in which leadership is practiced is critical. There is little point in implementing generic (and usually expensive) forms of 'leadership development' that fail to recognise this. Development must always be situation and organization specific, if it is to have any real impact on an organization's fortunes (Tourish 2012). It needs to be rooted in the real challenges that people face, rather than in having them attempt to master generic lists of competencies and behaviours that may not be applicable to their own unique situation. This is a tough proposition. It means that effective leadership development cannot be bought 'off the shelf' in a supermarket of ideas. Rather, each organization needs to improvise, adapt and grow distinctive forms of leadership development whose usefulness will most likely be time limited, since there is no one enduring key to long-term success. I would also suggest, in line with the central argument of this book, that it should reimagine what leadership means from the ground up, paying much more attention to the subtleties of leader–follower interaction than is normally the case. It needs to be accepted that leadership is inherently complex, contradictory, iterative, adaptive and contested. There is no one right way to lead or follow, no universal set of competencies or behaviours to adopt and no short course, book or article that can teach us what to do. Effectiveness, invariably elusive and transitory, is rooted in a profound appreciation of context, an understanding of the limitations inherent to leader agency and an acknowledgement of the agency of others.
- Spartacus was the leader of a slave revolt in ancient Rome from 73 to 71BC – a revolt that brought the Empire to the brink of collapse. History is written by the victors. But in this case Roman sources recorded that, before his final battle with Crassus, Spartacus's men brought him his horse. He ceremoniously

slaughtered it, to demonstrate that he shared their fate in either victory or defeat.[1] By contrast, many leaders today make sure that they have Golden Parachutes. In the event of failure they emerge from the wreckage with enough wealth to sustain them for the rest of their lives. Such differentials damage relations between leaders and followers. They also damage organizations and societies. A step change in practice is needed. Leaders need to be more willing to share the spoils of victory and the pain of defeat with their followers.

- There needs to be more emphasis on the role of followership as opposed to an infatuation with leadership (Kellerman 2012). But followership needs to be conceived much more broadly than it has in the past and to encompass the notion of proactive dissent. It follows that those who occupy formal leadership roles need to entertain a view of their role that embraces a culture of dissent and disagreement, rather than to pursue the illusory goal of a unified corporate culture, invariably characterised by excessive degrees of conformity around leader decreed values and norms.

- Leaders and non-leaders need to embrace uncertainty and to renounce their mutual quest for discursive closure. This means accepting that ambiguity and conflict are enduring traits of all organizational life, including interaction between leaders and non-followers. The more certain we are about something, the less open we are to critical feedback and the more likely it is that we are wrong. Doubt is a friend of clear thinking rather than its enemy. It is a quality that both leaders and followers need to cultivate much more deeply.

Conclusion

I suggested at the outset of this chapter that transformational and other models of leadership can be viewed as examples of '*The God That Failed*' (Crossman 1949). As this book has shown, much was promised but little has been delivered. A continued stress on unbridled leader agency is likely to produce further imaginary gods who will fail to meet the impossible expectations of their followers. Arguably, the greater the euphoria and hope that greets a new leader's appointment the more quickly disillusionment is likely to set in, as fantasy clashes with reality. Yet, as we have seen throughout this book, this does not mean that the potency of leader-centric visions has diminished. Such visions are promoted by many leadership researchers, who seem largely oblivious to the possibility that there are any downsides worth considering (for example, Antonakis 2012). As we have seen, followers, too, are not immune to risky infatuations with leaders who offer us cognitive closure.

It is easy to see why 'heroic' myths of leadership can be attractive to leaders as well as followers. As Haslam and colleagues note:

> First, it legitimises their position by providing a rationale for claims that they, rather than anyone else, should hold the reins of power ... Second, it frees

them from the constraints of group traditions, from any obligations to group members, and from any need to take advice or solicit alternative viewpoints. Third, it allows leaders to reap all the benefits of success while avoiding the pitfalls of failure.

(Haslam *et al.* 2011: 201)

We might wonder why anyone would not be attracted by such a perspective. Yet there are hazards in abundance. As these authors go on to point out, not least amongst these for leaders is that they may increasingly separate from the group from which their authority springs, thus risking the ultimate loss of their influence and power. Wretched outcomes for followers, as we have seen throughout this book, are also a frequent occurrence.

A different view of agency is central to any reimagining of leadership that can help avert the destructive outcomes repeatedly witnessed in the cases that I have examined. It is one that challenges the preoccupation with leader agency, including the hope that a leader will emerge who can offer a transcendental sense of purpose, save the planet – and double gross domestic product. In doing so, it recognises how crucial agency is when it is vested in non-leaders, acknowledges the productive potential of dissent and sees leadership and followership as co-constructed phenomena embedded in fluid social structures that we have barely begun to understand.

I hope that the journey undertaken in this book enables us to map at least the outline of some answers.

Points for discussion

1. In the light of this book, what do you think the role of followers should be in their dealings with leaders?
2. What are the strengths and weaknesses of Habermas's theories of communication, from a leadership perspective?
3. What does the communicative constitution of leadership mean to you, if anything?
4. What changes to the theory and practice of leadership would you make to overcome many of the problems discussed in this book?

Note

1 See *The Parallel Lives* by Plutarch, published in Vol. III of the Loeb Classical Library edition, 1916. Available online at http://penelope.uchicago.edu/Thayer/E/Roman/Texts/Plutarch/Lives/Crassus*.html. Last accessed 22 November 2012.

References

Aasland, M., Skogstad, A., Notelaers, G., Nielsen, B. and Einarsen, S. (2010) The prevalence of destructive leadership behaviour. *British Journal of Management*, 21: 438–52.

Aburdene, P. (2005) *Megatrends 2010.* Charlottesville, VA: Hampton Roads Publishing.

Ackers, P. and Preston, D. (1997) Born again: the ethics and efficacy of the conversion experience in contemporary management development. *Journal of Management Studies,* 34: 677–701.

Adams, D. and Maine, E. (1998) *Business Ethics for the 21st Century.* Mountain View, CA: Mayfield Publishing Company.

Agho, A. (2009) Perspectives of senior-level executives on effective followership and leadership. *Journal of Leadership and Organizational Studies,* 16: 159–66.

Algera, P. and Lips-Wiersma, M. (2012) Radical authentic leadership: co-creating the conditions under which all members of the organization can be authentic. *The Leadership Quarterly,* 23: 118–31.

Alvesson, M. and Sandberg, J. (2011) Generating research questions through problematization. *Academy of Management Review*, 36: 247–71.

Alvesson, M. and Spicer, A. (2012) Critical leadership studies: the case for critical performativity. *Human Relations*, 65: 367–90.

Alvesson, M. and Sveningsson, S. (2003) Managers doing leadership: the extra-ordinarization of the mundane. *Human Relations*, 56: 1435–60.

Alvesson, M. and Sveningsson, S. (2012) Un- and repacking leadership: context, relations, constructions and politics. In M. Uhl-Bien and S. Ospina (Eds), *Advancing Relational Leadership Research: A Dialogue Among Perspectives.* Charlotte, NC: Information Age Publishing, pp. 203–25.

Alvesson, M. and Willmott, H. (2002) Identity regulation as organizational control: producing the appropriate individual. *Journal of Management Studies*, 39: 619–44.

Amann, W., Pirson, M., Dierksmeier, C. and Kimakowitz, E. (2011) *Business Schools Under Fire: Humanistic Management Education as the Way Forward.* London: Palgrave Macmillan.

Amar, A., Hentrich, C., Bastani, B. and Hlupic, V. (2012) How managers succeed by letting employees lead. *Organizational Dynamics,* 41: 62–71.

American Family Foundation (1986) Cultism: A conference for scholars and policy makers. *Cultic Studies Journal,* 3: 119–20.

Amernic, J. and Craig, R. (2007) Making *CEO-speak* more potent: editing the language of corporate leadership. *Strategy & Leadership,* 35: 25–31.

Amernic, J., Craig, R. and Tourish D. (2007) The charismatic leader as pedagogue, physician, architect, commander, and saint: five master metaphors in Jack Welch's letters to stockholders of General Electric. *Human Relations,* 60: 1839–72.

Anand, S., Hu, J., Liden, R. and Vidyarthi, P. (2011) Leader-member exchange: recent research findings and prospects for the future. In A. Bryman, D. Collinson, K. Grint, B. Jackson and Uhl-Bien, M. (Eds), *The SAGE Handbook of Leadership.* London: SAGE, pp. 311–25.

Ancona, D., Kochan, T., Scully, M., Van Maanen, J. and Westney, D. (1999) *Organizational Behaviour and Processes.* Boston, MA: South-Western College Publishing.

Andriopoulos, C. (2003) Six paradoxes in managing creativity: an embracing act. *Long Range Planning,* 36: 375–88.

Antonakis, J. (2012) Transformational and charismatic leadership. In D. Day and J. Antonakis (Eds), *The Nature of Leadership* (2nd ed.). London: SAGE, pp. 256–88.

Armstrong, T. (1995) *Exploring spirituality: the development of the Armstrong measure of spirituality.* Paper presented at the 103rd Annual Convention of the American Psychological Association, New York, NY.

Arnulf, J., Mathisen, J. and Haerem, T. (2012) Heroic leadership illusions in football teams: rationality, decision making and noise-signal ratio in the firing of football managers. *Leadership,* 8: 169–85.

Aronson, E. (1997) The theory of cognitive dissonance: the evolution and vicissitudes of an idea. In C. McGarty and S. Haslam (Eds), *The Message of Social Psychology.* Oxford: Blackwell, pp. 20–35.

Aronson, E. and Mills J. (1959) The effect of severity of initiation on liking for a group. *Journal of Abnormal and Social Psychology,* 59: 177–81.

Aryee, S., Walumbwa, F., Zhou, Q. and Hartnell, C. (2012) Transformational leadership, innovative behavior, and task performance: test of mediation and moderation processes. *Human Performance,* 25: 1–25.

Asch, S. (1951) Effects of group pressure upon the modification and distortion of judgement. In H. Guptzkow (Ed.) *Groups, Leadership, and Men.* Pittsburgh, PA: Carnegie.

Ashcraft, K., Kuhn, T. and Cooren, F. (2009) Constitutional amendments: materializing organizational communication. *Academy of Management Annals,* 3: 1–64.

Ashford, S. and Tsui, A. (1991) Self-regulation for managerial effectiveness: the role of active feedback seeking. *Academy of Management Journal,* 34: 251–80.

Ashforth, B. and Pratt, M. (2003) Institutionalized spirituality: an oxymoron? In R. Giacalone and C. Jurkiewicz (Eds), *Handbook Of Workplace Spirituality And Organizational Performance.* New York: Sharpe, pp. 93–107.

Ashmos, D. and Duchon, D. (2000) Spirituality at work: a reconceptualisation and measure. *Journal of Management Inquiry,* 9: 134–45.

Avolio, B., Luthans, F. and Walumbwa, F. (2004) *Authentic leadership: theory-building for veritable sustained performance.* Working paper, Gallup Leadership Institute, University of Nebraska, Lincoln.

Awamleh, R. and Gardner, W. (1999) Perceptions of leader charisma and effectiveness: the effects of vision content, delivery, and organizational performance. *Leadership Quarterly,* 10: 345–73.

Bain, P. and Taylor, P. (2000) Entrapped by the "Electronic Panopticon"? Worker resistance in a call centre. *New Technology, Work, and Employment,* 15: 2–18.

Balch, R. and Taylor, D. (2002) Making sense of the Heaven's Gate suicides. In D. Bromley and J. Melton (Eds), *Cults, Religion and Violence.* Cambridge: Cambridge University Press, pp. 209–28.

Banks, S. (2008) The problems with leadership. In S. Banks (Ed.), *Dissent and the Failure of Leadership*. London: Edward Elgar, pp. 1–21.

Barker, E. (1995) The scientific study of religion? You must be joking! *Journal for the Scientific Study of Religion*, 34: 287–310.

Barker, J. (1993) Tightening the iron cage: concertive control in self-managing teams. *Administrative Science Quarterly*, 38: 408–37.

Barker, R. (1997) How can we train leaders if we do not know what leadership is? *Human Relations*, 50: 343–62.

Barmine, A. (1954) *One Who Survived: The Life Story of a Russian Under the Soviets*. New York: Putnam.

Barnett, C., Krell, T. and Sendry, J. (2000) Learning to learn about spirituality: a categorical approach to introducing the topic into management courses. *Journal of Management Education*, 24: 562–79.

Baron, R. (1996) 'La vie en rose' revisited: Contrasting perceptions of informal upward feedback among managers and subordinate. *Management Communication Quarterly*, 9: 338–48.

Baron, R. (2000) Arousal, capacity and intense indoctrination. *Personality and Social Psychology Review*, 4: 238–54.

Baron, R., Crawley, K. and Paulina, D. (2003) Aberrations of power: leadership in totalist groups. In D. van Knippenberg and M. Hogg (Eds), *Leadership and Power: Identity Processes in Groups and Organizations*. London: SAGE, pp. 169–83.

Bartel, C., Blader, S. and Wrzesniewski, A. (2007) (Eds), *Identity and the Modern Organization*. Mahwah, NJ: Lawrence Erlbaum.

Barton, D. (2011) Capitalism for the long term. *Harvard Business Review*, March: 85–91.

Bass, B. (1985) *Leadership And Performance Beyond Expectations*. New York: Free Press.

Bass, B. (1990) From transactional to transformational leadership: learning to share the vision. *Organizational Dynamics*, 18: 19–31.

Bass, B. (1999) Two decades of research and development in transformational leadership. *European Journal of Work and Organizational Psychology*, 8: 9–26.

Bass, B. and Avolio, B. (Eds), (1993) *Improving Organizational Effectiveness Through Transformational Leadership*. London: SAGE.

Bass, B. and Riggio, R. (2006) *Transformational Leadership* (2nd ed.). London: Erlbaum.

Baxter, L. (1984) An investigation into compliance-gaining as politeness. *Human Communication Research*, 10: 427–56.

Beer, M., Voelpel, S., Leibold, M. and Tekie, E. (2005) Strategic management as organisational learning: developing fit and alignment through a disciplined process. *Long Range Planning*, 38: 445–65.

Bell, E. and Taylor, S. (2003) The elevation of work: pastoral power and the new age work ethic. *Organization*, 10: 329–49.

Bell, E. and Taylor, S. (2004) 'From outward bound to inward bound': the prophetic voices and discursive practices of spiritual management development. *Human Relations*, 57: 439–66.

Bell, E., Taylor, S. and Driscoll, C. (2012) Varieties of organizational soul: the ethics of belief in organizations. *Organization*, 19: 425–39.

Bellow, S. (1977) *To Jerusalem and Back*. New York: Avon Books.

Bencherki, N. and Cooren, F. (2011) Having to be: the possessive constitution of organisation. *Human Relations*, 64: 1579–607.

Benefiel, M. (2005) The second half of the journey: spiritual leadership for organizational transformation. *The Leadership Quarterly*, 16: 723–47.

Bennis, W. and O'Toole, J. (2005) How business schools lost their way. *Harvard Business Review*, May: 96–104.

Benoit-Barne, C. and Cooren, F. (2009) The accomplishment of authority through presentification: how authority is distributed among and negotiated by organizational members. *Management Communication Quarterly*, 23: 5–31.

Bierly, P., Kessler, E. and Christensen, E. (2000) Organizational learning, knowledge and wisdom. *Journal of Organizational Change Management*, 13: 595–618.

Bies, R. and Tripp, T. (1998) Two faces of the powerless: coping with tyranny in organizations. In R. Kramer and M. Neale (Eds), *Power and Influence In Organizations*. London: SAGE, pp. 203–20.

Biesel, R., Messersmith, A. and Kelley, K. (2012) Supervisor–subordinate communication: Hierarchical mum effect meets organizational learning. *Journal of Business Communication*, 49: 128–47.

Blanck, P. (Ed.) (1993) *Interpersonal Expectations: Theory, Research, and Applications*. Cambridge: Cambridge University Press.

Blaschke, S., Schoeneborn, D. and Seidl, D. (2012) Organizations as networks of communication episodes: turning the network perspective inside out. *Organization Studies*, 33: 879–906.

Boje, D. (2001) *Narrative Methods for Organisational and Communication Research*. London: SAGE.

Boje, D., Rosile, G., Durant, R. and Luhman, J. (2004) Enron spectacles: a critical dramaturgical analysis. *Organization Studies*, 25: 751–74.

Bones, C. (2012) Bankers' bonuses – blame the 'because I'm worth it' generation. *The Guardian*, 20 February. Available online from: http://www.guardian.co.uk/commentisfree/2012/feb/20/lloyds-bankers-bonuses-loreal-generation. Last accessed 22 November 2012.

Bono, J., Hooper, A. and Yoon, D. (2012) Impact of rater personality on transformational and transactional leadership ratings. *The Leadership Quarterly*, 23: 132–45.

Borrus, A. (2004) Exposing execs' 'stealth' compensation. *Bloomberg Businessweek*, 23 September. Retrieved from http://www.businessweek.com/bwdaily/dnflash/sep2004/nf20040924_8648_db016.htm. Last accessed 22 November 2012.

Brake (2011) Drivers blame everyone else for bad driving. Brake.org.uk, 9 March. Available online at http://www.brake.org.uk/latest-news/drivers-blame-everyone-else-for-bad-driving.htm. Last accessed 22 November 2012.

Briñol, P., McCaslin, M. and Petty, R. (2012) Self-generated persuasion: effects of the target and direction of arguments. *Journal of Personality and Social Psychology*, 102: 925–40.

Brown, A. (1997) Narcissism, identity, and legitimacy. *Academy of Management Review*, 22: 643–86.

Brown, R. (2003) Organizational spirituality: the sceptic's version. *Organization*, 10: 393–400.

Bryman, A. (1992) *Charisma and Leadership in Organizations*. London: SAGE.

Burack, E. (1999) Spirituality in the workplace. *Journal of Organizational Change Management*, 12: 280–91.

Burke, K. (1937) *An Attitude Toward History*. Berkeley: University of California Press.

Burns, J. (1978) *Leadership*. New York: Harper and Row.

Burrell, D. (2006) Emerging options in doctoral study in management for international executives. *Vikalpa*, 31: 13–17.

Burrell, G. (1988) Modernism, postmodernism and organizational analysis, part 2: the contribution of Michel Foucault. *Organization Studies*, 9(2): 221–35.

Burris, E. (2012) The risks and rewards of speaking up: managerial responses to employee voice. *Academy of Management Journal,* 55: 851–75.

Byrne, D. (1971) *The Attraction Paradigm.* New York: Academic Press.

Byrne, J. (1998) Jack: A close-up look at how America's #1 manager runs GE. *Business Week,* 8 June, (3581): 92–104.

Cacioppe, R. (2000) Creating spirit at work: re-visioning organization development and leadership – Part 1. *Leadership and Organization Development Journal,* 21: 48–54.

Callaghan, J. (1984) *British Trotskyism: Theory and Practice.* London: Blackwell.

Callaghan, J. (1987) *The Far Left in British Politics.* London: Blackwell.

Cannon, M. and Edmondson, A. (2005) Failing to learn and learning to fail (intelligently): how great organizations put failure to work to innovate and improve. *Long Range Planning,* 38: 299–319.

Capra, F. (1982) *The Turning Point: Science, Society and the Rising Culture.* New York: Simon and Schuster.

Carsten, M., Uhl-Bien, M., West, B., Patera, J. and McGregor, R. (2010) Exploring social constructions of followership: a qualitative study. *The Leadership Quarterly,* 21: 543–62.

Case, P. and Gosling, J. (2010) The spiritual organization: critical reflections on the instrumentality of workplace spirituality. *Journal of Management, Spirituality & Religion,* 7: 257–82.

Cash, K. and Gray, G. (2000) A framework for accommodating religion and spirituality in the workplace. *Academy of Management Executive,* 14: 124–34.

Cavanagh, G. (1999) Spirituality for managers: Context and critique. *Journal of Organizational Change Management,* 12: 186–99.

Cavanagh, G., Hanson, B., Hanson, K. and Hinojoso, J. (2001) Toward spirituality for the contemporary organization: implications for work, family and society. Paper presented at *Institute for Spirituality and Organizational Leadership, Proceedings from 'Bridging the Gap'.* Santa Clara University, Leavy School of Business, Santa Clara, CA. Available online from http://lsb.scu.edu/ISOL/contemporary_organization.pdf. Last accessed 22 November 2012.

Chaleff, I. (2003) *The Courageous Follower* (2nd ed.). San Francisco: Berrett-Koehler.

Chemers, M. (2003) Leadership effectiveness: functional, constructivist and empirical perspectives. In D. van Knippenberg and M. Hogg (Eds), *Leadership and power: identity processes in groups and organizations.* London: SAGE, pp. 5–17.

Cheney, G. and Christensen, L. (2001) Organizational identity: linkages between internal and external communication. In F. Jablin and L. Putnam (Eds), *The New Handbook of Organizational Communication.* London: SAGE, pp. 231–69.

Chow, C., Hwang, R. and Liao, W. (2000) Motivating truthful upward communication of private information: an experimental study of mechanisms from theory and practice. *Abacus,* 36: 160–79.

Chryssides, G. (Ed.) (2011) *Heaven's Gate: Postmodernity and Popular Culture in a Suicide Group.* Farnham: Ashgate.

Chuang, A., Judge, T. and Liaw, Y. (2012) Transformational leadership and customer service: a moderated mediation model of negative affectivity and emotion regulation. *European Journal of Work and Organizational Psychology,* 21: 28–56.

Churchill, W. (1931) *The World Crisis.* New York: Scribner.

Cialdini, R. (2009) *Influence: Science and Practice* (5th ed.). Boston: Pearson.

Ciulla, J. (1995) Leadership ethics: mapping the territory. *Business Ethics Quarterly,* 5: 5–28.

Clegg, S. (1989) *Frameworks of Power*. London: SAGE.

Clifton, J. (2012) A discursive approach to leadership: doing assessments and managing organizational meanings. *Journal of Business Communication*, 49: 148–68.

Coates, J. and Herbert, J. (2008) Endogenous steroids and financial risk taking on a London trading floor. *Proceedings of the National Academy of Sciences of the United States of America*, 105 (16): 6167–72. doi: 10.1073/pnas.0704025105.

Cohan, J. (2002) 'I didn't know' and 'I was only doing my job': has corporate governance careered out of control? A case study of Enron's information myopia. *Journal of Business Ethics*, 40: 275–99.

Cohen, P. (1997) *Children of the Revolution: Communist Childhood in Cold War Britain*. London: Lawrence & Wishart.

Collins, J. (2001) *Good to Great: Why Some Companies Make the Leap ... and Others Don't*. New York: Random House Books.

Collins, J. (2009) *How the Mighty Fall: And Why Some Companies Never Give In*. New York: Random House.

Collins, J. and Hansen, M. (2011) *Great by Choice: Uncertainty, Chaos and Luck – Why Some Thrive Despite Them All*. New York: Random House.

Collins, J. and Porras, J. (1994) *Built to Last: Successful Habits of Visionary Companies*. New York: Harper Business.

Collins, J. and Porras, J. (1995) Building a visionary company. *California Management Review*, 37: 80–100.

Collinson, D. (1994) Strategies of resistance: Power, knowledge and subjectivity in the workplace. In J. Jermier, D. Knights and W. Nord (Eds), *Resistance and Power in Organizations*. London: Cengage Learning EMEA, pp. 25–68.

Collinson, D. (1999) Surviving the rigs: safety and surveillance on North Sea oil installations. *Organization Studies*, 20: 579–600.

Collinson, D. (2003) Identities and insecurities: selves at work. *Organization*, 10: 527–47.

Collinson, D. (2005) Dialectics of leadership. *Human Relations*, 58: 1419–42.

Collinson, D. (2005) Questions of distance. *Leadership*, 1: 235–50.

Collinson, D. (2006) Rethinking followership: a post-structuralist analysis of follower identities. *The Leadership Quarterly*, 17: 179–89.

Collinson, D. (2008) Conformist, resistant, and disguised selves: a post-structuralist approach to identity and workplace followership. In R. Riggio, I. Chaleff and J. Lipman-Blumen (Eds), *The Art of Followership: How Great Followers Create Great Leaders and Organizations*. San Francisco, CA: Jossey-Bass, pp. 309–24.

Collinson, D. (2011) Critical leadership studies. In A. Bryman, D. Collinson, K. Grint, B. Jackson and M. Uhl-Bien (Eds), *The SAGE Handbook of Leadership*. London: SAGE, pp. 181–94.

Collinson, D. (2012) Prozac leadership and the limits of positive thinking. *Leadership*, 8: 87–108.

Collinson, D. and Collinson, M. (2004) The power of time: leadership, management and gender. In C. F. Epstein and A. L. Kalleberg (Eds), *Fighting for Time:Shifting Boundaries of Work and Social Life*. New York: Russell Sage Foundation, pp. 219–46.

Conger, J. (1989) *The Charismatic Leader: Behind The Mystique Of Exceptional Leadership*. San Francisco, CA: Jossey-Bass.

Conger, J. (1990) The dark side of leadership. *Organizational Dynamics*, Autumn: 44–55.

Conger, J. (2011) Charismatic leadership. In A. Bryman, D. Collinson, K. Grint, B. Jackson and Uhl-Bien, M. (Eds), *The SAGE Handbook of Leadership*. London: SAGE, pp. 86–102.

Conger, J. and Kanungo, R. (1994) Charismatic leadership in organizations: perceived behavioral attributes and their measurement. *Journal of Organizational Behavior*, 15: 439–52.

Conger, J. and Kanungo, R. (1998) *Charismatic Leadership in Organizations*. London: SAGE.

Conger, J., Kanungo, R. and Menon, S. (2000) Charismatic leadership and follower effects. *Journal of Organizational Behaviour*, 21: 747–67.

Connor, J. (2011) Understanding the cognitive restraints of physicians. *Canadian Medical Association Journal*, E137–8.

Conrad, C. (2003) Stemming the tide: corporate discourse and agenda denial in the 2002 'corporate meltdown'. *Organization*, 10: 549–60.

Conrad, C. (2011) *Organizational Rhetoric*. Cambridge: Polity Press.

Coombs, W. (2007) Protecting organization reputations during a crisis: the development and application of situational crisis communication theory. *Corporate Reputation Review*, 10: 163–76.

Cooren, F. (2006) The organizational world as a plenum of agencies. In F. Cooren, J. Taylor and E. Van Every (Eds), *Communication as Organizing: Empirical and Theoretical Explorations in the Dynamic of Text and Conversation*. London: Lawrence Erlbaum, pp. 81–100.

Cooren, F., Taylor, J. and Van Every, E. (2006) Introduction. In F. Cooren, J. Taylor and E. Van Every (Eds), *Communication as Organizing: Empirical and Theoretical Explorations in the Dynamic of Text and Conversation*. London: Lawrence Erlbaum, pp. 1–18.

Cooren, F., Kuhn, T., Cornelissen, J. and Clark, T. (2011) Communication, organizing, and organization: an overview and introduction to the Special Issue. *Organization Studies*, 32: 1149–70.

Courpasson, D. (2011) 'Roads to Resistance': the growing critique from managerial ranks in organization. *M@n@gement*, 14: 7–23.

Craig, R. and Amernic, J. (2004) Enron discourse: the rhetoric of a resilient capitalism. *Critical Perspectives on Accounting*, 15: 813–51.

Cravens, K., Oliver, E. and Ramamoorti, S. (2003) The reputation index: measuring and managing corporate reputation. *European Management Journal*, 21: 201–12.

Crick, M. (1986) *The March of Militant*. London: Faber and Faber.

Crossman, B. and Crossman, J. (2011) Conceptualising followership – a review of the literature. *Leadership*, 7: 481–97.

Crossman, R. (Ed.) (1949) *The God That Failed*. London: Hamish Hamilton.

Cruver, B. (2003) *Enron: Anatomy of Greed*. London: Arrow Books.

Cunliffe, A. (2008) Orientations to social constructionism: relationally responsive social constructionism and its implications for knowledge and learning. *Management Learning*, 39: 123–39.

Currie, G., Boyett, I. and Suhomlinova, O. (2005) Transformational leadership within secondary schools in England: a panacea for organizational ills? *Public Administration*, 83: 265–96.

Daniels, D., Franz, R. and Wong, K. (2000) A classroom with a worldview: making spiritual assumptions explicit in management education. *Journal of Management Education*, 24: 540–61.

de Holan, P. (2011) Agency in organizational forgetting. *Journal of Management Inquiry*, 20: 317–22.

De Vries, R., Roe, R. and Thaillieu, T. (1999) On charisma and need for leadership. *European Journal of Work and Organizational Psychology*, 8: 109–26.

Deakin, S. and Konzelmann, S. (2003) After Enron: an age of enlightenment? *Organization*, 10: 583–87.

Deal, T. and Kennedy, A. (1982) *Corporate cultures*. Harmondsworth: Penguin.

Deal, T. and Kennedy, A. (1999) *The New Corporate Cultures: Revitalising the Workplace After Downsizing, Mergers and Reengineering*. London: Orion Books.

Dean, K. (2004) Systems thinking's challenge to research in spirituality and religion at work: an interview with Ian Mitroff. *Journal of Organizational Change Management*, 17: 11–25.

Dean, K. and Safranski, S. (2008) No harm, no foul? Organizational intervention in workplace spirituality. *International Journal of Public Administration*, 31: 359–71.

Deetz, S. (1992) *Democracy in an Age of Corporate Colonization: Developments in Communication and the Politics of Everyday Life*. Albany, NY: State University of New York Press.

Deetz, S. (1995) *Transforming Communication, Transforming Business*. Cresskill, NJ: Hampton Press.

Deetz, S. and McClellan, J. (2009) Communication. In M. Alvesson, T. Bridgman and H. Willmott (Eds), *The Oxford Handbook of Critical Management Studies*. Oxford: Oxford University Press, pp. 433–53.

Dehler, G. and Welsh, M. (2003) The experience of work: spirituality and the new workplace. In R. Giacalone and C. Jurkiewicz (Eds), *Handbook of Workplace Spirituality and Organizational Performance*. New York: Sharpe, pp. 108–22.

Delbecq, L. (1999) Christian spirituality and contemporary business leadership. *Journal of Organizational Change Management*, 12: 345–49.

Delves Broughton, P. (2010) *What They Teach You at Harvard Business School: My Two Years Inside the Cauldron of Capitalism*. London: Penguin.

Dent, E., Higgins, M. and Wharff, D. (2005) Spirituality and leadership: an empirical review of definitions, and embedded assumptions. *The Leadership Quarterly*, 16: 625–53.

Detert, J. and Edmondson, A. (2011) Implicit voice theories: taken-for-granted rules of self-censorship at work. *Academy of Management Journal*, 54: 461–88.

Dezfouli, A. and Balleine, B. (2012) Habits, action sequences and reinforcement learning. *European Journal of Neuroscience*, 35: 1036–51.

Díaz-Sáenz, H. (2011) Transformational leadership. In A. Bryman, D. Collinson, K. Grint, B. Jackson and Uhl-Bien, M. (Eds), *The SAGE Handbook of Leadership*. London: SAGE, pp. 299–310.

Dickson, D., Hargie, O. and Wilson, N. (2008) Communication, relationships, and religious differences in the Northern Ireland workplace: a study of private and public sector organisations. *Journal of Applied Communication Research*, 36: 128–60.

Donaghey, J., Cullinane, N., Dundon, T. and Wilkinson, A. (2011) Reconceptualising employee silence: problems and prognosis. *Work, Employment and Society*, 25: 51–67.

Driscoll, C. and Wiebe, E. (2007) Technical spirituality at work: Jacques Ellul on workplace spirituality. *Journal of Management Inquiry*, 16: 333–48.

Driver, M. (2005) From empty speech to full speech? Reconceptualizing spirituality in organizations based on a psychoanalytically-grounded understanding of the self. *Human Relations*, 58: 1091–10.

du Gay, P. (1991) Enterprise culture and the ideology of excellence. *New Formations*, 13: 45–61.

DuBrin, A. (2012) *Narcissism, in the Workplace: Research, Opinion and Practice*. Cheltenham: Edward Elgar.

Duchon, D. and Plowman, D. (2005) Nurturing the spirit at work: impact on work unit performance. *The Leadership Quarterly*, 16: 807–33.

Durand, T. and Dameron, S. (Eds) (2011) *Redesigning Management Education and Research: Proposals From European Scholars*. London: Edward Elgar.

Economist (2000) The energetic messiah. *The Economist*, 1 June. Accessed online at http://www.economist.com/node/334871. Last accessed 20 November 2012.

Edmunds, A. and Morris, A. (2000) The problem of information overload in business organisations: a review of the literature. *International Journal of Information Management*, 20: 17–28.

Edwards, M., Ashkanasy, N. and Gardner, J. (2009) Deciding to speak up or to remain silent following observed wrongdoing: the role of discrete emotions and climate of silence. In J. Greenberg and M. Edwards (Eds), *Voice and Silence in Organizations*. Bingley: Emerald, pp. 83–109.

Eisenberg, E. (1994) Dialogue as democratic discourse: affirming Harrison. In S. Deetz (Ed.), *Communication Yearbook 17*. Newbury Park, CA: SAGE, pp. 275–84.

Eisler, R. and Montouori, A. (2003) The human side of spirituality. In R. Giacalone and C. Jurkiewicz (Eds), *Handbook of Workplace Spirituality and Organizational Performance*. New York: M. E. Sharpe, pp. 46–56.

Eliot, T. S. ([1925] 2007) *Eliot's Poems: 1909–1925*. Bel Air, CA: Read Books.

Ellison, C. (1983) Spiritual well-being: conceptualisation and measurement. *Journal of Psychology and Theology*, 11: 330–40.

Enron (2000) *Code of Ethics*. Houston, TX: Enron. Available online at http://www.thesmokinggun.com/documents/crime/enrons-code-ethics. Last accessed 20 November 2012.

Evans, J. (2009) *Inspirational Presence: The Art of Transformational Leadership*. New York: Morgan James.

Fairhurst, G. (2007) *Discursive Leadership*. London: SAGE.

Fairhurst, G. (2011) *The Power of Framing: Creating the Language of Leadership*. San Francisco: Jossey-Bass.

Fairhurst, G. and Grant, D. (2010) The social construction of leadership: a sailing guide. *Management Communication Quarterly*, 24: 171–210.

Fairhurst, G. and Zoller, H. (2008) Resistance, dissent and leadership in practice. In S. Banks (Ed.), *Dissent and the Failure of Leadership*. London: Edward Elgar, pp. 135–48.

Fast, H. (1958) *The Naked God: The Writer and the Communist Party*. New York: J. Lane.

Fast, H. (1990) *Being Red: A Memoir*. New York: M. E. Sharpe.

Fast, N. and Chen, S. (2009) When the boss feel inadequate: power, incompetence and aggression. *Psychological Science*, 20: 1406–13.

Federico, C. and Deason, G. (2012) Uncertainty, insecurity, and ideological defense of the status quo: the extremizing role of political expertise. In M. Hogg and D. Blaylock (Eds), *Extremism and the Psychology of Uncertainty*. Oxford: Wiley Blackwell, pp. 198–211.

Ferlie, E., McGivern, G. and Moraes, A. (2010) Developing a public interest school of management. *British Journal of Management*, 21: S60–70.

Fernie, S. and Metcalf, D. (1999) (Not) hanging on the telephone: payment systems in the new sweatshops. *Advances in Industrial and Labor Relations*, 9: 23–68.

Festinger, L. (1957) *A Theory of Cognitive Dissonance*. Evanston, IL: Row and Peterson.

Figes, O. (2007) *The Whisperers*. London: Allen Lane.

Financial Services Authority (2011) *The Failure of the Royal Bank of Scotland*. London: FSA.

Financial Services Authority (2012) *Final Notice*. London: FSA, 9 March. Accessed online at http://www.fsa.gov.uk/static/pubs/final/bankofscotlandplc.pdf. Last accessed 22 November 2012.

Flauto, F. (1999) Walking the talk: the relationship between leadership and communication competence. *The Journal of Leadership Studies*, 6: 86–97.

Fleming, P. (2012) 'Down with Big Brother!': The end of 'corporate culturism'? *Journal of Management Studies*, published online 13 June, doi: 10.1111/j.1467-6486.2012.01056.x.

Flyvbjerg, B. (1998) *Rationality and Power: Democracy in Practice*. Chicago: University of Chicago Press.

Ford, J. and Harding, N. (2007) Move over management: we are all leaders now. *Management Learning*, 38: 475–93.

Ford, J. and Harding, N. (2011) The impossibility of the 'true self' of authentic leadership. *Leadership*, 7: 463–79.

Forray, J. and Stork, D. (2002) All for one: A parable of spirituality and organization. *Organization*, 9: 497–509.

Foucault, M. (1977) *Discipline and Punish*. London: Allen and Unwin.

Foucault, M. (1979) *The History of Sexuality*. London: Allen and Unwin.

Foucault, M. (1982) Afterword. In H. Dreyfus and P. Rabinow (Eds), *Michel Foucault: Beyond Structuralism and Hermeneutics*. Hemel Hempstead: Harvester Press, pp. 208–28.

Freshman, B. (1999) An exploratory analysis of definitions and applications of spirituality in the workplace. *Journal of Organizational Change Management*, 12: 318–27.

Frey, J. (2002) Water over the dam. *The Washington Post*, 17 April: CO1.

Friedman, M. (2002) *Capitalism and Freedom (40th anniversary Edition)*. Chicago: The University of Chicago Press.

Fry, L. (2003) Toward a theory of spiritual leadership. *The Leadership Quarterly*, 14: 693–727.

Fry, L. and Cohen, M. (2009) Spiritual leadership as a paradigm for organizational transformation and recovery from extended work hours cultures. *Journal of Business Ethics*, 84: 265–78.

Fry, L., Vitucci, S. and Cedillo, M. (2005) Spiritual leadership and army transformation: theory, measurement, and establishing a baseline. *The Leadership Quarterly*, 16: 835–62.

Fryer, M. (2011a) *Ethics and Organizational Leadership*. Oxford: Oxford University Press.

Fryer, M. (2011b) Facilitative leadership: drawing on Jurgen Habermas' model of ideal speech to propose a less impositional way to lead. *Organization*, 19: 25–43.

Fukuyama, F. (1993) *The End of History and the Last Man*. London: Penguin.

Furnham, A. (2010) *The Elephant In the Boardroom: The Causes of Leadership Derailment*. London: Palgrave Macmillan.

Fusaro, P. and Miller, R. (2002) *What Went Wrong at Enron: Everyone's Guide to the Largest Bankruptcy in U.S. History*. Hoboken, NJ: Wiley.

Gabriel, Y., Fineman, S. and Sims, D. (2000) *Organizing and Organizations: An Introduction* (2nd ed.). London: SAGE.

Galanter, M. (1999) *Cults: Faith, Healing and Coercion* (2nd ed.). Oxford: Oxford University Press.

Galbraith, J. (1977) *The Age of Uncertainty*. London: BBC/Andre Deutsch.

Galinsky, A., Gruenfeld, D. and Magee, J. (2003) From power to action. *Journal of Personality and Social Psychology*, 85: 453–66.

Gardner, W. L., Fischer, D. and Hunt, J. G. J. (2009) Emotional labor and leadership: a threat to authenticity? *The Leadership Quarterly*, 20: 466–82.

Garner, J. (2012) Making waves at work: perceived effectiveness and appropriateness of organizational dissent messages. *Management Communication Quarterly*, 26: 224–40.

Gemmill, G. and Oakley, J. (1992) Leadership: an alienating social myth? *Human Relations*, 42: 113–29.

Gergen, K. (2000) *Invitation to Social Constructionism*. London: SAGE.

Gergen, K. (2010) Co-constitution, causality, and confluence: Organizing in a world without entities. In T. Hernes and S. Maitlis (Eds), *Process, Sensemaking and Organization*. Oxford: Oxford University Press, pp. 55–69.

Ghoshal, S. (2005) Bad management theories are destroying good management practices. *Academy of Management Learning and Education*, 4: 75–91.

Giacalone, R. and Jurkiewicz, C. (2003) (Eds) *Handbook Of Workplace Spirituality And Organizational Performance*. New York: Sharpe.

Giebels, E., Noelanders, S. and Vervaeke, G. (2005) The hostage experience: implications for negotiation strategies. *Clinical Psychology and Psychotherapy*, 12: 241–53.

Gist, M. (1987) Self-efficacy: implications for organizational behavior and human resource management. *Academy of Management Review*, 12: 472–85.

Gladwell, M. (2002) The talent myth. *The Times (T2)*, 20 August: 2–4.

Godard, A., Lenhardt, V. and Stewart, M. (2000) *Transformational Leadership: Shared Dreams to Succeed*. London: Palgrave Macmillan.

Goffee, R. and Jones, G. (2006) *Why Should Anyone Be Led By You? What it Takes To Be An Authentic Leader*. Boston, MA: Harvard Business School Press.

Goffman, E. (1959) *The Presentation of Self in Everyday Life*. London: Penguin.

Goffman, E. (1968) *Asylums*. Harmondsworth: Penguin.

Goldhammer, J. (1996) *Under the Influence: The Destructive Effects of Group Dynamics*. New York: Prometheus Books.

Goldstein, N. and Cialdini, R. (2007) Using social norms as a lever of social influence. In A. Pratkanis (Ed.), *The Science of Social Influence: Advances and Future Progress*. New York: Psychology Press, pp. 167–91.

Gordon, R., Clegg, S. and Kornberger, M. (2009) Power, rationality and legitimacy in public organizations. *Public Administration*, 87: 15–34.

Gosling, J. and Mintzberg, H. (2006) Management education as if both matter. *Management Learning*, 37: 419–28.

Gozdz, K. and Frager, R. (2003) Using the everyday challenges of business to transform individuals and organizations. In R. Giacalone and C. Jurkiewicz (Eds), *Handbook of Workplace Spirituality and Organizational Performance*. New York: Sharpe, pp. 475–92.

Granberg-Michaelson, W. (2004) *Leadership From Inside-Out: Spirituality and Organizational Change*. New York: Crossroads Publishing Company.

Grant, R. (2000) *Contemporary Strategy Analysis: Concepts, Techniques, Applications* (2nd ed). Oxford: Blackwell.

Gray, J. and Densten, I. (2007) How leaders woo followers in the romance of leadership. *Applied Psychology: An International Review*, 56: 558–81.

Greenleaf, R. (1977) *Servant Leadership: A Journey Into The Nature of Legitimate Power and Greatness*. New York: Paulist Press.

Greiner, L. (2002) Steve Kerr and his years with Jack Welch at GE. *Journal of Management Inquiry*, 11: 343–50.

Greve, H., Palmer, D. and Pozner, J. (2010) Organizations gone wild: the causes, processes, and consequences of organizational misconduct. *Academy of Management Annals*, 4: 53–107.

Grey, C. (1994) Career as a project of the self and labour process discipline. *Sociology*, 28 (2): 479–97.

Grint, K. (2000) *The Arts of Leadership*. Oxford: Oxford University Press.

Grint, K. (2005) *Leadership: Limits and Possibilities*. London: Palgrave Macmillan.

Grint, K. (2010) The sacred in leadership: separation, sacrifice and silence. *Organization Studies*, 31: 89–107.

Guney, S. (2006) Making sense of conflict as the (missing) link between organizational actors. In F. Cooren, J. Taylor and E. Van Every (Eds), *Communication as Organizing: Empirical and Theoretical Explorations in the Dynamic of Text and Conversation*. London: Lawrence Erlbaum, pp. 19–36.

Guthey, E. (2005) Management studies, cultural criticism and American dreams. *Journal of Management Studies*, 42: 451–65.

Habermas, J. (1974) *Theory and Practice*. Boston, MA: Beacon Press.

Habermas, J. (1984) *The Theory of Communicative Action, Vol. 1: Reason and the Rationalisation of Society*. Boston, MA: Beacon Press.

Habermas, J. (1987) *The Theory of Communicative Action, Vol. 2: Lifeworld and System: The Critique of Functionalist Reason*. Boston, MA: Beacon Press.

Habermas, J. (1990) *Moral Consciousness and Communicative Action*. Massachusetts, MA: MIT Press.

Haidt, J. (2012) *The Righteous Mind: Why Good People are Divided by Politics and Religion*. London: Allen Lane.

Haigh, G. (2003) Bad company: the cult of the CEO. *Quarterly Essay*, 10: 1–97.

Hamel, G. (2000) *Leading The Revolution*. Boston: Harvard Business School Press.

Hamel, G. (2012) *What Matters Now*. San Francisco, CA: Jossey-Bass.

Hansbrough, T. (2012) The construction of a transformational leader: follower attachment and leadership perceptions. *Journal of Applied Social Psychology*, 42: 1533–49.

Hansen, M., Ibarra, H. and Peyer, U. (2010) The best-performing CEOs in the world. *Harvard Business Review*, January-February: 104–13.

Hardy, C. and Phillips, N. (2004) Discourse and power. In D. Grant, C. Hardy, C. Oswick and L. Putnam (Eds), *The SAGE Handbook of Organizational Discourse*. London: SAGE, pp. 299–316.

Hargie, O. and Dickson, D. (2003) Editorial introduction. In O. Hargie and D. Dickson (Eds), *Researching the Troubles: Social Science Perspectives on the Northern Ireland Conflict*. Edinburgh: Mainstream Publishing, pp. 11–14.

Hargie, O., Stapleton, K. and Tourish, D. (2010) Making sense of CEO public apologies for the banking crisis: attributions of credit, blame and responsibility. *Organization*, 17: 721–42.

Haslam, A. (2004) *Psychology in Organizations: The Social Identity Approach* (2nd ed.). London: SAGE.

Haslam, S. and Reicher, S. (2012a) Beyond conformity: revisiting classic studies and exploring the dynamics of resistance. In J. Jetten and M. Hornsey (Eds), *Rebels in Groups: Dissent, Deviance, Difference and Defiance*. Chichester: Wiley-Blackwell, pp. 324–44.

Haslam, S. and Reicher, S. (2012b) Tyranny: revisiting Zimbardo's Stanford prison experiment. In J. Smith and S. Haslam (Eds), *Social Psychology: Revisiting The Classic Studies*. London: SAGE, pp. 126–41.

Haslam, S. A., Reicher, S., and Platow, M. (2011) *The New Psychology of Leadership: Identity, Influence and Power*. New York: Psychology Press.

Hassan, S. (1988) *Combating Cult Mind Control*. Rochester: Park Press.

Hatch, M. J., Kostera, M. and Kozminski, A. (2005) *The Three Faces of Leadership: Manager, Artist, Priest*. Oxford: Blackwell.

Haugaard, M. (1997) *The Constitution of Power: A Theoretical Analysis of Power, Knowledge and Structure*. Manchester: Manchester University Press.

Hay, A. and Hodgkinson, M. (2006) Rethinking leadership: a way forward for teaching leadership? *Leadership and Organization Development Journal*, 27: 144–58.

Hayward, M. (2007) *Ego Check: Why Executive Hubris is Wrecking Companies and Careers and how to Avoid the Trap*. Chicago: Kaplan.

Heaton, D., Schmidt-Wilk, J. and Travis, F. (2004) Constructs, methods, and measures for researching spirituality in organizations. *Journal of Organizational Change Management*, 17: 62–82.

Hegele, C. and Kieser, A. (2001) Control the construction of your legend or someone else will: an analysis of texts on Jack Welch. *Journal of Management Inquiry*, 10: 298–309.

Hensmans, M. (2003) The territorialization of common sense. *Organization*, 10: 561–4.

Hicks, D. (2003) *Religion and the Workplace*. Cambridge: Cambridge University Press.

Hochman, J. (1984) Iatrogenic symptoms associated with a therapy cult: examination of an extinct 'new psychotherapy' with respect to psychiatric deterioration and 'brainwashing'. *Psychiatry*, 47: 366–77.

Hogg, M. (2001) A social identity theory of leadership. *Personality and Social Psychology Review*, 5: 184–200.

Hogg, M. (2007) Organizational orthodoxy and corporate autocrats: some nasty consequences of organisational identification in uncertain times. In C. Bartel, S. Blader and A. Wrzesniewski (Eds), *Identity and the Modern Organization*. Hillsdale, NJ: Lawrence Erlbaum, pp. 35–9.

Hogg, M. (2008) Social identity processes and the empowerment of followers. In R. Riggio, I. Chaleff and J. Lipman-Blumen (Eds), *The Art of Followership: How Great Followers Create Great Leaders and Organizations*. San Francisco, CA: Jossey-Bass, pp. 267–76.

Hogg, M. (2012) Self-uncertainty, social identity and the solace of extremism. In M. Hogg and D. Blaylock (Eds), *Extremism and the Psychology of Uncertainty*. Chichester: Wiley-Blackwell, pp. 19–35.

Hogler, R., Gross, M., Hartman, J. and Cunliffe, A. (2008) Meaning in organizational communication: why metaphor is the cake, not the icing. *Management Communication Quarterly*, 21: 393–412.

Holstrom, B. (1979) Moral hazard and observability. *Bell Journal of Economics*, 10: 74–91.

Hoopes, J. (2003) *False Prophets: The Gurus Who Created Modern Management and Why Their Ideas are Bad for Business Today*. Cambridge, MA: Perseus.

Hope, V. and Hendry, J. (1995) Corporate cultural change – is it relevant for the organizations of the 1990s? *Human Resource Management Journal*, 5: 61–73.

Hopfl, H. (1992) The making of the corporate acolyte: some thoughts on charismatic leadership and the reality of organizational commitment. *Journal of Management Studies*, 29: 23–33.

Hopfl, H. (2005) The organisation and the mouth of hell. *Culture and Organization*, 11: 167–79.

House of Commons Treasury Committee (2009a) *Banking Crisis: Volume 1 Oral Evidence*. HC144-1. London: The Stationery Office. Available online from http://www.publications.parliament.uk/pa/cm200809/cmselect/cmtreasy/144/144i.pdf. Last accessed 22 November 2012.

House of Commons Treasury Committee (2009b) *Banking Crisis: Reforming Corporate Governance and Pay in the City. Ninth Report of Session 2008–09*. Available online from http://www.publications.parliament.uk/pa/cm200809/cmselect/cmtreasy/519/51902.htm. Last accessed 22 November 2012.

House of Commons Treasury Committee (2009c) *Banking Crisis: Dealing With the Failure of the UK Banks. Seventh Report of Session 2008–09*. HC416. London: The Stationery Office. Available online from http://www.publications.parliament.uk/pa/cm200809/cmselect/cmtreasy/416/416.pdf. Last accessed 22 November 2012.

House of Commons Treasury Committee (2012) *Fixing LIBOR: Some Preliminary Findings. Second Report of Session 2012–13. Volume I: Report, Together with Formal Minutes; Volume II: Oral and Written Evidence*. London: The Stationery Office. Volume 1 available online from http://www.parliament.uk/documents/commons-committees/treasury/Fixing%20LIBOR_%20some%20preliminary%20findings%20-%20VOL%20I.pdf. Volume II available online from http://www.publications.parliament.uk/pa/cm201213/cmselect/cmtreasy/481/481ii.pdf. Last accessed 22 November 2012.

House, R. and Baetz, M. (1979) Leadership: some empirical generalizations and new research directions. In B. Staw (Ed.), *Research in Organizational Behavior*. Greenwich, CT: JAI Press, volume 1: 341–53.

House, R. and Howell, J. (1992) Personality and charismatic leadership. *Leadership Quarterly*, 3: 81–108.

Hudson (2007) *Cull or Cure: The Secret of an Efficient Company*. London: Hudson Management Consultancy.

Human Rights Watch (2002) *The Enron Corporation: Corporate Complicity in Human Rights Violations*. New York: Human Rights Watch. Available online at http:www.hrw.org/reports/1999/enron/. Last accessed 22 November 2012.

Hunter, S., Bedell-Avers, K., and Mumford, M. (2007) The typical leadership study: assumptions, implications and potential remedies. *The Leadership Quarterly*, 18: 435–46.

Hutson, M. (2012) *The 7 Laws of Magical Thinking: How Irrational Beliefs Keep Us Happy, Healthy, and Sane*. New York: Hudson Street Press.

Huxley, A. (2004) *Brave New World*. London: Vintage.

Hyde, D. (1952) *I Believed: The Autobiography of a Former British Communist*. London: MW Books.

Incomes Data Services (2011) *What Are We Paying For? Exploring Executive Pay And Performance*. London: High Pay Commission.

Introvigne, M. (2002) 'There is no place for us to go but up': new religious movements and violence. *Social Compass*, 49: 213–24.

Jackson, B. (2001) *Management Gurus and Management Fashions*. London: Routledge.

Janis, I. (1972) *Victims of Groupthink*. Boston: Houghton Mifflin.

Jenkinson, G. (2008) An investigation into cult pseudo-personality: what is it and how does it form? *Cultic Studies Review*, 7: 199–224.

Jensen, M. (1994) Self-interest, altruism, incentives and agency theory. *Journal of Applied Corporate Finance*, 7: 4–19.

Jensen, M. and Meckling, W. (1976) Theory of the firm: managerial behaviour, agency costs and ownership structure. *Journal of Financial Economics*, 3: 305-60.

Jetten, J. and Hornsley, M. (2011) *Rebels in Groups: Dissent, Deviance, Difference and Defiance.* Oxford: John Wiley.

Jetten, J., Iyer, A., Hutchison, P. and Hornsey, M. (2012) Debating deviance. In J. Jetten and M. Hornsey (Eds), *Rebels in Groups: Dissent, Deviance, Difference and Defiance.* Chichester: Wiley-Blackwell, pp. 117–34.

Johnson, B. (2011) How I did it: The CEO of Heinz on powering growth in emerging markets. *Harvard Business Review*, October: 47–50.

Jones, E. (1990) *Interpersonal Perception.* New York: Freeman.

Jost, J. and Elsbach, K. (2001) How status and power differences erode personal and social identities at work: a system justification critique of organizational applications of social identity theory. In M. Hogg and D. Terry (Eds), *Social Identity Processes In Organisational Contexts.* London: Psychology Press, pp. 181–96.

Kahneman, D. (2011) *Thinking Fast and Slow.* London: Allen Lane.

Kamoche, K. (2000) Developing managers: the functional, the symbolic, the sacred and the profane. *Organization Studies*, 21: 747–74.

Kanter, R. (1985) *The Change Masters.* London: Jossey-Bass, Wiley.

Kark, R., Shamir, B. and Chen, G. (2003) The two faces of transformational leadership: empowerment and dependency. *Journal of Applied Psychology*, 88: 246–55.

Kark, R., Waismel-Manor, R. and Shamir, B. (2012) Does valuing androgyny and femininity lead to a female advantage? The relationship between gender-role, transformational leadership and identification. *The Leadership Quarterly*, 23: 620–40.

Kassing, J. (2011) *Dissent in Organisations.* London: Polity.

Kellerman, B. (2004) *Bad Leadership.* Boston: Harvard Business School Press.

Kellerman, B. (2008) *Followership: How Followers Are Creating Change and Changing Leaders.* Boston: Harvard Business Press.

Kellerman, B. (2012) *The End of Leadership.* New York: Harper Collins.

Kelley, R. (1988) In praise of followers. *Harvard Business Review*, 66: 142–8.

Kelley, R. (2008) Rethinking followership. In R. Riggio, I. Chaleff and J. Lipman-Blumen (Eds), *The Art of Followership: How Great Followers Create Great Leaders and Organizations.* San Francisco, CA: Jossey-Bass, pp. 5–16.

Keltner, D., Gruenfeld, D. and Anderson, C. (2003) Power, approach and inhibition. *Psychological Review*, 1: 265–84.

Kerr, R. (2008) Discourse and leadership: using the paradigm of the permanent state of emergency. *Critical Discourse Studies*, 5: 201–16.

Kerr, R. and Robinson, S. (2011) Leadership as an elite field: Scottish banking leaders and the crisis of 2007–2009. *Leadership*, 7: 151–73.

Kerr, R. and Robinson, S. (2012) From symbolic violence to economic violence: the globalising of the Scottish banking elite. *Organization Studies*, 33: 247–66.

Kets de Vries, M. (1994) The leadership mystique. *Academy of Management Executive*, 8 (3): 73–89.

Kets de Vries, M. (2001) *The Leadership Mystique: An Owner's Manual.* London: Financial Times/Prentice-Hall.

Kets de Vries, M. (2004) Organizations on the couch: A clinical perspective on organizational dynamics. *European Management Journal*, 22: 183–200.

Kets de Vries, M. (2006) *The Leader on the Couch: A Clinical Approach to Changing People and Organizations.* London: John Wiley and Sons.

Kets de Vries, M. and Miller, D. (1985) Narcissism and leadership: an object relations perspective. *Human Relations*, 38: 583–601.

Khanna, H. and Srinivas, E. (2000) *Spirituality and leadership development.* Presented to the Roundtable Conference on Developing Leaders, Teams and Organizations: Meeting the challenges of global markets and technology, Management Development Institute, Guragon.

Khurana, R. (2002) *Searching for a Corporate Savior.* Princeton: Princeton University Press.

Kinjerski, V. and Skrypnek, B. (2004) Defining spirit at work: finding common ground. *Journal of Organizational Change Management,* 17: 26–42.

Kiser, E. (1999) Comparing varieties of agency theory in economics, political science and sociology: an illustration from state policy implementation. *Social Theory,* 17: 146–70.

Knights, D. and Vurubakis, T. (1994) Foucault, power, resistance and all that. In J. Jermier, D. Knights and W. Nord (Eds), *Resistance and Power in Organisations.* London: Routledge, pp. 167–98.

Knottnerus, J., Ulsperger, J., Cummins, S. and Osteen, E. (2006) Exposing Enron: media representations of ritualised deviance in corporate culture. *Crime, Media, Culture,* 2: 177–95.

Koestler, A. (1959) Arthur Koestler. In R. Crossman (Ed.) *The God That Failed.* New York: Harper, pp. 15–75.

Konz, G. and Ryan, F. (1999) Maintaining and organizational spirituality: no easy task. *Journal of Organizational Change Management,* 12: 200–10.

Korac-Kakabadse, N., Kouzmin, A. and Kakabadse, A. (2002) Spirituality and leadership practice. *Journal of Managerial Psychology,* 17: 165–82.

Krackhardt, D. (1994) Constraints on the interactive organization as an ideal type. In C. Heckscher and A. Donnellon (Eds), *The Post-Bureaucratic Organization: New Perspectives on Organizational Change.* Thousand Oaks, CA: SAGE, pp. 211–22.

Kraditor, A. (1988) *"Jimmy Higgins": The Mental World of the American Rank-and-File Communist, 1930–1958.* Connecticut: Greenwood Press.

Kruglanski, A. and Orehek, E. (2012) The need for certainty as a psychological nexus for individuals and society. In M. Hogg and D. Blaylock (Eds), *Extremism and the Psychology of Uncertainty.* Oxford: Wiley Blackwell, pp. 3–18.

Kruglanski, A. and Webster, D. (1991) Group members' reaction to opinion deviates and conformists at varying degrees of proximity to decision deadline and of environmental noise. *Journal of Personality and Social Psychology,* 61: 212–25.

Kuhn, T. (2008) A communicative theory of the firm: developing an alternative perspective on intra-organizational power and stakeholder relationships. *Organization Studies,* 29: 1227–54.

Kunda, G. (1992) *Engineering Culture: Control and Commitment in a High-Tech Corporation.* Philadelphia, PA: Temple University Press.

Lacombe, D. (1996) Refraining Foucault: a critique of the social control thesis. *British Journal of Sociology,* 47: 332–52.

Ladkin, D. (2010) *Rethinking Leadership: A New Look at Old Leadership Questions.* Cheltenham: Edward Elgar.

Lalich, J. (1992) The cadre ideal: origins and development of a political cult. *Cultic Studies Journal,* 9 (1): 1–77.

Lalich, J. (1993) A little carrot and a lot of stick: a case example. In M. D. Langone (Ed.), *Recovery From Cults: Help for Victims of Psychological and Spiritual Abuse.* New York: Norton, pp. 51–84.

Lalich, J. (2004) *Bounded Choice.* Berkeley: University of California Press.

Lammers, J., Stapel, D. and Galinsky, A. (2010) Power increases hypocrisy: moralizing in reasoning, immorality in behavior. *Psychological Science,* 21: 7373–44.

Langbein, H. (1995) *Against All Hope: Resistance in the Nazi Concentration Camps.* London: Constable.

Langer, E. and Benevento, A. (1978) Self-induced dependence. *Journal of Personality and Social Psychology*, 36: 886–93.

Langley, A. (2009) Studying processes in and around organizations. In D. Buchanan and A. Bryman (Eds), *The SAGE Handbook of Organizational Research Methods*. London: SAGE, pp. 409–29.

Langley, A. and Tsoukas, H. (2010) Introducing 'Perspectives on process organization studies'. In T. Hernes and S., Maitlis (Eds), *Process, Sensemaking and Organization.* Oxford: Oxford University Press, pp. 1–26.

Langone, M. (1988) *Cults: Questions and Answers.* Weston, MA: American Family Foundation.

Langone, M. (Ed.) (1993) *Recovery From Cults.* New York: Norton.

Layton, D. (1999) *Seductive Poison: A Jonestown Survivor's Story of Life and Death in the People's Temple.* London: Aurum Press.

Lenin, V. I. (1977) *Collected Works*, Vol 10. Moscow: Progress Publishers.

Levs, J. (2008) Big Three auto CEOs flew private jets to ask for taxpayer money. *CNN US*, 19 November. Available online at http://articles.cnn.com/2008-11-19/us/autos.ceo.jets_1_private-jets-auto-industry-test-vote?_s=PM:US. Last accessed 20 November 2012.

Lewis, D. (1992) Communicating organizational culture. *Australian Journal of Communication*, 19: 47–57.

Lewis, J. and Geroy, G. (2000) Employee spirituality in the workplace: a cross-cultural view for the management of spiritual employees. *Journal of Management Education*, 24: 682–94.

Lifton, R. (1999) *Destroying the World to Save It: Aum Shinrikyo, Apocalyptic Violence, and the New Global Terrorism.* New York: Holt.

Lifton, R. (1961) *Thought Reform and the Psychology of Totalism.* London: Gollancz.

Lipman-Blumen, J. (2008) Dissent in times of crisis. In S. Banks (Ed.) *Dissent and the Failure of Leadership.* Cheltenham: Edward Elgar, pp. 37–52.

Lips-Wiersma, M. (2003) Making conscious choices in doing research on workplace spirituality: utilising the "holistic development model" to articulate values, assumptions and dogmas of the knower. *Journal of Organizational Change Management*, 16: 406–25.

Lips-Wiersma, M., Dean, K. and Fornaciari, C. (2009) Theorising the dark side of the workplace spirituality movement. *Journal of Management Inquiry*, 18: 288–300.

Locke, R. and Spender, J. (2011) *Confronting Managerialism: How the Business Elites and Their Schools Threw Our Lives Out of Balance.* New York: Zed Books.

Lord, R. and Maher, K. (1993) *Leadership and Information Processing: Linking Perceptions and Performance*. New York: Routledge.

Lord, R. and Brown, D. (2001) Leadership, values and subordinate self-concepts. *The Leadership Quarterly*, 12, (2): 133–52.

Lord, R. and Brown, D. (2004) *Leadership Processes and Follower Self-identity.* New Jersey: Lawrence Erlbaum.

Lubit, R. (2002) The long-term organizational impact of destructively narcissistic managers. *Academy of Management Executive*, 16: 127–38.

Luthans, F. and Larsen, J. (1986) How managers really communicate. *Human Relations*, 39: 161–78.

Mabey, C. (2001) Closing the circle: participant views of a 360 degree feedback programme. *Human Resource Management Journal*, 11: 41–53.

McCabe, D. (2007) *Power at Work: How Employees Reproduce the Corporate Machine.* London: Routledge.

McCabe, D. (2011) Opening Pandora's Box: the unintended consequences of Steven Covey's effectiveness movement. *Management Learning*, 42: 183–97.

Maccoby, M. (2000) Narcissistic leaders: the incredible pros, the inevitable cons. *Harvard Business Review*, 78: 69–77.

Maccoby, M. (2003) *The Productive Narcissist: The Promise and Peril of Visionary Leadership.* New York: Broadway Books.

McGregor, D. (1960) *The Human Side of Enterprise.* New York: McGraw-Hill.

McKinlay, A. and Taylor, P. (1996) Power, surveillance and resistance: inside the factory of the future. In P. Ackers, C. Smith and P. Smith (Eds), *The New Workplace and Trade Unionism, Critical Perspectives on Work and Organization.* London: Routledge, pp. 279–300.

McKnight, R. (1984) Spirituality in the workplace. In J. Adams (Ed.), *Transforming Work: A Collection of Organizational Transformation Readings.* Alexandria, VA: Miles River, pp. 138–53.

McPhee, R. and Iverson, J. (2009) Agents of constitution in communidad: Constitutive processes of communication in organizations. In L. Putnam, L., and A. Nicotera (Eds), *Building Theories of Organization: The Constitutive Role of Communication.* London: Routledge, pp. 49–87.

MacLeod, A. (1997) *The Death of Uncle Joe.* London: Merlin Press.

Maghroori, R. and Rolland, E. (1997) Strategic leadership: the art of balancing organizational mission with policy, procedures, and external environment. *Journal of Leadership Studies*, 2: 62–81.

Magretta, J. (1998) The power of virtual integration: an interview with Dell Computer's Michael Dell. *Harvard Business Review*, March-April: 113–23.

Marshall, E. (2010) *Transformational Leadership in Nursing: From Expert Clinician to Influential Leader.* New York: Springer Publishing.

Martin, G. and Learmonth, M. (2012) A critical account of the rise and spread of 'leadership': the case of UK healthcare. *Social Science and Medicine*, 74: 281–8.

Martin, J. (1992) *Cultures in Organizations: Three Perspectives.* New York: Oxford University Press.

Martin, J. (1999) 'Come, Join our family': discipline and integration in corporate organizational culture. *Human Relations*, 52: 155–78.

Mason, E. and Welsh, A. (1994) Symbolism in managerial decision making. *Journal of Managerial Psychology*, 9: 27–35.

Mautner, G. (2010) *Language and the Market Society.* London: Routledge.

Maxwell, T. (2003) Integral spirituality, deep science, and ecological awareness. *Journal of Religion & Science*, 38: 257–76.

Mayo, M. and Pastor, J. (2007) A Follower-centric contingency model of charisma attribution: the importance of follower emotion. In B. Shamir, R. Pillai and M. Bligh (Eds), *Follower-Centered Perspectives on Leadership: A Tribute to the Memory of James R. Meindl.* Charlotte, NC: Information Age Publishing, pp. 93–114.

Mayo-Wilson, C., Zollman, K. and Danks, D. (2012) Wisdom of crowds versus groupthink: learning in groups and in isolation. *International Journal of Game Theory*, published online 20 April. doi: 10.107/s00182-012-0329-7.

Mehri, D. (2006) The darker side of lean: An insider's perspective on the realities of the Toyota production system. *Academy of Management Perspectives*, 20: 21–42.

Meindl, J. (1993) Reinventing leadership: a radical, social psychological approach. In J. Murningham (Ed.), *Social Psychology in Organisations: Advances in Theory and Research*. Englewood Cliffs, NJ: Prentice Hall.

Meindl, J. (1995) The romance of leadership as a follower-centric theory: a social constructionist approach. *The Leadership Quarterly*, 6: 329–41.

Meindl, J., Ehrlich, S. and Dukerich, J. (1985) The romance of leadership. *Administrative Science Quarterly*, 30: 78–102.

Mellahi, K. (2000) The teaching of leadership on UK MBA programmes: a critical analysis from an international perspective. *Journal of Management Development*, 19: 297–308.

Mcrolla, J., Ramos, J. and Zcchmcistcr, E. (2012) Authoritarianism, need for closure and conditions of threat. In M. Hogg and D. Blaylock (Eds), *Extremism and the Psychology of Uncertainty*. Oxford: Wiley Blackwell, pp. 212–27.

Michels, R. ([1911] 1962) *Political Parties: A Sociological Study of the Oligarchical Tendencies of Modern Democracy*. New York: Collier Books.

Milgram, S. (1974) *Obedience to Authority: An Experimental View*. New York: Harper and Row.

Miller, D. (1989) The limits of dominance. In D. Miller, M. Rowlands and C. Tilley (Eds), *Domination and Resistance*. London: Unwin Hyman, pp. 63–79.

Milliken, F., Morrison, E. and Hewlin, P. (2003) An exploratory study of employee silence: issues that employees don't communicate upward and why. *Journal of Management Studies*, 40: 1453–76.

Milliman, J., Ferguson, J., Trickett, D. and Condemi, B. (1999) Spirit and community at Southwest Airlines: an investigation of a spiritual values-based model. *Journal of Organizational Change Management*, 12: 221–33.

Milliman, J., Czaplewski, A. and Ferguson, J. (2003) Workplace spirituality and employee work attitudes: an exploratory empirical assessment. *Journal of Organizational Change Management*, 16: 426–47.

Mintzberg, H. (1989) Ideology and the missionary organization. In H. Mintzberg, *Mintzberg on Management*. New York: Free Press, pp. 221–35.

Mintzberg, H. (2004) *Managers Not MBAs: A Hard Look at the Soft Practice of Managing People and Management Development*. London: Prentice-Hall.

Mintzberg, H. (2011) From management development to organization development with IMpact. *OD Practitioner*, 43: 25–9.

Mirvis, P. (1997) 'Soul work' in organizations. *Organization Science*, 8: (2): 193–206.

Mitroff, I. (2003) Do not promote religion under the guise of spirituality. *Organization*, 10: 375–82.

Mitroff, I. and Denton, E. (1999) *A Spiritual Audit of Corporate America: A hard Look at Spirituality, Religion, and Values in the Workplace*. San Francisco, CA: Jossey-Bass.

Morrison, E. (2002) Information seeking within organizations. *Human Communication Research*, 28: 229–42.

Morrison, E. (2011) Employee voice behavior: Integration and directions for future research. *Academy of Management Annals*, 5: 373–412.

Morrison, E. and Milliken, F. (2003) Guest editors' introduction: speaking up, remaining silent. The dynamics of voice and silence in organizations. *Journal of Management Studies*, 40: 1353–8.

Morrison, E. and Rothman, N. (2009) Silence and the dynamics of power. In J. Greenberg and M. Edwards (Eds), *Voice and Silence in Organizations*. Bingley: Emerald, pp. 111–33.

Morrison, J. (2003) Leadership is our business. *Journal of Education for Business*, September/October: 4–5.

Morrison, J., Rha, J. and Helfman, A. (2003) Learning awareness, student engagement, and change: a transformation in leadership development. *Journal of Education for Business*, September/October: 11–17.

Morsing, M. and Rovira, A. (Eds) (2011) *Business Schools and Their Contribution to Society*. London: SAGE.

Mumby, D. (2001) Power and politics. In F. Jablin and L. Putnam (Eds), *The New Handbook of Organizational Communication: Advances in Theory, Research, and Methods*. London: SAGE, pp. 585–623.

Mumby, D. K. (2005) Theorizing resistance strategies in organizations: a dialectical approach. *Management Communication Quarterly*, 19: 19–44.

Myers, D. (1996) *Social Psychology*. New York: McGraw-Hill.

Neal, J. (2001) Leadership and spirituality in the workplace. In R. Lussier and C. Achua (Eds), *Leadership Theory, Application, Skill Development*. Boston: South-Western College Publishing, pp. 464–73.

Neal, J. and Biberman, J. (2003) Introduction: the leading edge in research on spirituality and Organizations. *Journal of Organizational Change Management*, 16: 363–6.

Nelson, D. and Quick, J. (1995) *Organizational Behaviour: Foundations, Realities and Challenges*. St. Paul: West Educational Publishing.

Nemeth, C. and Goncalo, J. (2012) Rogues and heroes: finding value in dissent. In J. Jetten and M. Hornsey (Eds), *Rebels in Groups: Dissent, Deviance, Difference and Defiance*. Chichester: Wiley-Blackwell, pp. 36–53.

Nirenberg, J. (1998) Myths we teach, realities we ignore: leadership education in business schools. *The Journal of Leadership Studies*, 5: 82–99.

Nutt, P. (2002) *Why Decisions Fail: Avoiding the Blunders and traps that Lead to Debacles*. San Francisco, CA: Berret-Koehler.

O'Creevy, M. (2001) Employee involvement and the middle manager: saboteur or scapegoat? *Human Resource Management Journal*, 11: 24–40.

O'Reilly, D. and Reed, M. (2011) The grit in the oyster: professionalism, managerialism and leaderism as discourses of UK public services modernization. *Organization Studies*, 32: 1079–101.

Oren, L., Tziner, A., Sharoni, G., Amor, I. and Alon, P. (2012) Relations between leader-subordinate personality similarity and job attitudes. *Journal of Managerial Psychology*, 27: 479–96.

Orwell, G. (1949) *1984*. London: Secker & Warburg.

Ospina, S. and Uhl-Bien, M. (2012) Introduction: mapping the terrain: convergence and divergence around relational leadership. In M. Uhl-Bien and S. Ospina (Eds), *Advancing Relational Leadership Research: A Dialogue among Perspectives*. Charlotte, NC: Information Age Publishing, pp. xix–xlvii.

Packer, D. (2011) The dissenter's dilemma, and a social identity solution. In J. Jetten and M. Horney (Eds), *Rebels in Groups: Dissent, Deviance, Difference and Defiance*. Chichester: Wiley-Blackwell, pp. 281–301.

Park, S., Westphal, J. and Stern, I. (2011) Set up for a fall: the insidious effects of flattery and opinion conformity toward corporate leaders. *Administrative Science Quarterly*, 56: 257–302.

Pelletier, K. (2010) Leader toxicity: an empirical investigation of toxic behaviour and rhetoric. *Leadership*, 6: 373–89.

Pentland, A. (2012) The new science of building great teams, *Harvard Business Review*, April: 60–70.

Perlow, L. (1999) Time famine: toward a sociology of work time. *Administrative Science Quarterly*, 44: 57–81.

Peters, T. (1992) *Liberation Management*. London: Pan Books.

Peters, T. and Waterman, R. (1982) *In Search of Excellence*. New York: Harper Collins.

Pettigrew, A. (1979) On studying organizational cultures. *Administrative Science Quarterly*, 24: 570–81.

Pettigrew, A. (1990) Is corporate culture manageable? In D. Wilson and R. Rosenfeld (Eds), *Managing Organizations*. London: Heinemann, pp. 267–72.

Pfeffer, J. (2003) Business and the spirit: management practices that sustain values. In R. Giacalone and C. Jurkiewicz (Eds), *Handbook of Workplace Spirituality and Organizational Performance*. New York: Sharpe, pp. 29–45.

Pfeffer, J. (2010) *Power: Why Some People Have It and Others Don't*. New York: Collins Business.

Pfeffer, J. (1998) Six major myths about pay. *Harvard Business Review*, May-June: 109–19.

Pfeffer, J. and Cialdini, R. (1998) Illusions of influence. In R. Kramer and M. Neale (Eds), *Power and Influence In Organizations*. London: SAGE, pp. 1–20.

Pfeffer, J. and Fong, C. (2002) The end of business schools? Less success than meets the eye. *Academy of Management Learning and Education*, 1: 78–95.

Pfeffer, J. and Sutton, R. (2006) *Hard Facts, Dangerous Half-Truths, and Total Nonsense: Profiting from Evidence-based Management*. Boston: Harvard Business School Press.

Pollach, I. and Kerbler, E. (2011) Appearing competent: a study of impression management in U.S. and European CEO profiles. *Journal of Business Communication*, 48: 355–72.

Pratto, F. and John, O. (1991) Automatic vigilance: the attention grabbing power of negative social information. *Journal of Personality and Social Psychology*, 51: 380–91.

Prentice, R. (2003) Enron: a brief behavioural autopsy. *American Business Law Journal*, 40: 417–44.

Putnam, L. and Nicotera, A. (2010) Communicative constitution of organization is a question: critical issues for addressing it. *Management Communication Quarterly*, 24: 158–65.

Putnam, L. and Nicotera, A. (Eds) (2009) *Building Theories of Organization: The Constitutive Role of Communication*. London: Routledge.

Putnam, R. (2000) *Bowling Alone*. New York: Simon and Schuster.

Rajagopalan, N. and Datta, D. (1996) CEO characteristics: does industry matter? *Academy of Management Journal*, 39: 197–215.

RealTimeLiveTV (2009) Enron – Vision and Values 1998 (VHS DUB). [video clip] Accessed online at http://www.youtube.com/watch?v=tc-l9J6WiMY. Last accessed 20 November 2012.

Reave, L. (2005) Spiritual values and practices related to leadership effectiveness. *The Leadership Quarterly*, 16: 656–87.

Reed, M. (2012) Masters of the Universe: power and elites in organization studies. *Organization Studies*, 33: 203–21.

Reiterman, T. (2008) *Raven: The Untold Story of the Rev. Jim Jones and His People* (2nd ed.). New York: Penguin.

Richardson, H. and Taylor, S. (2012) Understanding input events: a model of employees' responses to requests for their input. *Academy of Management Review*, 37: 471–91.

Richardson, J. (1980) People's Temple and Jonestown: a corrective comparison and critique. *Journal for the Scientific Study of Religion*, 19: 239–55.

Roberto, M. (2005) *Managing For Conflict and Consensus: Why Great Leaders Don't Take Yes For an Answer*. New Jersey: Wharton School Publishing.

Robichaud, D., Giroux, H. and Taylor, J. (2004) The metaconversation: the recursive property of language as a key to organizing. *Academy of Management Review*, 29: 617–34.

Robinson, S. and Kerr, R. (2009) The symbolic violence of leadership: a critical hermeneutic study of leadership and succession in a British organization in the post-Soviet context. *Human Relations*, 62: 875–903.

Rocha, H. and Ghoshal, S. (2006) Beyond self-interest revisited. *Journal of Management Studies*, 43: 585–619.

Rogoff, E. G., Lee, M. and Suh, D. (2004) "Who done it?" Attributions by entrepreneurs and experts of the factors that cause and impede small business success. *Journal of Small Business Management*, 42: 364–76.

Rosenfeld, P., Giacalione, R. and Riordan, C. (1995) *Impression Management in Organizations*. London: Routledge.

Rosenzweig, P. (2007) *The Halo Effect ... And The Eight Other Business Delusions that Deceive Managers*. New York: Free Press.

Ross, L. (1977) The intuitive psychologist and his shortcomings: distortions in the attribution process. In L. Berkowitz (Ed.), *Advances In Experimental Social Psychology, 10*. New York: Academic Press, pp. 173–220.

Ross, S. (1973) The economic theory of agency: the principal's problem. *American Economic Review*, 62 (2): 134–9.

Rost, J. (1991) *Leadership for the Twenty-first Century*. New York: Praeger.

Rost, J. and Barker, R. (2000) Leadership education in colleges: toward a 21st century paradigm. *The Journal of Leadership Studies*, 7: 3–12.

Rousseau, D. (Ed.) (2012) *The Oxford Handbook of Evidence Based Management*. Oxford: Oxford University Press.

Rudd, M. (2009) *Underground: My Life with SDS and the Weathermen*. New York: Harper.

Rynes, S., Gerhart, B. and Parks, L. (2005) 'Personnel psychology: performance evaluation and pay-for-performance'. In S. Fiske, D. L. Schacter and A. Kasdin (Eds), *Annual Review of Psychology*, 56: 571–600.

Salancik, G. and Meindl, J. (1984) Corporate attributions as strategic illusions of management control. *Administrative Science Quarterly*, 29: 238–54.

Salter, M. (2008) *Innovation Corrupted: The Origins and Legacy of Enron's Collapse*. Cambridge, MA: Harvard University Press.

Sanders, W. and Hambrick, D. (2007) Swinging for the fences: the effects of CEO stock options on company risk taking and performance. *Academy of Management Journal*, 50: 1055–78.

Sankar, Y. (2003) Character not charisma is the critical measure of leadership excellence. *The Journal of Leadership and Organizational Studies*, 9: 45–55.

Schabas, W. (2011) *An Introduction to the International Criminal Court* (4th ed.). Cambridge: Cambridge University Press.

Scheflin, A. and Opton, E. (1978) *The Mind Manipulators*. New York: Paddington.

Schein, E., with Schneir, I., and Barker, C. (1961) *Coercive Persuasion: A Socio-psychological Analysis of the "Brainwashing" if American Civilian Prisoners by the Chinese Communists*. New York: Norton.

Schilling, J. (2009) From ineffectiveness to destruction: a qualitative study on the meaning of negative leadership. *Leadership*, 5: 102–28.

Schley, D. (2008) Legal aspects of spirituality in the workplace. *International Journal of Public Administration*, 31: 342–58.

Schmidt-Wilk, J., Heaton, D. and Steingard, D. (2000) Higher education for higher consciousness: Maharishi University of Management as a model for spirituality in management education. *Journal of Management Education*, 24: 580–611.

Schrank, R. (1998) *Wasn't That A Time: Growing Up Radical and Red in America.* Cambridge, MA: MIT Press.

Schultz, M., Maguire, S., Langley, A. and Tsuoukas, H. (Eds) (2012) *Constructing Identity in and Around Organizations.* Oxford: Oxford University Press.

Schutz, A. (1998) Assertive, offensive, protective, and defensive styles of self-presentation: a taxonomy. *Journal of Psychology*, 132: 611–28.

Schwartz, J. (2002) Darth Vader. Machiavelli. Skilling Sets Intense Pace, *New York Times*, 7 February: 1.

Scott, M. and Lyman, S. Accounts. (1968) *American Sociological Review*, 33: 46–62.

Sebag-Montefiore, S. (2007) *Stalin: Inside the Court of the Red Tsar (New Edition).* London: Phoenix.

See, K., Morrison, E., Rothman, N. and Soll, J. (2011) The detrimental effects of power on confidence, advice taking, and accuracy. *Organizational Behavior and Human Decision Processes*, 116: 272–85.

Seibold, D. and Shea, B. (2001) Participation and decision making. In F. Jablin, and L. Putnam (Eds), *The New Handbook of Organizational Communication: Advances in Theory, Research and Methods*. London: SAGE, pp. 664–703.

Seligman, M. (1975) *Helplessness: On Depression, Development and Death*. London: W. H. Freeman.

Sen, A. (1977) Rational fools: a critique of the behavioural foundations of economic theory. *Philosophy and Public Affairs*, 6: 317–44.

Seteroff, S. (2003) *Beyond Leadership to Followership*. Victoria, BC: Trafford.

Sewell, G. and Barker, J. (2006) Coercion versus care: using irony to make sense of organizational surveillance. *Academy of Management Review*, 31: 934–61.

Sewell, G., Barker, J. and Nyberg, D. (2012) Working under intensive surveillance: when does 'measuring everything that moves' become intolerable? *Human Relations*, 65: 189–215.

Seyranian, V. (2012) Constructing extremism: uncertainty provocation and reduction by extremist leaders. In M. Hogg and D. Blaylock (Eds), *Extremism and the Psychology of Uncertainty*. Oxford: Wiley Blackwell, pp. 228–45.

Shamir, B. (2007) From passive recipients to active co-producers. In B. N. Shamir, R. Pillai, M. Bligh and M. Uhl-Bien (Eds), *Follower-Centered Perspectives on Leadership: A Tribute to the Memory of James R. Meindl*. Connecticut: Information Age Publishing, pp. ix–xxxix.

Shamir, B., House, R. and Arthur, M. (1993) The motivational effects of charismatic leadership: a self-concept based theory. *Organization Science*, 4: 577–94.

Shapiro, S. (2005) Agency theory. *Annual Review of Sociology*, 31: 263–84.

Sherman, S. (2002) Enron: uncovering the uncovered story. *Columbia Journalism Review*, 40: 22–8.

Siegel, P., Strohl, N., Ingram, L., Roche, D. and Taylor, J. (1987) Leninism as cult: the Democratic Workers Party. *Socialist Review*, 17: 59–85.

Simkins, T. (2005) Leadership in education: 'What works' or 'What makes sense?' *Educational Management Administration and Leadership*, 33: 9–26.

Simon, B. (2005) The return of panopticism: supervision, subjection and the new surveillance. *Surveillance and Society*, 3: 1–20.

Sinclair, A. (2007) *Leadership For The Disillusioned: Moving Beyond Myths And Heroes To Leading That Liberates*. Crows Nest, NSW: Allen and Unwin.

Singer, M. (1987) Group psychodynamics. In R. Berkow and M. Sharp (Eds), *The Merck Manual of Diagnosis and Therapy. Rahway*, NJ: Dohme Research Laboratories.

Singer, M. and Lalich, J. (1996) *Crazy Therapies: What are They? Do They Work?* San Francisco: Jossey-Bass.

Singer, N. (2012) In executive pay, a rich game of thrones. *New York Times*, 7 April. Available online at http://www.nytimes.com/2012/04/08/business/in-chief-executives-pay-a-rich-game-of-thrones.html?_r=1&ref=natashasinger. Last accessed 22 November 2012.

Singhal, M. and Chatterjee, L. (2006) A person-organization fit-based approach for spirituality at work: development of a conceptual framework. *Journal of Human Values*, 12: 161–78.

Sinha, P., Inkson, K. and Barker, J. (2012) Committed to a failing strategy: celebrity CEO, intermediaries, media and stakeholders in a co-created drama. *Organization Studies*, 33: 223–45.

Slater, R. (1999) *Jack Welch and the GE Way*. New York: McGraw Hill.

Smircich, L. (1983) Concepts of organizational culture and organizational analysis. *Administrative Science Quarterly*, 29: 339–58.

Smircich, L. and Morgan, G. (1982) Leadership: the management of meaning. *Journal of Applied Behavioral Science*, 18: 257–73.

Socrates (1993) *The Republic*, trans. R. Waterfield. Oxford: Oxford University Press.

Southern Poverty Law Centre (2009) *The Second Wave: Return of the Militias*. Montgomery, AL: Southern Poverty Law Centre.

Spears, L. (1995) *Reflections On Leadership: How Robert K. Greenleaf's Theory of Leadership Influenced Today's Top Management Thinkers*. New York: John Wiley.

Spicer, A. and Levay, A. (2012) Critical theories of organizational change. In D. Boje, B. Burnes and J. Hassard (Eds), *The Routledge Companion to Organizational Change*. London: Routledge, pp. 276–90.

Stapleton, K. and Hargie, O. (2011) Double-bind accountability dilemmas: impression management and accountability strategies used by senior banking executives. *Journal of Language and Social Psychology*, 30: 266–89.

Starbuck, W., Greve, A. and Hedberg, B. (1978) Responding to crisis. *Journal of Business Administration*, 9: 111–37.

Starbuck. W. and Milliken, F. (1988) Challenger: fine-tuning the odds until something breaks. *Journal of Management Studies*, 25: 319–40.

Starkey, K. and Tiratsoo, N. (2007) *The Business School and the Bottom Line*. Cambridge: Cambridge University Press.

Stein, A. (2002) *Inside Out: A Memoir of Entering and Breaking Out of a Minneapolis Political Cult*. Minneapolis: North Star Press of St. Cloud.

Stein, H. (2008) Organizational totalitarianism and the voices of dissent. In S. Banks (Ed.), *Dissent and the Failure of Leadership*. Chltenham: Edward Elgar, pp. 75–96.

Stein, M. (2007) Oedipus Rex at Enron: leadership, Oedipal struggles, and organizational collapse. *Human Relations*, 60: 1387–410.

Stein, M. (2011) A culture of mania: a psychoanalytic view of the incubation of the 2008 credit crisis. *Organization*, 18: 173–86.

Stein, M. and Pinto, J. (2011) The dark side of groups: a 'gang at work' in Enron. *Group & Organization Management*, 36: 692–721.

Stohl, C. and Cheney, G. (2001) Participatory processes/paradoxical practices. *Management Communication Quarterly*, 14: 349–407.

Stones, R. (2005) *Structuration Theory*. London: Palgrave Macmillan.

Strange, J. and Mumford, M. (2002) The origins of vision: charismatic versus ideological leadership. *The Leadership Quarterly*, 13: 343–77.

Sutton, R. (2010) *Good Boss, Bad Boss: How to Be The Best ... And Learn From The Worst*. London: Piatkus.

Swartz, M. and Watkins, S. (2003) *Power Failure: The rise and fall of Enron*. London: Aurum Press.

Taaffe, P. (1995) *The Rise of Militant: Militant's Thirty Years 1964–1994*. London: Militant Publications. Available online at http://www.socialistparty.org.uk/militant/. Last accessed 22 November 2012.

Taylor, K. (2004) *Brainwashing: The Science of Thought Control*. Oxford: Oxford University Press.

Thompson, P. (2005) Brands, boundaries and bandwagons: a critical reflection on critical management studies. In C. Grey and H. Willmott (Eds), *Critical Management Studies: A Reader*. Oxford: Oxford University Press, pp. 364–82.

Tichy, N. and Devanna, M. (1990) *Transformational Leadership*. New York: Wiley.

Tichy, N. and Ulrich, D. (1984) The leadership challenge – a call for the transformational leader. *Sloan Management Review*, 26: 59–68.

Tischler, L., Biberman, J. and McKeage, R. (2002) Linking emotional intelligence, spirituality and workplace performance: definitions, models and ideas for research. *Journal of Managerial Psychology*, 17: 203–18.

Tobias, M. and Lalich, J. (1994) *Captive Hearts, Captive Minds: Freedom and Recovery From Cults and Abusive Relationships*. Alameda, CA: Hunter House.

Tolbert, P. and Hiatt, S. (2009) Michels: on organizations and oligarchies. In P. Adler (Ed.), *The Oxford Handbook of Sociology and Organization Studies: Classical Foundations*. Oxford: Oxford University Press, pp. 174–99.

Tompkins, P. (1993) *Organizational Communication Imperatives: Lessons from the Space Program*. Los Angeles: Roxbury.

Tompkins, P. (2005) *Apollo, Challenger, Columbia – The Decline of the Space Program: A Study in Organizational Communication*. Los Angeles: Roxbury.

Tompkins, P. K. and Cheney, G. (1985) Communication and unobtrusive control. In R. D. McPhee, and P. K. Tompkins (Eds), *Organizational Communication: Traditional Themes and New Directions*. Beverly Hills: SAGE, pp. 179–210.

Tosi, H., Misangyi, V., Fanelli, A., Waldman, D. and Yammarino, F. (2004) CEO charisma, compensation, and firm performance. *The Leadership Quarterly*, 15: 405–20.

Toubiana, M. (2012) Business pedagogy for social justice? An exploratory investigation of business faculty perspectives of social justice in business education. *Management Learning*. Published online before print August 6, 2012, doi: 10.1177/1350507 612454097.

Tourish, D. (1998) Ideological intransigence, democratic centralism and cultism: a case study from the political left. *Cultic Studies Journal*, 15: 33–67.

Tourish, D. (2005) Critical upward communication: ten commandments for improving strategy and decision making. *Long Range Planning*, 38: 485–503.

Tourish, D. (2006) The appraisal interview reappraised. In O. Hargie (Ed.), *A Handbook of Communication Skills*. London: Routledge, pp. 505–30.

Tourish, D. (2011) Leadership in cults. In A. Bryman, D. Collinson, K. Grint, B. Jackson and Uhl-Bien, M. (Eds), *The SAGE Handbook of Leadership.* London: SAGE, pp. 215–28.

Tourish, D. (2012) Developing leaders in turbulent times: five steps towards integrating soft practices with hard measures of organizational performance. *Organizational Dynamics*, 47: 23–31.

Tourish, D. and Hargie, O. (1998) Communication between managers and staff in the NHS: trends and prospects. *British Journal of Management*, 9: 53–71.

Tourish, D. and Hargie, O. (2012) Metaphors of failure and the failures of metaphor: A critical study of bankers' explanations for the banking crisis. *Organization Studies,* 33: 1044–1068.

Tourish, D. and Irving, P. (1995) Group influence and the psychology of cultism within re-evaluation counseling: a critique. *Counselling Psychology Quarterly*, 8: 35–50.

Tourish, D. and Pinnington, A. (2002) Transformational leadership, corporate cultism and the spirituality paradigm: an unholy trinity in the workplace? *Human Relations*, 55: 147–72.

Tourish, D. and Robson, P. (2003) Critical upward feedback in organisations: processes, problems and implications for communication management. *Journal of Communication Management*, 8: 150–67.

Tourish, D. and Robson, P. (2006) Sensemaking and the distortion of critical upward communication in organizations. *Journal of Management Studies*, 43: 711–30.

Tourish, D. and Tourish, N. (2010) Spirituality at work, and its implications for leadership and followership: a post-structuralist perspective. *Leadership*, 5: 207–24.

Tourish, D. and Wohlforth, T. (2000) *On the Edge: Political Cults Right and Left.* New York: Sharpe.

Tourish, D., Collinson, D. and Barker, J. (2009) Manufacturing conformity: leadership through coercive persuasion in business organisations. *M@n@gement*, 12: 360–83.

Tourish, D., Craig, R. and Amernic, J. (2010) Transformational leadership education and agency perspectives in business school pedagogy: a marriage of inconvenience? *British Journal of Management*, 21: S40–59.

Tourish, N. (2007) *The Dynamics of Upward Communication in Organisations.* PhD Thesis, Robert Gordon University, Aberdeen.

Townley, B. (1993) Foucault, power/knowledge, and its relevance for human resource management. *Academy of Management Review*, 18: 518–45.

Townley, B. (1994) *Reframing Human Resource Management: Power, Ethics and the Subject at Work.* London: SAGE.

Townsend, P. and Gephart, J. (1997) *Five-Star Leadership.* New York: John Wiley.

Tracy, S. J., Lutgen-Sandvik, P. and Alberts, J. K. (2006) Nightmares, demons and slaves: exploring the painful metaphors of workplace bullying. *Management Communication Quarterly*, 20: 148–85.

Turnage, A. (2010) *Identification and Disidentification in Organizational Discourse: A Metaphor Analysis of E-mail Communication at Enron.* PhD thesis, North Carolina State University.

Turnbull, S. (2001) *Quasi-religious experiences in a corporate change programme – the roles of conversion and the confessional in corporate evangelism.* Paper presented at the Critical Management Studies Conference, Manchester School of Management, UMIST, July 2001. Available online at http://www.mngt.waikato.ac.nz/ejrot/cmsconference/2001/Papers/Change%20and%20Organisation/Turnbull.pdf. Last accessed 23 November 2012.

Turner, J. (2006) Tyranny, freedom and social structure: escaping our theoretical prisons. *British Journal of Social Psychology*, 45: 41–6.

Uhl-Bien, M. (2006) Relational leadership theory: exploring the social processes of leadership and organizing. *The Leadership Quarterly*, 17: 654–76.

Ulman, R. and Abse, D. (1983) The group psychology of mass madness. *Political Psychology*, 4: 637–61.

Valtin, J. (1988) *Out of the Night*. London: Fortress Publications.

van Dierendonck, D. (2011) Servant leadership: a review and synthesis. *Journal of Management*, 37: 1228–61.

Van Langenhove, L. and Harre, R. (1999) Introducing positioning theory. In R. van Langenhove, R. Harre and R. Harra (Eds), *Positioning Theory*. London: Blackwell, pp. 14–31.

Vanderbroeck, P. (2012) Crises: Ancient and modern – understanding an ancient Roman crisis can help us move beyond our own. *Management and Organizational History*, 7: 113–31.

Varey, R. (2006) Accounts in interactions: implications of accounting practices for managing. In F. Cooren, J. Taylor and E. Van Every (Eds), *Communication as Organizing: Empirical and Theoretical Explorations in the Dynamic of Text and Conversation*. London: Lawrence Erlbaum, pp. 181–96.

Vaughan, D. (1996) *The Challenger Launch Decision: Risky Technology, Culture and Deviance at NASA*. Chicago: University of Chicago Press.

Wagner-Marsh, F. and Conley, J. (1999) The fourth wave: the spiritually based firm. *Journal of Organizational Change Management*, 12: 292–302.

Waldron, V. and Krone, K. (1991) The experience and expression of emotion in the workplace: a study of a corrections organization. *Management Communication Quarterly*, 4: 287–309.

Wang, L., Malhotra, D. and Murnighan, J. (2011) Economics education and greed. *Academy of Management learning & Education*, 10: 643–60.

Ward, V. (2010) *The Devil's Casino: Friendship, Betrayal, and the High-Stakes Games Played Inside Lehman Brothers*. New Jersey: Wiley.

Watkins, J. (1976) Ego states and the problem of responsibility: a psychological analysis of the Patty Hearst case. *Journal of Psychiatry and Law*, 4: 471–89.

Watkins, S. (2003a) Ethical conflicts at Enron: moral responsibility in corporate capitalism. *California Management Review*, 45: 6–19.

Watkins, S. (2003b) Former Enron vice president Sherron Watkins on the Enron collapse. *Academy of Management Executive*, 17: 119–27.

Watts R. and Zimmerman, J. (1986) *Positive Accounting Theory*. Englewood Cliffs, NJ: Prentice Hall.

Webber, A. (1987) The CEO is the company. *Harvard Business Review*, January-February: 114, 116, 118, 122.

Weber, M. (1930) *The Protestant Ethic and the Spirit of Capitalism*. London: Allen and Unwin.

Weber, M. (1968) *Economy and Society: An Outline of Interpretive Sociology*. New York: Bedminster Press.

Weeks, J. and Galunic, C. (2003) The theory of the cultural evolution of the firm: the intra-organizational ecology of memes. *Organization Studies*, 24: 1309–52.

Weick, K. (1995) *Sensemaking in Organizations*. London: SAGE.

Weissman, R. Global management by stress. *Multinational Monitor*, 22(7–8). Available online from http://www.multinationalmonitor.org/mm2001/01july-august/julyaug-01corp2.html. Last accessed 23 November 2012.

Welch, J. with Welch, S. (2005) *Winning*. New York: Harper Business.

Werther, W. (2003) Enron: the forgotten middle. *Organization*, 10: 568–71.

Western, S. (2008) *Leadership: A Critical Text*. London: SAGE.

Westwood, R. and Linstead, S. (2001) Language/organization: introduction. In R. Westwood and S. Linstead (Eds), *The Language of Organization*. London: SAGE, pp. 1–19.

Wexler M. and Fraser, S. (1995) Expanding the groupthink explanation to the study of contemporary cults. *Cultic Studies Journal*, 12: 49–71.

Whitehead, A. N. ([1929]/(1957) *The Aims of Education and Other Essays*. New York: The Free Press.

Whittle, A. and Mueller, F. (2012) Bankers in the dock: Moral storytelling in action. *Human Relations*, 45: 111-139.

Wilkinson, A., Gollan, P., Marchington, M. and Lewin, D. (Eds) (2010) *The Oxford Handbook of Participation in Organizations*. Oxford: Oxford University Press.

Williamson, O. (1975) *Markets and Hierarchies: Analysis and Antitrust Implications*. New York: Free Press.

Willmott, H. (1993) Strength is ignorance: slavery is freedom. Managing culture in modern organisations. *Journal of Management Studies*, 30: 515–52.

Willmott, H. (2003) Renewing strength: corporate culture revisited. *M@anagement*, 6: 73–87.

Wilson, J. and Elman, N. (1990) Organizational benefits of mentoring. *Academy of Management Executive*, 4: 88–94.

Winkler, I. (2010) *Contemporary Leadership Theories: Enhancing The Understanding Of The Complexity, Subjectivity And Dynamic Of Leadership*. Berlin: Springer-Verlag.

Wong, E. (2001) A stinging office memo boomerangs: chief executive is criticized after upbraiding workers by e-mail. *New York Times, Section C*, April: 1.

Wong, P. (1998) Implicit theories of meaningful life and the development of the personal meaning profile (PMP). In P. Wong and P. Fry (Eds), *Handbook Of Personal Meaning: Theory, Research And Practice*. Mahwah, NJ: Lawrence Erlbaum, pp. 111–40.

Woods, A. and Grant, T. (1995) *Reason in Revolt: Marxist Philosophy and Modern Science*. London: Wellred.

Yukl, G. (1999) An evaluative essay on current conceptions of effective leadership. *European Journal of Work and Organizational Psychology*, 8: 33–48.

Zablocki, B. (2001) Towards a demystified and disinterested scientific theory of brainwashing. In B. Zablocki and T. Robbins (Eds), *Misunderstanding Cults: Searching for Objectivity in a Controversial Field*. Toronto: University of Toronto Press, pp. 159–214.

Zajac, E. and Westphal, J. (2004) The social construction of market value: institutionalization and learning perspectives on stock market reactions. *American Sociology Review*, 69: 233–57.

Zhang, X., Bartol, K., Smith, K., Pfarrer, M. and Khanin, M. (2008) CEOs on the edge: earnings manipulation and stock-based incentive misalignment. *Academy of Management Journal*, 51: 241–58.

Zimbardo, P. (2007) *The Lucifer Effect: How Good People Turn Evil*. London: Rider.

Zoller, H. and Fairhurst, G. (2007) Resistance leadership: the overlooked potential in critical organization and leadership studies. *Human Relations*, 60: 1331–60.

Zuboff, S. (1988) *In The Age Of The Smart Machine*. New York: Basic Books.

Index

Aasland, M. 4, 100
Abse, D. 165
Aburdene, P. 59
Ackers, P. 37, 73
Adams, D. 106
agency theory 106–110
Agho, A. 202
Alberts, J. (40)
Alon, P. 34
Alvesson, M. 14, 23, 41, 80, 132, 199, 211
Amann, W. 98
Amar, A. 11, 12
American Family Foundation, 29
Amernic, J. 4, 25, 106, 111, 113, 186
Amor, I. 34
Anand, S, 21
Ancona, D. 70
Anderson, C. 10
Andriopoulos, C. 84
Antonakis, J. 214
Arab Spring 17
Armstrong, T. 62
Arnulf, J. 10
Aronson, E. 34, 123
Aryee, S. 23
Asch, S. 46
Aschraft, K. 206
Ashford, S. 80
Ashforth, B. 64
Ashkanasay, N. 79
Ashmos, D. 60, 64, 68
authentic leadership 16, 202–03
Avolio, B. 20, 203
Awamleh, R. 24

Baetz, M. 24
Bain, P.
Balch, R. 167, 172
Balleine, B. 49

bankers 5–6; banking crisis 6–7; bankers'
    explanations for crisis 179–80; bankers'
    explanatory themes 180–91; leadership
    lessons of bankers' explanations
    193–96
Banks, S. 3
Barker, C. 36
Barker, E. 167
Barker, J. 44, 45, 47, 58
Barker, R. 97, 99
Barmine, A. 139
Barnett, C. 60
Baron, R., 46, 48, 80, 85
Bartel, C. 45
Barton, J. 7, 47, 56
Bass, B. 20, 22, 23
Bastani, B. 11, 12
Baxter, L. 81
Bedell-Avers, K. 98, 110
Bell, E. 63, 65, 66
Bellow, S. 201
Bencherki, N. 200
Benefiel, M. 67
Benevento, A. 9
Bennis, W. 98
Benoit-Barne, C. 210
Biberman, J. 60, 70
Bierly, P.65
Biesel, R. 82
Blader, S. 45
Blanck, P. 32
Boje, D. 120, 131, 212
Bones, C. 193
Bono, J. 199
Boyett, I. 111
Brake, 82
Briñol, P. 174
Brown, A. 84
Brown, D. 41

Brown, R. 74
Bryman, A. 24
Burack, E. 70, 71
Burke, K. 55
Burns, J. 20, 22, 23
Burrell, G. 51, 98
Burris, E. 86
Byrne, D.34
Byrne, J. 100, 111

Cacioppe, R. 66
Cannon, M. 193
Capra, F. 211, 212
Carsten, M. 201
Case, P. 76
Cash, K. 71
catastrophism 146–47
Cavanagh, G. 62, 65, 66, 67
Cedillo, M. 70
Chaleff, I. 111
Chatterjee, L. 60
Chemers, M. 22
Chen, G. 23
Chen, S. 9
Cheney, G. 12, 45, 50
Chow, C. 80
Christensen, E. 65
Christensen, L. 50
Chryssides, G. 158
Chuang, A. 199
Churchill, W. 94
Cialdini, R. 27, 36, 47, 48, 109, 160, 175
Ciulla, J. 21
Clegg, S. 40, 56, 58
Clifton, J. 207
coercive persuasion 40: affiliation
    42–5; alignment of identity 47–8;
    communication systems 49–50;
    limits of 55–7; peer pressure 467;
    performance assessment 48–9;
    psychological safety and conformity
    50–51; reference group role modelling
    45–6; reward systems 49; techniques
    43; with surveillance 40–41, 47, 52;
Coates, J. 10
cognitive closure 44
Cohan, J. 118, 131
Cohen, M. 66
Cohen, P. 155
Collins, J. 11, 54
Collinson, D. 4, 14, 54, 57, 58, 61, 64,
    66, 74, 81, 102, 122, 126, 176, 202,
    209, 210
Collinson, M. 54

Committee for Workers International
    136: traits of political cults 139–41;
    vanguard party 141–44
communicative constitution of leadership
    205–07
Condemi, B. 71
conformity, dangers of 22–23;
    manufacturing of 161–64
Conger, J. 23, 24, 26, 27, 28, 29
Conley, J. 65, 70
Connor, J. 85
Conrad, C. 133, 192
Coombs, W. 187
Cooren, F. 200, 204, 206, 211
corporate culture 35–6; 515
Courpasson, D. 9
Craig, R. 4, 25, 106, 111, 113, 186
Cravens, K. 4
Crawley, K. 46, 48
Crick, M. 151
critical leadership studies 14–16
critical performativity 14; and
    spirituality 69–72
Crossman, B. 201
Crossman, J. 201
Crossman, R. 200, 214
Cruver, B. 118, 120, 121
Cullinane, N. 82
cults 27: and charismatic
    leadership 31–2; and compelling vision
    32–3; and conversion 34; and individual
    consideration 33–4; traits of political
    cults 139–141; and transformational
    leadership 29–31
Cummins, S. 129
Cunliffe, A. 14, 101
Currie, G. 111
Czaplewiski, A. 64

Dameron, S. 98
Daniels, D. 62, 68
Danks, D. 84
Datta, D. 4
de Holan, P. 193
de Vries, R. 25, 27
Deaken, S. 133
Deal, T. 54
Dean, K. 70, 71, 74
Deason, G. 201
Deetz, S. 12, 83
Dehler, G. 71
Delbecq, L. 70
Delves Broughton, P. 99
Denston, I. 27

Dent, E. 61, 62
Denton, E. 64, 68, 70, 76
Detert, J. 82
Devanna, M. 23
Dezfouli, A. 49
Díaz–Sáenz, H. 20, 24
Dickson, D. 12, 63
Dierksmeier, C. 98
dissent 78; 126–29
Donaghey, J. 82
Driscoll, C. 60, 63, 69
Driver, M. 76
du Gay, P. 37, 54
DuBrin, A. 26
Duchon, D. 60, 63, 64, 66, 68
Dukerich, J. 26
Dundon, T. 82
Durand. T. 98
Durant, R. 120, 131

The Economist, 118
Edmondson, A. 82, 193
Edmunds, A., 80
Edwards, M. 79
Ehrlich, S. 26
Einarsen, S. 4
Eisenberg, E. 213
Eisler, R. 70
Eliot, T. 209
Ellison, C. 62
Elman, N. 51
Elsbach, K. 45
Enron: origins of 118; charismatic
    leadership within 119–20; common
    culture issues 126; role of compelling
    vision 121–22; conversion of recruits
    124; deception 13; individual
    consideration and love bombing
    122–24; indoctrination processes
    124–25; rank and yank
    systems 126–29
Evans, J. 20
evidence based management 13

Fairhurst, G. 12, 17, 57, 83, 110, 192, 199,
    205, 206
Fanelli, A. 111
Fast, H. 139
Fast, N. 9
Federico, C. 201
Ferguson, J. 64, 71
Ferlie, E. 98
Fernie, S. 56
Festinger, L. 31, 152, 173

Figes, O. 18
Financial Services Authority 193
Fineman, S. 212
Fischer, D. 203
Flauto, F. 20
Fleming, P. 209
Flyvberg, B. 83
followership 16; 201–202
Fong, C. 98
Ford, J. 48, 203
Fornaciari, C. 70
Forray, J. 67
Foucault, M. 47, 51, 52, 55, 64
Frager, R. 73
Franz, R. 62, 68
Fraser, S. 36, 152
Freshman, B. 70
Frey, J. 120
Friedman, M. 106, 108
Fry, L. 60, 65, 66, 70
Fryer, M. 200, 207, 208
Fukuyama, F. 47
Furnham, A. 4
Fusaro, P. 123, 124, 126, 127

Gabriel, Y. 212
Galanter, M. 158, 163, 165, 170
Galbraith, J. 75
Galinsky, A. 8
Galunic, C. 50
Gardner, J. 79
Gardner, W. 24, 203
Garner, J. 80
Gemmill, G. 26
Gephart, J. 202
Gergen, K. 205, 211
Gerhart, B. 194
Geroy, G. 60
Ghoshal, S. 97, 108
Giacalione, R. 34, 60, 67, 69, 70
Giebels, E. 42
Giroux, H. 205
Gist, M. 27
Gladwell, M. 127
Godard, A. 20
Goffee, R. 203
Goffman, E. 45, 51, 124
Goldhammer, J. 34
Goldstein, N. 160
Gollan, P. 91
Goncalo, J. 79
Gordon, R. 40, 56
Gosling, J. 76, 98
Gozdz, K. 73

Granberg-Michaelson, W. 62, 63
Grant, D. 199
Grant, R. 108
Grant, T. 142
Gray, G. 71
Gray, J. 27
Greenleaf, R. 204
Greve, A. 80
Greve, H. 57
Grey, C. 51
Grint, K. 21, 22, 87, 112, 208, 212
Gross, M. 101
groupthink 36
Gruenfeld, D. 10
Guney, S. 205
Guthey, E. 25

Habermas, ideal speech acts 207–10
Habermas, J. 207, 208, 209
Haerem, T. 10
Haidt, J. 150
Haigh, G. 98
halo error 10–12
Hambrick, D. 194
Hamel, G. 7, 120
Hansborough, T. 26
Hansen, M. 11, 25
Hanson, B. 65
Hanson, K. 65
Harding, N. 48, 203
Hardy, C. 130
Hargie, O. 12, 63, 78, 179, 180, 182, 183, 196
Harre, R. 184
Hartman, J. 101
Haslam, S. 46, 163, 164, 215
Hassan, S. 33
Hatch, M. 96
Haugaard, M. 50
Hay, A. 23, 98
Hayward, M. 111
Heaton, D. 60, 70
Heaven's Gate: ending of 172–74; origins of 159–60; rituals of confession 167
Hedberg, B. 80
Hegele, C. 100
Helfman, A. 98
Hendry, J. 36
Hensmans, M. 133
Hentrich, C. 11, 12
Herbert, J. 10
Hewlin, P. 80
Hiatt, S. 16, 138
Hicks, D. 69

Higgins, M. 61, 62
Hinojoso, J. 65
Hlupic, V. 11, 12
Hochman, J. 29
Hodgkinson, M. 23, 98
Hogg, M. 46, 72
Hogler, R. 101
Holocaust 17
Holstrom, B. 108
Hooper, A. 199
Hoopes, J. 54
Hope, V. 36
Hopfl, H. 100, 204
Hornsey, M. 22, 163
House of Commons Treasury Committee(a) 179
House of Commons Treasury Committee(b) 188
House of Commons Treasury Committee(c) 193
House of Commons Treasury Select Committee 191
House, R. 24
Howell, J. 24
Hu, J. 21
Hudson, 101
Human Rights Watch. 131
Hunt, J. 203
Hunter, S. 98, 110
Hutchison, P. 163
Hutson, M. 85
Huxley, A. 48, 49
Hwang, R. 80
Hyde, D. 139

Ibarra, H. 25
ideological totalism 32, 137, 141, 147, 149, 151; 153
Ingram, L. 139
inspirational vision 23–6
Introvigne, M. 56
Irving, P. 31
Iverson, J. 205

Jack Welch, presentation of in business schools 100–3
Jackson, B. 5
Janis, I. 84
Jenkinson, G. 34
Jensen, M. 106, 108, 109
Jetten, J. 22, 163
John, O. 86
Johnson, B. 4
Jones, E. 22, 33, 34, 81

Jones, G. 203
Jonestown: ending of 169–72; origins of 158–59; rituals of confession 165–67
Jost, J. 45
Judge, T. 199
Jurkiewicz, C. 60, 67, 69, 70

Kahneman, D. 85
Kakabadse, A. 72
Kamoche, K. 66
Kanter, R. 96
Kanungo, R. 24
Kark, R. 23,199
Kassing, J. 49, 77, 90
Kellerman, B. 4, 6, 100, 201, 214
Kelley, K. 82
Kelley, R. 65
Keltner, D. 10
Kennedy, A. 54
Kerbler, E. 4
Kerr, R. 25, 100, 176
Kessler, E. 65
Kets de Vries, M. 4, 81, 105, 106, 127
Khanna, H. 66
Khurana, R. 98
Kieser, A. 100
Kimakowitz, E. 98
Kinjerski, V. 70
Kiser, E. 108
Knights, D. 17
Knottnerus, J. 129
Kochan, T. 70
Koestler, A. 35, 139
Konz, G. 60
Konzelmann, S. 133
Korac-Kakabadse, N. 72
Kornberger, M. 40, 56
Kostera, M. 96
Kousmin, A. 72
Kozminski, A. 96
Krackhardt, D. 87
Kraditor, A. 142
Krell, T. 60
Krone, K. 86
Kruglanski, A. 26, 44, 49, 84, 201
Kuhn, T. 50, 206
Kunda, G. 45, 47

Lacombe, D. 47
Ladkin, D. 24
Lalich, J. 5, 29, 36, 48, 51, 73, 121, 122, 128, 131, 139, 151, 158, 161, 162, 167, 174
Lammers, J. 8

Langbein, H. 17
Langer, E. 9
Langley, A. 66, 83, 200, 204
Langone, M. 31
Larsen, J. 80
Layton, D. 158, 160, 165, 166, 175
leader agency 5, 97
leader charisma 23
leader influence 22
leader power 8–10: power differentials between leaders and non-leaders 38
leaderism 4
leadership: bad 4; dark side of 4; derailment 4; toxic, 4
leadership teaching in business schools 97–100; suggestions for improvement 110–12
Learmonth, M. 4
Lee, M. 192
Lenhardt, V. 20
Lenin, V. 142, 143
Levay, A. 26
Levs, J. 92
Lewin, D. 91
Lewis, D. 26
Lewis, J. 60
Liao, W. 80
Liaw, Y. 199
Liden, R. 21
Lifton, R. 31, 32, 36, 41, 56, 137, 138, 141, 144, 147, 149, 153
Linstead, S. 205
Lipman-Bluemen, J. 5
Lips-Wiersma, M. 70
Locke, R. 98
Lord, D. 24, 41
Lubit, R. 105
Luhman, J. 120, 131
Lutgen-Sandvik, P., 40
Luthans, F. 80, 204
Lynam, S. 183

Mabey, C. 89
Maccoby, M. 25, 55
MacLeod, A. 139
Magretta, J. 98
Maguire, S. 66
Maher, K. 24
Mahhroori, R. 65
Maine, E. 106
Malhotra, D. 97
Marchington, M. 91
Marshall, E. 20
Martin, G. 4

Martin, J. 47, 125
Mason, E. 62
Mathison, J. 10
Mautner, G. 97
Mayo, M. 102
Mayo Wilson, C. 84
McCabe, D. 17, 25, 195
McCaslin, M. 174
McClellan, J. 83
McGivern, G. 98
McGregor, D. 106
McGregor, R. 201
McKeage, R. 70
McKinlay, A. 47
McKnight, R. 62
McPhee, R. 205
Meckling, W. 106, 108
Mehri, D. 47
Meindl, J. 26, 27, 102
Mellahi, K. 99
Merolla, J. 201
Messersmith, A. 82
Metcalf, D. 56
Michels, R. 16
Milgram, S. 46
Miller, D. 47, 105
Miller, R. 123, 124, 126, 127
Milliken, F. 40, 79, 80
Milliman, J. 64, 71
Mills, J. 123
Mintzberg, H. 52, 92, 98
Mirvis, P. 60
Misangyi, V. 111
Mitroff, I. 64, 68, 70, 76
Montouri, A. 70
Moraes, A. 98
Morgan, G. 205
Morris, A. 80
Morrison, E. 8, 77, 79, 80, 81, 83, 94
Morrison, J. 98, 99
Morsing, M. 108
Mueller, F. 192
Mumby, D. 112, 211
Mumford, M. 54, 98, 110
Murnighan, J. 97
Myers, D. 27

narcissism 84–5; 103–06
Neal, J. 60, 70
Nelson, D. 100
Nemeth, C. 79
Nicotera, A. 80, 200
Nielson, B. 4
Nirenberg, J. 100

Noelanders, S. 42
Northern Ireland Troubles 12–13
Notelaers, G. 4
Nutt, P. 77
Nyberg, D. 47

O'Creevy, M. 91
O'Reilly, D. 4, 48
O'Toole, J. 98
Oakley, J. 26
Oliver, E. 4
Opton, E. 151
Orehek, E. 26, 44, 49, 201
Oren, L. 34
Orwell, G. 50
Ospina, S. 205
Osteen, E. 129

Packer, D. 87
Palmer, D. 57
Park, S. 81, 95
Parks, L. 194
Pastor, J. 102
Patera, J. 201
Paulina, D. 46, 48
Pelletier, K. 4
Pentland, A. 51
pay: performance related 193–95; top leaders' pay 5
Perlow, L. 65
Peters, T. 36, 47
Pettigrew, A. 125
Petty, M. 174
Peyer, U. 25
Pfeffer, J. 8, 27, 55, 64, 94, 98, 193
Phillips, N. 130
Pinnington, A. 39
Pinto, J. 118
Pirsin, M. 98
Platow, M. 215
Plowman, D. 63, 66
Pollach, I. 4
Porras, J. 11, 54
Pozner, J. 57
Pratt, M. 64
Pratto, F. 86
Prentice, R. 121, 131
Preston, D. 37, 73
process theories 204–05, 210–13
producing appropriate individual 132–33
Putnam, L. 80, 200
Putnam, R. 75

Quick, J. 100

Rajagopalan, N. 4
Ramamoorti, S. 4
Ramos, J. 201
RealTimeLiveTV 130
Reave, L. 62, 68, 73
Reed, M. 4, 48, 203
Reicher, S. 163, 164, 215
Reiterman, T. 169
Rha, J. 98
Richardson, H. 86
Richardson, J. 158
Riggio, R. 23
Riordin, C. 34
Roberto, M. 93
Robichaud, D. 205
Robinson, S. 25, 100
Robson, P. 22, 78, 83, 84, 95
Rocha, H. 108
Roche, D. 139
Rogoff, E. 192
Rolland, E. 65
romance of leadership 26
Rose, R. 25
Rosenfeld, P. 34
Rosile, G. 120, 131
Ross, S. 108
Rost, J. 99, 110
Rothman, N. 8, 83, 94
Rousseau, D. 13
Roviura, A. 108
Rozenzweig, P. 10
Rudd, M. 139
Ryan, F. 60
Rynes, S. 194

Safranski, S. 74
Salancik, G. 27
Salter, M. 128, 129, 132
Sandberg, J. 199
Sanders, W. 194
Sankar, Y. 57
Schabas, W. 202
Schein, E. 36, 40, 41, 42, 49, 51, 55,
    56, 57, 58
Schflin, A. 151
Schilling, J. 4, 26, 100
Schley, D. 63
Schmidt-Wilk, J. 60, 70
Schneir, I. 36
Schrank, R. 139
Schutz, A. 187
Schultz, M. 66
Schwartz, J. 120
Scott, M. 183

Scully, M. 70
Sebag-Montefiore, S. 19
See, K. 8, 83
Seibold, D. 78
self-persuasion 174
Sen, A. 106
Sendry, J. 60
servant leadership 203–04
Seteroff, S. 111
Sewell, G. 47, 56
Seyranian, V. 33
Shamir, B. 23, 24, 58, 200
Shapiro, S. 108
Sharoni, G. 34
Shea, B. 78
Sherman, S. 119
Siegel, P. 139
Simkins, T. 98
Simon, B. 55
Sims, D. 212
Sinclair, A. 111
Singer, M. 5, 31
Singer, N. 6
Singhal, M. 60
Skogstad, A. 4
Skrypnek, B. 70
Slater, R. 96, 100
Smircich, L. 73, 205
social identity theory 45–6; 72
Socrates, 37
Soll, J. 8, 83
Southern Poverty Law Centre 200
Spears, L. 204
Spender, J. 98
Spicer, A. 14, 26
spirituality in workplace 59–61: identity
    issues 66–8; inclusivity, tensions of
    68–9; managerialist biases of 65;
    religious definitions 62–3; secular
    definitions 63–4
Srinivas, E. 66
Stapel, D. 8
Stapleton, K. 179, 180, 182, 183, 196
Starbuck, W. 40, 80
Starkey, K. 99
Stein, A. 139
Stein, H. 25
Stein, M. 118, 196
Steingard, D. 60
Stern, I. 81, 95
Stewart, M. 20
Stohl, C. 12
Stones, R. 129
Stork, D. 67

Strange, J. 54
Strohl, N. 139
Suh, D. 192
Suhomlinova, O. 111
Sutton, R. 10, 94
Sveningsson, S. 23, 80, 211
Swartz, M. 118, 122, 125, 127, 128, 129, 130, 132

Taaffe, P. 154, 155
Taylor, D. 167, 172
Taylor, J. 139, 204, 206
Taylor, K. 42, 75
Taylor, P. 47, 56
Taylor, S. 63, 65, 66, 86
Thaillieu, T. 25
Thompson, P. 14
Tichy, N. 23
Tiratsoo, N. 99
Tischler, L. 70
Tobias, M. 36, 151
Tolbert, P. 16, 138
Tompkins, P. 40, 41, 45, 92
Tosi, H. 111
totalitarian state regimes 18: romance of totalitarian leadership 200
Toubiana, M. 98
Tourish, D. 4, 22, 25, 26, 27, 31, 32, 34, 39, 48, 58, 76, 78, 81, 83, 84, 95, 102, 111, 113, 126, 135, 155, 183, 186, 196, 213
Tourish, N. 76
Townley, B. 41, 47, 48
Townsend, P. 202
Tracy, S. 40
transactional leadership 38
transformational leadership, definitions 21–3; downsides of 28; similarities with cults – see cults
Trickett, D. 71
Tsoukas, H. 66, 83, 200, 204
Tsui, A. 80
Turnage, A. 117
Turnbbull, S. 52
Turner, J. 164
Tziner, A. 34

upward feedback, benefits of 79; availability error 85; fear of feedback 80; ingratiation theory 81; implicit voice constructs 82; power differentials 82–3; self-efficacy biases 82; suggestions for improvement 89–94

Uhl-Bien, M. 201, 206
Ulman, R. 165
Ulrich, D. 23
Ulsperger, J. 129

van Dierendonck, D. 204
Van Every, E. 204
Van Langhenhove, L. 184
Van Maanen, J. 70
Vanderboeck, P. 194
Varey, R. 206
Vatcha, N. 135
Vaughan, D. 40
Vervaeke, G. 42
Vidyarthi, P. 21
Vitucci, S. 70
Vurdubakis, T. 17

Wagner-Marsh, F. 65, 70
Waismel-Manor, R. 199
Waldman, D. 111
Waldron, V. 86
Walsh, E. 62
Walumbwa, F. 203
Wang, L. 97
Waterman, R. 36
Watkins, J. 42
Watkins, S. 118, 122, 125, 127, 128, 129, 130, 132, 133
Watts, R. 106
Webber, A. 98
Weber, M. 55
Webster, D. 84
Weeks, J. 50
Weick, K. 27
Weisman, R. 111
Welch, J. 101
Welsh, M. 71
Werther, W. 128
West, B. 201
Westney, D. 70
Westphal, J. 81, 95, 108
Westwood, R. 205
Wexler, M. 36, 152
Wharff, D. 61, 62
Whitehead, A. 111
Whittle, A. 102
Wiebe, E. 60, 69
Wilkinson, A. 82, 91
Williamson, O. 108
Willmott, H. 37, 41, 47, 53, 54, 72, 132
Wilson, J. 51
Wilson, N. 63
Winkler, J. 192

Wohlforth, T. 32, 126
Wong, K. 62, 68
Wong, P. 62
Woods, A. 142
Wrzesniewski, A. 45

Yammarino, F. 111
Yoon, D. 199
Yukl, G. 26

Zablocki, B. 34, 167
Zajac, E. 108
Zechmeister, E. 201
Zimbardo prison experiment 164–65
Zimbardo, P. 164
Zimmerman, J. 106
Zoller, H. 12, 17, 57
Zollman, K. 84
Zuboff, S. 47

Made in the USA
Middletown, DE
28 December 2023

46913220R00148